WALKING THE BROKEN ROAD

SEAN R. FOSTER

COPYRIGHT © 2026
SEAN R. FOSTER

Walking The Broken Road

NOTICE OF COPYRIGHT

All rights reserved. No portion of this book may be reproduced in any form without written permission from the publisher or author, except as permitted by U.S. copyright law.

This publication is designed to provide accurate and authoritative information regarding the subject matter covered. It is sold with the understanding that neither the author nor the publisher is engaged in rendering education, counseling, or other professional services. While the author has used their best efforts in preparing this book, they make no representations or warranties with respect to the accuracy or completeness of the contents of this book and specifically deny any implied direction or fitness for a particular purpose. No warranty may be created or extended by sales representatives or written sales materials. The advice and strategies contained herein may not be suitable for your situation. You should consult with a professional when appropriate. Neither the publisher nor the author shall be liable for any special, incidental, consequential, personal, or other damages.

AUTHORED BY:
Sean R. Foster

COVER PHOTOGRAPHY BY:
Sean R. Foster

INDEPENDENTLY PUBLISHED
Printed in the United States of America
Available from Amazon.com and other retail outlets

First Printing Edition, 2026
ISBN 979-8-218-91926-9

DEDICATION

To Yeshu'a Hamashiach (Jesus the Messiah) to Whom all glory, honor and power belong. I praise and thank You for trusting me with Your gifts, talents, and blessings.

To my father, the late Deacon James Allen Foster (1927-2020), whom I miss every day. Your prayers are still getting answered for me, Dad. Thank you and I love you!

To my Wife, my sweetheart, and my rib. I love you. You inspire me to reach higher.

CONTENTS

Walking The Broken Road

Preface

I first want to greet you in the Name of my Lord and Savior, Yeshu'a Hamashiach (Jesus the Messiah), The Christ, The Son of the only living and True God, Who is Adonai, Who is El Elyon, and Who is El Shaddai. The Three who are One, the Lord of Heaven's Armies, the God of the Bible and my everything. Without God I am ***NOTHING***. I am humbled and honored to be considered as one of His and I will never, ever compromise my faith and relationship with Him. My prayer is that I never step ahead or above His Wisdom and that I will never operate outside of His Will. I only desire to never outshine Him, but I live to be the wire that conducts His Power and that all the glory will forever belong to God. Period. I don't desire to be famous or rich from writing to sell books and being interviewed or featured anywhere because this is about ministry, and I am satisfied being wherever God wants me to be. If one person is forever changed and blessed, all of this is worth the while.

This book is deeply personal to me because I have been in these places in my life, and I have experienced pain and loss on a scale many that may or may not know me realize. When I began to author this book, I had no idea what God was going to do with what I was inspired to put into words. The only thing that I knew was that my heart was moved in this direction because of all the things that I had suffered and overcame during my walk with Jesus so far in my life. Being a follower of Jesus isn't a cakewalk, and it is a hard journey. Being saved isn't a paradise here on Earth, but it is where we punch our ticket for paradise in Eternity with Jesus.

It doesn't matter what other people try to say about faith and religion, but Jesus Christ is the only way to Heaven. Period. He is the literal road, and He has a plan and a path for each of us to follow as we walk the winding road to Glory. I know that I haven't gotten there yet, but where I have travelled and what I have experienced shaped me to be the person I am today. I am not perfect, and I am not the one ***ANYONE*** should pattern themselves after (which I will reiterate many times, so get ready), but it is Christ and Christ alone that we should run after with all our strength.

As I said in my last book, *Consecration in the Refiner's Fire,* I am not an expert or major theological scholar, but what God has given me I am releasing to the world because God has placed the desire in my heart to do so. I know that in my brief time on this Earth of nearly fifty years that I have seen sunshine, rain, and many things in between. Many times, in my existence I have questioned everything, shaken my proverbial fist at God, and had some of the greatest breakthroughs I have ever experienced. It makes me think of the poem *Footprints In The Sand* by Margaret Fishback Powers, but instead of a beach full of sand I pictured a long, winding road going to the horizon that was cracked, weather-beaten, and well-travelled. A road that isn't used by many people is lonely, and desolate. Just like the poem, I can look back over my journey, and I can see where I walked, ran, stumbled, fell, was wounded, nearly died, and even carried by Christ because I was never alone.

Yet, when I look at the road that I have travelled I realized that it wasn't always easy, and that this road had many pitfalls and spots where I was attacked by Satan and his demons. The image of the cracked asphalt and potholes reminds me that the walk of the Christian was never meant to be easy and smooth always. Just like a cracked and abandoned road would hurt bare feet my walk in Christ has been hard. Every step was full of struggle because I escaped the grasp of Satan and now, I had a greater enemy than I had ever encountered.

Thankfully, I was and still am destined to win because if God is for me, who could stand against me? Even so, there has been the entire spectrum that I have had to overcome, and I know that you are in the same situation as I am, along with millions of others. What stymied me the most about all of this was that there was very little teaching or sharing among others about this broken road that we all will walk to get into Eternal Life. When God moves your heart? You must do something about it and here we are.

Please don't misunderstand me, because all the Christian life is doom and gloom. We will have many more good days than bad days. We will have blessings on blessings because our God loves us and provides for us richly. Too often, we as Christians only focus on getting blessed, riches, and all the good things that our life can bring. Those things are still important, and God does faithfully give them to us. Yet our journey occurs in all areas and some of those areas are dark, lonely, and full of sorrows. No matter what happens to our lives, we should always be grateful and thankful to our God no matter what we experience because He deserves the praise in the sunshine and the rain. I have had to do that so many times in my life and I didn't understand it at the time, but God had a purpose for my life, and He does for yours as well.

This book was inspired by me having recovered from the worst of my life experiences and the experiences that others have shared with me over the years as well as direction from God. There are some controversial topics covered here and for some they may find them against God or find fault in their explanations. I pray that we all seek God for all the answers and for all the wisdom necessary to walk this broken road the way Christ has intended. God has allowed me to take the pain I experienced and turn it into my purpose. He taught me along the way that he didn't hurt me but allowed things to happen to me for His Glory and for His Purpose. I began to author this book soon after *Consecration In The Refiner's Fire* after teaching my then current worship team about drawing close to God despite the pain we face. That we need to improve our relationship with Him to not just work in ministry, but to live in this life.

We are all utterly helpless in this world and this broken road will show us just how desperate and lacking we are compared to our God. This doesn't mean that we are worthless, but it means that we are desired, and worthy and we need to realize what that means to us and to God. He gave His Son so that we could have life and that life to the full. The debt of sin is paid forever and because of that when we accept Him as our Lord and Savior, we are joint heirs with Christ. We don't deserve to be an equal heir to the Kingdom of God, but here we are. I see the broken road as a small price to pay for eternal communion with Christ forever in Heaven.

If you are reading these scribblings, I want you to know that I am not putting this to print to harm or insult anyone. There are some things about hurt and pain that may either trigger your past scars or make you feel that I may be targeting your way of life or belief system in Christ. I can assure you that this is never my intention. Reading some of these things may bring you back to a place that you never wish to return in your mind, and I understand that, and I pray that you find peace and healing. For others, certain things will make you angry and want to call me a heretic or a lost soul and I can handle that.

I am not writing to trash another person's church or blow up their belief system. Please, ***PLEASE*** do not take what I write that seems to identify you as a personal attack. I am eternally grateful for every person, place, or thing that has affected my life and regardless of the role that they played. I pray that everyone and everything will be blessed and prosper as God desires. I hold no ill will towards a soul or any place that I have lived or served.

Know that I have dug deep to author this book and the Holy Spirit has been my guide and my teacher. These are observations that I have made over my life and the testimonies of others I know. Instead, the focus should be on the methods of spiritual warfare that are being used. This war is unyielding, and we are in the middle of the oldest conflict in eternal history, and I don't and won't apologize for stirring the pot, per se, and sounding the alarm that we must stop taking things personal and see to the spiritual concerns to get the work done that we must do.

My sincerest prayer is that this book will help someone along this life's journey. That someone will get the courage to get up again after being knocked out. That someone would have the courage to not give up when it seems hopeless. This book is the pouring out of my heart because God has allowed my heart to be broken by the things that have broken His Heart. His Heart breaks for us and for our condition. No one cares for us like God cares for us and His Love never runs out and His Grace is longsuffering. Even though this book may be in your hands right now I want to let you know that this story will never end.

If there is life and breath, there will be pain as well as joy on this Earth. Those of us who belong to Christ will suffer in the same ways that He suffered. This is how we get to know Jesus and how we get to understand the depth of His Love and compassion that He has for everyone and why He ministered the way that He did. Still, this journey that will lead us to transition into eternal life in Heaven is not a fairy tale and for many the true details of that journey are obscured from view and I am praying that my humble words will somehow help someone out there who is having a rough time or may have tough times in the future.

Just know that your story is not over. If you are reading this, you are still breathing, and God is not done with you yet. I must tell myself that because I still have fears, I still have hang-ups, and I still have hills to climb in my life. Don't ever, ever look at me or anyone else as being perfect, because you will be disappointed. Only God is perfect and in Him is His divine perfection. Even though I authored this book to talk about pain and things that just aren't right, I want you to know that I have joy in Jesus and that He does reward us here on Earth. We all can be prosperous, happy, blessed, and whole while we live here. This book is for those who are in the middle of their storms and need to know that there is a way out of it all. Yes, there is, and God can turn it around suddenly or over time as He chooses for His Glory. Just be encouraged and know that I stand in agreement with you in prayer that God will not just supply all your needs but bless you beyond measure.

Know that you are loved by God and that you are His precious one in His sight. Those of us who renounced sin, repented of our sins, asked Him to be the Lord and Savior of our lives, and picked up our crosses to follow Him are His beloved. When we are his beloved, we are Hell's most hated, and we must be ready for that and a lot of us are not prepared for that reality. I know that I wasn't, and this book is the result of my errors and experiences and the lessons that I learned along the way. I took a lot of lumps and bumps that I never should have taken because I was either blind or arrogant to the reality of what was happening around me. Sometimes that blindness was due to fear or me making up a picture in my mind that was inaccurate yet satisfying to me and not the soul-crushing truth. Knowing who and what we are in this life is the first step to understanding how we fit into God's eternal plan. We are His beloved, but we must live a whole lot and do plenty to get to being the bride of Christ in eternity. Just know that we can only receive the revelation of the grand plan by being in relationship with our God and because of who we are as humans, God uses the road of relationship as the bridge builder that connects us from the Earth into eternal life with Jesus. This is why we are here, and this is why I authored this book which was to be an aid for people to use their time in this existence wisely and to their best potential.

My desire is that you see these words I have written, ponder in your heart and mind their meanings to you, and then consult the Holy Spirit for His guidance and wisdom. He is the source of all knowledge, and my scribblings are, but dust compared to all that He has to offer us. Although the Holy Spirit gave me wisdom and knowledge to assemble this book, know that for your life and situation there may be more to do than what is here. Seek The Lord in all that you do and don't lean on what you know or think you know. I pray that God uses this book to open your eyes and helps you on your journey on your broken road. I pray that something in these chapters will be what you need to make it over whatever obstacles or dark days that you may be facing. Even as I write this I am going through my own struggles and trials and they aren't easy, but because God is faithful, I will have to carry on just like everyone else. I know that I still have much to learn and don't be surprised that years from now I will write another edition of this work. This never ends until we return to God in Glory and until then I will keep walking my road as I pray that you will continue walking yours. Keep me in your prayers ***CONTINUALLY*** and I will pray for you as well.

Until then? Keep walking where He (God) leads you…

WALKING THE BROKEN ROAD

1

The Road & The Relationship

When we are born into this world, we are on a journey that will eventually lead to our deaths. I am sure that this isn't the way you might have expected a book to start, but the cold, hard facts are necessary to set this stage. We may be helpless and tiny beings that every need is taken care of by our parents, but we have entered the on-ramp to life and until our time to leave this realm we are on a spiritual journey that is like a highway. We enter at "Mile Marker Zero" in the battle for our souls even though we don't know what our feet are for as infants. The road is symbolic and helps us understand and relate to how the trip of preparation for Eternity will shape and mold us into who we will become in life.

We don't know where the road will take us, but all we know is that day after day, week after week, month after month, year after year, and decade after decade will pass us by as we can only move forward and never go backwards. We don't know what the weather will be, and we won't know what the terrain will look like. All we know is that from our first breath until our last we are in the fight for our eternal lives, and the road isn't as smooth and easy as we would like it to be. The road can have many holes and cracks that make it easy to stumble or fall. The road can have hazards that can hurt us just by passing by them. Even though these things are true, God has been there the entire time as He wants to have a relationship with each person born on the Earth.

Through many revelations from God, I had to understand that God as always had a relationship with humanity, and we were the ones who destroyed everything that God built with us. What I am about to say isn't popular, but the truth is the truth. We aren't "building a relationship" with God on this road. We are ***RECONCILING*** our relationship with God. He set up the relationship from the beginning when we were first made. God created everything for us and did so only asking us for our love for Him. ***WE*** are the ones who strayed from Him. ***WE*** are the ones who whored ourselves out to sin. ***WE*** are the ones who moved away from God, and ***we*** are the ones who needed to repent for our sins.

God came through forty-two generations of humans to send His only Son, Jesus Christ, into the world. He came and lived with His own created as one of them. He was slandered, abused, tortured, and sentenced to die when it should have been us to be punished. He died on the cross for us before we, in today's world, were born. He died for those who never accepted Him as their Savior. He rose from the dead so that we have a right to eternal life. God did everything right for all of humanity that time after time turned their backs on Him. God never had to apologize or repent for one single thing. Yet, we have the audacity to question His Love.

I have often wondered why we as Christians must be placed on a journey that is so hard and involves so much pain (it's not ***ALL*** pain, just remember that). My thoughts have spiraled around the fact that it doesn't seem right and fair that once we surrender and we give our lives to Almighty God, accept Him as our Lord and Savior, and live for Him we are subjected to pain and situations that sinners don't always seem to go through. While those who don't know God may still endure many of the same trials and tribulations that the true believers in Jesus Christ go through there are distinct differences. One being that we love and serve an unlimited God that has delivered many others from pitfalls and danger.

We know a God that has supernaturally transformed situations and shifted realities at His Will. Even those these things are true; this same God appears to be hands-off and silent when we go through some things in life. The unsaved don't have a Savior to rescue them like we do. It just doesn't seem equal. When I sit back and look over the timeline of Scripture there are things that begin to stand out as to the reasons why this journey on this broken road is what it is and how we are to handle it.

So, let's go to the beginning of scriptural history and see how all of this began. I thank God for the Bible because it is an exceptionally good record of many instances and examples of God's relationship with humankind. I want to go all the way back to the literal genesis of this relationship with our God that ironically starts in the Book of Genesis. From the first verse we see a world that is formless and void, God was there moving (Genesis 1:2). For six "days" God speaks conditions and things into existence. I would be remiss if I didn't take a few moments to describe the power of God's Voice. God said, "Let there be..." and every minute detail of His Words were created out of nothing. His intention down to the last molecule was shaped following His wishes. When I looked at all of this, I saw something that made me really see the depth of God's Love for us. I know that this is familiar, but sometimes we need to review what we already know just to be sure. Let's dig in...

On the first day God said, "Let there be light," and utter darkness was banished forever. Outer space was shaped over the Earth that was still unformed. Day and Night were created and no matter how dark the night might be it is never completely dark, and it will not be until God wills it so (Genesis 1:1-5). On the second day God said, "Let there be a firmament in the midst of the waters, and let it divide the waters from the waters." The old King James is a little unclear (Old English can be hard to read at times), but the liquid water was separated from the water vapor in the newly created atmosphere, and the sky was called Heaven. Water molecules took their respective places on the ground and in the air. Clouds, jet streams, cyclones and the weather were kick started from God's words (Genesis 1:6-8).

On the third day God said, "Let the waters under the heavens be gathered together unto one place, and let the dry land appear" and named the dry land Earth and the gathered waters Seas (Genesis 1:9-10). You would think that that alone was a miracle. God said these words and land masses rose out of the depths of the water and God set each boundary of every coastline, shoreline and riverbank, but it was just a part of this day.

God also kept speaking and said, "Let the earth bring forth grass, the herb yielding seed, and the fruit tree yielding fruit after his kind, whose seed is in itself, upon the earth" and from nothing sprung up plant life. The complexity of every plant that grows and how it is germinated, lives, reproduces and dies were created. From one sentence ***AFTER*** creating the ground and the water that these plants will live in God spoke into existence grasses, flowers, trees and their fruits to all be unique and diversified. Chemicals like chlorophyll were formed in every cell of every plant. Sugars and starches were created in every fruit. Plants are encoded with the ability to have roots that varied from organism to organism. Some had bark while others knew to creep up on other things. They created stamens, all the diverse types of pollen, what seasons to grow in and how long they can live. They knew how to bathe in various levels of light for their survival. They knew how to breathe in carbon dioxide to release oxygen. Every little thing about them came from one sentence from God's lips.

On the fourth day when He said, "Let there be lights in the firmament of the heaven to divide the day from the night; and let them be for signs, and for seasons, and for days, and years: And let them be for lights in the firmament of the heaven to give light upon the earth" (Genesis 1:14-15) molecules of hydrogen formed and swirled together in great masses all over the Universe and gravity took shape of these molecules into giant spheres that ignited in a nuclear fusion reaction that released heat and light from every star that formed from God's statement.

Stars began to rotate, and molecules smashed together to create helium at millions of degrees at their cores. The celestial body that we know as Luna, or the moon, gained its purpose as the lesser light of the night while Sol, our sun, became the greater light of the daytime. The laws of physics took shape, and these stars and heavenly bodies were markers for the change and behavior of seasons. Certain stars would only show up at various times in the sky while being billions of miles away from the Earth. The very tilt of the Earth now came into focus as the Earth orbits the sun in a precise dance to support the plants already thriving.

On the fifth day God said, "Let the waters bring forth abundantly the moving creature that hath life, and fowl that may fly above the earth in the open firmament of heaven" (Genesis 1:20) he then said in Genesis 1:22, "Be fruitful, and multiply, and fill the waters in the seas, and let fowl multiply in the earth." Every life form from the sea and their diversity was created. From the deepest depths to the rivers and streams in every detail and variety. The same for the birds and He instructed them on their mode of transportation.

From what God was thinking in His mind came into existence. Deoxyribonucleic acid (DNA) was transformed from just making plants that were rooted to the ground into creatures that swam, walked or flew. God did the same type of thing on the sixth day when He said, "Let the earth bring forth the living creature after his kind, cattle, and creeping thing, and beast of the earth after his kind" (Genesis 1:24) and every beast, insect and creature that was on the land was sprouted from God's intent. Every detail from skin to fur, scales to hides were commanded to appear, but again, that wasn't the end.

Then God said, "Let Us make man in Our image, after Our likeness: and let them have dominion over the fish of the sea, and over the fowl of the air, and over the cattle, and over all the earth, and over every creeping thing that creepeth upon the earth." (Genesis 1:26) Here is the beginning of the relationship that God has with us. Here is where I noticed the most interesting part about all of this. Notice the words God used when everything else was created. "Let there be..." or "Let the..." were what He said about everything else. From the most complex star and series of galaxies, the patterns on the wings of the honeybee and how nerves spider into every cell, blood carries nutrients, oxygen and water sustain life, He just said those words and all things were created.

They simply appeared at His command. God's intent was felt everywhere because He spoke it, and it was so. What fills pages and pages of our science to explain these things that God simply spoke cannot be fully contained. The depth of the details goes beyond our understanding. Orbits of electrons for every element were determined by His words. Gravity, light, energy, mass, time, and many other things came into existence by what He spoke. God's Words carry a power like none other and yet God did something different. He declared, "Let *Us **MAKE MAN***..."

Now when we go to Genesis 2:7 it gives a little clarification as to how He made humans. "And the Lord God formed man of the dust of the ground and breathed into his nostrils the breath of life; and man became a living soul." Still, we should give pause to the fact that God ***MADE US***. God has the power to invoke us into existence. We have blood, flesh, and intelligence just like many other life forms on the Earth. We have eyes, nostrils, and appendages like many other things that are alive. We, however, were made differently. There is no doubt in my mind about that, but what I see here is that God made it personal with us.

He ***formed us*** from the dust of the ground. I can imagine that God shaped Adam from the dust with His Own Hands. Not only did God shape Adam, but He made Him specifically "in His image, after His likeness" and that my friends are powerful things to take note of. Psalms 139:14 declared that the author was "fearfully and wonderfully made" and we were the only thing created on Earth by being formed. Formed in His image is a monumental concept that carries weight. In our realm today when we snap a picture of something on our lovely telephones what we have created is an image. That picture is a representation of what the eye of the camera saw when it was taken.

Here is what I know about an image. When I take a picture of a person, I take a living and breathing person and I make a representation of them, but it isn't them. No matter how many megapixels a camera has or how powerful and sophisticated that camera is it cannot and will not make another exact copy of what it captures. Here is the cool part. A person and everything in our reality has three dimensions: Depth, Width and Height. We call it 3D or three-dimensional. We love movies in 3D, and we love virtual reality which is 3D. Yet, when we take a picture, we ***LOSE*** a dimension. We still have height, and we still have width, but we no longer have depth. We can capture every color and every detail of that person, but they are not flattened. If we print that picture out on our printer it is flat. We can try and cheat and use a 3D printer and even that is not the same because we have the depth, but no life. We're not done yet...

Here is something else and I don't want to blow anyone's brain, but we have three dimensions, but we live in a fourth called time. Time is around our existence and affects us and the living and breathing person who exists in time is captured in that photo is now frozen in time. I can look at the picture years from now and it will remain the same while the person that was the subject will change. I don't want to make anyone's head spin, but an image loses two dimensions from the original. One is the dimension that is their existence, and the other is the dimension that surrounds their existence. A photo is two-dimensional and frozen in time compared to a three dimensional being carried by time. See if you can catch this. God thought so much of humanity that He made us in His image which means we look like God, but because we are an ***IMAGE***, we aren't but a snapshot of God. We lost two dimensions from God when He formed us. Let me explain...

God is beyond time. God is the holder and author of Eternity. God is the Alpha and the Omega, the beginning and the end, the first and the last. God is the bookend and bookcase of all reality. God walks in Eternity and even though we are in His image we lost the dimension of Eternity as we have a lifespan and God does not. He is infinite. We are finite. Our lives appear as vapor which is there for a moment and then is gone. God is everlasting and if we could have the ability to make an image of God like our photograph, we couldn't capture His Eternity.

The second dimension we lost is His unlimited power. I can take a picture of a lightning bolt, but if I hook up a voltmeter to a photo it will read zero volts. God has unlimited power, and He has shown that He does. He commanded the seas where to stop, and His Words caused matter to appear and be shaped as He wanted it. We can't do that in any way. We don't even control our heartbeats or how we breathe. God has the control, and we are just created beings. Our bodies are powered, but we cannot make our own power.

So, when God formed us, He made a much smaller version of Himself. He gave us our physical characteristics when we were shaped, but we are a slave to time versus its master, and we are powerless and depend on God for everything. We cannot create like God can. Everything we make is limited within the boundaries of what God sets. Yet He also made us with His likeness and that is also beautiful. We are the only created beings with true emotions and sentience or awareness of our existence. We are ***LIKE*** God in that we can reason with God with our own minds and emotions. He gave us the choice of what we want to do, and God gave us the power to speak things into existence if we do so by faith through His Name.

God made us special and just for Him. He walked with Adam in the cool of the Garden of Eden. He spoke with His servant Moses mouth-to-mouth. He carried

Enoch and Elijah away into Heaven. God loves us in a unique way, and we are not like anything else in Creation. It is when we understand that God created ***EVERYTHING*** out of ***NOTHING*** to give us a home and gave us dominion over the Earth? That's when we see how much God loves us and how much He cares for us!

The Bible clearly shows us how God initiated the relationship with humanity. He created us to love and live for Him, and we messed all of that up with bad decisions detailed in Genesis Chapter 3. He drove us out of Eden because we failed to resist temptation and own up to our errors, and we received the consequences of our actions. We lost the fellowship with God that we had because of sin, we suffered loss, and we now encounter pain and adversity for the first time. We messed up because we listened to the serpent, failed to be accountable for our lapse in judgement, and ever since that day humanity has been on a road of reconciliation back to God.

Because of what Adam and Eve did, we now must deal with all the pitfalls and trials that come to us all because of one bad choice. A choice that God allowed us to suffer for because we caused it but still loved us enough to give us a way back home to Him. Let me be clear, everything isn't bad on this journey. I want to be completely clear and let you know that the life of being saved isn't all doom and gloom, but the rough patches and difficult journey we face is an uphill battle because we are in a war with our flesh and Satan himself.

Lucifer is fighting us, too, and it is because of his unwise decision to rebel against God. Because of this and because we are in his territory on the Earth, we are caught in the middle of the oldest feud in all of eternity. Lucifer is jealous of us because God made us the way he did. That's my opinion and I am convinced that it is true. Lucifer, or Satan, even tried to trip up Jesus by tempting His flesh to get Him to sin. Satan has zero chill and knows that he has lost the eternal struggle and will be sentenced to Hell himself, and he wants to take as many humans as possible along with him. He is petty, limited, prideful and he hates us because we now have the relationship with God that he no longer has. He is still one of the "Sons of God" as depicted in Job 1:6, but he lost his place as the exalted one and he has engaged us to keep us from getting to know God on any deeper levels. The more he keeps us apart from God, the less we get to know Him which is why

God uses our journey on this road of life as a way that we get to know God in special ways.

I don't know about you, but I love road trips. I have been on a few with people I liked to be around, and they all have been an experience I have yet to forget. I once went on a trip many years ago to take a vacation in Orlando, Florida and all of us didn't have a lot of money, but we had a place to stay at a great price, if we could get there, so we drove. When we mapped it all out the estimated driving time was sixteen hours. If we could have flown it would have been about three hours, but due to our financial situations the road was the way we had to go. When we first got in the car we had fresh clothes, food and snacks and a full tank of gas.

Under the cover of darkness, we left our homes (IYKYK), and the first driver took the wheel, and we headed south. At first, we settled in our seats and although we all knew each other over the years, we had no idea what was in store for us on the road. After we crossed the first state line, we were still excited and still euphoric like we were when we left. We had many conversations about various things and music was playing and after a while something interesting began to happen.

We started to discover things about one another that we never knew just by association. We were all in one place and had time to kill so we talked about many things as the miles passed us by. We couldn't physically be separated, so we talked and talked about all kinds of stuff. Some "deep" things and some silly things. We shared perspectives that we never knew the others had. We laughed at stories that we had never told before. We shared some things we never told another soul, and we shared the Word of God too.

Each person chose a CD (yes, it was that long ago) to listen to and we all got to hear music we hadn't heard before. We sang well and sang poorly sometimes and yes; we even shared moments of worship. It was amazing. Some people took turns sleeping while others drove. Rest stops and bathroom breaks were often enough to stop at rest areas and road and fact markers, and we learned things we never knew before. We ate in the vehicle, and we stopped at various eateries for hot food and cold drinks. As each person drove, we learned about how they drove and their own quirks and each other's habits.

There weren't always good moments. We did get on each other's nerves at times and there were more than a few awkward moments and silences as well. We even had disagreements, and we apologized after thinking things over and we made things right since we had sixteen hours of driving each way to experience and a week to spend in Orlando. We grew tired, got uncomfortable at times and couldn't wait to get off the road after time went on. However, when we got to our destination our collective weariness was turned into joy as we pulled up to our destination. Then we began our vacation, enjoyed ourselves immensely, and then prepared for the return trip home to repeat the experience all over again of the journey. After a week of vacation and thirty-two hours of travelling together we were not the same. We learned to appreciate things about the other and we even learned some things that we never knew, wish we didn't know, but learned anyway. The journey transformed us and regardless of all that went down we were closer and knew each other more than we ever did before.

When we travel together with people, we learn more about them and we learn about ourselves. The key to every relationship is ***TIME***. The more time a person has together with one another the more they either grow closer to them or realize that they are not compatible and go their separate ways. As it is in the Natural Realm, so it is in the Spiritual Realm. When we are born into this world, we are born into sin by the legacy of the First Adam. We are disconnected from Christ from Day One and we are subject to the ruler of this sinful world Lucifer. While in our humanity we are servants of the flesh and our life's journey can be more influenced by Satan than anyone else (no matter how good or bad we are). As we progress, we are introduced to God in some form and if we choose to accept Him as our Lord and Savior, we begin a journey with Him along with the line between the two points that are our birth and death.

This is where the parallels start to make sense. Let's go back to my road trip as an example. All of us that traveled together ***CHOSE*** to interact with each other because we already knew each other. We decided on what level we would interact with them, and we pursued the avenues to us. Now imagine if we did that trip and never spoke to one another. Suppose that we stayed to ourselves and did only what we needed to do to complete the trip and nothing more. We communicated as much as we needed to function and left it at that level. Imagine that we just got on the phone and talked with someone else while we were with the others, or we immersed ourselves within ourselves and didn't bother to venture out. How do you think that the results would be different? Well, for starters, we wouldn't have discovered anything new about each other than what we already knew. We wouldn't have shared things with one another that we didn't know. We wouldn't have forged stronger bonds with the other travelers. We would only have the trip as a necessary avenue to get from Point A to Point B.

I want to show something about this broken road that many of us don't see until after we mature in our reconciliation of our relationship with God. The broken road is not a punishment, but it is an invitation to return to Jesus. This may seem strange to us humans, but God does and has done things differently than we would to get His point across. I know that many would not see this as positive, but here is a passage of Scripture from the Book of Amos that illustrates this perfectly:

AND I ALSO HAVE GIVEN YOU CLEANNESS OF TEETH IN ALL YOUR CITIES AND WANT OF BREAD IN ALL YOUR PLACES: YET HAVE YE NOT RETURNED UNTO ME, SAITH THE LORD. AND ALSO, I HAVE WITHHOLDEN THE RAIN FROM YOU, WHEN THERE WERE YET THREE MONTHS TO THE HARVEST: AND I CAUSED IT TO RAIN UPON ONE CITY, AND CAUSED IT NOT TO RAIN UPON ANOTHER CITY: ONE PIECE WAS RAINED UPON, AND THE PIECE WHEREUPON IT RAINED NOT WITHERED. SO TWO OR THREE CITIES WANDERED UNTO ONE CITY, TO DRINK WATER; BUT THEY WERE NOT SATISFIED: YET HAVE YE NOT RETURNED UNTO ME, SAITH THE LORD. I HAVE SMITTEN YOU WITH BLASTING AND MILDEW: WHEN YOUR GARDENS AND YOUR VINEYARDS AND YOUR FIG TREES AND YOUR OLIVE TREES INCREASED, THE PALMERWORM DEVOURED THEM: YET HAVE YE NOT RETURNED UNTO ME, SAITH THE LORD. I HAVE SENT AMONG YOU THE PESTILENCE AFTER THE MANNER OF EGYPT: YOUR YOUNG MEN HAVE I SLAIN WITH THE SWORD AND HAVE TAKEN AWAY YOUR HORSES; AND I HAVE MADE THE STINK OF YOUR CAMPS TO COME UP UNTO YOUR NOSTRILS: YET HAVE YE NOT RETURNED UNTO ME, SAITH THE LORD. I HAVE OVERTHROWN SOME OF YOU, AS GOD OVERTHREW SODOM AND GOMORRAH, AND YE WERE AS A FIREBRAND PLUCKED OUT OF THE BURNING: YET HAVE YE NOT RETURNED UNTO ME, SAITH THE LORD. – AMOS 4:6-11 KJV

Look at what God spoke through Amos and see what God did. God laid out how He allowed things to befall Israel that would seem to be punishments, but it wasn't God punishing them, but God was trying to get the people's attention to realize that they had strayed from God. God even demonstrating a supernatural-level of demonstration by raining on one field and not another. He allowed people to die and let some escape with scars. Then see the language that God used: "Yet, you have not returned unto me." God wanted Israel to return to Him. He did all that He could to convince them, and they ignored Him. God could have wiped them out, but He didn't. He gave them a chance to return, and they didn't do it. God got fed up and instead of killing them all He allowed captivity to come to them. God had made it apparent that He still loved His people, but He had to use the only thing at His disposal that seemed to work which was trouble manifesting in their lives. So, the question that arises now is how to we return to God after moving away from Him?

The Three Keys

There are many things that can happen to us on our road of reconciling our relationship with Jesus and many possible pitfalls, pit stops and scenarios of many dark days. Being saved isn't all doom and gloom and honestly, it is the best life that a person can live. Sure, there are circumstances that are tough, but our God has given us the way and the means to connect with Him as He leads us along where we must go. It isn't simple living this life, but it is more than worth it and not just for the reward of eternal life with God forever. The road may be broken, but God is not broken in any way. Yes, humanity failed Him, but He has never and will never fail us. In the Spiritual Realm there is one major difference when it comes to the journey with Christ. Jesus already knows ***EVERYTHING*** about us, and we relatively know little about Him. The ways we get to know Him are through His Word, through prayer and through worship. What is important to keep in mind is that each of these activities can lead to the others and they do not have to be independent of each other. I call these items the Three Keys of Reaffirming a Godly Relationship and without these Three Keys we cannot get to experience God in a meaningful way.

The Word of God

The Word of God is alive and is God Himself (John 1:1). What I am going to say here may shock some people and may cause you to question some traditions that you may believe. The Bible is the Word of God, ***BUT*** so is every Word that comes from the Mouth of God. The book that we know as the Bible is a collection of manuscripts that God inspired and spoke through regular people like you and me to write, transcribe and were collected (not without controversy) into a single volume. The key thing to remember here is that the Bible was constructed by humans, edited by humans and translated by humans. The hands of human beings have been touching, changing and modifying the Scriptures for millennia. The Word of God is perfect, but the Bible is not. I know that statement won't be well-received but hear me out. What God said and spoke to humankind is perfect in every way and is infallible. The human collection that is the Bible has been messed with for so long that we don't know what is really supposed to be in there except for what has been handed down by generations of humans. That doesn't mean that the Bible should not be revered and cherished as the Word of God.

From grade school I learned that the earliest stories in human history were first passed down via oral traditions. Elders, griots, or storytellers passed the history of a civilization down to be memorized by the next generations in succession. For the thousands of years that people have lived here on Earth the oral transmission of history was the only means of keeping the accounts of people until the invention of writing over six thousand years ago. As a Christian man who understands science, I know that Creation is more than six millennia old and by the time writing was invented what was recorded before that time was whatever was remembered by the people responsible for keeping the record as accurate as possible. Let's be realistic, there wasn't a stenographer present when God said, "Let there be light…" so what was written down was what was passed down from person to person.

Let me explain it like this. Have you ever played the "conversation game"? This game's premise starts when the first person in a line tells the next person something quietly and they must pass it down an extensive line of people until the end and the goal is to see if what was said makes it to the other end intact? I know I have, and I have seen everything from the last person saying something completely different than the first person or a paraphrase that is close, but that is not exactly what was said. To me, the Bible is exactly like that "conversation game" because we don't have existing copies of what each contributor to the Word of God wrote themselves as they have been lost to time.

We don't have the words transcribed by Paul's transcriber. We don't have any scrolls (or stone tablets) that Moses may have written on. We don't have anything physically written on by Joshua, Samuel/Nathan/Gad, Mordecai, the writers of the Psalms (David, Solomon, Moses, The Sons of Korah, Asaph [and family], Ethan the Ezrahite, or the ones who are still anonymous), Agur, Heman, Solomon, Isaiah, Jeremiah, Nehemiah, Ezekiel, Daniel, Hosea, Joel, Amos, Obadiah, Jonah, Micah, Nahum, Habakkuk, Zephaniah, Haggai, Zechariah, Malachi, Matthew, (John) Mark, Luke, John (also the Revelator), Paul, whoever wrote Hebrews, James, Peter, or even Jude.

We only have what was collected and written down by those who had it passed down to them. The Bible, as it stands, is still the most well-documented book in history. Where many religious texts have few copies (or non-existent ones) the Bible stands out as well passed down by the ages. I am not saying that the Bible is worthless, because it is so valuable and so precious to us, but what I am saying is that there may have been some things accidentally (or purposely) left out of it, or meanings twisted and mistranslated. If people are involved there will be errors. Then there were the many councils and versions of the Bible that I won't get into that determined which books were included and which were not.

There are things you might have heard of like the Apocrypha and Gnostic Gospels that are not included in most mainstream Bibles (often for good reasons). There are some texts listed in the Old Testament that are not included in the "official" canon or lost to the ages like the Book of Jasher (Joshua 10:13), the Book of the Wars of The Lord (Numbers 21:14), the Book of Nathan the Prophet (2 Chronicles 9:29), and the Visions of Iddo the Seer (2 Chronicles 9:29). I am not advocating for the inclusion of these texts, but I am just stating what is in the historical record.

I could go on and on, but there is something interesting that Jesus said while He was on Earth that I feel is so important. In John 14:26 Jesus said, "But the Comforter, which is the Holy Spirit, Whom the Father will send in My Name, He shall teach you all things, and bring all things to your remembrance, whatsoever I have said unto you." Beyond the fact that all Three Persons of The Trinity are in action in this verse (just like 1 John 5:7 says) the Holy Spirit was sent to teach us all things and bring all things to our remembrance that ***JESUS*** said to us. Think about that. Jesus knew that what He would say might get lost in the "Conversation Game" and that He needed God the Father to send the Holy Spirit in the Name of Jesus to keep us connected to the Word of God correctly. Christ knew that things would get lost in translation and sent the greatest Teacher ever known to us to keep us connected to the Word of God which is God Himself. Slow down, back up, and read that again. God confirms His Word, by the Word, through the Holy Spirit, Who is God. We get the Word of God straight with no chaser.

Combined with the Holy Spirit, The Word of God permeates every barrier and removes every stain in our lives. The Word can function as a medical kit to heal and as a chastiser and loving corrective instrument. When we seek The Word and delve deeper into its depths God reveals things that we never could have imagined. The Word of God is not just about answers, but is also about comfort, wisdom, power, and so much more. Whatever you need is in there. Whatever you are missing in your life is in there. The Word of God is full of testimonies of those who suffered abuse, rape, torture, suffering, sickness, and struggles with mental health.

There is nothing in this world that is more complete and more comprehensive than God's Word. The Bible is just the appetizer to the main course that is God Himself. What seems like a paradox makes so much sense when you look at things through spiritual eyes. God is everything and every Word He speaks is eternal. When God speaks things are either created or destroyed. When God speaks time can be altered and reality can be turned on its ear. The Word of God is the embodiment of ***POWER*** and there is nothing that can defeat it, nothing that can stand against it and nothing that is greater.

The Word of God is more than just writings on a page, but it is the essence and Presence of God Himself. The Word of God is rich and cannot be contained in the paper pages of a book or an electronic file or an app. The Word of God is like a battery. It is power that when we connect to that Word things begin to move and transform. The Word is needed on this journey and to connect with the Word of God we must be connected to the Spirit of God. When trouble comes, we may not have a printed Bible or an app, but we have Jesus. When we study the Word of God and when we meditate on the Word of God it becomes embedded in our spirits. When we absorb the Word of God and not just memorize words on pages, that Word becomes a part of our lives, our habits and our mindsets.

When the Word of God becomes integral to our lives no matter what comes we get to know His Power and we see it in action because His Word is an account of all that He has done for Creation. When we come across certain situations, we can rely on the Word of God to show us how He did things before and how He can do it always by faith. The Word of God is like a class that never ends and the Scriptures and what God reveals to us is His textbook. This is our research library, and our tangible anchor point when it seems that nothing else is around us and we are in the darkness and in total silence.

The Word of God is eternal and will never lie or break a single promise. I don't care what anyone says, or some secular scholar will try to deduce, the Word of God has never done these things. Ever. Anything that God promised to anyone always and I mean ***ALWAYS*** happened. The naysayers have tried to pick the promises of God apart and failed to see the part where the promise was a two-sided covenant. God promised His people things that depended on what they did for Him. The Word's promises teach us to trust in a God that has never lied to us and never broke a promise.

When we see how He promised things to the Israelites, the prophets, and even to people we can be sure that if God said and did it before that He will do it again for us! It is by a solid track record that we can rest assured that God is true, and He is eternal. Look at how Scripture has promised things over time. What He said to the prophets of old is happening right now. What He predicted with Christ happened. What He said about Israel betraying Him and turning to other Gods happened. When we see a God that over every lifetime has been truthful helps us get to know Him even better and allows us the bridge to trust God with a "right now" situation and every single one after that.

The Word of God is measurable, dependable, reliable, relatable, and durable. God has spoken in units of time that came true, and He has shown over generations what He can and will do for us. God is not a "one and done" God who will help us one day and quit on us another day. God's Word shows His personality and His emotions. Remember when He was angry and ready to kill everyone (many, many times) and Moses pleaded with God not to do it? Remember when God said that he was sorry for causing the Great Flood? How about when Jesus was baptized by John the Baptist and He spoke over His Son and said that He was very pleased with Him?

It is amazing to me to see a God that spoke everything into existence (except us because we were formed) allows Himself to talk to us about things like this. God has been consistent and with what is captured in Scripture, we can see that God is stable, and His ways are durable and withstand our test of time. We can see the consistency, and we can see what He did in the past can help us today paint the picture of what He can do in the future or even right now. I tend to feel that the Bible was compiled for our benefit to see the wonderful works of God. Our God didn't need printed words on pages, but we did.

The Word of God fulfills Itself. Remember that John Chapter 1 told us that the Word is with and is God. What we see, as I just said, as the Word of God is just a printed representation of the Word. It is the physical manifestation of the Word of God as it is printed for our benefit. Our flesh needs to access the Word via our physical senses before we can access the Word on a spiritual level. Remember in the Scriptures where it says that we need to be ***HEARERS*** and doers of the Word? Remember that we must ***HEAR*** the Word to receive it. Therefore, the Word of God is God, His actions, His person, and His actions. His Word is a movement of energy. It transforms and activates and what is spoken or said ***MUST*** come true.

What God's Word does is beyond our logic. When God speaks a promise, His actual words are that promise. When God blesses someone, His blessing is literally what that person will experience. His Word doesn't need our help, but by design can have us participating in what is beyond our control. Isaiah 55:11 states that His Word will never return void or empty. His Word never comes back defeated or without action. When we see the promises in His Word, we can know that when God says it? That's it. It doesn't matter what is happening at that moment or what anyone has said, ***IT WILL HAPPEN***. We thrive in relationships that have trust and when we can see God's Word fulfill itself it helps us to draw closer to Him because we know that we can trust a guarantee like that.

The Word of God satisfies every hunger. To some this may be a reach, but I can tell you that this is very true. The Word of God can satisfy every hunger and it's not the way that you may think. Let's first draw a line between physical and spiritual hunger. Physical hunger is directly connected to our flesh while spiritual hunger is connected to our spirits. Walking with God and digesting His Word can show us how to satisfy our physical cravings that can cause us harm. Being hungry for food is one thing, but too much food can cause harm. Desiring physical intimacy is natural, but unnatural and immoral cravings for intimacy can cause harm. It is expected for us to thirst for water to live, but too much water can kill us too.

The Word speaks of excesses, and it speaks of things that can harm us. We can see examples of people who went with cravings, and they went sideways. We can also see how God restored those who made mistakes and the consequences of those errors. Scripture talks about taming our fleshly desires and how to live a holy life. The Word of God not only talks about those things but also gives us a way to satisfy our hunger and thirst of spiritual things too. When we seek God through His Word, He will give us what we need to satisfy our bodies and souls, and that satisfaction is directly tied to our spiritual growth in Him. Jesus told the woman at the well that the water He offered would cause her to never thirst again. We can rely on that in our walk with God too.

The Word of God is a refuge in the time of storms. We can be thankful for Psalm 46:1 for that bold declaration that God is our place of safety. There are so many examples in the Psalms and in other passages of the Word of God that tell us that God is our safe space and strength. When we are in a crisis and need shelter from the storms of life, we can find that safety in the Word of God. Just as I have stated before, we can see how God has been that place of rest and comfort for many others throughout the Bible, and we can rest assured that God has no favorites. In the natural realm, we know where a rest area is by the signs on the roadway. We know where food or lodging is located by signs like that too.

The signage is not just there because someone put them there. They are standardized and recognized by those who have followed them before. If a sign is inaccurate or is pointing to a trap it is taken down. When we read Scripture, we can see where God was the shelter from storms and a secret place for us when the author needed one. We establish over time that God is dependable and reliable. We know where safety is and when we read the Scriptures, we can see the type of safe place our God can be. We can see the testimonies of those who wrote words that give witness to God being our hiding place and when we see those words we know that God can comfort us too.

The Word of God can be whatever God desires to be for us. I am bold enough to say that the Word of God can fit every situation and every scenario in our lives. The Word of God is universal because our God is universal. God is everywhere and He is everything and His Word is no different. When we flip through the printed Bible, we can see scenarios of faith being tested, people enduring struggles, folks who suffered loss, and many more different things. When we look closer, we see how God resolved their circumstances and gave them the resolution that they believed in Him for or needed. For myself, whatever I needed to find answers for or need help with I found in His Word.

From temptation to tragedy, the Word is complete and gives answers on many levels. Most importantly, it points us to the source of all things Who is God Himself. When we are on this road of relationship and when we run into whatever it may be that we encounter, God's Word has the answer, and that answer is God. When we see the witnesses in the Scriptures it comes alive and lets us know that there are answers and there are paths or restoration, and we can see how others experienced these things and overcame them. To sum it all up, the Word of God is more than just a collection of words, phrases and sentences. It lives, moves, breathes and demonstrates who God is and what He has done throughout all Creation.

Praying to God

If we don't talk to God (through prayer), we will never know what He is truly like. Prayer is not just about asking things of God. Prayer is not just a method to make special requests and is so much deeper than that. Prayer is a conversation from the heart, mind and spirit that connects us with God. Through prayer we can tell God our troubles and confide in Him. Prayer is a means to express your feelings towards God in a verbal way and yes, it is a way to ask God for help. A prayer could be a simple conversation between us and God that pours out our emotions or thoughts. Just like any other conversation, prayer allows us to vocalize what is inside of us to God in a meaningful way.

Prayers don't have to be "church formal," but they do need to be sincere and truthful. Prayer must not be a formality or strictly ceremonial but be from the heart. Prayers to God should never be full of empty words and platitudes with ulterior motives or deceptive meanings. God knows what we are thinking or feeling already, and prayer is our way with communicating to God what He already knows. While human conversation needs eye contact, prayer needs ***HEART CONTACT***. Our heart must point to God's Heart for prayer to be genuine. Prayer is something that allows us to communicate with God no matter where we are and no matter what we are doing. Prayer can be whatever we need it to be because God is always listening to us.

Every relationship, whether it be between people or inanimate objects, requires communication. The better the communication, the better the relationship. Let's look at nature. Two birds don't know that they want together and nest to have baby chicks unless they communicate through birdsong or through some sort of action. Two people don't get to know each other unless they communicate by language or actions. Even things that humans create require relationships. My secular career is in Computer Science and for two devices to interoperate with each other they must communicate with each other to work together. For a web browser to get a website to display the application it must send information over the Internet to a server which interprets what the browser has asked for and then the server sends it back over the Internet to the web browser for viewing.

To communicate two or more items must send and receive information and understand that information and meaningly convey whatever it is they need to achieve what they are trying to achieve. When it comes to people, the more they communicate, the more they learn to interact with each other. Let's use going to your favorite coffee shop as an example. When we first go into the shop, we read what is on the menu, pick what we want and tell the barista what we want, they confirm our order, and then we pay for it and wait for it to be ready. Then, after some time, the barista calls our name, gives our order to us, and we then get to enjoy our beverage. Now, let's tweak our scenario here. Let's say that the same barista is there every day at the same time, and we go there every day on our way to work to get the same drink. We become accustomed to the barista, and they get accustomed to us over time.

What started as two people who never met became of a sort of relationship. If the barista and we are friendly people, we get to know their name, and they get to know ours. If we are the type of customer that always thanks them for their service, tip well and always have a smile, things start to change. Soon, the barista gets to know our order without us asking and they might ask if we want the usual thing. After a longer period if we don't deviate, they will see us coming and put the order in before we get to the front of the line. After an even longer period, they will have the order timed to be ready at a certain time before we even arrive.

Even though the specific barista and customer scenario is not representative for everyone, it shows us that when people communicate, connect, and come together a relationship of some form is the result. In our little setting imagine if the barista doesn't show up for work one day? Or even if we don't show up for work for whatever reason. When there is a relationship, one will look for the other and miss them. When I relate this to the relationship that we have with God I know that God is everywhere and that He doesn't need us but loves us dearly. When we start praying to God at first it seems awkward to us, but over time we get closer to God, and we enjoy the communication with Him. It goes beyond being a chore and becomes a desire, pleasure and even a necessity. When we don't pray, we miss our time with God in prayer. I think that God misses us too in a way. God pursues us relentlessly. His Love is reckless and so deep for us that it doesn't make sense. Until we accept Him as our Savior He stands at the door of our heart and knocks.

When we talk to God in prayer for the first time, we really don't know what to say. I know I felt lost and intimidated by His awesome Presence. It still boggles my mind that the Creator of the Universe Who is so massive and so powerful allows me to speak to Him and pour out my heart, and He not only hears me but understands me. Here I am so small, flawed, finite, mortal, and God knows when I call out to Him. From my best days to my worst days, I can talk to God. Most of us first learned the Lord's Prayer or the traditional Sinner's Prayer as the first prayer we even prayed to God. I can honestly say that beyond these prayers I had to learn on the fly how to pray. I asked advice from others like my parents and other Christians and through teachings from church. As my relationship with Christ developed my prayers changed with it and will continue to evolve as I continue this journey. Every circumstance and every situation have changed my relationship with Jesus and that upgraded my prayer life.

When I pray, I try to first bless God for who He is first and not just for what He has done. I tell God how beautiful He is and how I appreciate His Mercy and His Grace. I profess my love to Him in every way that I can think of and let Him know that he is my all and all and that He deserves my every breath, my every thought and that my very life is His to use as ***HE*** sees fit. I then ask God for forgiveness for every sin, every fault and every shortcoming that I have whether it is intentional or not. I acknowledge that He is perfect and that I am a mess doing my best to serve Him the best I can. Depending on what I am praying about I will either just talk to Him like a son would talk to his father and vent, cry or share my feelings with Him or ask for what I am in need of, and I would do so with fear, reverence and respect, but still be raw, truthful and honest. I don't hold back with what I talk about to God because he already knows what is going on with me, but I tell Him anyway. I admit the faults and sin that I can see, and I ask God to reveal to me the things that I don't see. I pray for others more than myself and I ask for guidance, wisdom, and (gulp) correction for the areas where I am lacking.

I often find myself talking things out with God that I cannot share with another person. I can be honest and say that I love my wife very much and I know that I can tell her and talk through just about anything. Yet there are a few things that only God and I can talk about because they are things that only He can understand. That doesn't mean that my wife isn't important in my life. I married her because she is the best thing to happen to me from Earth, but God is the best thing to happen to me from Heaven. There are some things that only God and you can talk about because of what they are.

When we pray, we can share those thoughts that only He can understand or even help us with. God already knows so telling Him all about it shows our trust in

Him. God has proven Himself to us repeatedly and we have a choice to trust God with all we are. It doesn't matter how severe, sinful, painful or embarrassing things may be to us we can share them with God and He won't judge us, laugh at us or make us feel bad about ourselves. What He says to us is in love. What He shows to us He does in love. Even if it isn't what we expect or want God responds with love.

Here is the part that most people don't really talk about enough... God speaks back. God doesn't just answer prayer by giving us the things we ask for, but He also talks to us and reveals things to us. The more we talk to Him, the more He talks to us. The more we share with Him, the more he shares with us. Just like any conversational relationship (because prayer is not just one-sided) it grows between the two people it is occurring. When we pray to God without ceasing a transformation happens. Our eyes become opened to the things of God. The understanding that we thought we had will begin to change. When we converse with God like Adam used to do in the cool of the evening or like Moses did "mouth to mouth" it transforms us to seeing God as He is: a loving Father. A Counselor, a Healer, a Restorer, a Friend, a Savior and Master. We learn that we can talk to God when we are not just in need, but when we are basking in joy. We can come to God when we are in shame and when we are in strength. We can come to God about anything, and He will hear us.

It's beautiful and as we journey through life, we learn that God is our rock, sword and shield. We get to know more of His ways even though we will never completely understand them. We come to an understanding that He never leaves us even when we cannot hear Him or see Him. We learn that if He did it before that He will do it again. We learn how He answers prayer, and we learn how to pray more effectively. We learn how to hear His Heart because to pray sincerely our heart must be tuned in to His. We must touch His Heart with our heart to know Him. We must love God to be connected to Him and understand what His Will really means for us. Prayers can be spoken aloud, silently and in the Spirit. We learn that some prayers are communicated faster than human speech and the "Spirit Channel" through the Holy Spirit is required. Whatever the method and whatever the reasoning, prayer is the communication that with a natural or heavenly language with God that helps us to reconcile our relationship with Him.

Worship of God

For so many people worship is one of the most misunderstood of these Three Keys. Worship can "simply" be defined as intimacy with God on a spiritual level. When people hear the words "intimacy" and "God" in the same sentence some people make a connection to a sexual type of encounter, and it is nothing like that. Intimacy is just an encounter that is deeply personal, unhindered and mutual. Intimacy cannot be forced onto either participant. Intimacy involves a level of openness not shared with anyone else in a relationship. Worship is a major part of a spiritually monogamous relationship with God. When we worship privately or corporately, the only connection is between each person and God. Worship is unlike anything in this world when it is genuine and a part of a fulfilling relationship with God. As we travel on this journey through this world worship is a connection that cannot accurately be described with words and cannot be obtained by false pretenses. Worship is either real or fake. There is no in-between and worship without a relationship with God is no more than a ceremony. A person who "worships" and has no connection with God is no different than a pagan performing a ritual.

Being a Psalmist and Minstrel for many years now, I have a unique perspective of how worship is one of these Three Keys because it is very personal and very real to me. Leading others into the Presence of God is a level of ministry that is hard to quantify because of the nature of how worship transforms, heals and restores the spirit of people. Worship requires each person to put away their shame and strip away everything that can hinder them from connecting with God. Worship is humbling, revealing, and is not easy to explain, because God cannot be accurately described in human language. That's because when we worship God, we connect our spirit with His Spirit and willingly allow God to do whatever He wants to do during that time of closeness. It is a place and not a feeling as emotions don't have much to do with worship. Emotions get us there, but it is not what we feel, but what we experience in the Presence of God that makes worship so special and powerful.

When we are in a relationship with Christ, we have a spiritual bond with a God we cannot see with our eyes but feel with our soul. When we talk about worship it is something that can be described by many but experienced by one. As a

Psalmist, I teach worship leaders how to lead worship, but one thing that I tell them all is that they cannot lead someone where they have never been. I can teach them techniques to keep people engaged and how to not lose themselves until the room has entered the Presence of God together, but I can't teach them how to worship God on their own. We all can come into God's Presence, but only everyone can plunge in for themselves. I teach them that worship is a safe space in God and that they can "let their hair down" and not be ashamed of anything while their spirit connects with God intimately. In this life we all need a place to feel safe, comforted and welcome whether times or good or bad.

Psalm 91 is a powerful song that speaks to the power and refuge of God:

He that dwelleth in the secret place of the most High shall abide under the shadow of the Almighty. I will say of the Lord, He is my refuge and my fortress: my God; in Him will I trust. Surely, He shall deliver thee from the snare of the fowler, and from the noisome pestilence. He shall cover thee with His feathers, and under His wings shalt thou trust: His truth shall be thy shield and buckler. Thou shalt not be afraid for the terror by night; nor for the arrow that flieth by day; Nor for the pestilence that walketh in darkness; nor for the destruction that wasteth at noonday. A thousand shall fall at thy side, and ten thousand at thy right hand; but it shall not come nigh thee. – Psalm 91:1-7 KJV

When we live this life there is no better "secret place" to be than in the Presence of the Lord. When we worship, we are captured by His Spirit and we are in a place where there is no fear, no shame and no condemnation because where the Spirit of The Lord is, there is freedom. It is a guaranteed place of safety, protection and openness. When it comes to the renewal of joy, Psalm 16:11 says it best, "Thou wilt shew me the path of life: in Thy Presence is fulness of joy; at Thy right hand there are pleasures for evermore." In those dark days where pain and sadness seem to be the only reality where we can experience a worship experience that can restore joy in a targeted way. It doesn't matter how long we are in the state of worship because the result is that we get reconnected to God in a way that recharges us, restores us, protects us and reassures us that God is still there.

No matter what the Enemy is currently doing, he must flee from the Presence of God. Every demonic influence and every distraction must fall away when we are connected to God in worship. There have been services where I have seen demonic forces act out violently and try to disturb worship because it was driving them away from the property, a person or the room. The Worship of God is a weapon of warfare just like prayer and The Word of God is. Any connection we make to God is being actively fought by Hell and we need to understand that fact and be ready to fight. Walking this broken road, as I have said before, is a long march through a spiritual battlefield and there is an active war going on all around us. It is not easy, and we must know the tools at our disposal, and we must know how to use them.

The best time to learn how to fight is not during the war, but when there is peace. I'm not saying that you can't learn how to fight in a conflict, but it's just a fact. Basic training for new soldiers happens in a controlled environment where there is peace and no real fighting at all. Worship is the same way, and we need to enter our place of worship when days are good as well as bad. When we learn to worship with purpose it will determine what we encounter in the Spirit. I want to be careful and not say that it is "easier" to worship in the good times than when in the dark times, but there is a diverse set of variables that we face when we encounter God in different situations. Regardless of the time, learning how to connect with God starts with a heart that burns for God and desires to pour their love out on Him. While the Word of God gives us a model as to how we pray and the Bible is a book that we can read, there is not a whole lot that really speaks to worship, except for the Psalms and in various excerpts of Scripture.

Just in case you don't know the model of worship, I will explain the model how I teach it to the Worship Teams I have led. I call it the Psalm 100 Model and perhaps it can help you too. Let's start with Verse 1 of the psalm, which is how we begin worship. With joyful noise we worship Him (Psalm 100:1). Blessing the Lord with our lips. Opening our mouths and speaking out words of gratitude and thanks for what God is to us. Telling Him how marvelous and wonderful He is. Clapping our hands and being glad for He is our God and Savior! Having happiness and joy in our hearts and breaking out into a song of praise if we know one or make one up (Psalm 100:2) because there are no rules here.

Affirming that He is God, and He is the One who made us because we couldn't and no one else could either. We are His people and the sheep of His pasture (Psalm 100:3). This where we explicitly tell God about how we feel about Him. We must let it all out and not be afraid to say it aloud. Why aloud? Because the Adversary hates the praises to our God. Praise is a weapon, and Hell can't stand it and must leave the premises immediately. With this we can turn whatever place we are in into a temple unto The Lord. We must focus and be intentional and be persistent. We may start to feel foolish or even feel sick (the flesh will always resist us). We must keep pressing and not stop. It will be worth it. Here is where the model gets interesting.

The Temple of God that Solomon built was designed a certain way based on the Tabernacle of the Wilderness. There were five components of the structure: the pair of columns at the entrance or "gate" *(Jachin and Boaz)*, the Forecourt or "Outer Court" *(Ulam)*, the Outer Sanctum or the "Inner Court" *(Hechal)*, the Holy of Holies *(Devir)*, and the side chamber *(Yatsia Sovev)*[1]. For the sake of the Psalms 100 model, I will exclude (even though it is important, and you should look it up) the side chamber because I could author a whole book about it.

Verse 4 of Psalm 100 says to *"enter into His gates with thanksgiving"* which is what you do first. Thanking God. The same verse continues with *"and into His courts with praise"* and this is where it gets deeper. When we bless God for what He has done, something changes. Our praise turns from what God has done (Outer Court) into thanking God for who He is (Inner Court). Then the verse continues as we travel into the Inner Court you begin to *"be thankful unto Him and bless His Name."* When we bless the Name of God over what we have been blessed with and just focus our heart, mind, and spirit on Jesus alone we begin to lose ourselves to His Spirit and we plunge into a deep worship (Holy of Holies). We must give up control of ourselves and what we want to experience and turn our desires and affections to the Heavens. The atmosphere shifts, every demonic thing runs for its life, and God takes over and we should let Him.

Worship literally saved my life. In the darkest periods of my existence where I contemplated suicide[2] and where I began to lose my grip on my sanity, worship changed the game for me. I have been saved since I was a boy, and I know Jesus for myself. I have encountered God in varying degrees over my journey in life. I thought I was okay with my relationship with Christ. I thought I knew what trouble was in my life and I was wrong. Very wrong. I have been serving in church a long time and I love church, and I love God and when things got dark, I went into a shell. The sadness was so thick that it brought me to my spiritual, physical and mental knees.

I was being broken like I never had before. I stopped going to church because I felt that I was being a fake. I was angry at God, depressed over my losses, my heart was shattered beyond being broken, and I started questioning my faith. I was being deceived by Hell that I shouldn't be around real Christians because I would contaminate them with my downtrodden spirit. I stopped going anywhere except for work while those who hurt me seemed to be celebrating their lives and happy.

Here I was, coming home every night to sit in the dark and cry my eyes out and pigging out on comfort food and drink. I could hear the whispers of demonic beings telling me awful things about myself. How I deserved everything I got. I was told that I was alone and worthless. I was told that I was unloved and would never be truly loved. I was told that I was never saved, and that God was a lie. I wanted to depart this life, and I wanted to do it painlessly. My hope was gone, and my soul had turned cold. The one thing that never left me was music.

I would sit at my keyboard and play the saddest music you could imagine, and I remember that I (by reflex via the Holy Spirit) started playing the Shekinah Glory Ministry song, *Jesus*. Slowly all the darkness began to fade, and I played the song and started to hum the melody. I went from humming to weakly singing and from my quiet voice it began to grow louder and louder until I was singing again for the first time in months. Tears streamed down my cheeks as I sang the chorus which has just one word: ***JESUS***.

It went from just singing the Name Jesus to declaring His Name. The room was still dark except for the lighted screen of my keyboard, but the room felt as bright as the noon day sun. The atmosphere started to shift and every demon that tried to take me out had to leave long enough for the Holy Spirit to speak to my spirit. The fire in my heart was lit again, and I was at this point ugly crying and hardly singing. I don't even remember if I played the chords right, but it didn't matter. I was captured by His Presence, and I let myself go. I hadn't prayed for so long that I didn't even know how, but I just cried. I fell to the floor and just bawled, and I knew that the Holy Spirit understood exactly what I was saying. My heart poured out everything. Every dreary day and every gut-wrenching emotion that I had been feeling. I confessed to God that I had planned to overdose on over-the-counter painkillers. I told God everything I was feeling, and I wasn't ashamed. I literally could feel the arms of The Lord wrap around me and hold me close. I don't know how else to describe it. The suicidal thoughts fell away, and the gloom lifted from me.

At the point I don't remember everything else because I woke up face down on my tear-soaked carpet and I could still feel the Presence of God in the room. On my knees I just began to thank Jesus over and over for saving my life. I thanked Him for bringing things back to my remembrance. I learned valuable lessons that day and one that I want to share with you is that worship is needed, necessary and not to be taken for granted. I know that there are many controversies about worship and everything from where it can be done and what songs are spiritual enough to use in worship. I will say with certainty that it doesn't matter about any of these things.

What is more important is that we as people connect with God on a deeply personal level and worship is how we do it. Whether there are good times or not we as people need worship like we need to eat food or drink water. The Broken Road cannot be traveled without a connection to God on a spirit-to-spirit level. With or without music; alone or in a group; traditional or contemporary; none of these things are a factor. Worship is a source of life and when we learn to worship and connect with Christ on levels that surpass human understanding a bond develops between us and our Creator that becomes unbreakable.

The Paradox

After talking about the Three Keys of Relationship, I think that we need to look at the fact that these things are not as separate and distinct as they may appear. None of these keys are more important or more powerful than the others. I call this a paradox because we could go on and on in circles about how each of these things point at each other and rely or not rely on each other. A paradox is defined as someone or something with qualities or features that seem to conflict with one another. God is such a paradox in that He is described as three persons in One. Scripture is full of references and statements that seem to contradict themselves and to those who don't understand God it seems like our faith is built upon lies and twisted tales. When we try to wrap our human minds around how we can have a relationship with God we could easily fall into misconceptions and things can get lost in translation. It is exceedingly difficult for us to explain and understand how God works, but honestly just seeing God doing what He does is enough.

When we see the depth of His Love in John 3:16 (often overlooked for its sheer power and demonstration of God's reckless Love) that He gave His only birthed Son for us it doesn't make sense. When we look deeper into the Word of God for instance, It is God and is the record of who He is and what He has done. He always was, is and will always be, which breaks the human mind. God is a being that is beyond time, and He is a being that is everything and Himself at the same time. Let's go back, once again, to what John 1:1-4 says:

In the beginning was the Word, and the Word was with God, and the Word was God. The same was in the beginning with God. All things were made by him; and without him was not anything made that was made. In him was life; and the life was the light of men. – John 1:1-4 KJV

Examine what it says here… The Word was with God and was God. How can The Word be with and be God? All things were made by God, but it was His Word that created everything. See what I mean? If we try to make sense of this, it will give us a headache. From a human perspective, how God is illustrated in the Bible doesn't make sense to the natural mind. Those who do not believe in God will point at things like this and declare that our God cannot possibly exist, and they are ***WRONG***. Until someone has a relationship with God, they cannot understand Him. As complex and as large as our God is, He can be personal, and He opens Himself to us in direct relation to how we open ourselves to Him. That also doesn't make human sense. What other deity in other holy texts does what the true and living God of the Bible does? The answer is ***NONE***!

You could look at Allah (who is ***NOT*** the god of the Bible), to see how he related to humanity, but Muslims don't use the term *Walid Allah* (father god) or *'ab* (Dad). They believe that calling themselves the "children of god" presumes too much.

They don't believe Allah is knowable in an intimate, relational sense. They believe Allah reveals his will, but not himself[3]. Side note, the word "Islam" is literally defined as ***SUBMISSION***[4] and by its own name, is a religion of a form of slavery.

Voluntary or non-voluntary doesn't matter as Jesus told us that "whosoever will come after me, let him deny himself, and take up his cross, and follow me (Mark 8:34). Allah demands obedience and Christ gives us the option to love and serve Him. I challenge anyone to find anywhere in the Qur'an or any Muslim teaching where Allah gave any Muslim grace or showed unfailing love. Allah's love was conditional and was just a provider of everything while the Love of Jesus was unconditional and still gave us everything.

You could look at Baal who was prevalent during the time when the Israelites were conquering the land of Canaan. Baal was the supreme god of Canaan and Phoenicia, whose worship infiltrated Jewish religious life during the Judges and became popular in Israel during Ahab's reign. Baal means "lord" and was believed to be a fertility god who helped the earth produce crops and people have children.[5] The Bible has ***MANY*** references to the detestable nature of Baal worship and his consort Ashtoreth. Baal couldn't answer his 450 prophets when Elijah challenged Baal to send down fire from Heaven (1 Kings 18:20-40). He seems to be deaf or asleep.

You could look at Krishna who is considered an appearance or the descent of a deity (an avatar) to the earth. In traditional Hinduism, Krishna is considered the eighth avatar of the lord Vishnu. However, for Krishna devotees in Bhakti Hinduism this is reversed so that Vishnu becomes the avatar of Krishna[6]. Krishna's appearances through the ages are multiple while Jesus Christ came once and will physically return. The specific purpose of Christ coming was to reveal God to humankind and to reconcile lost sinners back to God through Christ's sacrificial atonement (Titus 2:13); none of the Hindu avatars of Vishnu provides revelation nor do they in any way make atonement for human sin. Many have erroneously compared Krishna and Jesus and there is no adequate comparison. Jesus came to save humanity and Krishna was just… There. Vishnu's "avatars" lived and died a lifetime repeatedly.

You could look at Ahura Mazda in the ancient faith of Zoroastrianism where it reflects the religion of natural man, and other works-oriented religions. Ahura Mazda does not offer any salvation and accordingly gives no assurance that a person will achieve heaven or paradise[7]. I couldn't imagine not having any assurances that Heaven would be my eternal home. I could not fathom the life of bondage wondering whether we were good enough or not. Ahura Mazda seems eerily like Allah of Islam in this way to me. Despite the calls to Heaven and the principles of living good and just where is love for humanity? From what I have read and studied I never saw anything that equated to wanting to know Ahura Mazda or having a relationship with them. What I see parallels what being a Christian is in many points, but what I also see is a clever counterfeit of the Gospel.

Whatever deity that one would want to call on, they will see that these false gods are nothing like the God of the Bible. The God of the Bible wants to know us and gives us a way to connect with Him. These other gods did not do this. These other gods stood afar off and didn't care about us the way that our God does. Look at every other deity in the world and ask yourself this one question: "Which of these gods laid down their lives for us like Jesus did?" I challenge anyone to research every faith (clarification on this… not including Christian cults) on Earth and find one where that god sacrificed themselves to redeem humans of their sins. I am bold enough to say that no one will ever find one example. That is also paradoxical as the God of the Bible is completely different from all the others represented on Earth. We, of course, know the reason for that in that He is the only true God.

From Adam until this very moment God has had a desire for us to relate to Him directly. We are not worthy of that relationship if we tally up the scores of who we are versus Who God is. God is eternal. God is Creator. God is so big that He can't be measured. God is all-powerful. God is all-knowing. God sees it all. God is perfect. God is everything. On the other hand, we are mortal. We make things that rust or decay. We are tiny, little bags of flesh. We are powerless. We are limited in understanding. We can only see what our tiny eyes can view. We are flawed. We are just ourselves and we can hardly be that. Psalm 8:4 says it best when it states: "What is man, that Thou art mindful of him? and the son of man, that Thou visitest him?" We were made from dirt. The dust of the Earth. The same Earth that God spoke into existence. We aren't made of anything precious like gold or platinum in vast amounts. We are not shiny and valuable like diamonds or rubies. Nope, we are made from dirt. Our life's essence is what God exhaled. We come into this world naked, defenseless, practically blind, and totally helpless and dependent on someone to care for us or we will die as fast as we were born.

Yet the greatest power in the Universe wants to know us on a personal level. God created everything in this existence just for us. We were shaped, not spoken into existence. We were desired by Him and designed by Him. It doesn't make human sense. Here's something else, we are the only thing that in Creation that God ever had conversations with. In Genesis Chapter 6, God commanded the animals to go to Noah before the Great Flood. In 1 Kings Chapter 17, God commanded the ravens to feed Elijah. In Jonah Chapter 1, God prepared the great fish to swallow the prophet. Even when God commanded His people to do anything He allowed them the ability to ask questions or speak back. We are the only beings on Earth that have the choice of free will. God allows us the ability to openly defy Him if we choose to do so (with consequences). God will allow us to disobey Him and then be able to be reconciled back to Him. God has the power to make us puppets to do whatever He wants us to do. We all could be actors in His own personal show, but He made us to have a relationship with Him. Thinking about this can break our brains.

God watched Adam screw up and even though he defied God, God made a way for him to still live and be as happy as possible. Look at Scripture and you will see repeatedly how we messed up, sinned, shook our fists at God, and did the most wicked and perverse things we would do, and God ***STILL*** had a plan to redeem us to Himself again. In one of the greatest paradoxes of them all, God disrobed His eternity and through forty-two generations of Abraham was born to a woman as Jesus, The Christ, The Messiah of us all to live and die on the cross at Calvary for the sins of the ***ENTIRE WORLD***.

Let's pause there for one moment. In all human history, how many times has a king (or queen) sacrificed themselves for their kingdom? Go look it up. Search for it and I would be surprised if you find one. Our God laid down His life for everyone. Christ died for Hitler. Christ died for Caligula. Christ died for Saddam

Hussein. Christ died for Osama Bin-Laden, Kim Jong-Il, Genghis Khan, Pol Pot, Joseph Stalin, Vlad Tepes, and many, many more of the evilest souls that have lived on the Earth. Jesus died for those who hated Him and even proclaimed to God before He died, "Father, forgive them, for they know not what they do." (Luke 23:34) While everyone else is petty and won't get a papercut for those that hate them, Christ sacrificed Himself for us all. It doesn't make sense by any measure.

The Love of God is so deep and so wide that it covers everyone and their sins (Romans 8:28). From the outside it looks insane, and it looks almost ridiculous. Let's take a human perspective of what lopsided love looks like. Imagine the richest person on Earth who can buy anything and enjoys things from the Dollar Store. Imagine a great chef who runs the finest restaurant in existence and only eats budget-priced frozen meals. Imagine the auto dealer of luxury cars who only drives a jalopy. Imagine someone in high society who wants a wharf rat as a pet.

The combinations of things are endless, but I think that you get the idea. Why would an omnipotent God love sculpted dust? Why would God go through all this just for a failure like us? We have nothing to offer God, and we constantly mess up His plans for us. God constantly makes ways for us when we don't deserve it. God rescues us from our bad decisions. God even cares about us when the terrible things happen to us that we didn't deserve and brings us comfort and healing. That is just the beginning that is His nonsensical love for us.

God knows who and what we are, and His Love never changes for us. When we get to know Him via the three keys of relationship, He shares Himself with us too. God reveals more of who He is that isn't "on the pages of the Bible" and He shows us just how much He loves us even when it shouldn't be that way. As we travel this road and draw closer to God, He becomes clearer to us than we could ever imagine. The reason, in my mind, that God seems so unlikely to those who don't know Him is because until you experience God is an unscripted way He seems unreal.

The words of the Scriptures become more alive when we suffer through things that are echoed in their words. We get to see what the characters in the Bible got to see and it becomes "real", and it still doesn't make sense as to why God does so much for us like that. No matter how badly we screw up and no matter what we do, God still loves us and died for us anyway. I could go on and on as the paradox wraps us up even more.

This journey of life that we are on is hard. Saved or unsaved, it is difficult. Every person has a road that has been tailor-made for them. No one can look at someone else's experiences and tell them that they don't have a difficult path ahead for them. Some struggles are open and public, and many others are private, and sometimes exclusive to the person at the epicenter. We cannot know and we should never assume the difficulty of another person's experiences. There is no way we can walk this broken road without Christ, and I wouldn't want to do this without Him being my God, my Master and my Friend.

God sees it all before it happens and knows my every want and need. God is so special to us, and we are special to Him. This is why this journey with Him is so important. This road we walk is designed to bring us to Him in Eternity. We start this walk here on Earth, but for those who are saved it ends right into the ever-loving arms of Christ. Regardless of that, the same God, the same Word and the same worship is for everyone and even these things don't seem to make sense to us because they are independent and dependent on each other. The Word allows us to define God and His Power. Prayer allows us to understand God and His Person. Worship allows us to know God and His Presence and being.

Even though none of this makes sense, what we need to realize is that we (while we are in human flesh) don't need to understand it all but just receive Christ's Love and accept Him as our Savior. In our limited view we can accept the laws of physics even if we don't understand them. We know that gravity pulls us downwards and water is wet, and we may not understand why; we accept it to be true. These things come from acquiring understanding. When we are born, we are clean slates and the only thing we have is the instinct to suckle to feed.

Everything that we learn is acquired through revelations. We don't understand that hot is the opposite of cold or that red is different than blue until it is revealed to us. Until we learn how to crawl, we don't know how to move to where we want to go. Crawling evolves into walking and walking into running. We don't learn anything about anything until we are taught, and the answers are revealed to us. Even the things we don't understand, we accept them as facts because we can see the end results of what they do or what they are.

That is how we must learn, and it is the same in the realm of the spiritual. We don't have the capacity to completely understand God, but we see the results of His power, majesty and love. It is needless to overanalyze why Jesus came to atone for our sins, but we need to accept the fact that this great gift was given to us freely and we don't need to understand why. All we need to do is love God back not because of what He has done, but because of Who He is. He gave us the ways to understand and love Him, and we should use them in every way we can to get closer to God so that He will get closer to us. The paradox fades into the background when we realize that we don't need to know why but be genuinely grateful that God is God and He loves us. Because of that we delve deeply into His Word, pray to Him to communicate with Him and because we don't understand, we are in awe of Him in our worship. Once we embrace Christ we will then marvel at another paradox: why go through life without Him?

The Warfare

The reconciliation of our relationship with God takes time to develop. Every day when we wake up and go through our normal routines, we tend to forget that we are spiritual beings living through a physical experience. From the moment we take our first breath to our last gasp, we are in a war that we cannot avoid. We are entwined in a battle that started long ago when Lucifer rebelled against God and was thrown out of Heaven (Revelation 12:7-12). We don't know exactly when it happened, but we do know that it was before we were created. Lucifer is insanely jealous of God and has been on a mission to mess up everything God has done for us.

From the first people all the way until today, Satan has been doing all he can do to destroy humanity, and he is quite good at what he does. He caused Adam and Eve to fall into sin and cursed our bloodlines to such a point that God Himself had to be born into this world and live a sinless life to be the perfect sacrifice to pay for the wrongs we committed against God. Even though the sin debt is paid, Satan will not stop his vendetta against humanity and because he is a fallen angel, and he fights us in the realm we aren't naturally equipped to deal with: the spirit realm.

It doesn't matter whether you believe in the Spirit Realm or not, because your belief or disbelief in something doesn't make it any less real. The war that Satan wages against us is spiritual warfare. Spiritual warfare is the act of fighting against Satan when he tries to keep us from God's purpose for our lives. The enemy comes to kill, steal, and destroy so when we are pursuing Christ, he tries to do all those things to stop us. Though encountering spiritual warfare is difficult, God uses it to grow us and draw us closer to Him.

Spiritual warfare attacks can look like thoughts of rejection, depression, self-doubt, loss of a family member, your head being filled with lies, or anything that could potentially prevent you from furthering your calling.[8] Spiritual warfare is intense, grueling and real. We aren't fighting humans here (Ephesians 6:12). Humans are involved, but this war is fought in a realm we have been made unaware of because of our flesh. Our five senses aren't equipped for the spirit realm, but thanks be to God that the Holy Spirit gives us a glimpse of that world. He gives us the time-tested toolset to win. To use those tools requires us to tame our flesh and our humanity as we allow ourselves to be integrated into God's Spirit.

So, yes, we are at war, and yes, we are outmatched and outgunned as humans. Hopefully, you don't get discouraged when you read this. Let me be real with you... I was terrified at first and I won't lie; it was tough, and it was a serious reality check for me. It still is harsh, and I believe that it always will be. The Enemy will attack your mind with crazy and damning thoughts. He will attack your body with sickness and pain. He will stir up passionate desires to sin. He will tickle your addictions with temptations. He will attack your family and cause Hell to rise in your home. He will attack your finances. It could, and usually does, get intense and nasty. It could get "off the chain crazy" and sometimes much worse. All these things can happen at any time, by any circumstance and during the good times as well as the bad. Satan doesn't wait for a time convenient to us and let's be honest, no war or conflict sets an appointment on their opponent's calendar. We were enlisted to fight from the first day and we will continue to do this until God calls us home so while we walk this road, we must be prepared and equipped to go to battle to win.

We need to understand a key fact: it is impossible to live this or any life without warfare and it doesn't matter whether it is in the natural or spiritual realms. On this road of life, we, as Christians, are called into this walk with God that also involves war. Here is the thing; to be victorious, we must show up on the battlefield and to fight effectively we must be ready and understand the nature of what that warfare is like. Thanks be unto God that we have been called into this life as Christians to walk in spiritual authority and power. Even though it seems like our journey is singular, it is not at all. Our walk may be personal, but the goal is cooperative, and that goal is to build the Kingdom of God on the Earth.

Remember, we are members of one body in Christ and just like the human body, we have billions of individual cells that do their own specific functions but together function as one. No matter what we do on this road, we are working with our Brothers and Sisters in Christ all over the world to advance the Kingdom of God. There are three different degrees I like to describe how we navigate this war: Pre-Consciousness, Becoming Aware, and finally, Eyes Wide Open.

Pre-Consciousness

Let's start with the first level that we all come to: Pre-Consciousness. Before we even know what the definition of spiritual warfare is and before we even know that Satan is real, he brings the battle to us. He does this the temptations and seductions of our flesh and all that comes with it. We cannot fight these things successfully in the natural world, but we must combat them in the Spirit where all warfare produces true authority and power. Romans 8:13 says, "For if ye live after the flesh, ye shall die but if ye through the Spirit do mortify the deeds of the body, ye shall live." When we are blissfully unaware of what the Spirit is we don't even know that we are in a war. A war that causes pain and suffering until we leave this Earth isn't really talked about that much.

Hell fights us from the moment we take our first breaths in this realm until we breathe our very last. Hell does all it can to stop us from knowing Christ and the things of God. As we develop as infants and then as children we are taught to rely on our senses and what we can determine to be true based on what our brains tell us is real. Seeing color or hearing a sound isn't theoretical, but it is actual. A good example is that to know that a stove is hot from feeling it versus being told about it registers it in our brains. Humans are trained to relate to the world around them by our brains, which to many is the greatest device known to humanity. The unexplained and the unknown are concepts that are too hard to grasp or understand and while we are maturing, they are prioritized lower until they have little significance.

Still, we as people have a deep-down feeling that there is more to all of this and as we grow, we begin to question what we don't understand or what we had blindly accepted as true. This is where the first attacks of spiritual warfare begin in my opinion. When humans develop the skill of independent thinking a transformation begins to take place. The blind faith of depending on our parents for everything begins to dissolve as time progresses and we start to decipher and process information on our own based on our own experiences. We become individuals and more independent people and begin to figure things out on our own. Lessons are learned as they happen in real-time, and impressions are made based on our personalities and our souls. We learn about emotional sensations like gain, loss, joy, pain, pride, regret, and many more as we become who we are destined to be. As we develop, the Adversary is watching us and waiting for each critical juncture to misdirect and hurt us to imprint into us ways that will stop us from seeing the things of God or wanting to learn more about the unseen.

The trick, I believe, is to not lie outrightly to us because a lie can be quickly disproved with evidence. This deception is to use a perceivable truth that can be "verified" by our minds which is not the whole truth or is a carnal realization of that "truth". For example, imagine a little child that tells their parents that they saw an angel. This can be a shocking thing for them to hear. Let me pause for a second and talk about children. Little ones are wide-eyed and believe what their senses tell them because they are trained to see them without bias. Children, in my opinion, are also perceptive to the Spirit Realm in ways that most adults are not. As children, they cannot explain what they experience as we do whether it be from Heaven or Hell. They are untainted in that way. So, when a child tells a parent that their angel talked to them many will tell that child that they didn't see anything or that they imagined what they saw and that it wasn't real. Some will panic and think that their child is crazy and will rush them to a psychotherapist or psychologist and have them medicated or counseled out of believing that what they saw was real.

That monster in their closet could very well be a demonic force or curse attached to a person, home, or object. That imaginary friend could be a real spirit, and we tell these children that this isn't reality and that they need to stop all this foolish talk. Many get punished or ridiculed by others because they tell those "tall tales" to people and these children learn to suppress what they have seen as nonsense and the brain will block them out to compensate. This doesn't only happen to children, but adults too. Especially adults who accept Jesus Christ as their Lord and Savior and are brand new to the faith. Remember the parable of the farmer and the seed?

He told many stories in the form of parables, such as this one: And he spake many things unto them in parables, saying, Behold, a sower went forth to sow; and when he sowed, some seeds fell by the way side, and the fowls came and devoured them up: Some fell upon stony places, where they had not much earth: and forthwith they sprung up, because they had no deepness of earth: And when the sun was up, they were scorched; and because they had no root, they withered away. And some fell among thorns; and the thorns sprung up and choked them: But others fell into good ground, and brought forth fruit, some a hundredfold, some sixtyfold, some thirtyfold…

…When any one heareth the word of the kingdom, and understandeth it not, then cometh the wicked one, and catcheth away that which was sown in his heart. This is he which received seed by the way side. But he that received the seed into stony places, the same is he that heareth the word, and anon with joy receiveth it; Yet hath he not root in himself, but dureth for a while: for when tribulation or persecution ariseth because of the word, by and by he is offended. He also that received seed among the thorns is he that heareth the word; and the care of this world, and the deceitfulness of riches, choke the word, and he becometh unfruitful. But he that received seed into the good ground is he that heareth the word, and understandeth it; which also beareth fruit, and bringeth forth, some an hundredfold, some sixty, some thirty. -- Matthew 13:3-8, 19-23 KJV

Notice the great lengths the seed is opposed to growing and attaching effective roots in the soil. God is broadcasting and planting His Word and awareness of His Presence to everyone, and Hell does everything it can to stop that from happening. So many people get saved in church or out of church and before they can be made aware of the battlefield they are summarily choked out and stifled before they can mature into great soldiers for The Lord. Satan devises the best plans designed for everyone to deter and defeat them and to get them before they even know that Hell exists the way that it does. It is expert spy craft at its finest and no humans are as efficient and devious as Hell is at this game. Hell knows no boundaries and will not just attack the person but will affect those around them (more on this later) or hold up the messengers of God just like demons did to the angel that was bringing Daniel an answer to his prayer.

When I think about these types of scenarios, I think about how a foreign, less powerful enemy would destroy another from within. What Hell does is like a foreign adversary infiltrating and destroying the schools and training facilities that produce soldiers and engineers to design the best defenses against them. Imagine that enemy destroying boot camps, compromising drill sergeants, and poisoning education and culture to cause people to be lulled to sleep and not pay attention to what is happening around them while that enemy makes shrewd and calculated moves to become stronger and harder to overcome.

Trapped in a lullaby of slumber, people are blinded by a false sense of security and never venture beyond the "woke" wall of truth staring at them in plain sight. Convinced that the truth is a lie, and the lie is the truth they will cling to what they can "see" and allow themselves to be cemented in a false truth with false pretenses that hide the real world from them. They have worn rose-colored glasses for so long that taking them off would cause them to see things in a different shade, making them afraid. So, they rush to put the filter of blindness on once again. In many ways this is happening right now in America, but I digress.

Another way Hell discredits and attacks us before we get started in spiritual things is whispering to us or suggesting that we do what they want us to do. Here is something that may shock some of you, but not all what Hell whispers to us is "bad" or evil. Yes, I said that, and I meant it. Remember, deception can only work if you mix in a little lie within a batch of truth. Sure, demons influence people to commit the most heinous and evil things known to humankind, but all influences from Hell start with a whisper, a gut feeling, a suggestion, or some sort of sequence of events that are interpreted as "signs" that "this is the way" and many choose to follow them. Though we mainly think that the whispers of evil only cause people to rape, pillage, burn, or drug themselves many of Hell's suggestions are to do seemingly what is right. Remember what Proverbs 16:25 says, "There is a way that seemeth right unto a man, but the end thereof are the ways of death." Why would the Scripture say such a thing? I believe that the answer is more complicated than people believe.

I don't believe that this verse is just talking about evil, but it is also talking about the things that seem like righteous living but are lies from the Devil. Think about one of the evilest premises that has fallen on the Earth: racism. The concept that one group of humans with a different skin tone is better, smarter, and more perfect than the others is straight from the Gates of Hell itself. The thought that people of "lesser" birth deserve to be enslaved and "taught" the right ways of righteousness and using the Bible as a justification is evil on a level that is worse than murder. To quote Scriptures to justify wicked and evil practices is shameful before God. To use racist tropes and call it righteousness is beyond the evil of any devil worship or witchcraft. To hate a person with real hate because they currently live differently than the Bible says is just as bad. To despise someone for their lifestyles instead of showing them the love that Jesus did is appalling and despicable. To try to force people to live a small group's standard of holiness at all costs instead of transforming one soul at a time with God's truth is reprehensible.

To despise other Christians because they don't follow their church's teaching about baptism, the Holy Spirit, or what foods we are to eat is ludicrous. Arguing over the roles of ministry regarding gender is just stupid. To fight against those who believe in divine healing, casting out of demons, or even prophecy is lunacy. People are groomed and taught before they can experience God in a raw and uncut way. People are manipulated or discouraged from encountering God on their own.

Some churches condemn spiritual warfare as witchcraft and keep congregations blind and happy that there is no war to fight. People will either embrace a false Christ or a false religion before the truth. Some people get so fed up that they believe that there is no God at all and throw their hands up and say that none of this makes sense. Hell sits back and laughs that it has destroyed people before they could even leave the starting line. He has either turned some away from the faith, blinded others with a false truth, or have some been entrenched in fighting everyone else because of pride. There are so many people caught in this conflict and have zero knowledge of what is going on and get lost forever.

Becoming Aware

This level of awareness is an in-between stage that is blurred by some gray areas and shifting boundaries. All of this revolves around an awareness of the Spirit Realm but being ill-equipped to handle or fully understand it. In many ways it is like seeing someone in a horrific car crash and the aftermath of being hurt versus being in the crash and living through it. There are many people who are saved and are aware that there is a Spirit Realm, and they know that it is real, but they have yet to fully experience it on a deeper level for themselves. Some have seen spiritual warfare in action, but they are spectators and not participants. This could be in the fact that they are inexperienced and rely on those who are stronger than they are, or they fear it after some sort of exposure, and they run from it. This, what I call the middle state, is either a place of opportunity or a place of spiritual defeat.

Let's start with the opportunity, a person who is becoming aware, but not yet strong in spiritual warfare has experienced it for themselves and they are open to learning more and growing more in spiritual things. These persons are on the cusp of being free of the bondage of religion and are primed to embrace the call of reconciling our relationship with Christ on a deeper level and are ready to receive the filling of the Holy Spirit, which begins their journey of spiritual maturity, and I will cover that in detail later in this chapter. My point here is that they are ***READY*** and ***OPEN*** for this next step, and this is where Hell steps in and tries its dirty tricks.

Fear is the greatest deception that Hell employs. There are many who believe that demons and Satan are all-powerful and cannot be stopped. They are made to believe to let the "sleeping dogs lie" and not punch above their weight. That challenging such powers will lead to destruction or death. The Enemy popularizes via the mass media movies and TV shows that show people basically running away from demons, ghosts, shadow people, Skinwalkers, and other malevolent entities that often show priests or people reciting the Lord's Prayer against supernatural entities. They make it seem like there is little that can be done. I have seen programs that tell people that they need to move because something is too strong to be fought against. Some of these people are Christians. Yes, Christians who listen to witches, mediums, and psychics tell them that its hopeless. Let the evil have this place. It can't be won.

We see other content that shows people who feel that once they tried to fight the demonic that their lives were now ruined. Some of these people wear their crosses and have their Bibles and they speak in defeat and regret that they stood their ground and tried to challenge Hell. Plenty of people see things like this and make up their mind that they will never go any deeper than they must go. They know the power at the tips of their tongues and in their spirits, but they choose not to risk the injuries that come with all of it. They may have already suffered some sort of loss in other areas of their lives, and it is very human to not want to rush into something to be hurt even more. It is when that conscious decision is made that they have limited their spiritual growth. They never took a moment to ask God where He wanted them to grow or to what level. The headwinds of adversity have stopped another soldier. This is where Hell gets its small victories.

Growing our spiritual muscles is critical to our progression in our everyday lives. All who are Christ followers are already reconciling their relationships with God and because God is a Spirit, we should desire to learn and grow more in the Realm of the Spirit. Our growth spiritually is directly correlated to our relationship with God. We cannot have one without the other. The closer we get to God and desire more of Him the more we will have to delve and thrive in the Spirit Realm. Hell wants to make the reality of the resistance to its power more real than us growing in the Grace of God. Because it is something that spills over into the Natural Realm, our flesh becomes conscious of that resistance, and our emotions kick in and try to stop us from taking the blows that could come from spiritual growth.

I feel that Hell's opposition to spiritual growth is a lot like the principles of wind resistance as it relates to a vehicle that is measured by what is called a drag coefficient. The drag coefficient is a common measure in automotive design as it pertains to aerodynamics. Drag is a force that acts parallel to and in the same direction as the airflow. The drag coefficient of an automobile measures the way the automobile passes through the surrounding air. When automobile companies design a new vehicle, they take into consideration the automobile drag coefficient in addition to the other performance characteristics. Aerodynamic drag increases with the square of speed; therefore, it becomes critically important at higher speeds. The reduction of drag in road vehicles has led to increases in the top speed of the vehicle and the vehicle's fuel efficiency, as well as many other performance characteristics, such as handling and acceleration[9].

Let's unpack that for a few minutes. Based on that information, it can be deduced that the air is the constant and the vehicle is the thing that is changing. Not to get into a science lesson, but if there is no motion? There is no wind resistance because the air flows around the vehicle as normal if there is no breeze and all is still. There are no sounds of the air moving and no vibration in the vehicle. No force is exerted on the vehicle except the normal atmospheric pressure. If we sat in a vehicle with the windows open in a calm wind no noticeable air would blow on us.

Now, the moment we start moving something happens. Air is still a state of matter even if we cannot see it. The vehicle is matter also and when matter moves against matter there is always friction, which is the foundation of what a drag coefficient is. As the vehicle moves through the air, the more the air affects it. Even though what powers the vehicle is stronger than the motion of the air, the vehicle is affected the faster it goes. Depending on the vehicle's design, a vehicle will be able to accelerate faster and faster until the air prevents it from going any faster. This is known as being drag limited.

In the spiritual realm, it can be said that if we aren't moving in the direction that God has sent us, Hell won't push up against us (remember that Satan is the Prince of the Power of the ***AIR***). However, the more we move forward, the greater the resistance. Just like that vehicle, what used to be silence will erupt into the noise of the wind fighting us. We can hear it in our lives and others can hear it too depending on our lives. There will be vibrations making us feel that we can't maintain this speed or direction because we may come apart or lose control. We may hit a wall and not be able to go any further because we can't seem to get beyond where we are, and we give up pushing harder. If our windows are open the sound of the air thundering in our ears may cause pain and discomfort. Whatever the means and whatever the methods. Hell finds a way to push against us to make us either stop or set the cruise control and go as fast as we ***THINK*** we can go in the Spirit.

This is the point of opportunity that I spoke of earlier. A vehicle designer can either accept what the circumstances are, or they can change them and find better ways to make things sleeker and more efficient. Here is something else interesting that I discovered. The deletion of parts on a vehicle is a straightforward way for designers and vehicle owners to reduce parasitic and frontal drag of the vehicle with little cost and effort. Deletion can be as simple as removing an aftermarket part, or part that has been installed on the vehicle after production or having to modify and remove an original equipment manufacturer (or OEM) part, meaning any part of the vehicle that was originally manufactured from the factory.

Most production sports cars and high efficiency vehicles come standard with many of these deletions to be competitive in the automotive and race market, while others choose to keep these drag-increasing aspects of the vehicle for their visual aspects, or to fit the typical uses of their customer base. When scientists add smoke to the air in a wind tunnel when they test vehicles discernible patterns can be detected. These patterns are either patterns of a smooth flow over a surface or a place of resistance that cause the air to build up pressure in circles called eddies. Eddies are points that effectively push back against an object and limit its potential of its motion.

Now, let's relate all of this to the spiritual realm. When we are born, we are in sin, and we have a spiritual "shape" as it would. We are not moving towards God and there is no resistance from Hell because we aren't going against the grain. When we accept Christ as our Lord and Savior, we are reborn and reshaped in the image that God desires us to be after we willingly submit to being converted. We then get in pursuit of the Heart of God, and we face the resistance of Hell wanting us to remain as we were in our sinful flesh.

The more we progress on God's path; the more Hell pushes back. There comes a point where we realize that we need to take some things off that we had before like we remove the things in our lives that hinder us from moving in the way God has intended. God will trim down our spirits, give us tools to help us stay stable as we go and will show us where we are making the most resistance and move them out of the way. The resistance still fights us, but as we learn from the journey, we must adjust if we are willing.

Some of us don't want to be modified because we realize that we will move differently, act differently and be different from others. This is that moment I spoke about in spiritual warfare. We see others that have been made to resist the Devil and move in the path set before them, but we are afraid that we won't be able to handle it. We are doubtful that it is for us. We don't want to be ostracized or isolated from what we have known all along. We know that we can go there if we want to, but many don't. The Enemy will plant seeds of doubt or fear that make us hesitant to change or make us content where we are.

To be comfortable even after change is still the goal of the flesh. A car we can get off the showroom floor can travel up to eighty miles an hour and for some that is enough. Some want to go faster so the car they get is ***DESIGNED*** to go up to let's say one hundred miles an hour. It's shaped differently, equipped differently and has an increased level of horsepower. Others want to go even faster and want a car that can go one hundred fifty miles an hour. All three of these cars are equipped with different shapes, more power, tires, attunements, brakes, and safety equipment. All are available, but ultimately the owner chooses the one they want.

Christians are the same in that respect. We can all be whatever we ask God to be, but even though God will call us and endow us with His gifts we still choose how far we go. If we ignore His higher calling God won't force us, but when we answer the call God will empower us. Some people enjoy being at the level of knowing that the spirit realm is real, can see it in others, and have enough faith to pray for protection and that's it. They have respect for those who do engage in spiritual warfare, or they know the demarcation line and won't cross it because they worry about retribution. I was there once as many people were or still are. It's "bad enough" being saved and opposed by Hell, but the pain and suffering that can come from spiritual warfare can be overwhelming. People in this state shouldn't be looked down upon but prayed for and encouraged. Many are dealing with traumas that go much deeper than just fear of spiritual warfare alone.

One more thing about spiritual growth and awareness. God has the plan that He has for us and where we need to grow. Going back to my sports car analogy, I would like to remind you that a person who orders a vehicle that has high performance should be able to handle such a vehicle in a safe manner. To take on the full potential of a sports car an operator should know how to drive it to get the most out of its performance. A person who thinks that they can drive a high-powered car and has never driven one can seriously get hurt if they drive too fast or the power gets away from them and they crash. The same goes with spiritual awareness of spiritual warfare. Attempting to wield weapons that are not understood could lead to very dire consequences. Look at this:

Then certain of the vagabond Jews, exorcists, took upon them to call over them which had evil spirits the name of the Lord Jesus, saying, We adjure you by Jesus whom Paul preacheth. And there were seven sons of one Sceva, a Jew, and chief of the priests, which did so. And the evil spirit answered and said, Jesus I know, and Paul I know; but who are ye? And the man in whom the evil spirit was leaped on them, and overcame them, and prevailed against them, so that they fled out of that house naked and wounded. And this was known to all the Jews and Greeks also dwelling at Ephesus; and fear fell on them all, and the name of the Lord Jesus was magnified. – Acts 19:13-17 KJV

Being aware and hearing and seeing what others have done can get us into trouble. The Sons of Sceva thought that they could cast out a demon and act like the apostle Paul, and you can see the results. Just being aware of spiritual warfare and wielding weapons that you don't have a relationship with will result in disaster. It's like the inexperienced driver who gets a hold of an expensive supercar and has a fender bender because the power was too much to control.

Awareness of spiritual warfare should inspire the desire to go higher in God. This is why the road of relationship is important to our well-being and our lives. God will allow us to grow as far as we desire to grow. We may miss what God truly has for us, but that doesn't mean that we wouldn't be blessed and happy. It all boils down to how much will we trust God and trust that He will take care of us. Either way, God doesn't condemn folks like that, and neither should anyone else.

EYES WIDE OPEN

To be made completely aware of our surroundings and all the things and consequences that come with them can be a humbling and frightening experience. It is like looking at a snapped photograph of someone that was supposed to be a wonderful time or event, only to notice something sinister in the background that no one had seen before. It can be a "spooky" feeling, but to understand the things around us comes with the price of knowing what is real and what is an illusion. When we, as Christians, become cognizant of spiritual warfare and all of what comes with it we embark on a part of our broken road that has the toughest challenges we have ever faced. It is here on this part of the journey that we need a strong relationship with Christ to be ever-strengthening and unwavering because now we are accountable and knowledgeable of what's really going on in this world and the Spirit Realm.

I would like to clarify what "eyes wide open" means because many occultist terminologies and concepts have crept their way into the Church. I have heard some people erroneously speak of the "third" eye being open in Christian circles and I want to caution everyone to discontinue the usage of that terminology. Why do you ask? Let's go to what it means. The third eye (also called the mind's eye or inner eye) is a mystical invisible eye, usually depicted as located on the forehead, which provides perception beyond ordinary sight. Hinduism relates the third eye to the *Ajna* (or brow) chakra[10]. In both Hinduism and Buddhism, the third eye is in the center of the forehead, slightly above the conjunction of the eyebrows (which some say is where is pineal gland is located), which is said to represent the state of enlightenment that can be achieved via meditation. The third eye is often associated with the doorway that leads to the inner realms and spaces of higher states of consciousness. In many occultist spirituality doctrines, the third eye often symbolizes the state of enlightenment. The third eye is often associated with supernatural visions, clairvoyant senses, the ability to observe chakras, categorize auras, precognition, and out-of-body experiences.

I want to be ***VERY*** clear here. This is the ***DOCTRINE OF DEVILS***. There is nothing Biblical about the third eye and I believe it to be a spiritual gateway to the occult and a backdoor for demonic possession. Some have erroneously linked the third eye with prophetic gifts, and this is not the case. Others have connected this demonic teaching with seeing angels and the supernatural and this is also false. We must be careful not to associate the principles of darkness and say that it is the Holy Spirit. Only the Holy Spirit can open our eyes to see the Spirit Realm as God desires us to see it. I encourage anyone who is saved and has subscribed to the third eye doctrine to repent from it and seek God to remove any spiritual backdoors that you may have opened. Don't feel bad about being duped because this is a part of Hell's plan.

When God opens your spiritual eyes, and you see all that He allows you to see the war becomes very real and it is very easy to be deceived and misdirected. Each step that we take when our eyes are opened requires that we not rely on our senses but stay reliant on Jesus and His Word. I am sure that many of us have seen movies or shows where there are hackers that tap into the CCTV system and instead of disabling the camera feeds, they inject a different set of looped videos that shows nothing happening to those who are paid to watch those feeds all while people are operating freely and doing what they have planned to do that they don't want seen. Hell is full of experts that know how to produce an altered reality and false flag operations that can blind us.

Satan knows that once our eyes are opened to spiritual warfare that we have become dangerous to his plans. He knows that if we are watching what's happening that we can not only act, but we can warn someone else that something is going on that needs to be stopped. Let me be clear, Satan knows that he cannot defeat you head-to-head, so he does what he does best which is to mislead. He will attempt to obscure himself from your view by deceptive doctrines like the third eye lie, perpetuate falsehoods that certain things like "angels" and "guides" can come from God, or worse, imitate the things of God and take credit for himself. All of that "New Age" nonsense is witchcraft and is meant to confuse and deceive people so watch out!

Let's start with the falsehoods. Remember, that in Matthew 24:24 it says, "For there shall arise false Christs, and false prophets, and shall shew great signs and wonders; insomuch that, if it were possible, they shall deceive the very elect." The very elect people are those who are the most mature, best equipped, and sharpest warriors of them all. There are things today that if we are not careful, we can fall under their spell and be misdirected from the real war. Being bombarded with all these things can make the spiritual walk of the "eyes wide open" person difficult. Why? Because we are still human and as humans, we have emotions, and we can make mistakes. It doesn't take but a slight slip in the wording or pressure from our peers to get us to be absorbed into what has a veneer of truth but is full of lies.

A good example of a blatant deception is that what happened in the days of the Acts of the Apostles doesn't happen today. This, of course, is a lie. Miracles, signs, wonders, prophecies, and the supernatural are just as relevant today as they were back then. Yet, these people, quoting Scripture and using flawed exegesis, have duped many into thinking that those who are fully persuaded by the five-fold ministry are the ones who are in the doctrine of devils. Imagine the strife and ridicule that can come from a person or a ministry that is full-bore into the Power of God as Scripture ***ACCURATELY*** declares being ridiculed, abused, and spoken evil of because they are working within God's unlimited power. It causes our emotions to be affected, even if it is temporary. No one wants to be humiliated or ostracized, but it happens.

There are some who are seeking answers beyond knowledge of the spirit realm and fall prey to the false teachers and prophets that Scripture has warned us about. I can tell you this from personal experience. There was a time when I was in a state of life transition, and I was attending classes at a "healing center" that dealt with spiritual issues and concerns. Even though I knew who I was in Christ I was intrigued and wanted to learn what people like that did to understand how to how to help someone else avoid it. Side note, I have a serious interest of understanding demonology and how we Christians can combat it and trust me,

I had to stay covered by the Blood of Jesus! So, if you aren't fully rooted in Christ, don't do what I did!

So, back to the "healing center", I remember that the instructor that led our classes also taught a ***BIBLE STUDY*** "to help people understand what the "Christian Church" was leaving out of what was being said in the Word. Here is the funny thing, this ***WITCH*** (I'm not being mean here, just truthful) knew Scripture better than I did at the time and I grew up in the church and was always studying God's Word. They could not only quote Scripture, but knew the references, understood the history, could exegete with textbook clarity, and if they were anywhere else, I would say that they were a solid teacher. Yet I knew better because they deviated into Gnostic and Spiritualist veins is when I knew they were incorrect.

They linked "angels and spirit guides" to the Scriptures with "precision" and made those who didn't know that much about the Word of God plunge into their teachings. Of course, I know that these "angels and guides" are nothing more than masquerading demons who possess or oppress people's souls. The people in these classes were hurt in their churches and were seeking God but were rebuked by church people because those churches were closed off to the spirit realm. They were sucked right in because God had opened their eyes to reality and the Devil swooped in to confuse them before they could get their proper footing.

I hate to tell you, but scenarios like this are only a part of the story. The other side of this coin are those whose eyes are wide open, fighting the good fight for Christ and they suffer under the weight of being in constant warfare. When Jesus said in Matthew 26:41 that, "the spirit indeed is willing, but the flesh is weak", He wasn't kidding. Those who are fully aware and fighting in this spiritual war have the Holy Spirit as their strength and shield. While He is strong, we are weak and can get tired or weary. We can still get hurt even if we have the Holy Spirit inside of us. The best soldier in the world with the best weaponry on Earth can still stub their toes and feel pain. They can still get tired from the long march or the extended battle. These things happen and yes, God is our strength and through it all, but that doesn't mean that we don't feel our flesh's sensations. We can still be betrayed, abandoned, lied on, misused, abused, and knocked down sometimes. We are still in the flesh.

Look, even Jesus had to rest. He was God in the flesh, and He still took time to recover from ministry. Jesus still cried at Lazarus' tomb even though He knew that He was going to raise Lazarus from the dead. Jesus still felt compassion for those who were hurting even though He knew He would heal them. Jesus still got angry at the money changers and was still the Son of God when He flipped tables and ran those crooks out of the Temple. Even with the greatest discernment that shows us that demons are closing in on us we still brace for the upcoming battle and pray for strength to make it through. Is it hard? Yes. Is it worth it? Yes. It pains us to see demonic forces attack our spouses and family. It grieves us to see the lost who refuse to come home. It angers us when we see folk in the church not acting right. Even if we don't want to admit it? It happens. We may not show it on the outside or act on that impulse that our old nature wants us to put in motion because the Holy Spirit grabs us by the collar and puts us in check if we let Him.

Part of putting us in check is to let us know that we cannot and should not do any of this without God. This is why we are on this broken road and as I have said earlier in this chapter it is about ***RELATIONSHIP***. We cannot call on the Name of Jesus unless we truly know Him for ourselves. We are not in the Sceva family, and we should know better. We have every opportunity to grow closer to our God, and we must not be afraid of what those entails. We need to acknowledge and get to know the authority that God has given us in the Earth. We need to know that the weapons of our warfare are not of the flesh (2 Corinthians 10:4) and that to use them we must embrace The One who made them and gave them to us. I could write a lot about spiritual warfare as I have experienced it and maybe, if the Lord says so, I will. Just know that God is our Teacher and will always be there for us no matter what.

Coming into the realization that spiritual warfare is literally everywhere can be overwhelming and daunting to a lot of people and I understand. For God to give us eyes to see what is out there can be hard to cope with and can shake us to our cores. It's like that famous movie where the guy took the red pill and was awakened to the reality of the world outside of the simulation. God will not abandon us when we come to full realization of the spirit realm and spiritual warfare. Arriving at this point of spiritual consciousness comes via the reconciliation of our relationship with God and travelling the road of life.

Seeing without blinders is humbling and terrifying at the same time, but we don't need to worry or fear. We have weapons at our disposal, and those weapons are found in the Word of God and within the Holy Spirit. We are far from defenseless, and we can wage war against the strongholds of the enemy. Satan wants us to fear the power and authority that God has given us in the Earth. He knows that when we get to the "Eyes Wide Open" stage that we are now direct threats to Hell. We are maturing soldiers of Christ. There is no way that we could have achieved this level of spiritual awareness unless we have journeyed this road with God. Not possible by any other means.

The road and relationship are necessary for us to be the people that God wants us to be. No one would voluntarily grow like this unless they go through it with God at their sides. The road must be rough and tough. The road must make us weary and break us down sometimes. It is necessary even though it seems unfair. The road and relationship have a purpose beyond our understanding and if we trust God, we will make it and come out like pure gold. Before we get to where we are going in life we will have to go through some things, and they will not and are not pleasant or easy.

CHAPTER REFERENCES

[1] Garfinkel, Y, & Mumcuoglu, M. (2019, March 15). The Temple of Solomon in Iron Age Context. Religions. https://www.mdpi.com/2077-1444/10/3/198/htm.

[2] Today, "988" is the three-digit, nationwide phone number to connect directly to the 988 Suicide and Crisis Lifeline. By calling or texting 988, you'll connect with mental health professionals with the 988 Suicide and Crisis Lifeline, formerly known as the National Suicide Prevention Lifeline. Pray, seek God and get help too! –SRF

[3] Chery, F., & Chery, F. (2024, February 19). Allah vs God: (8 key differences). Bible Reasons | Bible Verses About Various Topics. https://biblereasons.com/allah-vs-god/

[4] IslamFYI, & IslamFYI. (2017, September 19). *What does Islam actually mean?* | IslamFYI: An Educational Resource on Islam for the Public. https://islamfyi.princeton.edu/what-does-islam-actually-mean/

[5] Bolinger, H. (2023, October 23). Who is Baal in the Bible? Story and meaning. Christianity.com. https://www.christianity.com/wiki/bible/who-is-baal-in-the-bible.html

[6] Samples, K. (2021, April 22). *How Christ's Incarnation Differs from the Hindu Idea of Avatar.* Reasons to Believe. https://reasons.org/explore/blogs/reflections/how-christ-s-incarnation-differs-from-the-hindu-idea-of-avatar

[7] Samples, K. (2021, April 22). *How does Zoroastrianism compare to Christianity?* Reasons to Believe. https://reasons.org/explore/blogs/reflections/how-does-zoroastrianism-compare-to-christianity

[8] Swearingen, S. (2021, February 1). Spiritual Warfare: Definition, Viewpoints, and Why it Matters. Just Disciple. https://justdisciple.com/spiritual-warfare/

[9] Wikipedia contributors. (2023). Automobile drag coefficient. Wikipedia. https://en.wikipedia.org/wiki/Automobile_drag_coefficient

[10] Cavendish, Richard, ed. (1994). Man, Myth and Magic. Vol. 19. New York: Marshall Cavendish.

2

Brokenness

Broken. This word alone does something to the human psyche. To hear the word "broken" carries our minds to many things. It has taken me a very long time to understand this concept, but I am glad that I did come to an understanding of what brokenness means. It means two completely different things to a saved and unsaved person, and I would like to elaborate. Based on the definition by Merriam-Webster, the term brokenness is a variant state of the word "broken", and it has a whole host of meanings[1]:

- Violently separated into parts or shattered.
- Damaged or altered by or as if by breaking such as having undergone or been subjected to fracture.
- Not working properly.
- Being irregular, interrupted, or full of obstacles.
- Violated by transgression.
- Not kept or honored.
- Discontinuous or interrupted.
- Disrupted by change.
- Having an irregular, streaked, or blotched pattern especially from virus infection.
- Made weak or infirm.
- Subdued completely.
- Crushed or sorrowful.
- Bankruptcy.

- Reduced in rank.
- Cut off or disconnected.
- Imperfectly spoken or written.
- Not complete or full.
- Disunited by divorce, separation, or desertion.

I know that is a lengthy list, and I am sure that you can picture situations and scenarios where each of those things can happen to someone. It's harsh and it's not pretty. In the natural realm, brokenness can be seen as an end or lull state of being. In many situations in life being broken is usually the end of things as we know them. However, in the spiritual realm, brokenness is not an end state, but it is an opportunity. God uses brokenness to turn a very dark situation into a very beautiful beginning, and it can be difficult to see because of the gloom that brokenness brings.

Brokenness causes us to be desperate for things to change and get better and that is where the opportunity comes in. It doesn't matter whether someone is saved or not, being broken is the doorstep to God's transformation and transition into miracles happening right before our eyes. The key to being in a state of brokenness is what we do with it. Brokenness breaks us down to the "bare metal" and can either be where we corrode and rust away forever, or where we can be rebuilt and reestablished by God's miraculous power. God leaves it all up to us as to which way it goes. Yet, when we look at that definition it can be very hard to see the Hand of God while we are face down in the dirt wondering what just happened to us. Let's look at each piece of this definition and see where God can step in every situation and turn brokenness into blessings.

When we are violently separated into parts or shattered because life just rips our hearts, minds, and souls into pieces we can tend to fall into a daze-like state of numbness and disbelief. Situations will shatter our dreams and ruin our hopes in an instant and it's hard (yes, I said it) to keep your eyes and mind on God. It is very human to do this, but I didn't say that it is impossible. There isn't a person alive that can say that every "breaking" moment didn't faze them. Life can hurt badly and when it is violent or sudden it can knock the figurative wind out of us, and we hit the ground not really understanding why it went down that way. When the heart gets torn apart and life gets shredded, we can go dark and tune out or we can get angry, seek revenge, and try to heal by doing more harm. It makes me think of Jesus in the Garden of Gethsemane and the disciples scattered and ran for their lives. Peter had sliced off a man's ear and later denied he even knew Christ. Their leader, Jesus, was captured and they were scared that they would be next. You can't tell me that they weren't broken. They were emotionally destroyed and consumed by fear. Soldiers with weapons just took Jesus into custody and they were all alone.

Even so, look at what happened later in Acts, Chapter 2 when the Holy Spirit came and filled them up and they stopped hiding and they started proclaiming the Gospel like never before. Even though they had seen Jesus alive after the Resurrection, they were still in hiding but bust loose and evangelized the world after the Holy Spirit came and set things right. Sure, they may have still had their issues but look at what God did for them! He took their tragedy and made it into triumph and all they had to do was let God step in and heal their situations.

Being damaged or altered by something or cracked as if by breaking, such as having undergone or been subjected to fracture, is another form of brokenness. I think about going through a long-term situation where it seems like their whole life or extended season of their life is marked with terrible tragedies or less than ideal circumstances. I think of having a broken bone that never sets properly and doesn't heal right. There was someone I knew who, when I met them, were always hobbled with injury, and could hardly walk. They couldn't work and he was disabled for most of the time that I knew them. Yet, I heard stories of how they were a star athlete in school and was very active in their youth, but then tragedy struck, and they broke their foot in multiple places and because of society and medical availability at that time they didn't get the sort of medical care and treatment that we would get today.

Because of that they began a life of disability which persisted until their death. One act and motion changed everything, and it seemed to hobble them for life. One moment defined the rest of their days and because they couldn't get the care that would have changed everything for the best, and they were sidelined, and they accepted that as their lot in life. Life can be that way with many varying things where we have one snapping blow that cripples us, and we don't get the spiritual or physical help we need and we "stay broken" instead of being healed.

Let me clarify something here, God can take this situation and do one of two things. The first is that He can act like Christ did what He did with the man who laid at the Pool of Bethesda for thirty-eight years and heal him so that God can get the glory from it, or God can treat them like Paul and leave the messenger of Satan and let them deal with it for His glory. Either way, we must trust God because no matter what, the glory belongs to Him!

Being like a broken toy and not working properly can be hard to negotiate because it seems unfair. Let me explain. Sometimes we are in scenarios where how we work just isn't right. We may have some form of limitation or attribute that makes us operate differently than anyone else. It can be anything from being born with a disability to acquiring one. It can be a limitation of a person's being in the natural realm. It could even be an emotional trauma so deep and embedded that it moves and flows like it is that person. Whatever the condition might be, it is a set of circumstances where a person must operate differently than most other folks and it can affect that person deeply.

Things like this can cause a person to question themselves and their abilities, or they can be ridiculed by callous people about them being different. I think back to the prophet Samuel's mother, Hannah. She was "barren" and couldn't seem to have children and her husband's other wife tormented her about it. Hannah was loved by her husband, but it didn't change the fact that she couldn't have a child of her own. It hurt Hannah deeply and she was broken.

She went to the Temple to pray differently than most and when Eli, the High Priest, saw her he thought that she was drunk! In her experience, she wasn't working the way others did, and she turned to God and promised Him that if he gave her a son that she would give Him back to God. If she wasn't "broken" in what she couldn't do at that time, the world would have never had the prophet Samuel to instruct King David. From brokenness came a key to biblical history. When we feel limited and we feel that we just don't operate the way that everyone else does, it is an opportunity to show to the world that He can take anyone and anything and do wonderful things with and through them.

This is very similar to being irregular, interrupted, or full of obstacles. Sometimes it isn't being limited, but it's about being different. It is about life forcing us to take a pause from a goal or even having more obstacles than most people must go through. Having a "hard way to go" to get where one is going can occupy the mind and sometimes leave a stain on one's spirit. It is hard to fight your entire life to get where most people coast through to. It is hard be different than everyone else because God made you unique for His purpose and everyone doesn't get it. It is hard to have to scale and climb and jump over more obstacles than straight steps. It can take a toll on anyone, and we don't need to be ashamed to say it!

I think about Nehemiah and how he was a captive in a strange land and yet he stood out enough that Artaxerxes, the king, asked Nehemiah what was wrong (Nehemiah 2:2). We know the story about how Nehemiah went from cupbearer to governor, but we can see how hard it was for him to accomplish the goals of his vision. The adversity and challenges were immense and through it all the walls of Jerusalem were rebuilt, and God continued to give him strength to be the best version of himself. Nehemiah was not your average person and God used him to get major things done. He withstood being threatened and ridiculed for what he knew that he had to do. It's beautiful to go from serving at a table to being served at a table. God used Nehemiah's life to show us that it doesn't matter what happens, God will see it through no matter how irregular we are.

When we are violated by transgressions, it will form a level of brokenness that can be hard to shake. I don't want to (and cannot) speak for a victim of something like molestation or rape, but I have witnessed what that sort of violation can do. It changes people. It can cause a myriad of emotion and life states that it is difficult to account for them all. To be broken this way involves a very deep wound that rips open a person in ways that are rarely talked about publicly. When someone does something dastardly to another person it can cause someone to not want to live anymore. It can start them on a path of personal destruction that can lead to their deaths or even the deaths of others.

When someone takes something from our person's secret places it leaves a wound that is raw and unyielding. It is an injury that can cause a deep spiritual and emotional infection that only God can truly heal. The trajectory of that person's life will change and depending on how that brokenness is tended to, God will either heal them and restore joy, or He will set that before them as their personal ministry to help someone else. This doesn't matter whether a person is saved or not. When God gets in a situation there are no limits to what He can or will do.

When a person's word or trust is not kept or honored it too is a violation or transgression against someone, but the pain this causes is disappointment and rejection. I bless God that He has ***NEVER*** lied or ever betrayed our trust, Whatever he has said has always come true, but in the case of the serpent, it wasn't true. Deception is a weapon of brokenness that involves fraud. In the Garden of Eden, the serpent told Eve that if she ate the fruit that she would be as gods (Genesis 3:5). Obviously, he lied and because of that sin and spiritual brokenness entered the world. Everything that the serpent said destroyed everything for us. The direct spiritual connection between humanity and God was broken by sin and had to wait until the second Adam, Jesus Christ, came and redeemed us all to Himself (Romans 5:12-21).

Think of the pain that was caused by that lie. We all suffer that pain to this day, but only by God's Power can we be reconciled and brought back from disaster. I also think of Pharaoh in Egypt who said many times that he would let the Israelites go and he didn't. Yes, God was using him for His purpose, but the effects of Pharaoh's stubbornness were that it broke the spirits of the Israelites who feared that they would be slaves forever. They whined, complained, and doubted Moses and all of what he promised (Exodus 6:9). Breaking a promise and not keeping our word causes brokenness. When we callously hurt someone else because of what we didn't honor or do there will be consequences for us. We need to always keep that in mind because we don't want it to happen to us.

This brings me to the other form of brokenness which is the state of being discontinuous or interrupted. Let's look at the Israelites again for a moment. The trip from Egypt to Palestine is only a few weeks on foot, but Israel took ***FORTY YEARS***. Why? Because of sin. Because they were against the man of God, Moses, and because God was angry at their nonsense (Numbers 32:13). Disappointment because of a dream deferred can happen because we did something wrong or because something was done to us. The Israelites, sinning and missing out of forty years in their promised land is one thing, but let's look at a more personal example. I think about a person who is wrongfully convicted of a crime and sentenced to jail for something that they did not do. These folks go to prison and lose a portion of their lives; their rights and their hopes are postponed.

I know of people who do unappreciated work to help people who are wrongfully treated by the justice system and one of the things that they do is help these people keep their heads up and stay encouraged that they can get their lives back. People who get locked up and then get out of jail may have wanted to go to college or start a family, but they couldn't do those things because they were in prison. People who had a child unexpectedly stop their careers or had to change their lifestyle because of unanticipated events. Hopes and dreams deferred can expose a person to the root of bitterness or rejection too. Sometimes these interruptions are recoverable and sometimes they are not. Sometimes the new path is the right path that God wanted. Either way, until understood, being deferred in life can cause a person to be broken and dream of what could have been.

This leads directly into brokenness by being disrupted by change. These are very similar in nature, but they are different. Change can happen at any moment, and the results of change can sometimes be very different from our expectations. God promised that Israel would occupy their land forever but caveated His promise with the requirement that they continue to worship Him (which they didn't). The first major disruption was the splitting of the nation into the Kingdom of Israel and the Kingdom of Judah. When we read in 2 Chronicles in Chapter 13, we see Solomon dedicating the Temple and praying for unity, prosperity, and promise and God answers Solomon in Chapter 14. God knew that Israel would break their end of the bargain, but He did what He did anyway. He set them up for success and when they screwed it up God allowed consequences to fall.

Change is not always bad, but when it produces pain, it causes the breaking of minds, hearts, and spirits. Paul and Barnabas were a tag team and then suddenly, they weren't. We never heard from Barnabas in the biblical record again. Naaman was a proud officer, but when leprosy hit him, his life was devastated until he dipped in the Jordan River (2 Kings 5:11-12). When Elijah predicted that it wouldn't rain for three years, it caused starvation and most likely death (1 Kings 17:1). When we see how change can cause a disruption that causes brokenness, we can see how a sudden shift in our lives can break us into millions of pieces, just like that.

This part of the definition of brokenness needs a little spiritual imagination. Having an irregular, streaked, or blotched pattern especially from virus infection sort of situation can be harder to visualize, but I will say it in a way that it was revealed to me. When our lives have a "normal" rhythm and pattern we feel confident that all is well, but the moment we see that something is out of sorts or imbalanced we start to look around and try to figure out what has gone awry. Having a strange appearance spiritually that is different than what is expected can cause some of us to slip into brokenness.

A blotched "pattern" is usually not uniform and not as "pretty" as "normal" ones would be. The splotchy look of a guernsey cow can look graceful and beautiful for a cow, but not always on a human. When we clean a window and see streaks and spots, we consider it unclean, and we usually do it again. When we get sick and it causes a rash or spots on our skin, we know that we are unwell and will try to treat it. When life causes spots to show, or we are full of streaks and blemishes in our lives it can affect us if we listen to the whispers of the Enemy.

Our past lives can haunt us. Our bad decisions can come back and taunt us and make us feel shameful. It is like not realizing that we spilled food on our clean clothes, and we were walking around not knowing that we have been soiled. It causes embarrassment and we start to act and feel differently if we care about our appearance or if someone begins to taunt us. Our lives on this Earth are full of blemishes and spots no matter how holy we think that we are. All have sinned. All have fallen short of the glory of God (Romans 3:23). All. Everyone. What we do with knowing these things will determine if we get broken or restored. Hell wants us to feel shame and remorse. God wants us to trust Him with our mess and let Him have His way in our lives. It is up to us and how we respond, but there is not a spot or wrinkle that God cannot fix.

"To be made weak or infirm" is a tough situation to be in. No one wants to feel weakened or incapable. It doesn't matter about the type of injury or condition. Physical, mental, or spiritual infirmity or weakness can be hard to swallow, especially if you have been strong in the past. It reminds me of getting older and it is appropriate for this sort of discussion. When we are in the prime of our lives, we are strong, capable, sharp, and alert and we don't have much trouble moving, working, playing, or whatever we want to do. Yet, as the decades pass by, that spring in our step begins to wane.

When we could come home at 4 AM and sleep for ninety minutes and get up and go to work in our youthful days just can't happen anymore. When we could at one time spring out of bed in three seconds is just a memory, and we now must get up and sit on the side of the bed and warm up like a 1971 "Land Yacht" in January becomes a new level of reality. The days of sleeping through the night and not needing to use the facilities are long gone. Our perfect 20/20 vision has been replaced by bifocals and "Arthur Itis" invades our joints and becomes our new "best friend".

That's just one example, and there are many others. Simply put, some people fall into depression because of what it was and what now is. To go from healthy to sick can cause us to be broken and depressed. Going from being able to walk and run to being in a wheelchair can cause us to feel low. To once have had invincible faith and then run into a problem that faith didn't seem to work (even though God was still working, and we didn't see Him) can cause us to stumble. No one likes to feel like "we can't" anymore and the Enemy seizes on that situation and tries to keep us in bondage so that we simply give up or get overwhelmed with sadness. We will try to reclaim what we lost, and we can fail. Simply put, God doesn't care about what we lost, but He is concerned about what He can give us to continue to fulfill our destiny and His promises. We just don't always notice it.

"The state of being subdued completely" sadly resonates with all of us because it hits close to home. Every person that has lived, is living, or will ever live on this Earth will have that one moment where time halts and they will become paralyzed with the reality of what has just happened to them. This is not an optional event as if it hasn't happened to you yet? It will. A tragic death or a chilling medical diagnosis can cause fear, remorse, regret, and a broken spirit to emerge in us. When life can literally pin us onto the floor and cause silent screams to emanate from our souls. Life is hard and the life of a believer in Christ can be devastating at times.

The shocking nature of being broken can be so overwhelming that our spirits just quit functioning. We are so lost or so hurt that we feel like we can't get out of bed or face the day. I know that I have been there, and it is one of the worst feelings ever. We are children of God, but we still feel fleshly pain. I liken this to having the "wind knocked out" of us emotionally and spiritually. Because of that the physical body follows, and we collapse to the spot and barely move from it because of the terrible blow (or blows). The cruel part of being broken like this is that often it appears that nothing is wrong at all. From the outside, if someone didn't know you, the average person would think that everything is just fine and that there are no concerns with you.

This leads to the next part of the definition of broken. "To be crushed or sorrowful" is the purely emotional part of being broken. When the heart breaks, dreams are extinguished, or hopes are dashed, it can break a person into many pieces. To me, emotions are the connectors between our physical and spiritual bodies. Emotions can vary between person to person, as far as the intensity and strength of how they can affect someone. What can destroy one person emotionally is just a papercut to someone else. Yet, when the emotions are broken, and a person enters the stage of sorrow it is a completely different situation. Sorrow, in my view, is when sad emotions have not only been experienced, but continue to cycle repeatedly in the mind and spirit. Sorrow is a permanence of what sadness, hurt, or emotional pain can bring and usually stems from the mind being involved with remembering things. Let me explain.

When we think of a loved one dying, we can remember that sting of knowing that they just transitioned. That shock is like a spike driven into the heart, a blast to the gut, and an immediate sense of that loss is overpowering. Our emotions do what they are designed to do and release that sadness in response to what happened. For some, that moment passes quicker than others and after that initial release, it starts to get easier to cope with that death. Sorrow is when that initial feeling either never subsides and remains constant or grows and expands and becomes stronger. Whenever our hearts get preoccupied with an overwhelming emotion, we become fixed to whatever that emotion is. Sorrow is when sadness, regret, grief, pain, or whatever has happened that is not pleasant connects to memories of what was lost or what caused the pain and festers in the spirit. It can cause a person to stop functioning as they normally would and that is a state of brokenness that can be hard to endure without the help of God.

When we hear the word "bankrupt", we often think about one thing, which is money. I am here to tell you that being bankrupt can affect many areas of one's life and money is the least of them. Yes, we can lose all our money and property and be reduced to financial ashes but think for a moment about the other types of bankruptcy: Emotional and Spiritual. When I think of the word "bankrupt" I think about the state of which nothing is left to draw on to be sustained. Just like money, when the account is overdrawn and there is nothing to sell, we are immediately destitute and cannot spend or provide anything that needs money. When we speak of emotions and the things of the spirit, we are talking about nearly the same things.

Emotional bankruptcy is when we detach our feelings from our own humanity. We tend to say that a person has "gone cold" or is "cold-blooded" and they don't seem to feel anything like remorse, love, empathy, or anything at all. Being violated by someone you love can cause your heart to empty out for that kind of love again. Being mistreated or abused can cause one to lose empathy for another human being. The same goes with spiritual bankruptcy as Hell can turn up the heat so much that we try to solve it on our own and have our spirits emptied from trying to solve a God-sized problem with human hands. We can also become spiritually bankrupt by falling into sin and then turning reprobate and staying there because we choose it to be our home away from the Holy Spirit. When we choose to allow situations to empty our emotions and spirits and not rely on the Power that God holds us in His Hands is when we can get bankrupted and that can break us into many pieces.

No one wants to live through this next part of the definition, which is "to be reduced in rank." We all have "climbed up the ranks" in some part of our lives. We started school and were promoted to the next grade as we progressed after each year. We have started working on a job in an entry-level position and worked our way up to bigger positions and higher pay. As humans, we live for the state of being promoted. However, life isn't always fair, and we will all experience a demotion, or a reduction in some form of rank.

When it is insignificant things, it can be tolerated like being picked as a team captain for kickball in one game and then not being captain the next game with the same team. Then there are other scenarios like being promoted to a lead position only to have it stripped away for one reason or another. What can cause the brokenness is when the demotion is somehow seen publicly. The embarrassment can be hard to bear and for most of us, depending on the demotion will result in being broken.

This can happen in non-spiritual as well as spiritual things. Someone could be a pastor and lose their ministry, and they can be so devastated that it is hard to recover. Someone could make a mistake of some kind and lose that promotion they worked hard to achieve. Someone could be stripped of an ordination or be removed from a position in their church. Someone can lose their source of income and lose a home or vehicle and must "step down" to something like they once had. To go back to a level that they left can be difficult to negotiate in oneself, especially if it happened in the public. To see the looks in people's eyes or hear the idle chatter and gossip over what happen can break a person. For many, it can be hard to "arrive" somewhere only to be forcefully returned to where they started. Shame, regret, fear, and more can overtake us due to the severity of that event. Many can get depressed, angry, bitter, or worse. It can be a wound hard to heal from without God there to lay His Hands on us.

Being cut off or disconnected from something that gives a person "life" can break them and is closely related to the other portions of the definition of broken, but I would like to expand on this a little. We all know that God uses isolation as a growing tool, but the Bible shows us in many instances that everyone doesn't always handle that isolation well. In addition, being cut-off was also a punishment under the Law of Moses for committing sin. Either way, being disconnected is always a surprise and we rarely consciously see it coming. When I say this, I mean that we may have our eyes open and know that it is possible, but the reality doesn't hit until the deed is done. It's like not paying your electric bill and wonder why "out of the blue" the electric company vehicle happens to show up at your house, and the technician flips a switch and the power goes off. At the exact moment of disconnection, the situation around us changes with a jolt.

When we are cut off from loved ones, a situation, a job, or anything that we hold dear to us, that jolt can cause our emotions and spirit to break. Depending on what was disconnected means to that person it can cripple us in many ways. I tend to think of religious bodies that "shun" or "excommunicate" people for varied reasons. When the act of severance happens it abruptly takes away a source of comfort or sustainment that person once held dear. Whether its people or if people feel "cut off" from God because it seems that their prayers aren't answered anymore, we can feel the loss of those connections. They hurt and they burn us deeply inside our hearts, minds, or spirits. If we depend on something that gives us our purpose or meaning, and it is suddenly turned off it is like that power being shut off. Everything stops. A sudden change like that can break a person because confusion, regret, fear, and panic overwhelm the mind, heart and spirit. Some folks can negotiate situations like this, and some cannot.

I know that when you read this part of the definition, I am sure that you were wondering exactly where I would go with being "imperfectly spoken or written." This is what I feel about this, and it may be different than what you might expect. When God speaks a Word or gave us His Word, we know that everything that comes from His mouth is perfect and true. Even when God is chastising us and correcting us it is for our good and only for our good. His promises are the ones we can depend on, and they are perfectly written and spoken to us (regardless of the state of the Bible, we have the Holy Spirit, and He teaches us ***ALL THINGS!***) (John 14:26) Now, when we get a word that is ***NOT*** from God and is from humans or from Hell, I consider that an imperfect word or message. Anything that doesn't come from God will ultimately fail. When we as people fall prey to an imperfect word that is written or spoken it can cause brokenness.

A religious doctrine based on the opinions and machinations of humanity will always fail and leave a trail of brokenness. A curse from Hell will cause pain and destruction and will cause brokenness. The truth of the word of God tainted by a carefully placed lie will always cause brokenness. Everything that we as people try to rely on that did not come from God will ultimately disappoint us and will cause us to experience brokenness. When we depend on what humans say over what God says it will always end in disaster. Even what I write in this book can fail you unless it is compared to and connected to God Himself. We cannot ever cut God out of our life equations. Ever. When we lean on our own understanding it will lead to failure (Proverbs 3:5-8). Only God provides a final resolution of completeness which leads to the next part of the definition of broken.

The "state of not being complete or full" causes brokenness because of the presence of lack. When we lack, we yearn for whatever we don't have, and we have a need to be fulfilled. When we talked about bankruptcy earlier, we spoke of not being able to get what we needed to sustain ourselves. This is related, but slightly different. The yearning for more can cause hopelessness and sadness to permeate our very being and that can break us. Imagine watching your family starving and you seemingly can't do anything about it. How would one feel when we lose something or someone dear and we have this large emptiness inside and don't know how to fill it? What if we are lonely and downtrodden with no one to turn to for comfort or companionship? The condition of lack is a wide chasm that seems like it won't be filled, and it can break us as time passes.

What I also think about is spiritual deficiency or emptiness as well. When we don't have the Holy Spirit, we are incomplete, and we lack the substance that only He can bring us. People may not realize it or want to admit it, but without the Spirit of God a person is broken inside. Sure, they might hide it with sin, denial, or even ***CHURCH*** (yes, I said it), but the result is brokenness on a spiritual level and that can be coupled with emotional turmoil. When we are lacking anything, we will naturally begin to seek what we feel that we need. The search for completeness is where Hell steps up its game to distract or confuse us. There is a place in our lives that only God can fill and we, too often, fill it with the things that make us feel good and even then, we aren't complete. We can get caught up in the high feelings of a replacement, but there still an underlying brokenness that is subtle and under the surface.

The last part of this definition is being "disunited by divorce, separation, or desertion" and it's like being cut-off, but slightly different. I tend to see this as being cut-off up-close and personal. These things are usually slower than being instantly disconnected and, in many ways, carry a different level of pain and suffering. As someone who went through divorce, I know that it hurts deep down inside as I saw things unravelling before my eyes. After the deed was done it left me in a state of brokenness and situations like these can leave scars that only God can heal.

Take being abandoned for instance, I have met and known people who were abandoned as children and the wounds of that desertion run deep and permeate their entire lives. When something is a part of something and then separated like divorce or separation the root of that pain is rejection. One person will feel rejection and that rejection can break hearts and spirits. Unity brings comfort and strength, but this sort of brokenness makes one feel vulnerable, weak, and they can second-guess themselves in practically everything.

On a spiritual level, being broken this way leaves a scar just like an emotional one. We can never be separated from the love of God, but we can be separated from the love of people. When it comes to spiritual things like church, we can experience these sorts of things when we hold up leaders, principles and ideas to high regard and they either fail or cast us out. I have seen people who had a spiritual leader fail and fall and they were devastated. What they believed to be true was just washed away, and they were left dumfounded. The situations can vary and be severe or slight and either way a person can feel rejected and broken because of it. What's the common theme? Rejection! The cause of being broken is feeling ***REJECTED***!

As people, we do not like to deal with anything that is broken. When a glass that we drink out of gets broken, we do not keep it because shards of glass can harm us if we try to use it. We throw it away. If we break a bone, we no longer can do the things that we did before, we must wear a cast, let it heal, and we are sidelined until we are ready. We must be put aside. When we are broken by the betrayal of trust, our hearts are destroyed, and we are left with the scars and trauma of what happened. We are wounded. When our happy lives are broken beyond repair due to some tragic event, we are left to pick up the pieces. We are bewildered. When our spirits are irrevocably broken by tribulation, we can sometimes lose the will to fight on because of what appears to be overwhelming odds. We are defeated. When we are bullied and mocked for just being ourselves and we are made outcasts to society we can feel dejected, rejected and projected as failures we suffer. We are beaten.

Brokenness is a state that no one wishes to be in but will eventually have to endure. No one can escape a season of brokenness and if you have not experienced it, yet, you will. It is the way of the Christian and always will be.

True, we are to live victorious lives in prosperity and happiness, but here is a question to ask yourself: How can you be victorious unless you defeat something? How do we learn the difference between day and night? We see it with our eyes. How do we know the difference between wet and dry? We feel it with our skin. How do we know the difference between loud and silent? We hear it with our ears. How do we know the difference between salty and sweet? We taste it with our tongues. How do we know the difference between the odors of a skunk versus the perfume of a rose? We smell it with our noses. How do we know the difference between love and hate? We feel it in our hearts. How do we know defeat from victory? We must experience defeat to know and understand what victory is.

We can read all we want to read about how things can unfold in our lives, but until we live through it, we will never understand what it truly is like. It does not matter how long you have been saved or what office you hold in the church. Sure, you can preach about it, talk about it, pray about it, counsel about it, lead worship about it, but until you live through it, you cannot truly know it. I hate to burst anyone's bubble, but it is what it is. I saw pictures of Niagara Falls in encyclopedias as a child, but until I walked past it on the street, stood over it behind guardrails, and navigated the tunnels behind it did I truly understand its raw, awesome power that pictures could not capture. Just like those pictures, I did not know what it meant to be broken until I was shattered, destroyed, and beaten by life situations and felt so alone that the silence was deafening. It was not until that moment that I truly understood brokenness.

Many times, when we see people, we do not understand their situation or their lives. We must remember that life's journey is different and tailor-made for everyone. What may be the apocalyptic cataclysm for one person might be how life is regularly for others before lunch. It is important that we do not judge another person's trials and tribulations based on our own experiences. There are some things that took out many other people that you lived through. For example, a .22 caliber bullet shot at a leaf on a tree would destroy that leaf, but if shot at an old, healthy tree would not go all the way through and the tree would be just fine. What can destroy one person would be a "flesh wound" or even a scratch on another. Each person is different and each tolerance for pain and suffering is different. There is only one way to God, but many winding roads that are specific to each person and that includes the sorts of perils they might face.

Yet, in all the brokenness, God has a purpose and a plan. It seems like it is a strange way to do it to us, but when we stop and think about it, we as people only seem to learn through experience versus information. This also pertains to relationships as well. When a loving couple goes through situations together, they tend to lock arms with each other and fight their way through it. This builds the bond between them and solidifies their commitment to each other. Therefore, in the natural, it is in the Spirit. Facing the worst times of our life on this broken road are opportunities for us to strengthen and solidify our relationship with God as we endure trials, tribulations and pain. However, it is up to us as to what we do with these dark periods of our lives. Do we choose to embrace Christ and build a stronger foundation of our relationship with Him, or do we fall into a pile of defeat and grow distant from God? That depends solely on us. Life is unfair, but God is still God.

We will run into things on this broken road that will violently tear things apart. The chaos is more than real, and it seems that everything is shattered all around us. When the breaking happens, it is like a giant wrecking ball that swings in seemingly out of nowhere and nearly hits us as the wall is disintegrated. I have never broken a bone (bless God), but swift change like this happens like a broken arm or leg. Everything is fine and then a certain action or force causes us to be injured, and the break occurs. It could even be a slow process like a beam being stressed until suddenly it gives way. Breaking is unexpected when it happens even though it ***CAN*** be predicted. Life can hit us just like that and while the period of breaking is fast, the recovery is always slower.

Think about how it feels to have trust broken or a covenant being violated. I know how that feels when a relationship ends because of infidelity, which to me, is one of the greatest betrayals one can face. That dull ache in the gut and the chilling sensation in the heart are unforgettable. That moment when you realize that what you thought to be true comes crashing down, as the lies are revealed, it hurts and that pain cuts all the way to the bone. So many emotions flood your soul that the spirit gets lost in confusion. All that can be agreed on is that this pain us like none other. The spirit falls to the ground in agony and the heart shatters in so many pieces that it turns to dust. There are few things that ache like betrayal. The grief and sorrow are on a side note, I cannot imagine how God feels when we betray Him due to sin, but that is a whole other story.

When tragedies come that brokenness will affect our sleep and affect us in other ways physically, which can cause illness. How many sleepless nights have you had worrying or thinking about what is happening? Have you ever tossed and turned wondering how the bills would be paid if you were laid off? Have you ever cried yourself to sleep just to wake up screaming? Have you had dreams about the abuse that you suffered and woke up in tears from reliving the horror? Sleep is normally a refuge where the mind and body get not just rest, but recharge and even heal itself. Sleep plays a vital role in good health and well-being throughout your life. The way you feel while you are awake depends in part, on what happens while you are sleeping.

During sleep, your body is working to support healthy brain function and maintain your physical health. Getting inadequate sleep over time can raise your risk for chronic (long-term) health problems. It can also affect how well you think, react, work, learn, and get along with others. Sleep affects your heart and circulatory system, metabolism, respiratory system, and immune system. Sleep is necessary for us to be able to deal with life mentally, physically, and spiritually and when we do not get that sleep it causes us to break down.

Breaking down physically can create weaknesses in the body and that opens us up for more of an onslaught if we are not or adequately spiritually covered. It is almost like kicking someone when they are already down. When troubles come, the enemy uses everything that the human mind, body, and spirit goes through when trouble comes to his advantage. We must remember that when tribulation comes that brokenness is never one-sided, but a compounding of many layers and events. The weight that we feel on our hearts and in our minds is crushing to us if we have never felt that level of pain before. It is crushing, it is brutal, and it causes excessive amounts of sorrow. We often will feel isolated and alone as the Devil and his minions will whisper to our spirit that we are forgotten, unloved, unwanted, and unworthy. Brokenness can make us feel worthless. We feel empty, useless, defective, and undesirable. The feelings of being incomplete and damaged make us feel like that broken glass in that we belong in the trash.

Let me pause and say something that some folks may not understand. While we are being broken, it can feel that God is ignoring us and not answering our prayers. It can feel like even God Himself has left us to die and suffer. After all, we have called on the Name of Jesus in the time of our trouble and we expect Him to swoop in with the sounds of an angelic choir with a sparkling white light from Heaven as He picks us up as the tears are still fresh and crushes Satan and restores everything that we lost and heals everything instantly. Can that happen that way? Sure, it can, but most of the time it does not. There are many times that God has a plan, and our brokenness is within that plan. That plan on the broken road of relationship will build us up in Christ or shape our destinies if we allow God to finish His perfect work.

As crazy as it sounds, how we react to situations will affect the outcomes. Yes, God is in control, but how we use our faith and the decisions we make can possibly change the conditions and length of a trial. We must remember that every period of brokenness is a test. As I have said before these tests are because of what we did and sometimes not, but the situations are still tests. Life's exams are thankfully "open book", and God is the best reference text to use in life's situations. Why? Because God has the best seat in the house, and He loves us. He sees it all and knows how it all will unfold. More importantly, God uses brokenness in a unique way like how trainers "break" horses.

Being Broken

There is a wide range of techniques that can be used to break a horse, which affects the time the process takes. The timing will vary based on the handler's approach to horsemanship and whether they opt for a softer or more forceful approach. Depending on the horse's learning style and nature, the amount of time it takes for a horse to be broken varies. On average, it takes ninety days to break in a horse. The process can be as short as thirty to sixty days, but many professional handlers believe this is not a process that should be rushed. Besides the quality of engagement between a handler and a horse before being broken in, the length of time can vary based on the horse's age, environment, and natural temperament. The bond between a horse and the handler who breaks them in also plays a vital role in how a horse responds to the process of being more controlled and having a rider on their back. The overall aim of this process is to have a horse that is considered safe to be ridden and responsive to a rider. This process is sometimes also referred to as 'saddle breaking'. A successful backing process will result in a horse who is relaxed and comfortable to not only having a rider on their back but accepting commands to be steered, stopped and respond to requests from the rider on demand.

Breaking in a wild horse can take between four weeks to four months, depending on the approach. It is certainly no easy task, and it takes significantly longer than breaking in a horse that has grown up around humans. As herd animals, wild horses have an inherent "flight or fight" response to things they are unfamiliar. This can be quite dangerous for a handler as a horse may buck, kick, or attempt to bite them out of fear. Breaking a wild horse is a process that needs to be met with compassion and understanding from the handler for the process to be successful in the long term. These horses will have had little to no exposure to the surroundings and objects they may encounter when being domesticated and ridden. This means that before a handler can even consider putting a saddle on the horse's back, they will need to get the horse used to being handled on the ground[2].

There are a few things I want to put a laser focus on about horse breaking. The first being that the wide range of techniques to be used will vary depending on the handler's approach whether they want to be softer or forceful. After evaluation of a horse, an experienced handler should be able to determine whether a gentle or forceful action needs to be taken to break that horse. The amount of time and what needs to be done affect the length of this training. The next thing I want to look at is the "age, environment, and natural temperament" of that horse which is very interesting. That animal will have different experiences based on how old they are, what sort of stimuli they had, and what their natural personality is. These two things are closely related in my mind as how a handler approaches a horse is based on that evaluation of those few characteristics and tailors a breaking program for them.

With the goal of being a horse that is fit to operate the way that they are needed to function is why breaking is effective. I found it interesting that the bond between the horse and the trainer is critical to the success of the process. The stronger the bond between that horse and the trainer is the easier and more effective the training is. This is especially important when a wild horse is being broken. They have a built-in "fight-or-flight" response that makes them naturally distrustful of people. They will bite, buck and kick because of fear and patience and grace must be employed to get them first used to people and then used to instructions and learning. A good, and loving handler will take the time and patience to train that horse. They will endure dealing with tricky situations with them. They will feel compassion over what they must do to train them but will carry that training out because it is the result that is desired. They know that it is difficult for them, but the horse must be trained to serve its purpose.

The difference between a horse and us is that we are more intelligent, and we are made in God's image. God will break us to teach us to trust Him and grow closer to Him. What we must be reminded of is that while the trainer is breaking the horse that trainer does not do it to cause the horse irreparable harm. From the people I have encountered who train and participate in equestrian sports they all tell me that for that horse to perform and be what is desired of them that trainer must forge a unique and personal bond between themselves and that horse to be a success. In other words, the trainer must have a love for the horse and realize when it is at the point of pain beyond what the animal can stand. The trainer must employ ***GRACE***. Without grace, horse breaking is torture for them both. It is the unyielding power of one over the other and it is more akin to a sadistic relationship. God knows that what He is allowing us to go through is for our good and He will keep the worst away from us.

As I relate it to the broken road, I see that God gracefully breaks us. He knows our limits, He knows how much we can bear, and even when we think that we cannot go on we can push ahead if we trust God and rely on His strength. It doesn't matter what the test is, God is merciful and will never let a test like brokenness destroy us beyond repair. Satan indeed has the power to turn us all into RIP hashtags if he was allowed to do whatever he wanted, but God is still in control, and His Love for us will not allow us to be snuffed out because Satan has a vendetta against all of creation.

When we are at our most desperate, God is the most miraculous. We must be at our "last straw" and realize that we cannot do what is needed to fix our situations. We must recognize Who is really in control of everything in our lives and that is a humbling experience. It is a reality check that is not like any other. It is easy to say that we trust God with our lives and with everything and it is another thing to know what that means and how it applies to everything. That is when the flesh must take a back seat to our spirits, let God be God, and that my friends is not easy to do without motivation. Brokenness is that motivation.

Why We Must Be Broken

There is not a single person on Earth that one hundred percent desires to be broken by God. The word broken exudes pain and suffering and for many (including myself) and brings horrible flashbacks of past experiences that have impacted lives. It is hard to imagine that a loving God like ours would even think to put someone through awful times in their life to get them to grow and change into a different person than they already are currently. The question of why I was broken by God Himself is a difficult one to answer to any satisfaction that would satisfy a person's mind. In my other book, *Consecration in The Refiner's Fire,* I wrote about brokenness, but in this book, I wanted to expand a bit more on the reasoning of being broken by a loving and caring God Who is doing all of it for our good. It never seems that way at the time and many times afterwards, but it is for our benefit.

Let me say first that God does not enjoy seeing us suffer or in pain. This is not the way that God, who is a Father, loves us and cares for us. No parent enjoys seeing their children going through things in their lives whether it be a punishment or a learning curve that they must go through on their own. Yet, when I look at the big picture of this life, it bears noting that God is shielding us from the eternal consequences that we deserve. We are born in sin and shaped in iniquity (Psalm 51:6) and because of the separation from God in the Garden of Eden we were condemned to Hell via the rules of Eternity. Jesus Christ came to die for the sins of the world so that we would have Eternal Life (Romans 6:23). Frankly, we got off easily compared to what could have happened to us. Yet, being broken by God seems personal and to be honest, it is.

As I have said before, every set of circumstances that God has established for our lives has been made just for us. Within those circumstances there are scenarios that God has designed to "break" us out of the things in our lives that He knows will hinder us or will not allow us to function completely in our destiny. Since God is a being beyond time, He can see every scenario, every decision, and every outcome all at once. Simply put, God ***IS*** the definition of the multiverse. His omnipotence and omniscience include the knowledge of all of time. I liken it to a chess expert who can look at the pieces on the board and see every gambit and every strategy before a single move can be made. Because of this, God will orchestrate that we go through a season or seasons of our lives that will strip us down to bare metal and allow us to be rebuilt in the way that He has desired for us. It is very personal and crafted uniquely for each of us.

The "***WHY***" of being broken is tied up with many misunderstandings and falsehoods that have plagued us for many years. There is a great misconception, in my mind, which has permeated the Church that sounds great, but is not grounded in real-life truths. I know that we all have heard the expression that, "God will not put more on us than we can bear," and I am going to have to completely disagree with that statement and I have many reasons why I feel that this is wrong.

Let me put this in a general statement first: If God wouldn't allow us to endure more than we could handle, why would we need God in the first place? I mean, if life itself would test us to our limits and back away would we really learn anything? I would say that the answer is that we would not. God will always push us past our limits to allow us to grow. It reminds me of weight training. If one would continue to use the same weights repeatedly the muscles would not grow beyond the limits being set. To push the body to grow, we must push past the previous milestone.

Scripture has shown us that God will indeed push us past our limits because we were made to rely on Him (1 Peter 5:7) and depend on Him for our very being. Every breath that we take and move that we make is dependent on God allowing it to be so. We cannot live without Him. How does our heart pump blood as it does without our control? How do we breathe even when we are unconscious? How do our bodies process nutrients without our thoughts? Our living depends on God in the physical as well as the natural realm. We unconsciously depend on God for everything, but the great deception is that because we have free will, that we can control our lives in every other aspect and that my friends is a lie. Breaking turns our conscious mind and spirit to what our unconscious mind has known all along.

God is everything. We can't do anything without Him. Seasons of breaking bring the reliance on God for everything into a clear focus even when we have learned part of this lesson already. We will trust God with most things, but we desire to control the others. It's like being on a roller coaster and unconsciously "steering" the bar that keeps us in the car in the way we think it should go. It means nothing. It makes us feel better, but it changes nothing.

It's like being a passenger on a plane or a bus and thinking that what we do can alter the course or speed of the vehicle. It does nothing if we aren't the driver or pilot. Even if we go to them and ask them to do something differently, they have no obligation to change what they are already going to do. We can pray and plead the Blood of Jesus over avoiding the breaking, but that won't always work. If God says that you are going through? You are going through, and you better learn to rely on Him for everything. No matter how mundane or how simple you may think it is. When we learn how helpless and weak, we are compared to God and eternity it is humbling, and it is reassuring at the same time. When we see how big God is compared to our situations, it gives clarity that we never had before. Being broken by God does this very well in ways that self-study will ever bring us.

If we aren't pushed past the brink and broken, we would be slow to call on God for anything (Acts 17:26-27) and we would have other options than God (like our own methods) and that's not how this works (John 15:5 and 2 Corinthians 12:7). If we always knew where the safety net was and how it could be used, we wouldn't cry out to God for anything. Have you ever ridden a roller coaster? After riding on it a few times we get to know every drop, every curve, and every feeling as we whip around the track. We then stop fearing or being reverent of the ride and we can take it for granted and start to enjoy the thrill of coming to the point of disaster and no further. It's like knowing how to perform the parlor trick that used to confound us. We would then begin to know what ways that we could use the situation to our advantage, or we would recognize the signs of progression and know when things will end.

As humans we would also realize that since we know the solution to the puzzle already that we can use our resources as to how to get through things. We would calculate and know where the bumps in the road are and choose another route or resource. When humans know the limits, we can get dangerous. We would take for granted the power and majesty of God. We would conclude (erroneously) that God does have limitations, and, in a sense, we would lose some reverence for God. When there is a way for humanity to step in and handle anything we tend to cut God out of it. If we were to simply bend and not break, we wouldn't learn anything and we wouldn't grow. That's like getting a mild reprimand when we have an illegal arrangement with a judge. The moment that we realize that we have consequences that we can contend with, we as people start branching out into our own ways and that defy God.

Being broken by God also reveals why God is our only source for life, strength, help and understanding. God knows what we don't know (Jeremiah 33:3) and when it gets dark during our season of breaking, He can guide us along the broken road. Why? Because He can see the unseen (Psalm 77:19). What makes a period a "season of breaking", in my mind, is that when we are going through tough times and cannot see what is coming, and we immediately start looking for answers.

We as people want to understand why things are what they are and that is what being human is about. We can reason and think through everything and when we don't know what God knows? We can get lost quickly if we don't ask for help. Ever get lost in a strange place in the dark? I know that I have, and it is unnerving. Sometimes, the place doesn't have to be somewhere that you have never been, but in an area where you haven't been without the things you normally depend on.

Stumbling and fumbling in the dark is a scary thing when you are used to being able to see where you are going. With God breaking us, we don't know anything. What once was up, is now down. What was reliably left, is now right. What was comfortably level is now uneven. Even if we have been in certain situations in life, if God "turns out the lights" we can get into trouble fast. The sense of hopelessness can settle in and make our fear factors rise to incredible heights. Have you ever had your car broken down on the side of a country road? Or somewhere with few people, no lights, and animals howling in the darkness? What about being stuck in your home and the power goes out? Or getting stuck in an elevator? In a flash we can lose control of our surroundings and not know what is happening and it can be frightening. Being broken by God can have us stumble where we used to walk and fall where we once had sure footing.

I remember playing silly games when I was young where you had to put on a blindfold and trust the voice of someone to guide you to an end point. The game was simple; follow the voice you heard and hope that they give the right directions to get to the goal. Do you trust that the person guiding you can get you there safely? If that person didn't give you the directions that you needed, you could lose the game. The twist here is that the same directions didn't mean the same thing to each person. The same thing can be said in slightly diverse ways to get to the desired goal.

Before anyone thinks that I am speaking of many ways to God. I am not. The Bible says the same things, but in different contexts and levels of understanding that speak the same truth. That truth is that there is no other source of life and wisdom but God (Yahweh, Adonai, Jehovah, El Shaddai). How God guided King David wasn't the same method used for Paul, the apostle. How God led Joshua wasn't the same way He led Moses. Still, God knows us well enough to know how to speak to us to guide us.

When God breaks us, He uses the methods that will speak directly to our minds, hearts, and spirits. He doesn't have to do the same things for different people unless He knows that it is necessary. God knows the answers before we can think of the questions. When the darkness comes and the familiarity fades, the breaking is designed to get us to reach out to God who knows it all and will answer us when the time us right for us to know. He will help us when we call on Him and He will be there when we need Him the most. Even when we are beaten and broken. He never revels in our pain, and He never will. I am sure that God is grieved to see us hurting, but I also know that He is rooting for us to come through our breaking in victory. God is that source of victory and until we are broken, we don't truly understand that.

Even though we are being broken, God's kindness and compassion will never run out (Lamentations 3:21-24) and He will still be gracious to us even while we are wondering what went wrong (Isaiah 30:18). God's breaking is never meant to hurt us, but it is done with His Grace, kindness, and compassion. Yes, God sees our tears as we endure the season of brokenness that He orchestrated and even in the worst of it He will show us that He loves us, but that doesn't mean that the trials will end. When our children are being disciplined and they are punished, we don't always end the punishment because they cry or that they plead with us that they have learned their lesson. It doesn't work that way. Think about someone convicted of murder. Picture a scenario where they did the crime but were repentant and remorseful. Even though they have repented and have learned from their mistakes, they still must endure the time in jail or the penalty of what they did.

When God allows us to be broken, even when we say we understand why He still has the right to allow whatever course that He has designed for us to continue. Even if we break down and cry loud, sloppy tears God knows what's best for us. The breaking is meant to strip us down to the foundation and that must involve pain. The beauty all of this is that this breaking is still done compassionately by God and could always be worse. The breaking could hurt even more than it already does, but God doesn't break us to permanently hurt us. A skillful surgeon won't just hack away at us and leave ugly scars for us to be reminded of the horror of being operated on but will make cuts that even though they split us wide open, will leave a scar that we can see, but won't always leave us in pain thereafter. The cuts aren't jagged and uncaring but are done to minimize scarring even though at one time that flesh was wide open and work in the body was being done that hadn't been done before.

When God breaks us, He does so with precision. The recovery may be hard, but it will be worth it. A surgeon knows that the healing will hurt, but the results will be worth it. Uncaring surgeons don't care what they cut and don't care about the healing process while compassionate ones do care and design their operations to consider this. God is no different as even though the breaking can be hard and painful, it is designed to heal in a way that it won't scar us spiritually for life, but we can see what the Lord has done in our lives. Yes, it will hurt, yes it will change us forever, but it is done with His Grace and His way that even though it is arduous, it will not hurt us forever. The breaking is designed to remove the undesirable, put in what is needed to sustain us or to clean up damage done from something earlier. When Satan destroys our lives and leaves scars that affect us, God will come along and operates in His caring way that will remove the scars, repair the damage, and sustain us even though it will hurt. We must trust His process.

As I have said earlier, the season of breaking can happen even when we do all the right things in God's sight. Sometimes what went wrong is us (Hebrews 12:6-7) and this breaking is meant to clean us up and get us right with Him. Why? Because God always desires to bring us back to Him even if we have strayed imperceptibly (Luke 15:7). When we mess up, we must pay the price. God will not allow us to allow our deeds to be unpunished if we stray or sin. Yes, all sin must be forgiven, but we still must pay for the consequences of sin besides death because Jesus paid that price. Since Jesus paid the biggest portion of the bill, we must pay the rest. God will break us out of sin and straying because we cannot have the impurities of sin in our lives if we desire to be what God has called us to be. We ***MUST*** be purified, and God will break us to do that for His Glory.

Just because all sin was paid for on the Cross doesn't mean that we can act any way we want and be whatever we want to be. We must present ourselves to God with holiness, and God knows how to bring holiness out of us which involves being broken. We cannot pollute the works and people of God when we are rife with the errors that we created or committed. We can't reach the potential in God that He has for us when we have back doors and escape ramps with sin all over them. When a habit becomes deeply ingrained in us a season of breaking by God will follow sometime afterwards. Remember, God knows all about us and He alone knows the best way to purge us from the sin and mistakes that we make for us to be what He has called us to be. I like to use the analogy of a great football coach.

A great coach sees the potential of their players and when they try out for the team, they look at them with the eye of potential as well as what they are currently. Even if a player is exceptional at their position on a team a great coach will be able to see what in them is holding back their potential and conversely, a person with raw talent that can be shaped by training is also allowed to be on the team. For example, a prime athlete who is strong, fast, and agile is great before training, but that coach will see the small flaws in how they perform and train and focus on those to make them even better. A muscle-bound athlete may be powerful in moving obstacles but lack coordination and is clumsy. A player may not be able to throw a football for long distances, but the throws they can make are pinpoint accurate. A player may not be fast, but they can quickly calculate the next moves of an opponent and that makes them valuable.

That great coach will drill that athlete until they begin to perform to the potential that they never knew they had. The strong, with training, can become stronger. The fast can become faster. Wise people can become wiser, but until they are challenged, they won't grow and mature. All players in a sport like football may have played the sport before, but now they need to learn the system the coach has in place. They need to get rid of how they used to play and play the way the coach says to play. They may have had one diet before on another team, but they now must eat the way their current team eats.

The ways that they have that are done wrong must be made right to play for their current coach. The drills and practice will hurt the athletes as they will sweat, get tired, and tend to the pains of their training. If the team falls short and does something wrong? Punishment will happen. Stronger drills happen that reinforce the need to stick with the program and listen to the coach. When a player messes up in the game, they are corrected for what they did wrong and get training to help them bridge the gap between futility and victory. The great coach will observe it all and prescribe what's best for the players.

When we mess up on the road of life, God will often put us through the process breaking. He already knows what we can do if we depend on Him and Him alone. He knows that with the right scenario from which we will learn what we did wrong and come out stronger. We need this at whatever level God determines, and it is more than necessary. When we commit ourselves to God, we must be prepared to be broken when we step out of line. We can instantly regret our mistakes when the trial starts, but we must go through it until God is satisfied with our progress. We will endure the "breaking" until He sees that we have arrived where He has designed for us to go and not a moment sooner.

The preparation for destiny must be completed. The stain of sin must come out. The mark of errors we made must be removed because if not, we will do it repeatedly and unchecked, humanity is dangerous. God knows that we are imperfect, but He wants is to be the best that we can be in Him. Being broken for straying from God reminds us of what we endured to get back in good standing with God, and it helps others to either not to repeat those mistakes or how to endure the process because it is worth it.

When we get broken by God, He builds us up with the character He desires in us and gives us eternal hope in Him (Romans 5:3-4). Going through the breaking builds us up in ways that we never could have imagined. Godly character is not something that happens overnight. This comes from being in relationship with God and that comes through trials and tribulations. Reading the Word all day and memorizing every word doesn't make one live holy. Applying what is read in the Word and what God teaches in life is what causes us to choose holiness. When God breaks us, our holy character is built up brick by brick and floor by floor. Breaking clears away the hay and the stubble that God has burned away (1 Corinthians 3:12-13) and allows Him to build our character and our faith in the image that He has designed for us. It causes a transformation that reshapes and reforms our hearts and minds that "classroom" learning never can.

As a child I remember seeing the elders of our church who seemed to live right all the time and seemed to always have it together. The way they spoke, and handled life's situations, was so automatic that it was nearly unbelievable. I saw their integrity and I admired it, but I didn't understand why they were the way they were until I asked them and what they said was shocking to me at the time. Those who were open to share would tell us that God developed their character through trials and hard life lessons. I remember that one person I knew that handled money for a ministry was once a petty thief when they were younger, but God transformed them. A person that seemed to be faithful and steadfast in their marriage used to be "loose" and lived any way that they wanted. One who had incredible faith who seemed to be able to pray the paint off the walls was once timid and didn't believe that God could do anything. It was shocking, but I learned how this worked once I lived a little while.

What I learned is that they couldn't become what God had intended until they went through a God-designed breaking that drew out these characteristics that they were known for by going through dark times that God made for them to purify them of what held them back. The breaking in their lives was made to get them to the places in their character that God would use in their later lives. I learned that these same pillars in ministry had to learn to be what they were, and they also learned to keep their hope in Christ for ***EVERYTHING***. This took time and it took multiple life lessons to do it. God doesn't "snap us into place" in one life lesson unless He wants to do so. It is His call to make. However, breaking comes in waves and cycles. It's like purifying a substance of impurities. The more cycles something goes through, the more suitable or valuable it is to the owner.

In my professional life, I work with information technology and if anyone knows anything about computers one of the pieces of that computer that most people are most familiar with is the hard drive. The hard drive is where information is stored, and computers run from. What most people don't know is that every drive that is used (except for the very first time) contains information that most people don't get to see but can still be present. A hard drive works with a file system which is a collection of data that is chained together in a meaningful way. When data is written to the drive it is linked together with each piece of data pointing at the next piece wherever there is space to write it. This writing is not like a CD or an old-school record where information is sequential, but data can live anywhere on the drive if it is connected.

When we "delete" a file or data what happens is that the data isn't destroyed but the links between each piece of that data is disconnected from each other. This tells the computer that this space can be written to again. A savvy person who can access the drive and with the right software can read the drive piece by piece and can "reconstruct" what files were thought to be deleted. No problem, right? Just reformat the drive and all the data get wiped out! (Right?) That is not correct and is a myth. Reformatting resets what is called the file allocation table and doesn't erase the data on the drive at all. The smart and technical can still pull unlinked data together and see what used to be there. This is how law enforcement can "undelete" files removed by users. Here is where it gets interesting.

There is a way to truly clean a drive, and it isn't a quick process. A drive can be written over block by block with uniform data from the beginning of the drive all the way to end of the drive. It is done several times to be sure that orphaned data is truly erased and makes it like a drive that is brand new. When a drive is new, accessing the files is more efficient because the computer doesn't have to skip around to various locations for a file, but is more sequential. It runs faster and more the way it was designed to run. Junk information is eliminated, and performance is much better. When God breaks us, He strips us down to the tiniest building blocks of our lives and removes the junk. When we delete things from our lives, we disconnect what once was, but it is still there and can be rediscovered. When God works us over, He deletes things cleanly. The process is longer than a simple "snap of the fingers", but it is worth it overall.

I respected my elders because I saw how seamless they seemed to work through their lives in Christ. Yes, I knew that they were imperfect like I was, but I saw and admired how "cleanly" they lived and that was because they went through some things that God allowed them to endure to make them better. They were reformatted on a "molecular" level, and it hurt them for a time. It wasn't easy, but the results of who they were after going through those trials made them who they were in Christ. They had hope for the things of God because He taught them in their breaking not just who they were, but who God was. When that happens, it transforms us as people, and it builds the Godly character that God intended and designed for us. If it wasn't for the breaking season, there would not be a season of rebuilding. That is what we need and what God wants.

It is in the process of being broken that we build our testimonies in His Power and might and we can help someone else who is going through tough times (2 Corinthians 1:3-4). Those elders would tell the public parts of their testimonies to us, and it encouraged and helped fortify us. Until we go through something we can't really speak convincingly to it. We can't bear witness to things that we didn't suffer through or trusted God to deliver us from. Experience makes for a convincing testimony because the conviction that can pour from us when we are sharing with someone else conveys to that person the tears that were shed and the pain that was felt in the midnight hour. Anything less than an authentic testimony is just another story. Any actor can tell a tale, but a witness who lived through something that should have taken them out, but survived and recovered because of the Grace of God? That's totally different and the Holy Spirit will activate from us when we share with others of the goodness of God. There is absolutely nothing like it in the world!

The breaking is meant for our good even when we don't feel like it is (Romans 8:28). It is very hard to read Romans 8:28 and believe it deep down in our spirits while we are being broken down by God's desire. In the next chapter I am going to cover brokenness at length, but for now I want to talk about how we feel about it and the reason we cry out to God "***WHY***?" I know for myself that while I was enduring tribulation, I asked myself how in the world is this for my good? How is it that I love God, serve God, and go through all of this for God to say that it was for my best?

Let me be honest with you, there is a very fine line where the devil will try to convince you to be angry at God. He will try to convince you that the Word of God must be a lie because a loving God wouldn't do this to you. Honestly, our flesh can believe that because in human terms it seems horribly unfair and even cruel. If you study the Scriptures, you will see where God has punished people and every instance of God doing that could possibly rush in to your mind because don't forget, Satan knows the Word of God too. He knows how to twist it to try and fool us and when we are in the middle of breaking, we may not be at our best strength.

That truth of God that all things work together for the good is a hard pill to swallow. It is hard to comprehend at ground zero of a situation that has the potential to take us out of commission. When we are in the worst situations of our lives that God has set up to break us our vision will be short-sighted. We, in the flesh, won't be able to see God in the middle of the storm. We won't always be able to stop and thank God because the pain that we feel is very real and very present. We won't be able to look past what we believe is our righteousness before God. Often, we didn't do anything to be punished or anything to "deserve" tough times. If we were to write it all out on paper it would seem like God hates us and we are being mistreated. We don't see that God is preparing us for our next level, and we can't see that God is putting us through the fire to purify us.

Breaking is more than unpleasant, and it is grueling and can drive us outside of the realm of sanity because it doesn't make sense at the time. We can be living holy, righteous, and still be placed in a season of brokenness. The reasons for God doing this is up to Him and only He knows the genuine answer as to why.

There is not another way to explain it, but we, as Christians, just need to accept that it is what it is. I know that many want a soothing and calming answer, but there isn't one. Sorry to burst your bubble or let you down, but when we say that God knows best? God knows best. Period. If we are desiring or destined for greater in God, we will go through periods of breaking. There isn't any way around this. We can refuse to endure the breaking, but we will lose out of what God has promised us.

This is what I have discovered on my walk on this broken road. Brokenness is a blessing in disguise. Read that again and meditate on that for a few minutes. Yes, brokenness is a blessing and here is how that is true. Brokenness is a sign that promotion is coming. It is the result of being chosen to ascend to the next level in God and in life. Brokenness is much like an interview for a job promotion. How one responds to the questions and their qualifications are the keys to getting the job. I have interviewed people for positions and hired them. One thing that I have learned from interviews is that a stacked resume is not always the thing that gets people hired.

The Interview

There have been people that I have interviewed for open job openings that had a stellar and superb resume with all the right details, education, and experience that seem to match exactly that for which the position is being advertised. When I conduct an interview, I ask questions that are beyond the description of the job, and I ask them for deeper details about their experience and give them a scenario that is closely related to the job I have available and see how they respond. Often, those with a flowery resume with all the trimmings do not give the responses I am looking for. Their statements don't line up with what I know that person would endure on the job if they truly knew what they were doing. The interview goes beyond the claims made in the resume and often it goes beyond the accolades of what is being advertised by the candidates. The real person shows himself or herself based on how they respond to an interviewer and will show himself or herself as fit to be hired.

The interview can be hard on a candidate. Having been on both sides of the interview table, I know that seeing a person sweating or nervous because of the challenging questions and being the one having questions fired at me is a kind of stress unlike any other. I have felt like I bombed an interview when I struggled to answer questions or when I look at the interviewers, I get non-emotional expressions on their faces. The candidate does not know whether they got the position or not as the dreaded words "we will be in touch" are spoken, hands are shaken, and the period of uncertainty can begin. Doubt can set in. Fear can set in. We can start kicking ourselves in our rear ends because we felt that we should have said something else or not said certain things at all. We do not want to be rejected, but we will have to know whether we get the job or not.

The question is when. When will we find out the answer we seek? As it is on the broken road, we never know how long God will take to answer our questions. We do not know how long we must travel through the darkness. We do not know how long we must stumble in the rain. We do not know how long we must hobble along in pain. What we can be certain of is that God has not forgotten about us. He knows where we and where we will be when the trial is over. He has the promotion waiting for us, but we must endure. The breaking process is needed to prove that we are the one "fit for the job" and ready to receive what God has for us. There is no entitlement on the broken road. No seniority or express lane is available. From the Apostle to the saint in the pew, there is a period of testing and road of brokenness that must be traveled.

God gives us the choice to go through it all now. We can say that we do not want to endure tribulation, but keep in mind that it will be there until we take that test. We can stand still, or we can venture off the main road. Yet, no matter what we think, the fact is that whatever God has for us to endure to break us down from our humanity into His Holiness will be waiting if we desire to go higher in Him. Sadly, we often look at the possibility of the pain instead of focusing on the guaranteed promise. That is our flesh talking to us. Remember, as I said before, our flesh will never see Heaven, so it does not have any incentive to endure discomfort in spiritual things. Have you ever seen a marathon? Ever notice how hundreds of people start, but only a smaller number finishes? There is something to take note of about such a long race. The runner is not alone.

Every few miles or so there are little stations set up with water for either a runner to grab which they drink or the splash on themselves. I do not believe that there has been a single runner in a marathon that has never taken a drink of water in history. That refreshment is needed to keep running the race. There is also something else along the way helping the runner. There are nurses and medical professionals to help someone who is showing signs of distress or illness. There are folks there to cheer them on. These folks that are not in that race are clapping their hands and helping them along the way. Some of those encouragers are running the water stations filling and setting out cups for runners to pick up. Some racers in the contest will even encourage others that are racing with them and will help another if they were to show signs of trouble. If it were not for others encouraging and helping runners along fewer people would finish or even, make it to the finish line.

Let me pause here for a second and connect this with the spiritual. In our life's race, God has placed other people to encourage us in our trials for us to survive. Sometimes they are angels or even God Himself encouraging us to continue forward in His Strength. There are places where we can get refreshment through His Word, worship, prayer, or an encouraging message from someone who has been where they are or even if they have not. There are some in our race that are sent to pray for us and with us when we are in greatest need. There are people that sometimes only need a hug or a shoulder to cry on to stay in the fight. Then you have those who are going through things at the same time, and they can encourage each other to keep the faith and carry on. Just like a marathon, these people and helpers are along every step of the way.

Unfortunately, there are heckling spectators there as well. Some just observe and some even heckle runners. Some will simply watch us struggle and say nothing to us. They do not pray for us and poke some fun at us while we are going through things. You have people that "mean well" or are out as predators and do everything they can to take advantage of other peoples' distress. There can also be other runners that are trying to "win" and discourage or sabotage others on the same course. Many come looking like help but are wolves in sheep's clothing. Many have been hurt in the past or taught incorrectly and they pass on the same bad teachings and advice along to someone else sending them into a tailspin.

Here is the most encouraging part of it all. The Bible passage in 1 Corinthians 9:24 talks about many runners running, but only one gets the prize. Even though the broken road we run, or walk, is for others and us may be going through similar circumstances, the road we are on is for us and us alone. We are going for the ultimate prize in Christ Jesus, and I tend to think of races like the Tour de France where the contest is done in stages. When we are in the press to that next level, to finish that portion of a dark road we should be running for daylight as if we are in the fight for our lives. Whether or not we get a little help or encouragement along the way or not we have to realize that at the end of this leg of the race will be not just a prize, but there will be some rest and a chance to recuperate. At the end of a marathon, there is usually a recovery station where runners (once they cross the finish line) can go for oxygen, medical attention, or just a place to lay down if they need it.

Going back to the interview, we must keep in mind that the race ***IS*** the interview. What I didn't talk about when I used a marathon as an example is that there are also judges along the way. The judges or officials ensure that runners stay on the course and have the power to disqualify a contestant that doesn't follow the rules. The entire race is observed and just like the marathon our walk on the broken road is observed by the only One I would ever want to judge me, and that is God Himself. God is always watching, and His Eyes never miss anything. I know that the focus here is on the runner, but the officials also watch the spectators and other contestants. God makes sure that Hell doesn't rise more than they are allowed. God ensures that anyone who tries to harm us is dealt with accordingly. There is not a single scenario in existence that God doesn't moderate and watch over us in love. None.

Remember when Christ was tempted for forty days in the wilderness? Remember what happened after those forty days? When we read Matthew 4:11 we see that angels came to minister to Him. The same thing happened after Jesus prayed in the Garden of Gethsemane on the Mount of Olives asking for the cup to be passed from Him in Luke 22:43. Even JESUS needed some comfort after going through a rough patch. After great, God-ordained challenges in our lives, there is comfort for our souls. There is reward for our endurance. There is peace in the middle of and after the storm. God has never and will never leave any of us to be battered alone without there being comfort and rest. The demanding thing to realize is that sometimes that relief may be transitioning into Glory. The test and the road are not up to us, but God gets all the glory no matter the circumstance.

The walk on the broken road of our relationship is not like anything else in the world. It doesn't ever seem like it makes any sort of sense, but it does. What God has designed for us is bigger and greater than we are right at this moment. None of us have arrived at our destination which is eternity. Because of this, we are always in the process of "the interview". We are never done with being reshaped and remade in God's desired image for us to be. We need to understand that just because we made it through one level, that another is not coming. We aren't finished until God is finished with us. I will use my professional career again as an example. For every position I went higher I had to participate in an interview. Even when I was told that the position was mine, I ***STILL*** had to interview for it because it was a part of the process.

This is the same thing for our walk in Christ. It has and never will change. It is necessary and we must keep in mind that God will never fit us, but we must fit God. We must be bent into the shape that He desires for us if we are willing to endure His process. This will cause us to be broken like the horse to be disciplined and discipled correctly. The difference here is that we have a choice. We can choose not to show up to the interview. We can choose not to be discipled, and we can choose not to endure the brokenness. There are benefits, but God won't force us. We need to change our perspectives on what brokenness is because many have wrong ideas about what this painful process really is.

What Brokenness Is Not

Brokenness is not a punishment. Brokenness is beautiful, because God shows us and the world that no matter what we may be or what we may be going through God is still on the throne and His Power cannot be matched. Where humans see failure, God sees potential. When others see us as disappointments, God sees us as champions. Fear and hesitation will make us leery of going through the trials God has for us and fleshly self-preservation will cause us to miss what God intends for us. God will not force us to go where we are not submissive to His Will. We must surrender our lives in every aspect to Christ. We must submit to

His teachings. We must yield to His ways. We must agree to walk this road to where God wants us to go. We are the ones that need to engage God and take a hold of His promises.

The faith that God is in control and will restore us is hard to visualize until we go through tribulation and come out on the other side victorious. If we could talk to any of the saints in the Bible, they would bear witness to the promises of God. If we could talk to Paul, the Apostle, he would tell us that even if you were going the wrong way that God can turn us around. If we could talk to Moses, he would tell us that even if we messed up God will still use us for His Glory. David would tell us that even if we had sinful habits that we struggled with that God will still bring royalty and majesty through our families. If we could talk to Naaman he would tell us that God will ask us to do crazy things to get what blessings, healing, and restoration that He has promised. If we could talk to Esther, she would tell us that we must put our lives on the line to get what God said He would do for us because His Word is unbreakable. Until we endure the tests, we will not truly believe what it feels like. Until we realize that others have gone through and come out on the other side? We will not do it.

We are creatures of "wait and see" because it is human nature. Until our faith grows, we will not step out and trust God in the way we later learn. It seems barbaric and even cruel to someone who does not believe in God that God seems to enjoy seeing us suffer. The concept that God is somehow toying with us instead of helping us is hard to wrap our minds around. That is so far from the truth. It is like watching another parent teach his or her child. Some things look cruel because we do not understand that child the way that their parent(s) know(s) them. A ***GOOD PARENT*** that loves their children will teach them in a way that they can and will learn. Some children learn by talking, some by demonstrating, and others through adversity and challenge. A wise parent who has known their child from birth knows how they respond and understand how they learn things.

I remember one of my nephews as a little one who was learning how to crawl. He would get in the crawling position and instead of going forward, he would go backwards, and this frustrated him to howling tears. When I say he was wailing, I mean ***WAILING*** with loud crying and snot running out of his little nose going everywhere. I remember the first time I saw this I was rushing to pick him up, but my sister told me, "Nope, leave him there and don't look directly at him, but keep an eye on him because he learns by getting frustrated and figuring it out." I did what my sister asked, but man, was it hard hearing that little man crying. It broke my heart to see him going backwards increasingly and his cries getting louder and louder. My heart started pulling for him, telling him in my heart that he could do it. He kept going in circles as we watched with a side eye and then something happened.

Little man fell on his belly, started to cry less, got back up again, and tried repeatedly. I watched as he started going sideways at first, then backward, sideways, and then he nudged forward. Tears still streaming, he nudged forward again. Then again, he nudged forward until he started plodding along in the right way and then he started giggling. Then he was ambling at a faster rate and crawled over to us laughing all the way and it was at that moment we picked him up and showered him with praise to his delight. We hugged him and celebrated his achievement, and he never looked back. As the years have gone on, I have watched that little man become so wise and so quick to learn anything that he touches. Why? Because instead of giving him shortcuts to bypass his challenges he was allowed to fail, allowed to get frustrated, allowed to cry until he learned what he had to do. His mother knew that him learning the "hard way" was not a punishment, but a teaching tool.

I am sure that God does not enjoy seeing us in pain. He does not get any happiness in watching us wandering around in the dark. I do not see how God enjoys seeing us lose the important things in our lives, but I do see God pulling and rooting for us. He gave us the tools, He made the way, and we must choose to use what He gave us and get through it. God gives us the answers repeatedly and has made our lives an open book exam. In Deuteronomy Chapter 30, He told us that He has given us the choice between life and death and that we should choose life.

After Adam was tricked by the serpent to sin, God sent His only Son to redeem us all and that all we must do is accept Him as our Lord and Savior and we would earn the right to Eternal Life. He sent the Holy Spirit, The Comforter, to be with us after Christ left the Earth to teach us everything and help us remember what he taught us. All we must do is accept what God has provided. Willingly receive these gifts in a loving covenant with the Creator of the Universe.

It is within this covenant that Jesus came to Earth and allowed us to execute Him for our benefit. Jesus came to die so that we wouldn't have to pay the actual cost for what we deserved. When we look at the account of Jesus in the Bible what we see is an innocent Jesus being tried, convicted, and murdered unjustly. If we really sit down and look at the whole scenario, we see the injustices that befell Jesus as He was tried. We can see how people abandoned Him and lied on Him all for our redemption. We can see how the soldiers mocked Him, stripped Him naked (just search the Internet for the details on crucifixion), and laughed at Him. Jesus died for them too. Jesus carried His cross despite being whipped to the point of near death. He was nailed and hung up for all of us. We can look at the entire thing and see how Jesus didn't deserve any of what He went through, but He did anyway. Jesus endured what He endured so that we could return to Him of our own free will.

Because of our sin, we as humans, must be reconciled with God and we must earn our way back to Him. We must reestablish the bond that was broken between Adam and God. We must come to full knowledge of life and living to accept Christ. We must make all the moves to go back to The Father. Part of that is the broken road. How else can we know an unseen God Whose Presence is felt everywhere? How else can we get to know Him except through the fellowship of suffering? How else can God be real to us until we learn to tap into Him? Relationship is the way, and the broken road is a method. Brokenness is the tool and our love for Him is what binds us to God forever. We must know that God is on our side and as a good Father wants what is best for His children. We may never understand how and why, but we must understand that His Love for us burns brightly for us like ours for Him must burn through our souls.

Because of His Love, we must never forget that the state of being broken is not because God hates us. Hell wants us to feel that way and when we do, we tend to miss out on what God has intended for us to achieve. The closer that we are to Jesus we will learn and understand that brokenness is not a punishment or death sentence. I know that it can feel that way at the time, but we must remember Who God is. Our seasons of brokenness will escalate and even if we overcame a prolonged test before, it does not take much for our flesh to want to forget that God is not only real but loves us so deeply that He chastens us. Fake "churchianity" wants us to believe that God only allows the good, but reality lets us know that rain must come before and after sunshine, if we desire growth.

One more thing, brokenness does not originate in Hell. It can feel like Hell, but brokenness is allowed or sent by God in Heaven. Satan cannot harm us without permission. Hell cannot orchestrate a single scenario even if we have spiritual backdoors and allow access by demons. The Dominion of God is so powerful that every created thing ***MUST*** wait until God permits them. Let's not forget that in Philippians 2:10-11 the word says:

THAT AT THE NAME OF JESUS EVERY KNEE SHOULD BOW, OF THINGS IN HEAVEN, AND THINGS IN EARTH, AND THINGS UNDER THE EARTH; AND THAT EVERY TONGUE SHOULD CONFESS THAT JESUS CHRIST IS LORD, TO THE GLORY OF GOD THE FATHER. – PHILIPPIANS 2:10-11 KJV

If ***EVERY*** knee will bow and proclaim that Jesus Christ is Lord, what do you think that Satan does right now? He may be in open rebellion of God, but he ***STILL*** knows God's Power. He still knows God's Authority. Frankly, I would be the same way, because I know that if God spoke everything into existence and that God, with the same mouth, could utter words to blink us out of existence. We need to keep these things in mind because God is in ***TOTAL*** control of everything. This includes seasons of brokenness. Satan is the author of confusion, but he doesn't own brokenness.

Sure, he is an expert in causing pain, but he cannot originate any of what he does without God not just saying if he is allowed, but also how far he can go. Satan, as we all know, has had more time and experience with God than anything or anyone else in all of Creation. Because of this Satan has a vendetta against us. He wasn't made in the Image of God, but we were. I believe that this is the reason Satan tempted Eve to wreck God's very personal creations. Because we messed up and believed Satan's lies, I feel that God allows Satan to be one of the vehicles delivering brokenness to all of Humanity. We don't understand why God allows this, but we just must accept the fact that God knows what He is doing. God isn't punishing us, per se, but allowing Hell as one of the options to refine us and shape us in ways a simple lecture of instruction would never be able to do.

His Refining Fire that burns on the inside will also burn on the outside and as we allow Him, He will burn through our foolishness, eradicate our shame, and purify our hearts. Brokenness exposes what has been hidden or dormant that we were unaware of its existence. When we allow Christ to burn us from within, He will destroy the hay and the stubble in our lives and allow rejuvenation to occur. We may cry and we may endure pain during this process because just like fire in the natural realm a purifying flame will cut deep. I think about how in the old war movies a lone soldier has a wound, and they heat a bowie knife in the fire until it glows red and cauterizes a wound to save their life. That may leave a scar, but they will live to fight another day. Brokenness does cause wounds, but the Fire of God is there to purify them and seal up the injuries. Yes, it will scar, but God delivers the healing afterwards.

Beautiful Imperfections

God gives us beauty for our ashes, He mends our broken pieces with His Spirit, and it reminds me of the Japanese art of Kintsugi. Kintsugi (golden joinery) is also known as kintsukoroi or golden repair. It is the art of repairing broken pottery by mending the areas of breakage with lacquer dusted or mixed with powdered gold, silver, or platinum. This ancient Japanese tradition highlights imperfections rather than hiding them. The broken pieces' gilded restoration usually takes up to three months, as the fragments are carefully glued together with the sap of an indigenous Japanese tree, left to dry for a few weeks and then adorned with gold running along its cracks. What was broken and destroyed is made beautiful again and in today's world, pottery pieces repaired with kintsugi are highly valued and sought after[3].

When I think about how God makes us beautiful again after going through the muck and mire of the broken road, I am reminded as to how kintsugi pieces do not hide the flaws or breaks in the objects. Normally in western culture, we want to use glues, adhesives, and cover-ups that make repairs look seamless, and like they never happened. Yet, with kintsugi, the gold shines from where there was brokenness. Where there was chaos is now strength. The gold shines first and allows us to see that what was destroyed at one time has now been brought back from the brink. When it was broken, it was destined for the trash heap. Now?

After a time of being separated from the point of impact and placed where other broken vessels are being repaired, and there an expert artisan takes an ordinary repair and makes it art.

Being destroyed and shattered hurts, but God will take every place that we have been broken, apply Himself to every crack, crevice, and hole, and assemble us the way that He has intended for us to be. His loving Hands will shape us, mold us, and make us valuable and useful to build up the Kingdom of God on Earth. It does not matter where we come from, and it does not matter what we think that we are worth. God will do what is necessary (if we let Him) to set us apart and fill us with His Spirit and renew our lives and our purpose, but we must be understanding that it all takes time.

It takes time, but it also takes obedience and submission. God will allow us to be broken, but it is up to us to allow ourselves to be reshaped into what God wants for us. Unlike human materials such as clay or broken pottery, we as humans must submit to allow God to mold us and restore us. Too often we fight against the Hands of God and He will let us resist even though it will get harder until He lets us alone. I know that this may be a bit challenging to agree with but hear me out. God gave us free will as individuals. God has ***NEVER*** mandated salvation or restoration for us. Yes, I said it. Look at the examples in the Word of God:

"…I HAVE SET BEFORE YOU LIFE AND DEATH, BLESSING AND CURSING: THEREFORE CHOOSE LIFE…" – DEUTERONOMY 30:19 KJV

"…IF THOU SHALL CONFESS WITH THY MOUTH, THE LORD JESUS…" – ROMANS 10:9 KJV

"…WHOSOEVER WILL, LET HIM TAKE THE WATER OF LIFE FREELY" – REVELATION 22:17 KJV

We were not made to be robots, but individuals. God gives us the choice to decide what we want in our lives. God has the power to make us, but He gave us the wonderful gift of the choice to live for Him or not.

I firmly believe that when we choose how deeply we want to relate to and grow in Christ we also are choosing the level of brokenness that we receive. This is what I mean by that statement. The closer we want to get to God we must allow

God to remove and purge all that is detestable and unacceptable to Him as we journey into covenant with God. It's like a roaring campfire on a winter night. The closer one gets to the fire the warmer they will get. I also think of an igloo dwelling built by Native Americans in the far reaches of the north. Their dwelling is made of snow and blocks of ice, and yet, they can build a fire in the middle and stay warm and even cook food. The walls of the igloo are far enough from the flames to not melt the snow and ice and keep the dwelling warm inside.

Think also about celestial bodies like the planets and comets. The closer that they are to the Sun, the warmer they are, and their atmospheres and climates are different. The same sun that heats up Venus to melt lead is the same one that shines on bitterly frozen dwarf planets like Pluto and Haumea. Their experiences with their seasons are based on how close they are to the Sun and the tilts of their axes. Our experiences with our seasons of life are based on how close we are to The Father and how much we lean towards Him. We can be in God's orbit and stay just enough on the outside that we still belong to Him but not let His Holy Fire burn away only what His Presence can remove. As living beings God made in God's Image, we can choose our orbit around God and when we do, we can only receive from God what we have chosen.

Let's look at the planets in our solar system, for example. Each of them rotates for a different period for their "day" and tilts at different degrees for their axes.

- Mercury: 58 days 15.5 hours, 0°
- Venus: 243 days 26 minutes, 177.3°
- Earth: 23 hours 56 minutes, 23.4°
- Mars: 1 day 36 minutes, 25.2°
- Jupiter: 9 hours 55 minutes, 3.1°
- Saturn: 10 hours 40 minutes, 26.7°
- Uranus: 17 hours 14 minutes, 97.8°
- Neptune: 16 hours, 28.3°[4]

The Sun is always in the same place, and the planets are different distances away from it. Their axes tilt at different angles and their rotations are different lengths as well as how large their circumferences are. Each of the planets is different in what they experience too. Mercury is slow to spin, is straight up and down and has very little atmosphere with temperatures as high as 800° F and as low as -300° F. Unbelievably, Venus is the hottest planet in our system with temperatures that can melt lead with over ninety percent carbon dioxide and sulfuric acid clouds in its atmosphere. Venus also seems to rotate backwards but is nearly upside down.

We live on Earth and know how it can be, but Mars is a rusty, chilly, and barren rock with very little atmosphere, Jupiter is the biggest planet with the most moons and a hurricane called the Great Red Spot that's been churning for over three hundred years. Jupiter is the biggest planet with the shortest "day". Saturn has the most pronounced set of rings and is almost twice as far away from the Sun as Jupiter. Uranus is the coldest planet in the solar system but is the only one practically lying on its side. One side of Uranus stays frozen for decades before warming up again. Neptune rounds out the bunch and has the fastest winds in our star system at over twelve hundred miles an hour.

What does this mean? Each one of those planets is different in many ways and yet, they are beautiful in their own ways. Only one of those planets was made for us, while the others are not. Still, God made each of them and while they may not be perfect for us, they are perfect in God's sight because He made them. He knows what they are and what they aren't, and it only matters what He thinks about them. We are very much the same way. God knows what and who we are. He knows how much we can shine and how hot or cold we can get. The difference between us and the planets is that we can change from where we start to where God desires for us to finish. We can start out like Venus and by His Power, we can turn into an Earth or whatever God needs us to be. While Earth gives us life, Jupiter is so massive that it protects us from wandering stellar bodies that may try to smash into us. Venus is beautiful and known as the Evening Star. Saturn may be cold but looks graceful with its shimmering rings. Each planet has a purpose and because God made them, they are beautiful despite what they may be.

God knows how broken we can be, and He knows us as we are. He will restore us or make us beautiful if we desire it from God as He is the only one who can. This is not a limitation of God's Power, but God respecting our boundaries. It seems like we are holding God hostage, but we aren't at all. As I have said many times before, God is not a rapist. Even when He yanks our chains and drags us to His calling and higher purpose we still get to choose if we will answer the call or follow the path that He has set.

Unlike the planetary bodies, there is no such thing as being "too close" to God and His Presence. Yielding even to the pain of being broken, humiliated, or embarrassed shakes things out of us that would not have if the status quo ruled the day. If we had our choice we would bathe in sunny days, embrace nothing but good times and we would never grow, never change, and most likely never have a desire to love God because we would be spoiled brats. God knew better.

He knew that we would be individuals and that we would have distinct aspects in each of us that were cut from the same cloth. He knew that we would have to be dealt with differently and that meant that we would each have imperfections unique to each person. He knew that He was the only One Who could make us beautiful again if we made mistakes. He knew that He was the only one qualified to do it because He knew us better than we knew ourselves. He knew that each of us would have unique ways that we could be a blessing to the Kingdom and that we would be able to give God glory in how we would live, imperfections and all. Even after we were broken, God already knew how we would be repaired and made alive again, if we were willing to be fixed.

To sum it all up, it is for our good to be as God intended with our beautiful imperfections, which is God's desire for us. If we want to be effective and in the mold of what His desire is for us, we must allow ourselves to be razed to the foundation and re-architected as God wants us to be. Our relationship with God gives us beauty for our ashes, He mends our broken pieces with His Spirit. Being destroyed and shattered hurts, but God will take every place that we have been broken, apply Himself to every crack, crevice, and hole, and assemble us the way that He has intended for us to be. His loving Hands will shape us, mold us, and make us valuable and useful to build up the Kingdom of God on Earth. It does not matter where we come from, and it does not matter what we think that we are worth. God will do what is necessary (again, if we let Him) to set us apart and fill us with His Spirit and renew our lives and our purpose, but we must be understanding that it all takes time.

When Things Happen To Us

Everyone wants to have a good life, and everyone wants nothing but peace, prosperity, and joy for our entire lives on this Earth. Who wouldn't want that? No one wants dreadful things to happen to them or their loved ones. Yet, as I paraphrase a common slang saying, "stuff happens" and it doesn't matter if one is saved, or unsaved because incidents will occur. Our lives in Christ can be surprising and eventful as we progress along the way. Just like any other journey, we will have difficulties, and we will have days of sunshine and rain. When we get saved, we hope and pray for only daylight and never ask for darkness because that isn't the norm. We should have faith and believe that life in Jesus will be beautiful and blessed (and believe me, it is). There are times, however, when the storms of life will rage, and the darkness eclipses the light and takes us into an undiscovered land. Anyone who has been saved for a while will tell you that we must take the good with the bad because it is a blessing just to be alive. Yet, as humans, we will not have everything come up daisies and roses and some unbelievably dreadful things will befall us.

I can say that in my own life; it hasn't always been a wonderful experience. Walking this broken road is a long march through a spiritual war zone. When I sit and ponder my personal pain and my life experiences, I can say that my existence hasn't always been fair to me. I have had some things that I chose on my own to do that wrecked my life and caused me deep pain that only now has been healed. Other things that have happened to me were done to me and I did nothing at all to cause them, but others had the pleasure of twisting the knife and inflicting pain and breaking my spirit.

You can best believe that my soul bled, and I cried many tears because of my own bad choices and the evil and malicious intent of others that caused me harm. Then I realized that there was a third category of incidents and that was the hardest to accept and understand. That was the fact that God allowed certain things to happen to me to fulfill a purpose that at the time I couldn't understand, but after some time realized that it was for my good.

When the darkness of tragedy overshadows our journey on this broken road it makes every step, every day, and every moment feel like pure Hell. It is often inescapable and inevitable to endure dire situations in our lives or have pain descend on us like rain when we desperately want and need sunshine. Pain does not discriminate. Pain does not favor one over the other and pain is relative to the one experiencing it. Depending on the person, what is a pin prick to one is impalement to another. No matter what the situation hurt is hurt and we need to always remember that. Nevertheless, where we are in our walk with God or walk in life is stuff will hurt, and we will keep reaching points where it is "the greatest pain" we have ever felt. This is never a "one and done" experience and we need to prepare for its eventual arrival in our lives.

When We Did It to Ourselves

Now, before we get to this, feel that I need to clarify something important first. Every choice does indeed have a consequence. Every action has a reaction. As we are human, we will make ***UNWILLING*** mistakes, and this is not what "When We Did It to Ourselves" is all about. We will make errors, and we will fall into things that we still have to deal with the aftermath of, and I want to let you know that God will always bless the penitent heart. So, when you go further into this section, please know that I am not talking about when we made an honest mistake out of lack of understanding or if we were deceived into a messy situation. God's Grace will wipe away our mistakes, but some consequences cannot simply disappear. This doesn't mean that God hates us or is punishing us, but we must keep in mind that God is fair and just. Let's not forget this fact as you read further. Look through Scripture and you will see that God is gentle to us no matter what, but especially when we make a mistake, and we quickly repent and get back in line. Still…

This is difficult to write, because we all have messed up ***WILLINGLY*** in the Eyes of God. All have sinned and fallen short of the Glory of God. All of us. Yet there are times when we go through Hell because we caused this Hell on our own because of sin or bad choices. From the Apostles all the way to the parking lot attendants everyone has gone in the wrong direction. No one is immune and no one is beyond veering off the straight and narrow road. Just like a flood starts with one drop of rain, so does a tragic story start with one small action in our lives and at the time we can't see it.

I liken it to the Butterfly Effect. The Butterfly Effect rests on the notion that the world is deeply interconnected, such that one small occurrence can influence a much larger complex system. The effect is named after an allegory for chaos theory; it evokes the idea that a small butterfly flapping its wings could, hypothetically, cause a typhoon. Or it could not – the overwhelming part of the butterfly effect is that it is virtually impossible to predict whether a small system will lead to chaotic behavior.[5]

I know that's a lot to unpack but let me explain this the best way that I can. One small, inconspicuous action could in theory cause a chain reaction that could lead to a colossal and catastrophic event. Let's relate this to just everyday life and see how I can relate to people like you and me. When we trace our steps back from everything in our lives, we can identify one single thing that started it all. A casual conversation in a grocery store parking lot lead to my wonderful marriage with my soul mate and beautiful wife. When I was a little tot my wide-eyed gaze at my father playing his guitar led to me being a psalmist and minstrel. When Neil Armstrong took his first steps as an infant, who knew it would lead him to being the first human to take steps on the moon? See what I mean? One seemingly innocuous thing can lead to a mind-boggling remarkable thing!

Or it could go sideways fast. A child born out of wedlock started from a lustful glance at a friendly stranger. A DUI that kills an entire family started with taking a tequila shot on a dare at a party. Dying from HIV/AIDS could have started by stepping out on a committed marriage with another person and having sex. Every action we take has a reaction and consequence. Remember, the Scripture says that the ***WAGES*** of sin are death (Romans 6:23), which means that we earn the consequences of sin over time. We run up the tab of sin by our own volition. One split-second choice can change any outcome that God urges us to choose correctly. How many sports plays would have been different over a slight change of motion? How many races would have changed if the one in the race took one misstep or pushed themselves over the limit? The possibilities are endless, but everything starts at "one".

When we choose to disobey God and go in our own way, God sets off the warning bells in our spirit warning us to not do it. For every temptation He supplies a means of escape (1 Corinthians 10:13). For every situation there is an ejection seat to bail out, but when we decide that we are big and bad enough to do what we want starts a chain reaction that if we don't quit while we are ahead and repent? The consequences keep snowballing and get larger and larger. Let's look at the classic marital affair model in greater detail. If we reciprocate that "look" with another who we aren't married to and stop there? We have our conscious to deal with because we know better. If we ignore it and go have coffee or lunch with someone and we know we shouldn't because there is a mutual attraction, and things could get messy? Their conscience may be damaged, but if someone saw them together there would be some explanation that has to be given to their spouse.

If there is some physical contact like a kiss or romantic touching, a line is crossed, vows, and promises are broken to their spouse and even if they get caught now there is a connection that isn't easily broken. If things lead to sexual intercourse of any form? Now there is adultery to deal with and possibly pregnancy. If there is more sex and more connections on a physical and emotional level? Now there is a marriage that is now an afterthought and deliberate cheating (because of a hard and recurring choice) is now happening and now it may be impossible to get out with willpower alone. This entire time God was warning us, and we knew it.

I didn't touch on every consequence, but I hope that you get the idea. All these things were done in ***SIN*** and besides the human aspect, there needs to be repentance on a spiritual level as well. For every level of escalation there was a growing set of consequences. In the beginning these consequences can be handled internally to the person, which for some can be manageable. After while the consequences can get too big to hide any longer even if you repent to God and their spouse. A child conceived out of wedlock won't disappear because they asked God and their spouse for forgiveness. An incurable sexually transmitted disease ***CAN*** but won't necessarily vanish (unless God wills it so for healing). The damage to their reputation won't go away overnight and even if the couple reconciles the affair will linger in the back of their human mind and heart. All of it could have been avoided if they didn't return that glance or that conversation or whatever it was. It could have been cut off before it started and for those who are saved this is the point where we must learn to listen to Him.

God lovingly warns us through the Holy Spirit. God will keep cautioning us until He sees that we just won't listen to Him anymore and let us go and do our thing knowing what lies ahead for us. God will watch us screw up our lives because we made a conscious choice and then be ready to catch us when we fall and when we fail. Oh sure, we will claim that "the devil made me do it" or "God didn't caution me", but all those things are lies. We chose to do what we wanted. We listened to our flesh versus our spirit which is connected to God. We knew what we were doing (most of the time) when we make that first misstep and everyone after that God opens an off-ramp, put the light on and begs us to change course. It reminds me of a GPS when we miss a turn it will say "recalculating" until it gets to a point where it stops suggesting we turn around and just let us go where we are going. God does that too, you know. He will do so until we ignore Him so much that we forget to hear the gentle sound of His Voice.

I'm sure that when King David saw Bathsheba, he knew that he shouldn't want another man's wife, but he did anyway, and he suffered for it. He had Uriah killed after he found out that she was pregnant and eventually the baby he conceived died (2 Samuel 12:19). Yet, David repented, got back in line with God and God ***STILL*** blessed him even though David had to pay for it. It hurt him and it grieved him and even down the road Absalom rebelled and raped his other wives later in life and David was still a man after God's own heart he still had to pay for his bad choices. King David would lament over his choices, but still God favored him and loved him. How do we think that we would be any different than David and every other example in the Scriptures? God allows us the privilege of choice and when we choose to make bad ones, we will reap what we sow.

When Scripture said in Galatians 6:7-8, "Be not deceived; God is not mocked: for whatsoever a man soweth, that shall he also reap. For he that soweth to his flesh shall of the flesh reap corruption; but he that soweth to the Spirit shall of the Spirit reap life everlasting", God wasn't kidding around. Whatever we sow into is what we will harvest. It is our fault if ***WE*** mess up ***OUR*** lives with ***OUR*** bad choices. Not God, not anyone else, but ***US***. We must be spiritually and physically accountable (that's a word the Church today doesn't like) for our actions and inactions. It is when we get into a mess that ***WE CHOSE*** to get into by defying the Will of God and thumbing our noses at God's Word and His Precepts that we get what we get. No cutting cards or softening the blow. It's all on us.

We need to stop being like Adam and stop shifting the blame to someone else. Adam chose to eat the fruit. Noah chose to get drunk and lay out naked (Genesis 9:20-21). Moses chose to strike the rock (Numbers 20:11). Hezekiah chose to be proud and show off to his enemies (2 Kings 20:12-14). Judas chose to betray Jesus for a bag of silver coins (Matthew 27:2-4). All of them made a choice and they got what they paid for and so will we. If you were looking for a comforting "feel good" message here, you won't find it when it comes to consequences that we earn ourselves. Today's society has a problem accepting responsibility for its actions and it shows and we, the Church, need to break this cycle and get real and get right in God's eyes!

We are liable for the mistakes that we make and the sins that we commit, and we have no one to blame, but ourselves. Because we were big and bad enough to do what we did we should be ready and accept the penalties for all of it. When we deliberately make these bad choices, they won't just hurt us, but they can hurt those around us even many generations after we are gone. Thomas Jefferson had unlawful relations with Sally Hemings and now there are generations of people hurt by what he did to one slave woman who was treated like a play toy. It hurt all those descendants all because of the conscious choice Thomas Jefferson made to violate that woman.

Think about the families that have had infidelities, and the children learn years later that their father isn't who they were thought to be. What about those people who discover that they were molested, but had mentally blocked it out? What about the family that lost someone in a car accident you caused because of poor judgement? What about the person that was rejected by one person that started them on a chain reaction of hurt and pain that lead to murder? In our lives it only takes one idle word. One drink. One look. One disgusting act. All it takes is one unwise decision to follow it with another while we ignore God's warnings and entire futures can be altered forever.

When It Was Done To Us

When we don't have any control over a situation, we feel powerless, and we don't know where to turn. Being on the business end of tribulation is one of the worst experiences that we can have in this world. Everyone has had things happen to them and everyone knows what it is like to lose control of their lives whether they admit it or not. It feels even worse when we didn't deserve or ask for what happened to us. There are so many scenarios of how this can happen and what can happen that it could take years to tell them all, but when it all comes down to the root of it all they are all spiritual attacks usually by demonic forces. Nothing evil comes from God and spiritual attacks and situations that can hurt and nearly destroy us are not just powerful, but they can cut to the deepest layers of our being. Not being able to fight off what happens to us makes us feel alone, ashamed and often abandoned like the Samaritan who was beaten, robbed and left for dead on the side of the road.

When a person is saved and running for Jesus, dealing with things that were done to us can be an overwhelming experience. Most of the time we either never saw it coming for us, or it happened before we were saved by grace and now, we are dealing with the remnants of things that happened in our past. Before, during, and after a trauma a Christian must carry the weight of the circumstances, and we can either let it defeat us or make us stronger. The problem with things that happen to us is that very rarely is it our unwise decision alone that caused circumstances to occur, but it is the decision of someone else who has targeted us as their next victim.

Sometimes it's neither and it is not about us being a victim by a person, but the receiver of a bad circumstance that we cannot control. Despite what the situation may be, not being in control of what happens to us is a completely unique viewpoint to experience tragedy. God will always bring us through things because the journey that we are on will have sunshine and rain; and God knows about it all.

I never want to minimize the sufferings that people can feel, nor do I want to gloss over the true depth of the traumas that befall so many people in this world. So, I ask for your prayers and for your understanding as I write this section of the book. I know that I have had things happen to me that nearly broke me, but the things that have happened to so many others are much worse than I could imagine.

When we are saved, persecution through tribulation hits a little harder, I believe. Here we are saved, and loving Jesus and a darkness comes against us that injures us well beyond human repair. These are the types of things that are hard to talk about and even harder to cope with unless we turn it all over to Jesus. One of those things that exists in that realm is that of child molestation.

To be violated in such a way makes a person feel desecrated in a way that robs them of innocence and opens spiritual doors that are hard to close on one's own. The victim is taken advantage of by someone who is bigger than them or more knowledgeable than them (because some children can molest other children too). It doesn't matter at what age it happens, and it doesn't even matter whether that child grew up in the Christian way or not when it happens, but the aftereffects of molestation are deep, cavernous wounds that can affect a person throughout their whole life. Young victims don't really know what is happening (even though they may know that it is not right) and those who come into understanding of what sexuality means do know and all of it is trauma.

When a sick and twisted individual molests a child, I am convinced that they are being controlled by a demonic spirit. A child was never designed to be a sexual partner in any way, shape, or form. For someone to prey and molest a child to me means that they are mentally unstable due to some sort of past trauma themselves that opened a spiritual doorway into their lives that breeds perversion. I think many of us have heard the expression, "Hurt people hurt people", and it is more than true.

I see molestation as a form of rape and I may be wrong about that, but it is just what I feel. It is an exercise of dominance over a weaker person who cannot truly fight back. It is also a crowbar and lockpick to open a person up for demonic manipulation and torment. I believe that when something like this happens and the flesh of one who is possessed enters the flesh of a victim a transference happens on a spiritual level as well. That is the doorway. Sexual acts are more than just physical, and the demonic world knows this and uses it to their advantage.

Let me pause for a second and share some of the lessons I have learned and experienced in spiritual warfare. Demons can possess the unsaved but cannot possess a Christian. A Christian can be ***INFLUENCED*** and fall prey to a demon if they have a spiritual doorway open to a demonic force which is mostly associated with a trauma or negative set of emotions or habits. I say all of this to say that a person can be saved, sanctified and filled with the Holy Spirit and still struggle with a demon. Yes, I said it. If that spiritual doorway isn't closed, they will struggle with it until they are delivered from it. Casting it out is only temporary if that spiritual door is still open. God will deliver them, but the door must be closed first by releasing what happened to God.

Confronting the issue and renouncing its hold on a person is the only way it can be cast out, and the person be set free. There are many Christians who are living for Jesus and are dealing with the effects of molestation in their lives. It affects their romantic relationships, their sexuality, and even their self-esteem. The wounds can rob them of their happiness, joy and sometimes their lives. Depression, rage, and even perpetuating the same sexual dysfunction can manifest. It is the goal of every demon to keep the state of oppression going. Humans don't live forever and because of that demons will attack whole families or keep passing and multiplying the damage to keep victims in full supply for them. It's sick, and it is wicked.

Neither molestation, nor rape have a gender preference. The belief of one gender identity or another being more prevalent with gender of the initiator of these deviant acts is dependent on the victims coming forward to confront their abusers. Regardless of any of that, both molestation and rape are heinous and abominable acts. They differ in the fact that molestation is usually by coercion and rape is by force. All sexual based attacks bring the same basic emotions: shame, fear, anger, and sadness. Just like molestation, the act of rape can deposit demonic visitors that torment the victims.

Rape is the act of enforcing the appearance of dominance and power to force a sexual act on them. Rape is violent and disgusting, and I can't imagine in my wildest imagination what that could feel like. The flesh is violated, but so is the mind, the heart and the spirit. It is dehumanizing, humiliating and demoralizing. It has been used as a weapon of war as well as a tool of control and abuse. I know several people who were raped (both men and women) and they all have similar outcomes. The wounds are multidimensional and just like molestation, the saved are not immune to them all. These types of things can potentially change a person, and the scars are the result of jagged wounds being healed to varying degrees.

Also, like molestation, the spiritual backdoor that was opened because of rape must also be closed or the wounds may never heal. I hate using that word, but until we shut the doors to demonic influence after a trauma happens to us, we will keep reliving or feeling that pain repeatedly. Just remember that all forms of abuse are not just sexual in nature. Other forms of abuse cause damage to the whole person as well. Regardless of the form of abuse that a person suffers there is a single constant that causes many Christians to still deal with the pain even years after it happens and that is because most churches don't talk about it, but I will cover this in-depth later on in the book.

Abuse is very real and very prevalent in our society. I believe that most people today have suffered from one form of abuse in their lives. Whether it be verbal, physical, financial, or emotional -- abuse is abuse and it breeds pain. All forms of abuse affect people on a psychological level. It infects the spirit, and things begin to fester and get spiritually diseased. Abuse is not fair to the victim by any measure, and most victims are made to feel that no one can help them, and no one can understand what they are going through. Saved or not, no one should experience abuse. It is cruel and it has no place in society, but it happens anyway because of a demonic chain reaction that perpetuates damage from one soul to another.

Before I leave this topic, I want to talk about torment, and it is not insignificant. A tormented person is one who is under constant siege by another. It doesn't matter what the form of torment is, but legitimate torment is a horrible form of abuse that plenty of people suffer under. What makes it particularly evil is that the tormentor does this out of pleasure, and it is not just wicked in my mind, but it is abominable. I tend to think of it as bullying on a greater scale. When someone is in a situation of torment it can literally shatter a person's existence. It can cause long lasting damage, and as Christians, even though we may be saved, we can feel hopeless just as much as anyone else. It isn't fair, just like everything else that we have talked about, but torment can inhabit any form of abuse. Torment goes beyond the physical and rests in the realm of the mental. It transcends into a person's spirit which makes it deadly if it isn't remedied by God.

There are a few notable examples of torment that a lot of people in the world do not wish to speak of, and I do mention them here because I feel that they are necessary to discuss and not sweep under the rug. One I can address better than the others, but I want to convey to the reader that I am not bringing these things up to harm, shame or mock anyone. Sadly, two of these examples were carried out under the banner of the Cross of Christ which is disturbing. This is not a part of some "woke" agenda or anything like that. Part of understanding where we must go as humanity means that we must confront the sins of the past and understand the hearts of the perpetrators and know in our hearts that we must never allow ourselves to sink to such levels of cruelty. These examples I'd like to briefly discuss are Western Colonialism, Chattel Slavery, and the Jewish Holocaust.

Western Colonialism, a political-economic phenomenon whereby various European nations explored, conquered, settled, and exploited large areas of the world. The age of modern colonialism began about 1500, following the European discoveries of a sea route around [Alkebulan's] southern coast (1488) and of America (1492). With these events sea power shifted from the Mediterranean to the Atlantic and to the emerging nation-states of Portugal, Spain, the Dutch Republic, France, and England. By discovery, conquest, and settlement, these nations expanded and colonized throughout the world, and spreading European institutions and culture[6].

You could search the Internet or read a reputable history book and see the far-reaching results of the evils of Colonialism. Entire societies were devastated, exploited, and decimated because of people who felt that it was their destiny to conquer humans who weren't from where they were from or had their skin tone. It was evil and today the results of it still scar many nations around the world.

Within that process many nations were stripped of resources and people were stolen from their homes in the name of European "progress". Millions of people were oppressed and taken advantage of and one of the most heinous institutions to come from Colonialism is Chattel Slavery. People were taken from their homes in Alkebulan[7] and were broken into being free labor in a place far from where they originated. Human beings were treated as property and regarded as mere beasts or objects for their twisted desires.

They were stripped of their identities, denied access to education, denied access to wealth, and whipped or mutilated for even thinking about being free. These people were tormented into believing that they were less than human (many nations even legislated that to be so) and were forced into the lowest realms of society. Painful legacies such as the Three-Fifths Compromise, Jim Crow, the KKK, and many more hateful and wicked things I refuse to mention because they are too heinous to repeat.

The enslaved people from Alkebulan were not the only ones who were harmed. Many native peoples in the Americas around this same period suffered the result of what is basically genocide as they were pushed off their lands. I see my Native American brothers and sisters and see how they were marginalized and pushed to the side, and it breaks my heart. They live in a Hell that few live through today and it is completely unfair. The Trail of Tears alone is more than enough to see how they have suffered. To this very day many descendants of the victims of colonialism are still being held hostage by socioeconomic torments. These are torments that have lasted for decades, and the aftereffects have been long lasting. Spirits and hearts have been broken for so long, many feel that there is nothing else to life, but this torment. Despite its all, God has been faithful and those descendants of slaves like me have still been blessed, yet we still ask how all of this could have happened.

[The] Holocaust, the systematic state-sponsored killing of six million Jewish men, women, and children and millions of others by Nazi Germany and its collaborators during World War II. The Germans called this "the final solution to the Jewish question." Yiddish-speaking Jews and survivors in the years immediately following their liberation called the murder of the Jews the Ḥurban, the word used to describe the destruction of the First Temple in Jerusalem by the Babylonians in 586 BCE and the destruction of the Second Temple by the Romans in 70 CE. Sho'ah ("Catastrophe") is the term preferred by Israelis and the French, most especially after Claude Lanzmann's masterful 1985 motion picture documentary of that title. It is also preferred by people who speak Hebrew and by those who want to be more particular about the Jewish experience or who are uncomfortable with the religious connotations of the word Holocaust.

Less universal and more particular, Sho'ah emphasizes the annihilation of the Jews, not the totality of Nazi victims. More particular terms also were used by Raul Hilberg, who called his pioneering work *The Destruction of the European Jews*, and Lucy S. Dawidowicz, who entitled her book on the Holocaust *The War Against the Jews.* In part she showed how Germany fought two wars simultaneously: World War II and the racial war against the Jews. The Allies fought only the World War. The word Holocaust is derived from the Greek *holokauston*, a translation of the Hebrew word *'olah*, meaning a burnt sacrifice offered whole to God. This word was chosen because in the ultimate manifestation of the Nazi killing program (the extermination camps) the bodies of the victims were consumed whole in crematoria and open fires[8].

Since I am not of Jewish descent, I will not elaborate more than the quoted material above out of respect. However, I will say that the Jews were tormented then and now just because they are Jewish, and that is abominable. What they experienced was just as real as Colonialism and Chattel Slavery. It was a horrifying ordeal, and the aftershocks are still affecting good people to this modern day. Neither of these groups deserved what happened to them. None of them provoked torment except for being who they were. With some of these dastardly acts being done plagiarizing the Name of Jesus Christ makes it painful and it causes those who aren't Christians to avoid Jesus because someone misused His Name. Among all these people I mentioned, there are those who are saved and have a relationship with Jesus Christ. I am sure that many have prayed and believed God for resolution, and it has yet to come. Imagine what that road of relationship with God is like. I don't have to imagine it because I live it.

There are many other examples that I could speak about, but any situation where a person was innocent and a tribulation like situation happens to them unjustly is the same. It doesn't matter, as I have said before, that whether they are a Christian or not. Unfair things happen and it can make life very hard and when it is waged against us by someone who wishes to inflect pain on us takes it to an entirely different level of pain. When we are saved, it makes it even harder to wonder why a good God would allow such things to happen and it is a fair question to ask. God does have an answer for us, and it isn't what we think. More on that later.

When God Allowed It To Happen

As humans, when we see consequences coming for someone else and we either say nothing or move to the side and let it get that person, we can consider that cruelty. If we were watching something like this happen most of the time, we would wonder what sort of person that is, especially if you know that they know that person and even more if you know that they have a relationship. We would say that this person who knew that it was coming and let someone get caught in a dire situation was either "teaching them a lesson", "minding their own business", or "was sadistic" and let things happen when they could have intervened in some sort of way. Now, let's substitute that person with God… Now what would we think?

We tend to, as humans, see God as either hands-off and aloof when it comes to our plight or as an angry and vindictive God. Those who aren't in Christ ***SEE*** God this way and when we are walking this broken road of relationship, we must be careful not to feel this way about our God. We can feel like God doesn't care or hates us when He allows things to happen to us, but we must keep our faith in Jesus stronger than we had ever had it before. It doesn't matter whether we deserved it, or we didn't deserve it, we cannot allow our spirits to be lied to by Hell that God is hurting us. It is very human and very understandable to feel this way because of our emotions, but we must invoke our spirit to cancel that out immediately.

I never understood the "why me" until it "was me" that had to endure tragedy. I had seen people go through things, but I truly didn't understand the plight of the downtrodden until I had to live within it second by second and moment by moment. Tribulation is not an easy thing to go through, and every waking moment slowly ticks by almost like time itself has gotten stuck in the mud and can't get any traction. The piercing feelings of dread and the flooding of emotions of anger, sadness and even happiness swirl around you as the mind, body and spirit are trying to rationalize what is happening. We tend to fashion a porcelain mask of our ideal selves that we can wear around others to hide what our spirit is truly wrestling with inside of ourselves.

The Adversary sits and waits for us to crack and become vulnerable just like a turkey vulture will watch carefully as an animal will collapse from some sort of condition, barely clings to life, and finally dies before casually fluttering down to pick their corpse clean. It is hard enough being unsaved to go through such a trial, but it is worse, in my mind, when one is saved, loves Jesus and serves God faithfully. It feels like we are being punished, and it seems like we have been abandoned by the One who promised that He would never leave us or forsake us. It is in that loneliness that the demonic vultures circle us and wait to see what we do next. They will intimidate us mockingly as we seem to be circling life's drain. We can feel overwhelmed and desire to release ourselves from this reality and allow circumstances to swallow us whole.

We can pray, cry, shout, and worship God and sometimes get zero relief. Yes, connecting with God will refresh us and give us healing and rest so don't think that I am denying these facts. God is our refuge and strength and our very present help in the time of trouble (Psalm 46:1) so don't get it twisted. Yet there are times when going through certain trials it feels like nothing is changing. It seems like prayers are unanswered and that God doesn't even seem to care. To the Believer this is the worst of times and yet, it may all be by God's design and His plan and even hearing those words while in the worst of scenarios is hard to swallow or understand.

When God allows things to happen to us it feels like a cruel joke, but it has a purpose that we will never truly see while we are at Ground Zero. God knows our limits better than we do. God knows us better than we could ever know ourselves because it is He that made us and not us ourselves. God knows what we can stand and what we can't which is why what is a gnat bite to us is a cobra bite to another. Every situation we are in is tailor made just for us and to me that shows the depth of God's love that He has for us. This alone proves that God will allow us to bend and not break because He won't allow us to go where we couldn't go. Even though Satan and his minions are at work God will stop them when we are about to break, and God knows the sincerity of our hearts. We must be faithful to complete the course to get our reward. Today if a team or athlete walks off the field before the game is over, they forfeit and the opposing team wins. We must not quit and even though we may have lost so much of everything that we may have; we must know that we will still come out as a winner.

This may be cliché for many, but when we live through a horrific experience and live to talk about it openly it changes us in one of two ways. We will either become lost in the struggle and never come out of it and lose ourselves to the challenge God put before us or we will come out, scars and all, stronger and closer to God than we could have ever imagined. The biggest thing that I have learned about these kinds of experiences is that even though we couldn't "see" God moving on our behalf, He never left us at all. God is always watching over us even if He has allowed calamity to enter our lives. That seems a bit sadistic, doesn't it? The God of Love and the Lord of Mercy allow us to suffer pain and utter destruction, and it doesn't seem fair. It seems like God is cruel and treats us like rats in a cage or fish in an aquarium. It seems like God is just making us puppets on a string to dance for His amusement and all these things are not true ***AT ALL!***

Yes, God allows us to go through things and suffer, but He also gives us the ***CHOICE*** as to whether we learn to trust and love Him or reject Him altogether. God ***NEVER*** tells us what to do while we are suffering. Look through all of Scripture carefully. God not one time told anyone how to feel, how to act and what he ***HAD*** to do. God will tell us about who He was and what He stood for and allowed us to choose what to do next. Even though the tether between our love for God may have been at one last solitary fiber we must chose not to let go, and God always restores us.

I've lived through Hell, and I almost gave up. I was in utter pain and still lead worship while I was dead inside from my own grief. I was allowed to feel and experience loss and tragedy. I nearly gave up and I nearly let Hell swallow me up whole while I was surrounded by Christians who meant well by telling me to pray about things, but they weren't in my story. They couldn't understand what I felt. Not completely anyway.

They were right by encouraging me to pray and to seek God, but sometimes you don't know how to pray or how to call out to God for help. When you cry so much that our tear ducts swell shut, and your screams make no sound at all it is beyond pain but crosses into anguish. All this time while I felt alone God was still there. Watching and listening to me suffer not as a sadist, but like a loving parent. I believe (based on my relationship with God now) that He too was sorrowful seeing me hurting, but He knew that it was His plan and purpose to chart my destiny. Like a parent who knows that their child must endure certain things to grow up healthy and strong God did the same for me. Many of you have had the same sorts of experiences.

It is even more difficult to explain this to those who don't have a relationship with God. How often have we all heard people saying things such as: "How can a loving God allow such pain in the world?" It doesn't matter what the scenario is the question is heard by many secular folks and sadly, it is also prevalent in Christian circles as well. Some use this thought process to try and deconstruct or disprove that God either exists or cares about us. These people erroneously say things like, "If God is so powerful why do such heinous things happen to good people?" Some people even wonder why God allows things as Christians who pray, fast, worship, or plead with God and things still happen no matter what we do.

Brokenness is something that will find its way into all our lives. We don't understand why it does at first because as humans we don't wish for terrible things to happen to us. It is far easier to see them happen to someone else, and I know that this is somewhat harsh. The reality is that living in brokenness and experiencing things that seem like it shouldn't happen to us while we walk this broken road is one of the toughest things we experience within our walk with Christ Jesus. It is more than hard enough to be a Christian in today's world, but to then go through all sorts of pain and suffering while you are trying to serve the Lord in the best way that you can is a tough challenge. This is happening all while Satan is laughing in your face and brings Hell to you on Earth.

We are being tried, and we are being tested. Yet it seems contradictory because if we are supposed to have God living on the inside of us, why do we need to be tested like this? Is this necessary? Is this what being a Christian means? I know that for myself, I went in many circles asking myself these questions because I just didn't get it, and it shouldn't be this way. At least, I felt that it shouldn't, but we must remember that God has better plans than we do. God is still in control and God knows what He is doing. When the pain is severe, no one is thinking about how God is going to renovate our lives as the first thing that comes to our minds. Is it okay to be honest? We need to realize that all people who are in Christ are just as human as every other person on Earth and we all ask these things at some level.

In this chapter I know that some of the things I talked about have a bit of overlap and that is by design. The ultimate statement that must be made about all these things is that God's plan is best for us. I know that we feel lost, alone, and desperate as we walk on the road to relationship with God. I know that we feel like we are the worst people in the world or maybe that salvation is a lie. Believe me, Satan loves to torture us about leaving him. Satan specializes in wielding the first and best weapon that was used against humanity: The lie. Lies must be laced with a bit of truth to be palatable. Lies must ring true in some parts of our being for us to come to a logical conclusion and accept them. Satan is the best at doing this and to thumb his nose at God he will use brokenness as the greatest justification that being saved is a waste of time.

There is nothing that happens in all the Universe that God doesn't know about. Period. God knows and sees everything, and he sees you and me. We are not discarded, and we are never alone. I know that we feel like trash, and we feel rejected and dejected, but we must keep in our spirits that change is coming, and redemption is close. God is in control and despite what He allowed, He will make it right. If I say this more than once, I apologize, but we must drill it into our spirits that God has us in His Hands. That He knows and He cares. That Satan knows that his time will soon be up, and he will fight us tooth and nail because he just wants to confuse, trick, and bamboozle as many people as he can before he is thrown into the Lake of Fire. Satan wants to stop the agenda of the Kingdom of God. For you to build God's Kingdom, we must be purged and broken out of our sinful natures and brought into a state where Christ can use us.

Whether or not your journey leads to a testimony that will affect billions or just one person is irrelevant because God has positioned us and ordained us to live this life for His Glory. I know that I have taught this many times before, but we need to realize that God is a being that is far beyond time. God knows all because He is all, and He knows just how much we can handle. He knows the weight that we can carry even if we have no clue as to how strong we really are. To be as powerful as He is He still gives us the choice to love and trust Him or turn our backs on Him. God could make us robots, but instead he made us autonomous and fully able to appreciate Him for who He is. That seems messed up to the unbeliever, but to the Christian it is a demonstration of God's confidence in us and how His Love is beyond comprehension. The dark days on our journeys will and must come to all of us, but as humans we will still want to know "***WHY***"?

CHAPTER REFERENCES

[1] Broken. (2024). In *Merriam-Webster Dictionary.* https://www.merriam-webster.com/dictionary/brokenness

[2] Plakson, K. (2020, November 13). Horse Breaking Techniques: How long does it take to break a horse in? *Horse Bonding Success.* https://horsebondingsuccess.com/horse-training/horse-breaking-techniques-how-long-does-it-take-to-break-a-horse-in

[3] Sho, T. (2022, February 25). Kintsugi: Japan's ancient art of embracing imperfection. BBC Travel. https://www.bbc.com/travel/article/20210107-kintsugi-japans-ancient-art-of-embracing-imperfection

[4] Nevres, M. Ö. (2023, January 10). The Sidereal Days And Axial Tilts Of The Planets - Our Planet. *Our Planet.* https://ourplnt.com/sidereal-days-axial-tilts-planets/

[5] *The Butterfly Effect.* (n.d.). The Decision Lab. Retrieved October 12, 2022, from https://thedecisionlab.com/reference-guide/economics/the-butterfly-effect

[6] Webster, R. A., Nowell,. Charles E. and Magdoff, Harry (2024, September 6). *Western Colonialism. Encyclopedia Britannica.* https://www.britannica.com/topic/Western-colonialism

[7] The African History. (2020, July 3). *The Ancient Name For Alkebulan Was "Alkebulan" Meaning "Mother Of Mankind."* https://theafricanhistory.com/770

[8] Berenbaum, Michael. "Holocaust". *Encyclopedia Britannica*, 29 Sep. 2024, https://www.britannica.com/event/Holocaust. Accessed 29 September 2024.

3

Why...

From the very beginning of our lives our senses are ablaze with wonder as we discover the world around us. With our sight we see colors, patterns and shapes. With our hearing we hear tones, noises and speech. With our tongues we taste bitter, sweet and sour. With our flesh we can touch smooth, rough, cold, hot and sharp. With our noses we can discern flowers, petrichor and waste. As our brains develop and we learn to reason with ourselves the simple, one-word question will come after every explanation: ***WHY***? To ask "why" is to satisfy the need to understand and comprehend what we are experiencing or have experienced. ***WHY*** is the sky blue? ***WHY*** is water wet? ***WHY*** does this bird sing differently than this bird? ***WHY***? ***WHY***? ***WHY***?

To learn anything in life we must ask the six questions to begin to understand anything, which are: Who, what, when, where, ***WHY***, and how. The interrogatives in the English language are the basis of learning. The word "who" determines the person or being. The word "what" determines the material or substance. The word "when" determines the time or period. The word "where" determines the location or place. The word "how" shows us the method or vehicle that it happened. Finally, the use of the word "why" desires answers. To know why is to understand the circumstances, the existence and reasoning behind it all. The word "why" is a powerful question asked, and many times never answered.

Even beyond our formative years and throughout our lives we will ask the question ***WHY***. We do so because we want to know and understand who was responsible for it, what it was, when did it happen and where it happened. The word ***WHY*** brings it all together as to the purpose. Why can be imagined as being after the "equal sign" like a math problem because the other four (who, what, when, and where) are the equation. ***WHY*** is the explanation and summation of it all and until we are dead, we will ask ***WHY*** for whatever reason it may be. As human beings this doesn't change in our spiritual lives either as we ponder the meanings of the experiences that we all have in our walk with Jesus Christ.

The wild thing about it all is that it was "easier" when we lived in sin, even though we had issues, problems and situations that were killing us. Sure, we asked this same question even back then when we didn't understand what was happening, but we didn't have the only wise and true God as our Lord and Savior. We didn't have a shield of defense or the Holy Spirit to guide us. Still, that question seems to ache and bleed in our hearts more once we get saved and start living for God because we get caught in the crossfire of spiritual warfare. It makes us truly wonder why life must be so hard. It just doesn't seem fair.

Let's be honest with ourselves and truly know that it really doesn't feel good when we get saved from a life of sin and darkness only to come into a life full of temptation, pain, suffering and the constant buffering from all of Hell's special forces. Sure, we may have had a life of utterly burdensome sin all around us, but many of us were told that things get better in Jesus with no suffering. Most of us were told that life can now truly begin, but many of us didn't get told that because we are now living for God that Satan was going to use every tactic that he could to stop our progress and neuter our zeal. Let's not get it twisted because life in Jesus ***IS MUCH BETTER*** than any life in sin, but the one thing we may not have been taught was that the real fight for our lives would now begin and we would be fighting this war until we close our eyes to this world.

Being a follower of Jesus Christ in a world full of people who misunderstand Him is a difficult experience to live through. This is especially true if we try to live this life by ourselves because it is the epitome of being alone. Being in fellowship with other believers makes it easier to cope, but it doesn't erase the reality that we are wanderers in a strange land. Society today is so Christ-adverse that even the mention of the Bible, its principles or saying that we are Christians causes pushback and retaliation. Standing for Jesus today can feel like a warzone and most of it is due to those who have perverted and twisted the message of Christ into a mess that seems like a hypocritical cult. All of this can sometimes make a person not want to stand for Christ at all. The enthusiasm for being saved can dwindle over time and digging deeper into the Word and living as Scripture says can sometimes fade away. Most of us don't know that this is the Enemy's plan and sadly it works on many people.

Yet the pain and suffering are not because of the Adversary. There are some things that we will go through in this life that are God-ordained for us to endure for His Glory. That statement is a mouthful to swallow. It seems unfair and it seems sadistic that God would allow dreadful things to happen to us. Trust me that our God doesn't play by those rules. Honestly, we need answers to these questions, and we need to get a complete understanding from God as to why things happen the way they do. The question of whether it is worth it, and what the outcomes are going to be are important. The answer to that ***WHY*** defines our walk with God and tests our faith to a higher level. However, God reveals the answers to us is critical to our spiritual growth. To do this we need to ask ourselves a few questions as to why things have happened to us that are common to most people in their walk on this road with God. So, ***WHY***…

…Was I Hurt?

Let's talk about the general question of why I was hurt first. This is a general question that leads to many others, but before we get to the specifics, we need to examine the general thing first. Honestly, no one wants to live a life of pain and virtually no one volunteers to be tortured for any reason. When we got saved, we knew that living a life for God was going to be better than earning the wages of sin that would lead to spiritual death (Romans 6:23). Salvation is a step up from a life of sin that only rewards in this life and denies bliss in the next life. This is what we are taught, and this is what the Bible says. The Bible isn't wrong and regardless of what the naysayers may say the Bible doesn't contradict itself.

There is a twist, however, in the fact that Scripture also shows us that trials and tribulations will come. Verses throughout The Word of God detail people and situations where we are either in trouble or near trouble as the normal way of life. Psalm 23 says that even when we walk through the valley of the shadow of death, we would fear no evil. I love that personally because it doesn't say we ***SHOULDN'T*** but that we ***WOULDN'T*** fear evil because God is with us.

Life is going to happen, and we need to be prepared to face the proverbial music. From Adam to John the Revelator you will find accounts of those who went through suffering. While they were going through their situations God didn't always tell them why they were in them. God told them to trust Him if He said anything at all. For those that don't know God, it seems like God can be cold-blooded because as the Creator of the Universe He can start and stop anything He chooses. God can stop time or redirect anything from us if He so chooses.

Sometimes, it seems personal. Those who are unsaved seem to have better lives than the saved folks. Have you ever noticed that? Here you are, living for Jesus and doing your absolute best and then ***BOOM*** you have a deep pain hit your life or your families' life while the unrepentant sinner seems to be living in paradise. Whatever Hell you are going through they seem to thrive. What you are struggling with doesn't seem to bother them at all. Even though we are going to get to specific scenarios later we all (regardless of whether we say it aloud) wonder why did it have to be me? We will answer that question later…

It hurts to wonder why sometimes. Time passes slowly while our pain gets worse without relief or resolution in sight. We pray and pray, and it seems like our prayers turn into ashes in the wind. Heaven seems closed and God seems deaf to our cries. The Adversary will sneak in and whisper to us that God isn't real or that God can't help us. Sometimes we physically get sick from the stress of what we are going through. Our emotions are running wild, and our sanity seems like it is hanging by a fraying thread. We go to church, and we feel good for a little while, but after the benediction our suffering is waiting for us at the exit doors of the church. Our friends may comfort us, but it's only temporary. We may stray into things that we shouldn't do and that may pacify us for a little while, but we are still staring down the barrel of a gun known as pain. It creepily breathes down our necks and won't let us go until it is done with us. It's awful. It's beyond real.

I have lived this existence. I know what it feels like to question everything about the "why" and it hurts beyond any words that I could use to describe it. I can be real and admit that I drifted for a while when the worst Hell of my life stopped by my address for a little while. I went over and over in my mind where I went wrong and wondered why God would do this to me and I came up with nothing. I would receive comfort from others and reassurances, but it never lasted. I remember that I asked God, and I never got any answers. At the time I was frustrated and angry, but now I know why God was silent. I forgot that the Teacher is always silent during the test. I was so wrapped up in wondering why I was going through so much that I forgot how God works.

I would never dare assume what another soul thinks, and I want to emphasize that regardless of your situation and how it may feel to you there is common ground. We all wish to understand the reasons behind what is happening. We may not say it the same way. We may not express it like others may share it, but deep down inside it is within us all. This chapter makes many generalizations, but I pray that you, the reader, will find a commonality in these few scenarios so that God can open your eyes to your why. None of this will ever make the pain feel any less intense. None of this will make us long for the earlier days when blessings and joy seemed to be the most prevalent happenings in our world. Looking back like that can cause us to stray and miss the mark that God has for us to hit (Philippians 3:14).

Regardless of the hurt and despite what happens to us we need to not fall to the wayside and lose our faith. When we ask God why we were hurt and don't get answers that satisfy us our faith can get stretched so thin that we can see through it like a plate glass window. It gets so fragile that the slightest thing makes it sway and tremble in the winds of tribulation. Being hurt will put us in a dangerous position where Satan can hijack us and divert us away from God's true intentions of us being hurt which can vary. Our faith being tested is not meant for us to break, but we can be fooled into thinking that we are broken beyond repair. Satan will have us focusing more on the pain instead of the path. Everything in his toolbox is meant to distract and redirect us from God's truth and we must keep that in mind. The enemy will do all that he can to rob us of the foundations of our faith to paralyze us in our struggles. As I have said earlier, it doesn't matter whether what's in this chapter is representative of your story or not.

So, in the next few sections I would like to cover some general scenarios that I have either witnessed personally or seen others endure in their walk with God. Some of these things may overlap and sometimes all of them happen all at once, but the point I would like to make is that the hurt and the pain do come in distinct flavors, and each can do damage in similar and yet different ways and that no matter what the situation God is still in control of it all. Most importantly is that God ***SHALL*** bring you out of it!

...Was I Betrayed?

Betrayal is a pain that cuts us down to our spiritual bones. Bewilderment and disbelief can shake even the strongest person's faith. No one is immune and no one can avoid this horrible pitfall that will at one point happen to us all. One of the pillars of humanity is being in relationships with other people. When someone we trust or rely on turns around and stabs us in the back? It is utterly devastating. That swelling feeling in the pit of your stomach can hurt worse than any pain we can experience.

The moment that you discover the truth that the ally you trusted was a double agent that set you up for failure strikes like lightning. To look them in the eyes while they revel in your demise or pain can break us down if we let it. Some folks never trust another soul again because of such pain. Others have future relationships forever poisoned because of being hesitant to trust another person ever again the way you did before. All while we sit there and ask God why this did happen. If you have ever been hurt like that you know what I mean.

From the first day we meet other people, we run the risk of being betrayed by them. It could be a broken promise, a lie, or a ruined covenant that sends us down the path to pain. It makes our hearts bleed because we have emotionally, physically, financially, or spiritually invested in a person or organization (like a person or church and I will talk about church later in much more detail). We are usually betrayed by the people we invested in or nurtured. It could be time, talents, money, or emotions and when we sow into a situation, we feel that we should reap the harvest that we expect. What unfortunately happens in betrayal is that we glean something different than what we planted.

Sometimes we don't reap at all because what we planted is stolen by the ground that we planted it in. The pain of betrayal can be so overwhelming that we can literally feel it physically. I honestly don't know what's worse; finding out you were betrayed by the traitor or discovering it via a third party. Depending on the circumstance it could hit us differently. Either way, we saw it coming whether we believe the signs or not. You realized what just happened and it feels like that movie effect where the camera zooms in on you and the things around you fade into the background and the truth cuts you like a knife.

Being flayed wide open by betrayal hits like a horrific car crash. It is sudden, and the injuries and future recovery are challenging. We talk a lot about when God shifts an atmosphere to His Will, and betrayal is similar, but in a very painful way. A car crash comes so quickly that our brains can sometimes fail to register that it is happening until it is over. It makes me think about that deep sea submarine accident where the experts said that the destruction of the sub happened so fast that the passengers' brains didn't have time to even process the pain of the collapse[1]. Betrayal stuns us and being shocked like that can knock us off our spiritual feet. In my experience, the pain that follows hits like a flash and grows with intensity with every waking moment.

This sort of pain makes us question why God would allow us to experience it just like every other pain we can feel. After all, the first humans in the Garden of Eden betrayed God and sinned against Him. God knows every pain that we feel, but the first betrayal in all of Creation was done by us. Our betrayal of God changed the course of Earth's history. God knew it was to happen because of His relationship with time, but I can imagine that it on some level hurt God's Heart. (No, I am not saying that God is human like us, but we ***ARE*** made in His image, right?) All the intentions that God had for us were wiped out because of what we did. In an instant all plans that God had for us were destroyed by us because sin entered the world. All this because Adam and Eve listened to a serpent's bad advice over God's instructions.

Every form of betrayal is rooted in envy, jealousy, greed, malice, apathy or even fear. Jesus was betrayed by Judas Iscariot, a man that He chose to be one of The Twelve. Judas walked with Jesus every day, oversaw the finances (he was also a thief, by the way) (John 12:4-6) and cast out demons like the other Disciples

(Matthew 10:1). Judas was one of the Brothers and I am sure that he had relationships with Peter, James, John, and their circles. Yet Judas sold Jesus out for thirty silver coins (Matthew 26:14). Here, betrayal came from greed. When Absalom staged a coup d'état against his father King David, Absalom wanted the power and position that his father earned rightfully, and Absalom had sex with his father's concubines in full view of the public on the palace rooftop to humiliate him (2 Samuel 16:21-22). Absalom betrayed King David because of envy and jealousy.

Joseph dealt with betrayal on a seismic scale. First, his brothers sold him into slavery (Genesis 37:18-36). Then, Potiphar's wife wanted Joseph while he worked for her family. Joseph wasn't going to take liberties with another man's wife and was trying to stay honorable. When she pressured him to sleep with her, he refused her, and as he ran away from her, she grabbed his garment and Joseph left it behind. Realizing that she was rejected she betrayed Joseph, and he was thrown in jail for being an honest man (Genesis 39:12-20). Joseph was betrayed because of malice. Joseph was betrayed again and after he went to jail, he met Pharaoh's chief cupbearer and baker who told Joseph about bad dreams they had that Joseph interpreted for them. All Joseph asked was to be remembered when the cupbearer saw Pharaoh again and after the cupbearer got freed, he forgot Joseph (Genesis 40:9-23). Apathy was the cause of betrayal here.

There are so many other ways that we could be betrayed. Some of us were cheated out of money, property or by someone we trusted. Some of us were betrayed by someone we thought was a friend, but they had ulterior motives and used us to get what they wanted from us or used our talents to help themselves. Some of us were cheated on by someone we loved, and, in some instances, it was with a friend or acquaintance. Some situations involve when we share a deep and dark secret with someone, and they release that secret, and it causes us pain. I could go on and on about it, but the premise is still the same. Regardless of how it happens, deception and revelation are hard to deal with when we are the target. When we cry out to God and ask Him why it happened and to please heal our hearts. God is a healer, but we also must understand why God allowed such a thing to happen to us.

Once we get past our emotions, which is easier said than done, we can then seek God for the answers we need as to why you were betrayed. I had to do it, and I know that you will too. This doesn't mean that our flesh won't try to rise and betray our hearts and act out when we see that person or even hear their name. I say this repeatedly, but we are still human. We are fallible and we can and will make mistakes. I know that I did, and I learned my lessons from God about it all. My betrayal hurt, but I had to forgive them despite never getting an apology from all the parties involved. I know that I may never get an apology, but I had to move forward, and God has done nothing but bless me.

Still, we as humans want closure and often our flesh wants revenge. Our humanity, no matter how saved we are, will, even if for a moment, want to fight fire with fire. A betrayed heart is fertile ground for either a vengeful spirit or an opportunity for God to bless us. You may say that that is a pair of very opposite paths, but it does make sense. David was betrayed by his own son Absalom. In 2 Samuel chapters 13-19 Absalom tried to usurp the throne of his father King David. Jesus was betrayed by Peter who denied Him (Mark 14:66-72) and instead of hurting Peter, He taught Him about the depth of His Love (John 21:15). For every betrayal we have a choice as to how we respond. We can fall into the desires of our flesh, or we can trust God and let Him handle everything. This doesn't necessarily mean that we would look for God to exact revenge on our behalf. God can choose to let the vengeance be His or He can seemingly do nothing. Even if He does the one thing we don't need to do is gloat in what someone may have deserved.

In this life with our journey with God, we will feel the pain of betrayal, and we will have to keep going even if we stumble a bit. Our spiritual foundations can be shaken and our desire to trust people damaged, but thankfully God never leaves us without a plan and a means to be restored. This part of our journey can be rough to travel as we will have good days and bad days. There will be times where we seem happy and others where we don't even want to get out of bed. We just must know that being betrayed is not the end. It will feel like everything is ruined and that everything will never recover but let me encourage you and let you know that God has not forgotten you and who betrayed you. Every betrayal is an opportunity for God to grow us and transform us. We must learn to trust the Spirit of God more and listen carefully to what He has to say to us.

We will mature in the natural and in the Spirit and even though it will feel like punishment I can assure you that it isn't.

...Was I Abandoned?

Who in our existence wants to be left behind? Chances are, no one. Abandonment is a feeling that makes the victim feel unloved or unwanted. As people, we all want to feel like we belong or that we are cared for by someone. It doesn't matter who you are, we all want to be surrounded by love. We want to be included, and we want to feel like we have worth and value to at least one person in this world. This is just the human condition, and I find it hard to believe that there is someone out there that doesn't feel like this. But what happens when we are left behind, left for dead or emotionally, physically, and spiritually left to be on our own? How can one cope? How can one understand something clearly at last amid what appears to be pure darkness? How do we answer the questions swirling around in our mind, heart and spirit? Being abandoned is an awful feeling to process and is one of Satan's greatest weapons that he uses against us. It is the lie that he uses to weaken our faith and allows the spirit of rejection to take a firm hold on us. Abandonment is a wound that only God can truly heal within us, and Satan knows how to wield abandonment is many ways to hurt us past, present, or future.

For example, some folks are abandoned as children by parents that either don't want them or cannot take care of them. Some are abandoned by loved ones who have rejected them for various "reasons" and spurned them. There are some who are literally left to die because someone couldn't or wouldn't risk themselves for another person. Whatever the cause and whatever the circumstance may be, being abandoned can affect a person's self-esteem, self-worth and mental health. The moment that we find out that we have been abandoned grips our hearts and chokes the life force out of our souls. The feeling of loneliness is terrifying and is gut-wrenching on many levels. Often, when circumstances arise that have us in a bind or in severe trouble the one thing we do not just want, but need is to know that someone out there in this world cares about our welfare. Someone is there at the end of the phone or that when we call in the middle of the night, sobbing and in tears, that someone will answer the phone. Sadly, that doesn't always happen.

Sometimes we will rush towards a crack of light in that darkness and knock on a door that will either remain shut for us or it will open and then be slammed in our faces. We will reach out or grasp at anything we can that could possibly take the pain away. The emptiness is deafening, and the emotions flooding us are a wellspring of sorrow. Hope can be used against us by Satan, which can cause us to lose it all together. It is a lot like the Titanic tragedy where people supposedly stayed on the ship while it was sinking and hoping that some feature or some mechanism was going to save them even as the lights went out and the ship was breaking apart. Hope in Jesus is amazing and never lets us down but hope in the natural realm can give rescue or let us down and we have need of resuscitation. Life is not simply hard, but it can feel like it is impossible. When we are left behind because of whatever the situation is we get desperate, and we can begin to rationalize in our hearts what we did wrong to deserve this or what we can do on our own to get out of it. This constant see-sawing of emotions can be devastating and can scar us if we don't activate our faith and trust God and His process.

As Christians we experience many difficulties, and it doesn't matter whether we are a new Christian or a mature Christ follower. We are prayerful and hoping that help, comfort, or love is (or will be) there when we need it. This goes to another level when we feel that the one that left us was God. Who has ever looked over their lives and just felt like they were God's punching bag? Has anyone been made to feel worthless and worthy of the abandonment that they were facing? Who has gone to see a pastor or a spiritual leader for comfort or guidance and were brushed off or ignored? Who has seen others in similar situations seem to get the help, support or love that they needed and yet we received nothing? It seems unfair, unjust and cruel. So many folks have been a help for others when they were in trouble and when it is their turn on the Potter's Wheel no one seems to be near; no one answers their phones. During a crisis, it seems that we are alone, left to suffer and left to withstand the worst of the storm.

The familiar word comes to our lips: Why? Lord, why am I alone right now? Why am I the best friend to so many and ***NONE*** of them are being friends to me right now? Why does it seem that my prayers aren't getting to You? Being abandoned makes us very vulnerable and it also makes us very receptive. We can go over and over in our minds about the causes while we sit alone and in serious pain. Abandonment causes us to want to reach out and grasp whatever comes our way that seems like comfort or peace. The Adversary will sneak in and begin to whisper to your spirit that God doesn't care or even real. He may slide that thirst for hard liquor back into your mouth because at least it can numb the pain. That old dealer might run into you at the gas station and offer you a taste for old times' sake. A future toxic relationship will hit your inbox with a "WYD" message. An opportunity for the "quick fix" may arrive right in front of you which is the worst move that could be taken. The wrong person who is hell bent on your destruction arrives with detailed plans on how to destroy you while they smile, hold your hand and wipe your tears knowing that within their hearts they want to see you fall and never get up again.

Being abandoned affects our spiritual, mental and emotional health. When we are abandoned, our anxieties can begin to go out of control and our emotions can range from sadness, to anger and low self-esteem. Even though God was with Adam, He knew that Adam should not be alone. The emotional damage can be disastrous when it comes to being abandoned. A young child abandoned by a parent can develop unhealthy attitudes towards that parent or even the gender of that parent. This can become one of the consequences of being abandoned, which is the void left from the departed. In nature and physics every void or vacuum desires to be filled. When a glass incandescent light bulb is broken the sound that we hear is the air rushing in to replace the vacuum. When a submarine goes below its defined crush depth the water around it will crush it and the air being replaced by water is an implosion. Notice that the void is filled by whatever is surrounding it when the vessel cannot withstand the pressure.

When we have a void in our lives, we need something to fill it. When we are abandoned and the place that was held in our lives is suddenly gone, we will often search for anything that can possibly fill it so that we won't feel so lonely or left behind. This is where the enemy is a specialist at sliding in to try and fill our voids with the wrong things first. We can want our comfort back so badly that we could possibly grasp at anything to replace what we have lost. It is almost like getting out of one unhealthy relationship and settling for one that is just as bad or even worse.

It reminds me of a child who was abandoned by a parent, and they seek out love, guidance, and presence in the worst of ways. When we are abandoned or feel abandoned, we tend to want to fix that as fast as we can. The depth of that void can cloud our judgments if we aren't careful. Even those who are in Christ can make tragic mistakes and even the "strongest" in The Lord can falter. Sometimes we can recognize that and do our best to allow God to fill our empty space and sometimes we can be fooled. Still, since we aren't perfect, this can be a haphazard thing. Take the apostle Thomas, for example…

I have always been fascinated about the man we call "Doubting Thomas" because his story is one of a flawed person who God called and despite his shortcomings God still used him. Thomas did indeed have a faith problem, but when I looked carefully, I could see something else that Thomas was dealing with. He was dealing with being abandoned. Thomas was recruited by Jesus just like the other of The Twelve and had been with Jesus for three years just like everyone else. All the Apostles had to grow into who they became, and Thomas was not any different.

Jesus had recruited a group of the most imperfect men that were comprised of fishermen, a thief, a tax collector, some ruffians, and a hot head. Jesus had taught them and guided them, and they witnessed things that were and were not written down in the Gospels. By the time of Jesus' capture and crucifixion, the Apostles had come to love and depend on Jesus. They needed Him and seemed to not thrive without Jesus being there or close enough to being there. Jesus foretold of His death, and I am sure that they weren't expecting Jesus to die so young. They had only known Him for three years and in their minds, I am sure that they felt that this was a far off.

The Apostles attended the Last Supper and even after Judas went to do his dirty deeds none of them seemed to show concern. It was just another day in the life of walking with Jesus. They went to the Garden of Gethsemane, and everything seemed okay. I mean, they went to sleep while Jesus went to pray. In my mind, the fact that they could sleep shows me that none of them thought that anything bad was going to happen that night. Then when the platoon of soldiers came for

Jesus, a cold reality smacked them in the face and Jesus was taken into custody. They went hiding and scattered like roaches.

We all know the accounts in Scripture about Peter denying Christ three times and such, but nothing was said in detail about the rest of them, especially Thomas. Now, if a large group of soldiers came for your mentor in the night and people were gossiping and relating the events about what was happening to them, I think that anyone would be terrified that they were going to be next. Christ had the Apostles and ***MANY*** disciples and detractors who were talking about what happened. I am sure that they detractors were acting like it was open-season on Jesus followers and many of those Christ followers went into hiding.

Fast forward to the crucifixion itself. Remember that Jesus' mother was there, and I am certain that the Apostles were there too. Let's go back to Doubting Thomas once again. If you read Thomas' words in John chapter twenty, he knew what wounds Jesus had and how they were caused. I truly believe that Thomas was there watching his beloved Jesus hung high and saw Him die. I believe that Thomas was dealing with trauma on a scale he had never experienced before. Jesus was gone, and Thomas was isolated and alone. In a sense, he felt abandoned, and he had retreated into a shell. Think about this for a moment, even after everyone had assembled after The Resurrection, Thomas wasn't with them.

I am sure that the same machine that was relaying the details of Jesus' death was relaying that He had risen from the dead. That Jesus had been seen in various places and that Jesus had done various things was probably quite the norm. Then Thomas hears it from the Apostles themselves, and he still didn't believe anyone because he hadn't seen Jesus for himself. Thomas saw Jesus die on the cross. Thomas saw when he was prepared for burial and buried. Thomas saw the seal that the Roman government put on the sepulcher. Thomas' faith was shaken, and he knew what he saw before.

Let me be clear, Thomas' lack of faith is legendary, and I agree that he should have believed his fellow apostles. He should have remembered when Jesus said that He would rebuild His temple in three days. Thomas flunked "Unwavering Faith Class", and I am not disputing any of that. What I can understand, from a human perspective, is that Thomas was severely affected by seeing Jesus captured, tortured, murdered and buried. One day his Mentor and Savior Jesus Christ was with all of them and the next day He was gone. In a way, Thomas was most likely feeling abandoned because it all happened so fast in Thomas' mind. Sure, he was afraid for his own life, but Jesus was gone and, if I can use my imagination, Thomas may have felt like the cohesive glue that held everything together was now gone.

To hear that Jesus was alive could have been a bit too much for Thomas to believe on someone else's words alone. It is faulty thinking, but I can understand it. If we really got real about it, we would feel the same. I mean, we have the expression, "I'll believe it when I see it", and that's just our humanity showing itself. Before Thomas could truly believe all of this, he had to see Jesus for himself and touch Him in the places that Thomas saw the wounds that killed Jesus with his own senses. Thomas was wrong, but he was human, and we shouldn't completely berate him.

Thomas wanted to fill the void of Christ being dead badly and he didn't want to just take someone else's word for it because once he committed that faith in Christ being alive, he probably didn't want to get let down again. A personality like Thomas probably had heard that Jesus was alive, and it wasn't true. He may have heard it several times and let down each time. When Jesus did appear to the Apostles and Thomas was there with them, I noticed that Jesus didn't really come down hard on Thomas.

AND AFTER EIGHT DAYS AGAIN HIS DISCIPLES WERE WITHIN, AND THOMAS WITH THEM: THEN CAME JESUS, THE DOORS BEING SHUT, AND STOOD IN THE MIDST, AND SAID, PEACE BE UNTO YOU. THEN SAITH HE TO THOMAS, REACH HITHER THY FINGER, AND BEHOLD MY HANDS; AND REACH HITHER THY HAND, AND THRUST IT INTO MY SIDE: AND BE NOT FAITHLESS, BUT BELIEVING. AND THOMAS ANSWERED AND SAID UNTO HIM, MY LORD AND MY GOD. – JOHN 20:26-28 KJV

What I noticed here was that Jesus gave Thomas exactly what he needed. Jesus told Thomas to do everything that he said that he required to believe that Jesus was alive. Yes, Jesus told him not to be faithless and believe but noticed that once Thomas did those things his faith was restored, and his personal void was filled. In our walk with Christ, it is more than possible that we will encounter a situation where we are abandoned, and it will at once create an empty place in our lives.

Just like that child left behind by a parent or even if a spouse simply leaves for whatever reason and doesn't return creates a void in the soul. We wonder why and then whatever is surrounding us begins to work to break us down to implode us from the inside. We pray to God and ask for His help and depending on the situation He may or may not come when we want Him there, but thanks be unto God, He always shows up on time.

Even if our spirits are being crushed by depression, temptations, hatred, loneliness, addictions or whatever is around us God won't let us implode, but we may or may not have some damage that only He can heal. There is never a time limit on our experiences. It depends on God and the road that He has designed for you to travel on. Somethings are for a season, and some are for a lifetime. Regardless of all of this and how long we ask God why because the life of being saved is supposed to be much better and not feeling wanted, loved or included hampers our feelings and affects our faith. Our walk can be forever changed depending on how we respond and survive being abandoned. God has and never will abandon us even though in the natural realm in our belief He did. God never leaves us alone. Never. Not once.

...Did I Lose Everything?

When we lose "everything" we have a loss of basic needs along with safety and security. Wants are one thing, but when we don't feel safe or feel like we are destitute we enter a very dark place. The fear of loss is a powerful state of anxiety that can cause anyone to act desperately and do things that they wouldn't normally do. Trust me when I tell you this because when I nearly lost everything I nearly did things that weren't legal or moral to survive. I can be honest about that now because God helped me overcome it all. Yet, while we are in the quagmire, it is hard to feel anything but gloom when one day we have what we need or want and the next minute it seems that it all falls away and crashed down around us.

Mind you, I know that these are needs in the natural realm and not the spiritual one, but since we are spiritual beings in a physical realm experience it doesn't make these things any less important or needed. We are still people, and we must balance these things as we walk this broken road when times like this arrive. Just like any other situation we feel and believe and trust that God will insulate us from being righteous and destitute and our children begging for food (Psalms 37:25). Yet, when the reality of the fact that God does allow such situations to happen sets in it can be jarring and hurtful. Just like the other examples thus far it can be a deeply painful situation to be in as a follower of Jesus Christ. To lose everything means that our next meal may be in question. It may mean that we lose our mode of transportation or our housing. It can cause us to get desperate and sorrowful, which is fertile ground for the Enemy to sow his seeds of discord inside of our hearts and minds.

As Christians, we should not be defined by our things but defined by Jesus Himself. However, we still have the need to have some form of income, food to eat, water to drink and a place to sleep safely. As humans, we have the hope to not have to worry about these things because we want personal security. Sure, we want greater for ourselves, and we want more than the bare minimum, but what happens when circumstances in our lives cause us to lose both our wants and our needs? I believe that many of us know how it feels to lose a job, receive an eviction or foreclosure notice or get a dire diagnosis that the good health we once had has now been put into question with a serious challenge. To lose what one holds dear is a feeling that one never forgets, and it can shape us for a lifetime.

To face a season of lack or want is not in anyone's playbook and when it happens when we are Christians, it automatically registers us for one of life's hardest exams. A test that most of us pray never is set before us because of the pain associated with it. When we, as humans, don't feel secure in our basic needs of income, shelter, food, and safety our reflexive actions can sometimes overcome us, and the Adversary will use them against us. When the chips are down, and our faith gets tested like this it can leave deep penetrating wounds to our emotions and spirits. No matter where we are in our walk with Jesus this can make or break us. Tough challenges show us exactly who we truly are and when it comes to our relationship with Christ it also shows us where our strengths and weaknesses are in our relationship with God and with others.

Sometimes we will see it coming and sometimes we don't. Either way it can be challenging to one's faith because if we are in relationship with Jesus we can feel let down because He didn't protect us from losing everything. The "why" question becomes as prevalent as we can expect, and we can fall into a spiral of doubts and depression, and it can be hard to come out of. As I said earlier, I have been in that place and nearly lost my home, lost my previous level of income, and many other things that went wrong and that took a toll on me. I know the pain of waking up every morning and praying that it all was just a bad dream, and it's not. I know what it feels like to cry yourself to sleep while consumed with worry and fears. I've been fearful to look in the mailbox because there may be another bill I can't pay there.

In a season where one loses everything all feelings of desperation and panic are "good friends" who like to break down our doors and visit us. They bring doubt, fear, anger, and rage along with them as gifts. Sometimes we will get angry at God (yes, I said it) because we did everything right and we still ended up losing all that we have. I will be honest, I looked back to that time and realized that I wasn't alone, and God was with me just as He promised, but at the time I felt isolated and rejected. Here I was, serving God and no matter how much I prayed, sowed seed, or served God nothing changed instantly. I knew that God could perform a miracle in my life, and I know that His Power is unlimited, and I had seen Him do it before, but when it was my turn? I felt like I did something majorly wrong. When I did my own poorly executed self-audit, I questioned God as to why He was doing this to me? I was baffled and bewildered because I had loved Jesus from my early years, served God faithfully, gave my tithes and everything! It didn't make sense!

Life can be hard enough on its own, but to see the things you had before vanishing creates an instant void in one's life. Something as simple as getting gas at the gas station had new meaning. At one time I could put my card into the pump and get all the gas I wanted with no worries. When my money was gone, I remember collecting spare change in my house just to get enough gas to get to church. I remember in the good times when my pantry was full, and my refrigerator was overflowing. I also remember when my shelves were bare, and my refrigerator only had ice water in it. I remember getting the bills that had "Cutoff Notice", or "Action of Foreclosure" printed on the ***OUTSIDE*** of the envelopes. It was so embarrassing and humiliating. I felt helpless and hopeless even though I had Jesus in my heart and in my life.

As humans we are naturally possessive of our things. It is truly human nature. Even when we are in Christ and spiritual a part of our humanity tries to bleed through, and it takes our faith to keep those fears and emotions from taking us over. It is a test of our faith and when we feel isolated the test gets converted into an exam. When we lose everything, Satan will use our memories against us. He will allow our minds to reflect and imagine all that we have lost and then go in for the kill with the reality that it is all gone and oh yes, God doesn't care about you. Satan would try to convince you that if God really loved you that you shouldn't go through this kind of pain. He will twist the knife and try to kill your spirit and continually lie that your faith was misplaced and that your prayers are useless in various degrees.

Depending on where one is in their walk with Jesus, Satan will either try to say that salvation is a lie and that you are wasting time all the way to the "you have failed God and now you are being rightfully punished." Satan uses the cold, hard reality of what we lost and directly ties it to God not loving us. He will use all your good memories to remind you that a loving God would never do this to us. This would cause us to bring up the ***WHY***. Our minds need to process changes around us and, in my opinion, losing everything will cause us to go into a mental recall process. We possibly may know the chronological events as to what happened, but "the ***WHY***" it happened will remain a mystery which is where Satan thrives.

We all know that Satan is an expert manipulator and illusionist. As I have said before, he knows how to mess with our minds and our hearts to try to get us to stray from the path of the road of life. I remember my Dad telling me stories of people during the Great Depression who took their lives because they felt like they could no longer provide for their families. We have seen television programs and movies where someone simply disappeared and started a new life because they either lost everything or became a colossal failure. Every program is designed just for us and is made to get us to stumble and fall.

Losing it all feels like a heavy cloak of despair that tries to smother us with fear and desperation. The season of loss usually starts suddenly and brutally. When we are in Christ we will at once pray and make petitions before God to take us out of this test. We cry, snot and lay on our faces begging God to let this cup pass from us. We quote Scripture and call God's words back to Him which is Biblical and should be our first response. We stand on our faith and sometimes no matter what we do, nothing changes. We pray for a "suddenly" miracle just like we may have done before, and Heaven seems silent. It can feel like God has left us and is ignoring us. It can feel like our faith isn't enough or that it's fake. The Adversary does his best to whisper to us that God is either deaf, doesn't care about our situation, or that God never really loved us. Satan will even "open" doors for us of opportunity that are either traps or dead ends to get us to stray from God's intended plan for this season. Oh wait, I forgot to mention that there is a purpose for all of this didn't I? Don't worry, I will get to the reasons why later.

I will be honest and say that I know that I have faith in Christ, and I have been there before, but I am human and so are you. I don't care how "saved" you are and how much Scripture you can quote, but when it is meant for you to go through something like this you will not avoid it. Still, we have questions about all of this. If you have been there before you know exactly what I mean. We start going over and over in our heads about what we did wrong. What did we do to deserve all of this and more importantly, why are we, a Christian, suffering like this? It is perplexing and sometimes while we are at our lowest it seems that the unsaved and those who persecute us seem to be getting blessed.

At the time we don't have a clue as to what we should do. We don't know which way to turn. To have at least something and then have nothing changes the game for anyone who goes through it. Up becomes down. Down is now up. Left is right and right is left. Nothing makes sense anymore. It feels unfair and unjust. It sometimes even feels like being saved isn't worth it. Walking this road means that we must face the fact that we are still human beings. Yes, we are saved, and yes, we have the Holy Spirit, but the flesh can still fail. I don't care who you think you are, we don't know what it feels like to hit that one obstacle that has our name on it that is meant to test us beyond the limits of where we think we can go.

When we are desperate for answers, we will often cling to whatever is the first seemingly conclusive answer to satisfy our minds and even our spirits. Satan knows this and will send the counterfeit answer that is rooted in truth but is a poisonous lie. This lie is meant to relate to our loss and try to trick us into giving up and being defeated. Things and people will come and go, but our God is forever. Losing it all can make us question our faith and we need to be honest with ourselves about something like this. We may bend, but we don't have to break and that is what we need to remember. Yes, we must endure the lashes of pain that comes with losing everything and trust me, there will be a time in everyone's life that this will happen, but most importantly we must remember that God's eyes are not dim, and His arms are not too short to reach us to pick us up and act on our behalf.

...Did They Die?

The unfortunate side effect of living is dying. This is a fact that we all must prove one way or another in this existence in our reality. We don't like talking about death because frankly there is not a future in it. Death is absolute, finite, and is the gateway for the transition to Heaven for the Christian. Even though death is a part of our lives we still can be affected by the death of someone who means a great deal to us. In many ways death can be tied to being abandoned as well as losing everything (depending on who that person was to them). A parent, a friend, and family member or even a child can devastate us and break us in two, depending on the relationship we have with them. Our lives are full of relationships and some of them are closer than others and some of them are the foundations of our being.

Each person is like a tower like that favorite party game where a piece is taken from one part of the stack and placed on top. Take a specific piece that's critical to the balance of the stack and it will teeter and fall over, and the game is over. We all lose people in our lives as we go through this journey. It is guaranteed there will be one person that transitions from this life into the next that will cause our lives to topple over and crumble to the ground.

I say all this about losing people like this because I have experienced it myself, and I am sure that this is the truth because if it hasn't happened to you yet? It will. As my elders would often tell me when I was a young man life isn't promised to us and "just as sure as you were born to die" it could be over and repeatedly those words became true. One doesn't have to be saved to have a person who is critical in their lives pass away and it wrecks them on many levels.

Each human has "their person" who is their "rock" or stability in this world and to do so is being human.

Saved or not we have people in our lives that God has blessed us with that are integral and important pieces of our lives. It could be a parent, a spouse, a mentor, a sibling, or friend. It doesn't matter about the relationship from the outside; we all have people who are partly responsible for who we are and that is okay. God will place people in our lives like that and use them greatly. However, as much as we don't want to acknowledge this fact it is in God's Will that that person that is our foundation in this world will be called into Eternity, and we will not be ready for that to happen.

From a human perspective, it doesn't make sense. Why would our loving God let someone die that we depend on so much in our lives and seem to need? Why does He allow someone whom we love to sometimes suffer through various forms of illness and then leave this world? God told us that His thoughts are not our thoughts, neither are our ways His ways (Isaiah 55:8), which can seem cold and distant when we are in the middle of our grief. Believe me, I know this on a very personal level as I said earlier. When I lost my father in 2020, I secretly questioned why God would take him when He did. Yes, I knew that Dad was in his nineties and that I should have expected his death at any time, but even in my forties I depended on my dad's wisdom and because of the COVID-19 Pandemic that was raging at the time I couldn't see him, or talk to him at the time of his passing. I still needed my Dad, and he was such a large part of my life even though I was a grown man with a wife and family of my own.

Thankfully, I visited him two weeks before the pandemic officially started, but the facility was under a lockdown due to an alleged "flu outbreak" and I was told to not stay long and wear a mask. That day I saw him was unusual because his condition normally had him out of it. That day, he was more lucid than usual. My mom wasn't feeling well either, so I went in to visit him alone that day. My uncle and aunt were already there visiting with him and when I came in my Dad perked up when I entered the room and didn't say a word at first but then called my name. His eyes fixated on me with the sparkle that I hadn't seen for many years, and it was a welcome sight.

I had a conversation with him that was short, but powerful where he was thankful that I was there with him and that I had a wonderful Christian wife, beautiful family, and that I was a happy man like he was. He told me how he prayed for my Mom and how God answered his prayers. I knew that I couldn't stay long, but I fought back the tears as I ended my visit and he said to me, "I love you, Sean, you are my son." I didn't know it then, but I look back now and see that he was saying goodbye. There are so many things that I didn't say that I wish that I did and so many things that I wished I had had asked him that I never got to ask. All these thoughts hit me all at once when I got the call from my Mom that my Dad had transitioned.

The first thing I asked God was, "***WHY***?" In my tears my mind was racing like a thoroughbred. My emotions were spiraling out of control and on the outside, no one knew what I was feeling. I was angry at God because I felt that God took Dad from me too soon. Yes, I knew the reality of his condition, but my grief did not understand logic and wanted what it wanted. At a time when Dad was the one who I turned to when I was upset that I didn't have him with me anymore. There were so many times when Dad had a bad turn that God had brought him out of it. I had prayed for him over and over and he always pulled through by the grace of God. Yet, when my Mom called me and let me know that he was being transported to the emergency room neither of us were concerned about it.

This was the man whose appendix burst years ago, and he drove himself to the hospital. Dad was the epitome of tough as well as favored by God. I went to lay down to sleep and was certain that all would be well. When my Mom called back, I expected that everything would be fine, but instead I was greeted by her uncontrollable tears and her uttering the words "Daddy died," and it slammed into me like a ton of bricks. That feeling was constant and increasing by the minute. I just wanted to see him one more time. Hear him tell me that he loved me one more time. I still have a voicemail saved on my phone with this voice, and it's been years since he passed away.

As I write this, I can feel my emotions welling up inside of me, but I am reminded that God is in control and that He has a plan for my life. When God calls someone into eternity that we love dearly the effects are widespread and various, but they all activate pain in our hearts, minds, and spirits. To know that you will never see them again on this side of reality is a truth that can be hard to accept. To see that person being lowered into the ground for the final time or in that urn is symbolic to your heart being buried with them or up in smoke and turned into ashes.

Satan will attempt to sow seeds of discord using whatever emotions we are feeling at the time. Anger, rage, depression, sadness, grief, and so many more. The last, and more effective, emotion that he will stir up is loneliness. Satan will make us feel alone, vulnerable, and ill-equipped to live this life anymore. He will make us begin to fear of what God will allow to be taken next from us. The pillar that we could see, and touch is now gone, and Satan will attempt to exploit our momentary weakness because of such a loss.

Let's look at the biblical account of Lazarus. Mary and Martha's brother meant the world to them just like a sibling means to any of us. Lazarus, as we know from the Scriptures, was sick and getting worse and Mary and Martha sent word to Jesus that their brother was dying. Jesus heard what was said and stayed where he was. Of course, everyone around Him was puzzled, but He is Jesus, so they let it go. Finally, Jesus signaled that He was going to go to Lazarus because he was dead. As Jesus was travelling word got to Mary and Martha that Jesus was heading their way, and Mary ran out to meet Him. The famously quoted John 11:21 verse comes into view with the words: "Lord, if thou hadst been here, my brother had not died." They were receiving friends and loved ones to console them because Lazarus was dead and buried. Let's pause here for a moment and look at the situation. Mary and Martha knew who Jesus is and they knew that their message had gotten to Him that they needed His help.

Could you imagine what Martha was feeling? She never left the house. She was grieving and she possibly felt that Jesus left them hanging in the wind. They knew that Jesus was the greatest healer that they had ever seen, and we know that Mary knew that He was the Son of God. Many of us condemn Martha a bit too much, but she was very human. She was hurt. She felt the loss because her brother was gone. She missed him and when they called on God, He didn't come when they wanted Him there. They wanted a miracle because they knew that Jesus had the power to do it. Then for Jesus to show up "late" was probably even more painful to these sisters, but Mary ran to see Jesus anyway. She told Jesus that Lazarus' death was His fault. We know that the account ends with Lazarus being raised from being dead for four days, but for most of us that doesn't happen.

The person that dies stays dead and we know that God has the power to raise them up again. It is a hurtful thing to know that God could either prevent them from dying, heal them from dying, or raising them up from death. When we lose someone, any one of those three feelings will float through our minds. As I have said before, it doesn't matter how saved they are. We are still in the flesh, and we have feelings. When we see the part of where Mary and Martha were grieving their loss all of us can identify with any part of that story. We don't know what they felt during those four days before Jesus arrived, but we do know how we feel when someone that we loved died. Even though Mary and Martha's ordeal was only four days, the ones we suffer can go on for years where the thoughts of that loss can stir up emotions that Satan will try to manipulate us with.

Ultimately, we will not know why God choses to end the life of people on the Earth because frankly, it's His call to make and we don't have much to say about that. It is hard, from a human standpoint, to trust in a God that will allow someone we need, love, or depend on to leave us when we still need them or love them. Yes, we can read the Scripture that says:

For my thoughts are not your thoughts, neither are your ways my ways, saith the Lord. For as the heavens are higher than the earth, so are my ways higher than your ways, and my thoughts than your thoughts. – Isaiah 55:8-9 KJV

At the same time, we can feel confused and bewildered that all of this is still happening. That reason being that we don't see things from God's point of view. We don't hold all of eternity in our hands and the death of one person at a particular time is miniscule in the grand scheme of things. Now, let me pause and say that this doesn't mean that the person isn't important to God. Satan wants us to feel that way, but that isn't the case because there is an overall plan at work that we cannot see. We have little choice, but to trust God because He made everything, and He knows what He is doing better than any of us.

This is not a definitive answer as to why someone we loved died and left us. This is not the neatly-wrapped up solution that we so desperately crave to satisfy our human minds and hearts. The only answer that we have access to is to trust that God has our best interests at heart. We must believe and know that God is in control. We must accept that whatever comes next is what God has intended so that He receives the glory. We must know that what God has planned with us trusting and relying on Him is greater than what we could imagine.

This still doesn't mean that there isn't a hole left in our lives. When that hole appears when someone we held tightly leaves this Earthly existence, we must remember to fill it with God and not just our feelings. This can be difficult because we are still very human. After losing Dad I was lost for a while, and I was devastated. I was hurt, but I really didn't show it much because I wanted to be strong for my family. Still, I am beginning to see what God is up to with me losing my Dad. I grew closer to God and some people dropped out of my life and others came into it. The greatest change for me was that I finally accepted my call into the ministry as an ordained Elder in the church. I surrendered to God and allowed Him to fill the void that my Father left after his passing and while it may seem sadistic and cruel, I have never been better in my spiritual life.

Now I am the husband and father that my Dad would be proud of. I have learned to fall into God's Hands more when I have doubts about being the best man that I can be. Even though my memories of Dad are still strong, and I still catch myself acting like him I realize that God has been my constant help that I can reach through prayer versus the telephone. I haven't completely gotten there yet, but I am well on my way on this road of life after I asked why did my Dad die. I know that you will too one day.

Just like any trauma be sure to guard your emotional and mental health too. Death of those we loved imprints on our minds and hearts like few things can. I know that all of us have heard of a person having a nervous breakdown or drastically changing their personality and habits after someone died. This is also fertile ground for Satan to step in and keep us distracted or break us and it could cause us to step out of God's Will. When we are questioning God as to why we can take our focus from what God has intended for us.

We cannot let our minds spiraling as to why someone died eat us up from the inside to the outside. We need to remember that we don't control life or death. We can't dictate our birth or life nor can we for someone else's. It is normal to wonder why, but we can't let that questioning rip us from God's destiny for us. We can process the pain as we need but not stay there. That is what Satan wants us to do. Believe me, I was there, and I pray that I never do, but I know that losing people will still happen. It feels just like a paradox.

I know that I spoke this from my perspective, and I dare not try to tell anyone how they should feel or how they should process feelings like this. When a loved one dies it will affect each person differently and I get that. Please don't try to do what I did down to every minute specific detail. If anything, please don't forget God. Don't abandon God. It is okay to wonder why, but to abandon God and believe the lies of Hell that He no longer loves you or left you is where you must draw the line. Grieve. Don't stop up your emotions and hide them. It is normal and okay to cry and to miss people. It is okay to not be superhuman and like what many Christians wish for you to imitate. Nine times out of ten they are just as torn up as you are. It is a very fine line to live human as well as in Christ and this is one of those times. You may never understand why they died but just know that God is still in control.

...Did I Fail?

The act of failure is a concept that is difficult to absorb and grasp. In our lives we must understand the fact that everything that we will do in this life will hit a speedbump or not end the way that we desire. It is a part of being human, and it is a hard experience to live. Our culture and our lives are based on success or the appearance of success. Rational people do not seek to fail, but it is something that we must experience. While we must learn from our failure to succeed the emotions and situations associated with failure can be too great to bear. Life will throw us the worst of the worst of situations, and it is unfair. When we as people do our best and try hard and it still ends in disaster? It hurts deeply and it can cripple our spirits for a long time. One would think that if we serve a God of possibilities and a God that rewards the faithful that success is always on tap for us. That is not the case, and I would like to explain.

First, we must establish the irrefutable fact that there is no failure in God. There will never be failure in God, and we need to realize that when things fall apart and we don't achieve what we set out to do or even directed by God to do, God was not the one who failed. Period. We have no right to blame God for something because He didn't mess anything up. He is perfect in all His ways and that's that. Lastly, when we fail, we need to realize that everything is still in God's plan and that we need to trust Him.

Still, it is very hard to accept these facts when everything is literally crashing down around us, and embarrassment starts to set up shop in our hearts and minds. The questions we have about why this happened start to rise in us as we question God about why we failed and believe me; it is a hard pill to swallow. Failure feels personal, and it indeed is personal. When we fail, Satan gets to work to stir up our flesh (as he always does) to either distract us or keep up pinned down in an invisible emotional prison. Failure makes us feel like we don't measure up and that we aren't or didn't do enough and even failing for a second is unacceptable.

No one wants to be at the receiving end of anything that failed. Whether it was asking someone out for a date, falling off a bike, or a multi-billion-dollar business venture. There isn't any scenario or setting where a person will want to fail and cause themselves harm. So, when failure comes to our lives, we are usually wondering what happened and why. This doesn't get easier when we get saved and start living for Jesus. No one wants to be a "loser". No one wants to feel the crushing weight of losing or of loss. Still, when failure comes calling, we tend to not take it well in any way.

Sure, we may shrug it off and try to learn from it (as we should), but there does come that failure that makes us question any and everything that we knew before. This is the type of failure where it seems that there is no hope of either survival or recovery. That's the level of failure that I want to talk about here. When we learn how to do anything, we must fail first to learn how to get things right. Rarely do we get things right on the first try. So, we have learned as humans, that failure is a part of education and that is how God designed it. Trial and error are the fundamentals of building any skill or achieving any task. It is when the error or the failure is so great that it cripples us like nothing we have experienced before that has severe impacts.

As we go along life's journey, every person will sadly meet up with such a level of failure. As Christians, we know that God can never fail, but we are prone to it daily. We know that our flesh can betray us and let us down. We know that any wrong step can cause us to stray away from God which would be a disaster. We live with that little reminder in the back of our minds and to be honest, it keeps us humble and seeking God. As we go, we learn to avoid pitfalls and even when we make those missteps, we can find our way back. In the natural world, we learn from falling on our diapered behinds as we learn to walk as babies. We learn that the black and yellow buzzing thing that flies has a stinger that causes us pain if we try to pick it up with our hand. We learn that we can't do what we want because there are consequences to our actions. Spiritually or naturally, failing is meant to perfect us, but sometimes the feelings of failure are too much to bear.

The enemy knows how to prey on human emotions as I have said before. He is an expert at turning our emotions against us, and the feelings of failure and being a loser are one of them. Look, it is not a question of "if" we will fail, but "when" we will fail. Failure in the Christian life is usually divided into two parts: Sin and Circumstance. Let's deal with sin first. Failure due to sin is very personal because it starts and ends with us. It was we who committed the sin and we who must endure the consequences of that sin. Even when sin is forgiven by God, the consequences will remain as a reminder of our past transgressions. No matter who we may think we are in Christ we will mess up and sin. We don't always intend to go that way, but we all are prone to stumble and lose our way. God does always provide a means of escape for us, but it is up to us to heed the warnings of the Holy Spirit and make a quick exit from screwing up. Still, it can and will happen.

There is a beautiful part of this scenario in that God will warn us and set off alarm bells that we are not going where we need to go. His Grace will try to lead us back on track, but if we choose to ignore God's warnings, He will let us go where we have chosen and wait for us to hopefully repent and turn back to Him. Yet, when the chances of escape have been ignored, and we find ourselves in a disaster where everything has crashed all around us and we have fallen to sin it is at that point that we have utterly failed. We know the usual failures of infidelity, sexual perversion, addiction of various kinds, spiritual compromise, or whatever you want to put here, but what we need to remember is that the failure didn't happen when we got caught, but it occurred the moment we made the first wrong move. Infidelity doesn't happen in a split second. Addiction doesn't happen just by looking at whatever it is. The failure of sin begins and ends with our action away from God's principles. We measure it when we get caught.

Yes, you can be saved, anointed, and appointed and still sin and fail. It doesn't matter how long you've been saved or what your position is in God's Church. If we are human, we can fail to sin. If we are progressing on this broken road, we will meet obstacles that Satan has put there to trip us up and move us off course from our God-given destinies. It is now when the consequences hit us while our world is collapsing that the enemy really gets to work on our hearts and minds. The core effective spiritual attack of failure is the feeling of rejection. In this case it's not when we are rejected by others, but when we reject ourselves. We see ourselves as a perpetual sinner and a failure. Satan makes us feel like there is no hope of getting out of this and that we should just stay here in our mess. Failure is like a spider's web. Even if we get out of it the strands that held us bound can stay with us until we are washed clean of them.

When we are caught in sin's web we are dazed, confused, angry, embarrassed, and afraid. We usually don't understand how and why we got where we are. At first, what we thought was innocent has now turned dire. What was something we could escape from or not get caught doing has finally come back to haunt us. We feel exposed and we are compromised. Shame sets in and regret tries to overrun us with guilt and sadness. This can be hard for anyone, but it is harder for the Christian.

When confronted with their sin "church people" can sometimes be the worst and the cruelest of anyone. They will shake heads at people who fall into sin. They will wag their tongues and their fingers at them telling them that they should have known better. Some of these "church people" will give bad counsel, beat them up with Scripture, or talk about them mercilessly behind their backs. Satan uses that to the finest degree as he deepens the gloom of those caught in sin's web. He lies and tells them that there is no recovering from this. There is no hope and that whatever God told you or has planned for you has vaporized.

Satan will even quote every verse of Scripture that tells us that we must be holy like God is holy. That we should not sin and that we must present ourselves faultless to God with exceeding joy. He will weave the truth into a quilt of lies and try to bury us with it where we fall. The emotions of our failure will swirl about us as we seem to go down the spiritual drain to drown and never rise for air again. That is Satan's plan, and he has been executing it perfectly for millennia. From the first to fall to sin until the very last he will use his expertly crafted playbook against human emotions and frailty.

Some people seem to never recover from falling into sin. We have seen big televangelists who were caught in the act to fall from grace and lose followers. We have seen preachers who messed up badly quit the ministry because they can't take the pressure of what they did. Spouses who slipped up hurt the other so badly by breaking trust and vows can sometimes never recover. There are countless other scenarios that can be used here, but the key ingredient of them all is Satan's meddling with the hearts and minds of people.

Failure to sin isn't restricted to just the sins the church has adapted as the worst but can be anything that is contrary to the Word of God. Whatever the sin is there is a failure level that can paralyze us from moving forward in God. How we respond is the key. We must break through the lies of Satan to survive. We will be in an endless loop of wondering ***WHY*** and it can hurt badly. Satan will have us running over in our heads about every bad choice and misstep with clarity. He will try to make us feel like we were never ready to walk with God. He will try to lie to us that there is no way that we can ever get out of this, so we might as well stay where we are. The consequences are too severe to try and make a comeback. Satan will try to convince us that failure is our only option. Satan will hide verses in the Word of God like this:

THE STEPS OF A GOOD MAN ARE ORDERED BY THE LORD: AND HE DELIGHTETH IN HIS WAY. THOUGH HE FALL, HE SHALL NOT BE UTTERLY CAST DOWN: FOR THE LORD UPHOLDETH HIM WITH HIS HAND. – PSALMS 37:23-24 KJV

Or this:

REJOICE NOT AGAINST ME, O MINE ENEMY: WHEN I FALL, I SHALL ARISE; WHEN I SIT IN DARKNESS, THE LORD SHALL BE A LIGHT UNTO ME. – MICAH 7:8 KJV

Satan will try to make us forget that every test can turn into a testimony and every mess can become a message. We will continue to incessantly ask ***WHY***, but when it comes to failing to sin, we and God only know the answer to that. We may not want to come to terms with the answers, but we need to understand that like Psalms 37 says, the Lord will hold our hands through it all. We can get back up again:

LAY NOT WAIT, O WICKED MAN, AGAINST THE DWELLING OF THE RIGHTEOUS; SPOIL NOT HIS RESTING PLACE: FOR A JUST MAN FALLETH SEVEN TIMES, AND RISETH UP AGAIN: BUT THE WICKED SHALL FALL INTO MISCHIEF. REJOICE NOT WHEN THINE ENEMY FALLETH, AND LET NOT THINE HEART BE GLAD WHEN HE STUMBLETH: – PROVERBS 24: 15-17 KJV

We can and we will rise from a sinful disaster and in the natural world we can get up again from failure in a circumstance. These sorts of failures can be situations like getting fired from a job, going bankrupt, foreclosure, repossession, a business going bankrupt, a parenting mishap, saying the wrong thing at the worst time, or an accidental destruction or even death. We can be in situations in life where we can do everything right and everything still fails. There are some situations that are beyond our control, but we can still find ourselves at the epicenter of the destruction and it is unavoidable. As Christians, we must face an unwinnable situation and there is nothing we can do about it except go through it. Sure, we can pray to God with all the faith in the world, but sometimes God will allow us to fail no matter what we do. Can He rescue us? He can and will save us from failure, but some fails are meant to be endured for many reasons.

We will still be plagued with the "***WHY***" and it can haunt us. We can receive a prophetic word that we are destined to open a business and encounter failure. We can be careful, skilled, and safe and still miscalculate and cause an accident that takes a life. We can get fired unexpectedly and be living our most upright life before God and people. Satan uses the same thought spiral that he uses in a sin failure here with perfection. While we are caught in the paralysis of analysis Satan will pounce and try to pound us into the ground. He will use our feelings against us as he always tries to do. He will attempt to sow seeds of doubt and regret in the hope that they will overtake us and cause us to give up.

I don't know about you, but I have failed a class before. It didn't happen until I went to college and believe me it was an eye-opening experience. The class was Physics with Calculus and even though it was hard, I understood the material. I went to class every day and I studied hard. I took pages and pages of notes during the lectures, and I participated in study groups with others. I turned in extra-credit work and worked long hours into the night doing practice tests and going over every example. When the exams came around, they were remarkably different, and I struggled.

I applied every principle and precept I knew, and I gave it my all. When the grades were posted I discovered that I failed big time. I tried to see the professor during office hours, but they were never available. I kept going to class and I kept trying to adapt to what I learned from the first failed exam. I worked harder than ever. I studied on my work breaks and when I ate meals. I asked for outside help and a tutor. Next exam? I failed again.

I was confused and getting ticked off. I complained to the Physics Department who said that this professor had great marks and reviews and that I should work it out with them. I tried repeatedly to do so to no avail. Others in my major were struggling too so I knew that it wasn't just me. I prayed to God and believed that He would help me. As a class we complained to the professor, and they said they would offer us a bonus exam to help our averages. I failed that one too.

I had taken Physics and Calculus for years and never had a problem until this one professor. The day for the final exam came and I was a wreck. I studied for over twenty-four hours straight. I fasted, prayed and cried out to God for a miracle. I had memorized every formula and every concept. I could go through problems and scenarios backwards and forwards. I could explain every detail and remembered every trap I had fallen in before because the professor would show us what we did wrong in each exam.

The day for the Final Exam came and I came in the class battle-ready. I was focused and prepared for the fight of my Physics life. The professor came into the classroom. I was sweating and my stomach was in knots. I knew that I was prepared to the best of my ability. I had followed the lectures and the textbook. I worked hard and I felt that I was going to be okay. The exam was handed out and I froze. This exam was unlike anything I had ever seen, but I remembered all my hard work studying. I could see through the traps. I remembered my formulas and I began to tackle this monstrosity. After nearly two hours of suffering and giving my hand cramps I turned in my answers. I was tired, but I felt good about what I did. Lo, and behold when I got my grade back, I was pleased that I didn't fail the final, but my course average was a big fat "D" which was a failing grade at my university for a core class. I was devastated.

I knew that I tried hard, and I studied more than I ever had in my life. I understood the lectures, but the exams sank my battleship. I was angry and depressed at the same time. I didn't know how to feel about this. I remember some others who didn't show up at each lecture, and they had passed the course. I didn't get it, and I felt lousy. I had never failed like this academically and it hurt badly. Me not graduating "on time" hovered over me and I was in despair. It was my senior year, and I hadn't filed for financial aid. The deadline had passed, and it was too late, and college was ***EXPENSIVE***. My proverbial goose was cooked, and I felt alone and rejected. Was I good enough for this? Was I smart enough? Was I fooling myself? Why did I fail? Why am I here? Questions swirled around in my head for weeks as I was in a state of disbelief. I had failed. Big time. I didn't know what to do. I did it all the best way I knew how, and I even did it the way the professor said to do it, and I failed miserably. It was awful.

I questioned everything. I asked God why did I fail? I searched my heart to see where I went wrong. I second guessed everything in my life because I had never failed a class before. I was so embarrassed. I was compromised and I felt rejected by God. I knew how to pray. I knew that God loved me, but I just didn't get why this had to happen. I saw those who cared nothing for God, and they passed. I got wrapped around questioning and meanwhile I didn't realize that Satan was there laughing at me. My world had collapsed, as far as I knew it, because being successful in academia was all that I knew at that time. God had rescued me many times before, but this time I fell flat on my face, and I felt that I didn't deserve it. It was an arrogant thought process, but God was teaching and molding me the entire time.

Here is where the story gets better. I took the class again, but I got a different professor. I remembered all of what I learned, but then I learned the material the way it was being taught by this new teacher. I was afraid of that first exam, but I knew that if I wanted my degree I had to do my best. I passed that exam. I kept going and came to the next exam and I passed that one too. At the end of the semester, the final exam I put my soul into studying and when I looked at the grades posted a wave of relief washed over me. I got a B-minus and I was ecstatic! I finally was on the winning side of Physics with Calculus! I found out later that the first professor I had hated people from my major in their classes and graded us much harder than the actual physics majors. I heard rumors that they were dismissed because of that and other concerns. Either way, I was at the center of my failure, but even though I did everything right, outside forces guaranteed my demise.

Look, I know that I am talking about a class here, but your failure could be tied to something like a business, a ministry, a marriage, or a host of other things. My failure cost me graduation time, but your failure could cost someone their life. It could cost a future or success. It doesn't matter what it is, but what does matter is our response to that failure. Whether it is sin or circumstance that happens to us to cause failure doesn't matter. It doesn't matter whether we did things to make us fail or if failure happens because of outside circumstances. We must keep in mind that God is still on His throne. We must not allow our spirits to sink in the mire of rejection and keep reaching out to God no matter what happens. We must stay steadfast in our faith in God's Power to turn everything around in His time.

As we walk along life's journey on this road it will happen no matter what we do or don't do. It makes no difference that we chose it, or it chose us we all must face this thing called failing. The key to this is what we do after we fail. What is our response to God? What do we do next? Do we allow failure to keep us in the grave that it dug for us, or do we fight our way back to the path God has set for us? Do we allow our failures to define us, or do we allow our recovery from failure define how good God is? Do we reach into the pit of despair that Satan wants us to dwell in, or do we reach up to God Who is our Help? Do we stay in the "Why did I…" or do we allow God to show us the "How He will…"? That choice is entirely up to us.

...Is Life So Hard?

This is a hard question to ask because there seems to never be the right answer. This comes from the deepest part of a person who has been through an extended amount of Hell in their life, and it seems to never let up or let go. It's true that life is not easy, but when it becomes the average and every day that troubles seem to come out of nowhere continuously. This question comes from the broken heart of a person who is "normal" who seems to perpetually live a life of sorrow and suffering. Our existence isn't fair, and it seems like we get the worst of it all sometimes and it is hard when we are saved and living our best lives in Christ. "Why is life so hard" is the question that can wrap all the earlier questions (and quite a few more) all up into one horrendous package. It goes beyond one test and one season and seemingly appears endless in duration. The level of anticipation for understanding can greatly increase because the pattern is so long that it feels like this is "just how it is" and there appears to be no end in sight.

When we live through a part of our lives where it seems that nothing goes right, or trouble never seems to take its foot off the gas, it can feel like a punishment. It seems like God doesn't care about our suffering and that somehow, He loves to see us suffer just like our enemies. I can assure you that this is not the case, and I will get deeper into that later. What we experience when life seems hard is the realization that this is pure Hell on Earth and when we are saved and walking this broken road it doesn't make sense. It can feel like we are being targeted for punishment or last-place treatment. When we look around, we can see those who don't love God who seem to have everything go their way it can anger or demoralize us. The Enemy will even giggle in our faces because he knows that what we are going through isn't what we want, and he is salivating at the chance that we turn our backs on God.

Living like this can be suffocating and oppressive. Often it feels like just existing is too hard because things seem to be continually against them. When life is hard, it can almost feel like it was always destiny that failure was the guaranteed lot in life. It can be said that those of certain genders and ethnic backgrounds fall into this category, and I know that all too well. Being African-American I can identify with that in ways that I wish that I did not. For many people who are who they are, and they have a relationship with Jesus Christ, the results and feelings are still the same. The feeling that obstacles are guaranteed for them or that they can only get to a certain point and no further is more real and more poignant to them than anyone. Socioeconomic factors are also linked to this as if a person is born in a certain area where they will either always stay in that area, or they would only achieve certain outcomes.

What makes it difficult is that a substantial majority of others will see the situations of those whose life is hard and not quite understand their struggles or their pain. From the outside, every person should be able to succeed or accomplish whatever they desire. Alternatively, some of those folks would say that terrible things are happening to them because they are either doing something wrong or they aren't trying hard enough in life. Lots of people living hard lives are told to "just try harder" or "stop making excuses" and these are the wrong things to say. Nonetheless, when life seems to be at a disadvantage it is painful to endure and from the people in the middle of it, fairness is the farthest thing from them.

What makes it seem worse is when we know the Word of God and we know the ways that we can achieve a better life and still nothing seems to change. Let me explain. I will use myself for example, no matter how much I pray and how many sacrifices I make giving God won't change my ethnicity. Why? It's not that God ***CAN'T*** do it because God can do anything. It's that He won't do it because who I was made as was for His divine purpose. Living in poor ways is something that God will change, but ***SOMETIMES*** God won't change those situations because for whatever reason, God has a purpose and plan for every season in life.

As a man I cannot speak about gender related issues, but I can speak about discrimination and how it can make life very unfair and quite difficult. As a proud man of color, I stand here today realizing that the strength and resilience that God has blessed me with did not come into my life by accident. It was God and God alone that has allowed me to get where I am today despite all the difficulties that I have faced. However, compared to some of my Caucasian brothers and sisters, my life has had many disadvantages that are prevalent in America and permeate throughout the entire fabric of our society. Regardless of whether anyone reading this thinks that these things are in our country's past, I can assure you that they are not. There isn't a single white person in the United States that would trade their life with a minority. Not even one.

This isn't some "woke" agenda or my way of trying to slander or hurt any white person, but this is just the experiences of an African-American in the United States, which I am sure mirrors most people of color around the world. According to the *Journal of Human Rights and Social Work*:

STEREOTYPES ARE INGRAINED IN THE FABRIC OF THE USA AND COINCIDE WITH THE INSTITUTION OF SLAVERY. THE EXPECTED BEHAVIORS OF AFRICAN-AMERICANS ARE FUELED BY STEREOTYPES MAINTAINED BY THE STATUS QUO. THROUGHOUT US HISTORY, THE STEREOTYPING OF AFRICAN-AMERICANS, PARTICULARLY MALES, HAS HAD A NEGATIVE IMPACT ON AFRICAN-AMERICAN FAMILIES AND COMMUNITIES. FOR INSTANCE, THE BELIEF THAT AFRICAN-AMERICANS ARE UNINTELLIGENT, LAZY, VIOLENT, AND CRIMINALS HAS AFFECTED EDUCATIONAL OUTCOMES, EMPLOYMENT OPPORTUNITIES, SOCIOECONOMIC STATUS, AND THE DISMANTLING OF AFRICAN-AMERICAN FAMILIES AND COMMUNITIES. EDUCATORS, BUSINESSMEN, AND LAW ENFORCEMENT OFTEN BELIEVE THESE STEREOTYPES, WHICH INFLUENCES THEIR TREATMENT OF AFRICAN-AMERICANS[2].

In American society the deck was stacked against me even before I was born. I grew up in an area that still flies the confederate traitors' flag at nearly every entrance by road into the county. My hometown is literally less than ninety minutes from Richmond, Virginia, the former capital of the traitorous confederacy. The same confederacy that was founded on the cornerstone that Black people were inferior to White people[3]. The deep-seated love for the confederacy and its treacherous history is still celebrated to this day.

A place where a disgusting memorial to confederate soldiers still stands on the town square allegedly guarded by the local "militia" around the clock. A place where there is a sign that welcomes you to the county and commemorates a female captain who was the first woman officer in the traitor's army. When I went to elementary school, I entered a building that was most likely built by Black people and full of White people that most likely were groomed to hate them. I went to a school named after Robert E. Lee and Stonewall Jackson. Even though the original building was torn down, the new school carried the same name until 2021 after a long fight to get the names of those scoundrels removed.[4]

It was in that school as a child that I learned really fast that having my skin tone was not to my advantage. On my first day I was called the N-Word for the first time in my life by a white child. I was poked and ridiculed by those same kids, and it hurt. I was a very smart kid, but my white teachers always seemed to check if I was cheating to get my answers. I was suspected more about doing mischief than the other children. I was sent to the principal's office or had confrontations with my instructors there, but thankfully, my first principal was African-American, and it made it better, but not the best.

What made it bad for me was the fact that I had an indomitable fire within me. My family is full of strong people, and it seemed that some of those white teachers didn't like that attribute in a Black child. It was fine for a white kid to be a go-getter, but not a Black one. I noticed as a child that many Black people didn't look white people in the eyes and seemed to be more passive. I wasn't like that at all, and I think it rubbed people the wrong way.

Most Black kids were excluded from some activities or shoved into more demeaning ones. Most of the time African-American kids weren't included in things that were the most interesting or enriching. I remember asking my parents why things were the way that they were, and my folks were very direct with me about it. They told me that it was because they didn't like Black people. While this wasn't every teacher that I had, because believe me, I had some great, loving and incredible white teachers that didn't care about race.

Yet I never saw most of them be a champion for equality or take a stand against racism while I was in school. I remember seeing circumstances where things happened and I would look in the face of some of these white teachers and they wouldn't stand up for the Black kids, especially when the racist teachers or staff were involved. It's like they didn't want to rock the boat and fall out of favor with those who were in power. If things happened in the background, I know that we wouldn't see it, but what we saw was not white teachers coming to our defense when we were wronged equally.

If I tried to achieve and excel in school, I was seemingly set up by others to try and make me fail. I didn't truly understand back then why it was so hard being a smart Black male kid. I'm not saying that I was the only one, because we had very smart Black children in our school. I sometimes feel like it was because I dared to be what others thought that I shouldn't be that I had such a tough time. When I was in the fifth grade, I took a test that exempted me out of the entire reading curriculum through the twelfth grade. They made me take it twice and I got the same results. The school system never honored it. I was one of the few Black kids in the Gifted and Talented Program and soon, no Black kids were in it.

I had a teacher chase me down and accuse me of stealing a needle from a sewing machine. A white student would pick a fight with me, but I would get in school suspension for defending myself and they got away with zero penalty. When I was in a class, I was a friend of a white student, and we got the same question wrong on a math exam. He got five points off, but I got twenty. I was on the Drama Team in High School and a teacher thought that I would be ***PERFECT*** for ***ME*** to do a piece as Uncle Remus, to which I vehemently refused. What made it worse was their justification for why it wasn't racist was because a white student in the past did the same piece.

Speaking of that, I remember when I went to the Virginia state finals for Dramatic Poetry Reading. I came in third place. I did *"Go Down Death"*, by James Weldon Johnson. I'm not bragging, but I made nearly every person in that room cry. When I got my scoresheets, I saw that one judge marked me as first place and the other as last place. When I saw that judge driving away in his pickup truck, I saw the confederate losers' flag on a bumper sticker. He simply said in the comments "Didn't like the piece." I was devastated and hurt. I told my parents about it, and I heard the same thing I had heard my entire life about how they didn't like Black people.

When I graduated from high school I couldn't wait to leave and never come back to live there and frankly, they couldn't wait either. My life in school there was the worst. I was seemingly hated and mistreated, and it didn't make sense. I still have my high school yearbook without a single signature in it after graduation. When I was growing up, I always wondered why my life was so hard to live. I was tortured tremendously and even though my home was happy and stable, life outside of my house was terrible. If it weren't for having a household raised in the Church, I would have succeeded in committing suicide. Yeah, I thought about it a lot as a child. Thank God I never acted on it.

My story is just one of many others. In fact, everything from education, economics and social status are affected by discrimination that affects African-Americans. Black people even have trouble being born in America and the statistics are shocking. Based on most recent estimates, non-Hispanic Black women are 2.6 times more likely to die from pregnancy-related complications than white women. For Black women 25 and older, pregnancy-related mortality is about four times higher than it is for white women of similar ages, according to data from 2007 to 2016. The maternal mortality rate for Black mothers doesn't improve with socioeconomic status or educational level.

For example, data from 2007 to 2016 show that among women with a college degree or higher, the pregnancy-related mortality ratio was five times higher for Black mothers compared with white mothers[5]. The data shows that racial and ethnic minority groups, throughout the United States, experience higher rates of illness and death across a wide range of health conditions, including diabetes, hypertension, obesity, asthma, and heart disease, when compared to their White counterparts. Additionally, the life expectancy of non-Hispanic/Black Americans is four years lower than that of White Americans[6].

I wondered why this was the case because I saw family members die younger than they should, and it bothered me deeply. I still feel that way today even though the United States claims to have the best healthcare in the world. Yet it doesn't seem that these wonderful resources are for all people. In fact, it's the same form of discrimination that is felt in school that fuels the disparities. This quote in the New York Times Magazine summed up the differences between Black people and Whites as it relates to healthcare and why it is that way:

One hundred and fifty years after the freed people of the South first petitioned the government for basic medical care, the United States remains the only high-income country in the world where such care is not guaranteed to every citizen. In the United States, racial health disparities have proved as foundational as democracy itself. "There has never been any period in American history where the health of blacks was equal to that of whites," Evelynn Hammonds, a historian of science at Harvard University, says. "Disparity is built into the system[7]."

Even though I have been blessed to have good health I saw people around me die because they felt that they wouldn't get good medical attention because they were African-American. The converse was that they couldn't afford decent medical treatments, so they just lived with things until they killed them. Suffering in open silence because of the lack of access to what they needed. The bar always seemed to be out of reach and those who want to keep that bar too high fight against programs that would allow all people to have access to great healthcare. The biggest deterrent is the money and economic access.

A racial salary gap has persisted in the US for more than 50 years among minority groups, with Black people currently earning 30 to 35 percent less than Whites. Now new research shows that in addition to receiving smaller paychecks, Black workers are also less likely to have supportive bosses, a positive work culture, and a healthy work-life balance[8]. In the United States, the average Black and Hispanic or Latino households earn about half as much as the average White household and own only about 15 to 20 percent as much net wealth[9].

Personally, I have not had it as badly as it relates to financial stability since I have a decent job, but I am far from being rich. I have, however, experienced discrimination in my career and getting access to financial gains. I will never forget years ago when I was getting my annual review for my first professional job out of college. I had an extensive list of accomplishments just like my white peers and it was known that after a certain number of years people with great reviews would get promoted to a project management level. I had those reviews, and I had stellar accomplishments to go along with it.

The Customer loved my work, and I was critical to the project as its architect and innovator. My reviewer, who was an older white man, sat me down and praised my accomplishments and gave me great marks. I was excited and happy that I would finally get my reward. When he gave me the review sheet it showed a three percent raise and no position change. Before I had a chance to even say a word, he looks at me and says, "You are not getting promoted and you should not seek to be in management. You should be happy just where you are." He then got up and walked out of the room.

All my white counterparts were getting promoted and I was seemingly stuck. This isn't just my experience as discrimination of Black people in professional jobs is quite prevalent. The higher you go, the fewer Black professionals you see. At the senior manager and VP level, Black workers make up just 5% of the workforce, and at the SVP level, just 4%. At the very top, only around 1% of Fortune 500 CEO spots are held by Black leaders. If the current trajectory continues, McKinsey & Company estimates that it could take 95 years before Black employees reach parity at all levels in the private sector[10].

I was on another job where they had a "reduction on the contract" where I found out I was the only person laid off. I was the only Black person on the team. The people who I was more senior than at the time are now senior and highly paid leaders in their professions. The only time in my career that I got a high-level position was one where I was hired sight unseen (my name sounds very European). Once, I interviewed over the phone with a government agency and was brought in for a face-to-face interview where I was told that I would see where my office would be. When I didn't get the job, I asked why I wasn't selected and I was told, "After reviewing the other candidates it was determined that you wouldn't fit our office culture."

I could go on and on, but the point is that from the first day until now I have always felt that life for me has been unfair because of who I am. It weighs on me a lot and even though God has brought me through it all I still feel slighted sometimes in moments of weakness. Sure, I have prayed for many things in my life and God turned them around, but He hasn't changed my ethnicity, and I am not currently a CEO of a multi-billion-dollar company. I am where God has desired for me to be even though I have felt that it wasn't fair when I compare my life to others. I'd like to pause and clarify what I am saying here. God doesn't ever want anyone to be poor or disadvantaged.

God wants us to have the best life possible and with God that is unlimited. God doesn't want us to live in pain or suffering of any kind. God only wants the best for us, especially those who believe in Him and serve Him. What is important to see here is that everything that happens to us is for a purpose that we don't understand. When we are going through a hard life it is difficult to understand exactly why God is allowing us to exist in such a state. In fact, it can sow seeds of anger and rage towards God because it doesn't make sense as to why we were the lucky ones selected for such an awful life. One of two things will happen when people get to this point: One, they will continue to trust God and seek to finish His process or, two, they will fall by the wayside full of bitterness, sadness, and disbelief.

Your experience could be very different or a part of the same as I went through. A hard life of whatever it may be is difficult to navigate. Some are born into abject poverty and disadvantages. Some are born with disabilities and struggles that others don't have. Insert your situation anywhere in this argument and the results are still the same. The feelings of hopelessness and endless struggles are a part of some people's everyday life. I can honestly say that it seems unfair, and, in many ways, it is. These aren't little events that happen every now and then, but it is what every moment of every day is like. The reality is that as Christians this can be hard to fathom. Why won't God deliver me from this? Why does God seem to heal or improve others, but not me? When it seems that hopelessness is perpetual, it can warp and negatively transform a person's spirit.

This transformation of a person's spirit can inhibit one's faith in God or anything else. It is so easy to miss opportunities to turn things around when life has been one big letdown or disappointment. When life is hard, everything seems like it is too good to be true, and we can be skeptical of things that God may have sent us as a way out. When we lose hope and faith, we become fertile ground for Satan to rake us over the coals of life and keep us in a negative mindset, and the broken road will feel like more broken than ever. The Enemy uses people enduring tough times as the perfect tool to try and distract us from our destinies. He is perfect at whispering lies in our ears to tell us that God hates us and that He isn't there.

It can be easy to believe the lies when every single day of life is a reminder of how awful things are. I feel that you could attribute living a hard life to be described like enduring mental torture. Unrelenting and always present, a hard life makes living seem like a waste of time. No matter what is tried? It fails. No matter what is done? Success seems to be denied. Which is the reason the question of "why" comes about as often as possible. Even those with the faith of ten people will every now and then ask the question of God. I have seen some people who never seem to ever get a fair chance. Sometimes it isn't just them, but their whole family or community. Despite all they do in their relationship with

God change is either slow or absent. They still come to church, still praise God, and things are always less than ideal.

This despair can bleed into every aspect of a person's life. A hard life can merge with a person's personality, goals, dreams, and accomplishments. What makes it seem worse is when the Scripture speaks of unwavering faith and asking that anything be asked in the Name of Jesus Christ that He would do that, and nothing seems to happen. It is taught that nothing is impossible for God and that the Word of God doesn't lie. It is demonstrated that God is a champion for the poor and disadvantaged.

The Bible chronicles miracle after miracle of people who had awful lives that recovered. The man who was by the pool for thirty-eight years or the woman with the issue of blood come to mind. They endured awful things and by their faith, they were well again. The Shunamite woman lost her son, but he was resurrected (2 Kings 4:8-37). All the examples of faith overcoming tragedy, loss, and lack are everywhere, but none of that faith described seems to change anything for the better for everything. Why?

...Not You?

No one likes to be on the receiving end of a tragedy. Nobody wants to be the one to endure pain while others seem to just sit there and watch. No one dreams and aspires to endure pain publicly or privately. Who in their right minds wants to see the stares of pity or have overwhelming feelings of dread and anguish? I know that I didn't want to endure the public embarrassment of some of the things I endured. All while I was serving God by leading worship and teaching the Word of God. I was broken and torn to pieces on the inside and that crept to the outside. Sure, I had good friends and family that surrounded me and loved me, but at the end of the day I was at ground zero and I had to endure what was happening in real-time. I continually prayed and continued to lay on my face before God and asked Him repeatedly, "Why me God? Why me? I serve You and accepted You as my Lord and Savior! Why do I have to continually go from tragedy to tragedy in my life?" God calmly and gently replied with three words that stunned me... Why not you?

Now, I know that there was a show on cable television some time ago that a notorious gangster asked this question to his therapist and the answer was the same, but when we compare apples to apples the gravity of this answer is much different. A therapist who can only "control" what is in their environment is one thing, but when the God of all of Creation tells us, "Why not you?" it stings just a little bit more. Isn't this the same God that gave us life and life more abundantly? Isn't this the same God that said that He would never leave or forsake us? Isn't this the same God that said that He would fight our battles? Yes, He is that same God and yes, He did say what He said. When I let His words ring in my ears and in my mind, I was not just stunned, but I was taken back. At that moment I saw ***NO REASON*** that I had to suffer like I was and here was God telling me that I had to endure this pain. It made no sense to me at all. I was furiously angry with God. My brain was burning out because I didn't understand it.

I don't think that I am the only one that has felt like this. I don't care how holy and righteous a person is no one just hears God tell them why not them and they just humbly bow down quietly with the "traditional" praying hands stance and tell God, "Be it unto me" and that's it. We may say something like that on the outside, but on the inside, we are at DEFCON 1, but in a bad way. I, personally, felt hurt that God was allowing these things to happen to me.

I was in the worst pain I had ever felt in my existence. I was embarrassed, exiled and secluded and all my life I tried to live the best I could for God. I grew up in a Christian home. I served God from an early age. I never did a single drug, got arrested, engaged in outrageous sexual practices and continued those practices throughout my adult life. I was a faithful husband, diligent worker, and faithful tither. I lead worship, taught Bible Study and didn't lead a double life. I thought that I did all I could do to shield me from tragedy and pain. There were people out there who were living anyway they wanted to live and had ***NOTHING*** but good things happening to them. They seemed to be living their best life, but here I was in ruins pondering where I went wrong.

I questioned my faith, and I questioned God role in everything. At the time I was wondering what I had to have done to deserve this sort of torment. I believed in God strongly. I had prayed for others by faith calling the Name of Jesus over them and watched miracles happen. I experienced things before my eyes, and I knew that there is power in the Name of Jesus. Yet, when I prayed for myself and my own situation there was nothing. Not a peep from Heaven. No peace for my soul. No deliverance from my circumstance. No changes in my situation. I would be in torment and would pray for others and their situations would change, but not mine. I was confused. I was bewildered and when God said, "Why not you?" I was devastated. I literally didn't pray for weeks after that.

There was a pivotal situation in my life where everything was so dire and so serious that I wanted out of this life. Things continued to get worse in my situation and I was ***ALMOST*** at the point of thinking that God hated me for some reason. Satan had been doing his best to cultivate doubt, fear, and despair from the day that I was born in my life to prepare me for this moment where he thought that he could snuff me out. The Enemy crept in for the killing blow and for a split second? I almost broke. I almost wavered. I was tired and I had no strength of my own left. I delt that I could no longer stand. I almost fell for the last time to never get up again, but as my faith was slipping away from my grasp, I held on for just one more second. I could see the life fading from my spirit and my heart and I desperately was searching for any ray of hope that God would provide. I had nothing left, but God was all I could reach out to. I had no choice but to pray one more time.

I told God something I had never said before which was this: "God, You are God, and Your Word doesn't lie. If my suffering is meant for Your Glory, then I accept it willingly because if I leave this Earth, I will be with You". As soon as I spoke those words my life began to change, and things turned around. Peace washed over me like a wave breaking over shipwreck survivor on a sun-beaten beach. I was still hurting, but I felt God's Presence again and though my wounds were still fresh and bleeding I knew that the healing was starting to occur. I knew that I wasn't perfect, and I knew that I wasn't blameless in my situation. I knew that despite it all that God must have some sort of purpose for my life even if it was to end in shame. My mind began to ponder what was happening and then I remembered my Bible and I began to read the Word intently like it was new to me, and I saw things like I never did before.

Everything that I struggled with began to reveal itself in a different light. Every place where the enemy would lie and tell me was a disadvantage or pitfall became a way God used me for His Glory. Let me get personal for a moment. When I was young, I felt that God had cursed me with an attribute that is very personal to me, and I don't talk about very much. There is a genetic trait that has been passed down to me (albeit dubiously, but I won't discuss that here) that affects my fingers. My hands are very different (while completely functional), and I used to be made fun of and repeatedly referred to as "disabled" even though I that I wasn't and despite a few small things like wearing gloves and playing guitar like my Dad did, I could do anything that I wanted to do. Still, as a child I wondered why God allowed me to be born this way.

My life as it stood was already disadvantaged in many ways. First, being African-American (or any person of color) is a hard burden to carry in today's world all by itself. I dealt with self-esteem issues, constant bullying, and on top of all of that I inherited the intellect of my parents, and I was, by definition, intelligent and gifted. I was hated by basically everyone and I felt like I was alone and isolated. I remember one day when I was outside alone, and I was so fed up with my life I looked up at the sky and I yelled at God. I was angry at Him for all that I was and dealt with because I felt that it was unfair. I didn't care about anything else, but what I was feeling.

I felt that I was singled out for nothing with disadvantages that I felt I didn't deserve. I looked to my left and my right, and I saw everyone else living what I thought was a better life. I questioned God why I had to be the way that I was. Why did I have to be so different that I stuck out like a sore thumb. I asked God why I had to be persecuted, hated, teased, bullied, and scorned just for who I was. It didn't feel right and no matter how much I prayed my situation didn't get any better. I was mad and I let God have it because I couldn't take it anymore.

When I look back, I realize that God could have killed me without delay for being so rude and obstinate with Him. Here I was, angry at the God of Creation for how He made me. I wasn't having a tantrum, but I was seriously mad, and I started to hate God. You heard me, I started to hate and resent God because I felt that I was a freak that no one wanted. I was the one who had to struggle and strain over everything. I wanted to be normal, and I wanted to blend in with the crowd and not be like I was. I had accepted Jesus as my Lord and Savior, and I knew how to pray. I knew how to believe, and I knew that God said that if I asked ***ANYTHING*** in His Name that He would do it.

I remember how I would pray and cry out to God. I remember what I learned in church, and I had a fundamental understanding of the Bible. I read and knew that God performed miracles. I knew that God could do ***ANYTHING*** and all I had to do was do what the Bible said. I did everything I knew how to do, and nothing changed. I was still who I was, and I was furious.

At first, I was wondering why it didn't work. Did I mess up? Was I kidding myself? Was God even real? (I wasn't an ordinary child.) I would sit for hours before I shook my fist at God pondering these things. I would be in my room or outside sitting on the old picnic table that my Dad had built for us. I would think and think and think about these things and my mind would swirl in countless circles. I never told anyone what I was thinking or feeling because I felt that no one could understand. When it all finally boiled over and I let God know how I felt about my life and Him was when, for the first time, I heard the Voice of God.

His voice was not like anything I had ever experienced before. His Voice, to me, was a combination of thunder, peace, and images. It was like I was too slow to capture all that God was saying, but just enough for me to understand. I knew that He was real and that it was His Voice and not my own. I heard that same voice before when I was being prayed for by my Aunt Sarah once at my grandmother's house. I knew who it was, and He wasn't playing around with me. I was humbled and folded like an envelope because I was afraid of what was about to happen. All God told me in that moment was, "Trust Me…" Not a single explanation or justification, but that I was to trust God. Period. That's it.

I remembered what God said, and I remembered all the many times that God had rescued me, and I had to take what He said to heart and hold it there. I didn't understand anything, but I knew that God was real. I had to convince myself that no matter what was happening and how long it was going to happen that God loved me and was in control. I had to understand the gravity of my situation and realize that God is still in control, and He is still on His Throne. He has not forgotten any of us and His Eye is still on the sparrow, and we need to remember that He is still watching over us. He loves us and He cares for us. We are not pawns on His chessboard, but we are His children.

So, let's go back to the question: "Why not you?" God uses life situations to grow us in faith and practice. Faith is something that is built or grown and never given. Read Hebrews Chapter 11. All those people had to ***GROW*** faith and earn their stripes. I've yet to see anyone in the Scriptures that just magically had strength and faith to do it all. Sorry to disappoint, but that is not real life. Even Jesus had a moment in His flesh. "Father, let this cup pass... Not my will, but ***YOUR*** Will be done" is what He said (Matthew 26:39).

His flesh said no, but His spirit said yes. Let the pain come and your mind and body may feel every drop, but let your spirit say, "it is well" and keep it moving. We are chosen. We are made for this. The walk is hard, but God is there to give us what we need to overcome it. If it is for restoration? To God be the glory! If it is a loss? To God be the glory? Why? Count it ***ALL*** joy. Not just the flashy parts, not just the good parts, but ***ALL OF IT***.

Remember these words that the apostle Peter shared with us:

BUT YE ARE A CHOSEN GENERATION, A ROYAL PRIESTHOOD, AN HOLY NATION, A PECULIAR PEOPLE; THAT YE SHOULD SHEW FORTH THE PRAISES OF HIM WHO HATH CALLED YOU OUT OF DARKNESS INTO HIS MARVELLOUS LIGHT: -- 1 PETER 2:9 KJV

When God chooses us, we must be ready to accept all that comes with Him calling us to be His people. We must understand that being chosen comes with a very high price. We don't always understand what that price can be until we live our lives in Christ. This is the answer to "why not you"! For everything that God allows us to endure is for His Glory and for our story. Our testimonies can be more powerful to those who don't know Jesus than anything that could be said from a pulpit. When we are chosen to go through things God knows that we can make it through, but we must put our full trust in His processes. Look, it is a myth that God won't put more on you than you can bear. Stop believing that lie. God will put on you what He desires for you to grow and be shaped in His plans for us. I believe that He desires for us to encounter situations that only He can step in, intervene, solve, and show us how much we need Him.

God knows what our story will do for others. We don't suffer just for God to sit back and gloat that we are helpless without Him. Our lives can be the only Bible some people will read before they encounter Christ. Our stories prove the goodness of God. Our testimonies show others that despite the tribulation, God will bring you out. God also needs for us to cultivate a level of faith or anointing that He will allow us to use to uplift the Kingdom of God. There are people waiting on what God is shaping us to become. It doesn't matter whether it is millions of people or just one, God can and will use us in the Earth to gather in the harvest of souls before it is too late. Every life has a purpose and every situation, good or bad, is for God's Glory. Rest assured that God knows what He is doing!

Stop second guessing God. Stop allowing Satan to corrupt your faith despite the times being so tough that you want to give up and quit. Don't allow seeds of doubt to sprout up weeds to choke out your faith. The broken road of life is hard to walk many days, but God will take us through. We are still blessed, and we are still favored by God. No matter the situation, God is your biggest cheerleader, and He loves you unconditionally. Your story isn't over yet, and the chapter currently being written in your book of life may still be in progress but change the narrative in your mindset and let go and let God. Let God finish the story His way and trust His ending. Even if you don't like what He does with your life know that it is for your good. Know that it is all for God's glory. Rest assured that you aren't forgotten, and I cannot say this enough. Trust God and keep praying even if you don't hear anything back from Him. God heard you. God sees you in the darkest of midnights and He hears you even if you don't say a word. If I can impart just one thing from all that was said in this chapter, just remember this: ***DON'T GIVE UP!*** God is far from being done with your life and what He desires you to be.

CHAPTER REFERENCES

[1] Fusil, E. (2023, June 23). *Titan sub: Expert explains what 'catastrophic implosion' means and the final moments.* Nationalpost. https://nationalpost.com/news/titan-sub-expert-explains-what-catastrophic-implosion-means-and-the-final-moments

[2] Taylor, E., Guy-Walls, P., Wilkerson, P., & Addae, R. (2019). The Historical Perspectives Of Stereotypes On African-American Males. *Journal of Human Rights and Social Work*, 4(3), 213–225. https://doi.org/10.1007/s41134-019-00096-y

[3] Alexander H. Stephens - Career, Facts & Role in Confederacy | HISTORY. (2009, November 9). *HISTORY.* https://www.history.com/topics/american-civil-war/alexander-h-stephens

[4] Jones, E. (2022, May 5). In Mathews, A Heated Debate Over Lee-Jackson Elementary Resurfaces. *Daily Press.* https://www.dailypress.com/2020/07/22/in-mathews-a-heated-debate-over-lee-jackson-elementary-resurfaces/

[5] Noble, Dana. (2023, August 4). *Why Are Black Maternal Mortality Rates So High?* Mayo Clinic Press. https://mcpress.mayoclinic.org/women-health/black-maternal-mortality-rate/

[6] Centers for Disease Control. (n.d.). *Racism Is A Serious Threat To The Public's Health.* Racism and Health. Retrieved December 26, 2023, from https://www.cdc.gov/minorityhealth/racism-disparities/index.html

[7] Interlandi, J. (2021, November 9). Why Doesn't America Have Universal Health Care? One Word: Race. *The New York Times.* https://www.nytimes.com/interactive/2019/08/14/magazine/universal-health-care-racism.html

[8] *Black Employees Not Only Earn Less, But Deal with Bad Bosses and Poor Conditions.* (2023, August 8). HBS Working Knowledge. https://hbswk.hbs.edu/item/racial-inequality-in-work-environments

[9] Aladangady, A. (2021, October 22). *Wealth inequality and the racial wealth gap.* https://www.federalreserve.gov/econres/notes/feds-notes/wealth-inequality-and-the-racial-wealth-gap-20211022.html

[10] Connley, C. (2021, May 4). Why Black Workers Still Face A Promotion And Wage Gap That's Costing The Economy Trillions. *CNBC.* https://www.cnbc.com/2021/04/16/black-workers-face-promotion-and-wage-gaps-that-cost-the-economy-trillions.html

4

Hurt From The Church

I would like to take a moment and explain a few things that I will cover in this chapter. This is about ***REAL*** hurt from the church and not the "hurt" that comes from being exposed to the truth. The truth does convict and that can feel like being hurt because it turns their world upside down. If someone feels "hurt" because they have been exposed or because they are living contrary to the Word of God, this chapter is not referring to you. I also wish to clarify that I am not attacking any denomination, ministry, tradition, or faith. I am not here to say who is wrong and who is right. Only God can do that, and I am not Him.

When I speak about these things I am speaking of things that can cause harm for people in and out of the church house. This is not me levying intention on anyone, but I am sharing examples of situations that can cause hurt from the church. Please do not feel that I am targeting anyone. I have experience with talking with and counseling people who have gone through many of the things I am about to speak about, but I am not placing blame. God is the judge and not I. As a human, I can only know the side of a situation as I can see it.

If your life is contrary to the Word of God and what is said and done causes you to feel like you are being picked on and scrutinized, I want to warn you about what lies ahead. If where you are being convicted is God-breathed and God-ordained I suggest you sit through it and let God work on you. No one likes feeling spiritually convicted for the right reasons. The old folks used to call it "getting their toes stepped on" and we need more of that today. No one likes when God is chastising them for being wrong. Wrong is wrong and if people claim they were hurt because of people and they go to a church that tickles their ears and powders their backside with a "comforting" message instead of the unadulterated truth that "hurt" is on them their own delusion and they have successfully been conned by Hell.

There isn't a single ministry that won't hurt someone somewhere. It will happen because there are people in those ministries. The only ministry that never hurt anyone was the one that was operated by Jesus. Some things are inadvertent, and some things are blatant and only God knows which is which. Unfortunately, even the truth with the best intentions will cause someone to be hurt. Let us all pray for every ministry around the globe for God to do what must be done to preserve the souls within the Kingdom of God.

A lot of today's churches do not want to undergo being corrected. I am not speaking of leaders who use their pulpits to slander or manipulate people, but I am talking about they who speak and teach the truth straight from the Word of God and not their opinions on how people should live. For anyone looking for an excuse to escape from the truth? Don't do it. It may seem harsh at the time, but it is necessary. Don't use my words in this book to attack your church leaders because if they are doing the work they were called to do? You just put yourselves in the crosshairs of being corrected by God. Believe me, you do not want to go through God's correction. It will either be harsh, or it will be invisible, but He takes His Hand of protection from your life and will allow painful lessons to be taught and learned. Be aware and be careful.

Don't touch the truly anointed of God. If a ministry and the people are using pure, Godly principles and doctrine it will "hurt" because the flesh doesn't want to change. Don't be fooled and don't run away to spare your feelings. Also, even if the church and the leaders are abusing their position or principles go where God says go. If you aren't sure about anything, ask God or someone you trust spiritually. If your intentions are right and your relationship with God is growing, please trust the process. Even in persecution God can grow you and teach you. If God opens a door for you to leave a church? Go where God sends you. This is more difficult for the unsaved so for those who are saved and connected to Heaven please pray not just for your church or ministry, but every church and ministry. Be prepared to be an impromptu mentor and counselor as God leads. This is a tricky process, but we all must trust God and do what He says.

Now that I have prefaced this chapter let me clarify some things with you, the reader:

1. I passionately believe in the whole Gospel of Jesus Christ and the Word of God.
2. I passionately believe in the workings of the Holy Spirit.
3. I passionately believe in the workings of the Five-Fold Ministry.
4. I passionately believe in the Spirit Realm and Spiritual Warfare.
5. I passionately believe that the promises of God don't expire (e.g., tithing and first fruits).
6. I passionately believe in the sowing of seeds of faith to reap spiritual harvests.
7. I passionately believe in taking care of the men or women of God who serve as pastors.
8. I passionately believe that most people of God are not racist or discriminatory.
9. I passionately believe that there is only one nation established by God, which is Israel.
10. I passionately believe that the Kingdom of God is only spiritual and not political.

I say all of this because this chapter will examine churches and leaders who ***ABUSE*** the Scriptures and the Name of Jesus Christ for their personal gain or for power. I am not speaking of legitimate ministries who are truly hearing from God and working for His cause. Just know that whenever we do good evil is always present. Some good people do unintentionally legitimately hurt people and then there are real crooks and shady characters that know what they're doing and don't care. Wherever the true Church is working the Enemy is doing all he can to corrupt and destroy what God has intended. Satan is using good, Godly principles and is twisting them just enough that they aren't perceptible as deceptions and traps. There is no one in existence that is as good as the Enemy when it comes to making a lie look like the truth. Only he can take bitter poison and make it taste as sweet as sugar. He did it in the Garden of Eden and he is still doing it today and so many ministries don't even realize that the shift they are making is destroying the Kingdom of God instead of building it.

So many ministries with good leaders and good intentions are spiraling down the drain because they don't know that they have been duped into a false doctrine, hurtful practices, or a perverted gospel. To every church leader, pastor or whatever you are please understand that I am not attacking anyone or their ministry. I am simply pointing out the fact that legitimate hurt from the church can happen whether you intentionally do it or not. People will always have their feelings hurt because they are made uncomfortable. That's okay because you won't please everyone. Nonetheless, collateral damage from church hurt can have far-reaching implications that can affect many people in many ways. This doesn't make the road of relationship any easier and believe me, it is more prevalent than you think.

Hurt from the church is a subject that is widely experienced but quietly spoken of in the circles of the Church itself. No one wants to deal with it, and no one wants to acknowledge its depth and its severity. One would think that the words "church" and "hurt" would be opposites of each other. The assumption is that the "hurt" come to the "church" to be healed and while that is true it is also factual that most of the hurt in today's church comes from those working in today's church. Let's pause and unpack that for a moment. Most of the hurt felt in churches comes from the church itself and that's not just disturbing, but it's outrageous. In this chapter we will go over the many facets of being hurt in the church, hurt by the church and how it has gone so long unchecked because it is either dismissed or blatantly perpetuated due to the ego and power-lust of church leadership.

So, let me also say this to be very clear: Hurt from the church is a life-changing thing. Don't dismiss it as anything but what it is because ***LEGITIMATE*** hurt from the church is tangible and widespread and yet, it is unseen and the breeding ground for evil. Don't dismiss what could be the truth. We must seek God's discernment of situations and hear from the Holy Spirit for the truth. This is so covert and so well-hidden within the church that only true victims of this pain truly understand it. Here is an obvious statement that will clarify everything: If there are humans involved there will be pain. Plain, simple, and to the point. It is unavoidable, yet God is always there to pick up the pieces and help us along to heal.

While that is true, just like any doctor, unless we are unconscious and unresponsive the doctor won't act on our behalf. Our houses of worship are consciously run by people who may or may not understand what they are doing to people. Some of it is because of old traditions that won't die. Some of it is by lack of understanding and spiritual naiveté. Some of it is because of manipulative spirits. Regardless of the causes, we will delve into the world of hurt from the church, which I will divide into these classes:

1. Out-Dated Traditions
2. Lack of Spiritual Connection
3. Lack of Understanding
4. Ministerial Manipulation
5. Apathy
6. Politics
7. Racism
8. Sin

It is impossible to cover everything in each of these sections, but I will pick a few things I have experienced or have heard from many others about how they experienced hurt from the church. The experiences that you may have could be different or a combination of many varied factors and I pray that you will find the relief that you need. God sees true legitimate hurt from the church, and He will make all things right in the end, so please trust Him to do what you need versus what you may want.

Out-Dated Traditions

Before anyone blows a gasket, let us define exactly what is meant by the term "outdated traditions". Foremost, the ***WORD OF GOD*** is not outdated, it is true, and it is the standard for our lives and our houses of worship. Period. I will always stand with the Word of God and will not water it down or dismiss its powerful and relevant guidance. Scripture is fresh, current, and ahead of its time. There are no other ways to say this, and I will say it loudly and boldly declare it to any and everyone who wants (or doesn't want) to hear it.

There is, of course, a problem in our houses of worship. It is not that the Bible is outdated, but how we have interpreted the Word to suit our needs versus allowing Scripture to speak for itself. We have levied what ***WE*** feel is holiness or what ***WE*** feel is the way people should develop in church or even approach church. It is so unnerving and ridiculous how some folks treat others outside and especially inside the church walls.

The biggest complaint I have heard from people who went to church (including myself) was what the people were wearing. When inviting someone to a church, one of the things that they will often say is that they do not have anything to wear. This is not the case for some churches, but it is for many of them. People from the type of churches that are so judgmental will tell people that if they are "clean and presentable" that they will be welcome at their church. I bristle every time I hear that because in many cases there is an undercurrent that comes with those words. "Clean and presentable" is anything from suits and near-formal dresses to button-up shirts, slacks, long below-the-knee dresses, and dressy shoes. News flash, not everyone has those items. Not because they are poor, but because it is not in their family or household culture.

I, personally, am a pair of blue jeans, polo shirt, tennis shoes, and stuff like track suits kind of guy at church. I wear a tie to work and rarely wear one to a house of worship. Unless, as an Elder, I must be in Civic Attire, I will rarely wear a suit. I have been serving in ministry for years and I would rather be comfortable to worship God, than all starched-up and in business attire. If that is your preference? Do what is good for you. However, when I visit some churches, I have memorized "the look" of judgement on the faces of folks as they see what I am wearing. The eyes moving vertically, sometimes the gaping mouth, the shaking head, or the obviously fake smiles as I approach them. It gets even worse if I am going to an instrument or the podium. I have seen that look given to the regular people, the poor family or worse the "sinner" who is searching for answers. Some of the biggest offenders of this are the "friendly" church ushers.

I am more than aware of what an usher does and the role they play. I used to be an usher, and I remember all the Scriptures, and such used to describe them in the traditional sense. Of course, I also know who the gatekeepers were at the temple and trust me, today's ushers would not like to do the things they did back then like verify every male's circumcision status, but I digress. I have seen some ushers give the dirtiest looks to people when they come in the church. Have you ever seen them before? Picking a guest's wardrobe apart with their darting eyes and the torn-up look on their faces.

God forbid the guest is a female with a skirt above the knee or noticeable breasts. I have seen ushers give females a "modesty drape" to cover their legs so that the elders or pastor will not get an up-skirt view of their valuables. Most guests who are not in "church attire" get paraded and sat up front to be on display or far away from everyone to be made to feel unwanted. The hurt starts and grows from the first moments they arrive to that church and most never come back.

Let us just start with the most obvious things first. Why are females judged so harshly over their attire? Why do many churches home in on skirt length or exposed cleavage to the point that they make people uncomfortable? Look, I am not talking about the church temptress who is flaunting their goodies to everyone to cause people to drool and lust over them. People need to have spiritual discernment and recognize that, but I will save that discussion for later. What if "club attire" was all that they had? The fact that if they came with the intention of getting answers for their life from a forgiving Savior who are you to judge them? At least they came! Leave people (especially females) alone and how they dress. I do not see these habitual judges giving modesty drapes to males that wear super-tight pants or wear gray sweatpants and no underwear.

For the record, ***I AM NOT*** talking about ushers who are rightfully doing their jobs when someone is ***OBVIOUSLY*** trying to cause trouble in the church with their too revealing attire. There is just the ***RIGHT WAY*** to address people in that situation. Show grace. Be kind. Be in the Spirit when talking to people. If they get offended after that it is because of their rebellion. It is just so easy for people to do the right thing in the wrong way or the wrong reason that causes someone who truly doesn't know that they may be offensive in their clothing choices. Otherwise, let people come as they are (not just on special Sundays) and show people the love of Christ.

The same goes with people who are poor, dirty and may even stink of drugs and alcohol. Treat them like the father did the prodigal son. Wrap your arms around them and love them with the love of Christ. Who cares if their shoe has a hole in it! Who cares if there are shirts outside of pants or if someone comes in with shorts? Let them come hungover, let them come still on a lingering high. They could have just turned a trick or just shot up. Let them come as they are. They may never have been to a church before and show up wearing baggy jeans and tennis shoes. Let them come.

Someone could have run from an abusive situation and came with what was on their backs. Let them come. Gay, straight, queer, transgender, transsexual does not matter. Let them come. If we set an atmosphere that allows God be God and draws people to Him? Do that. Those are souls that need Jesus. They came looking for Him to make them feel welcome. Because if we do not, they may never come back. They may never meet Jesus because we didn't greet them in the love of Christ. Jesus hung with many diverse types of people and not one time did He judge them. He met them where they were, and we need to meet people as they are.

Do patients come into the Emergency Room all neat and clean after an accident? What about a woman who is giving birth? What if her water broke in the parking lot? Should she be expected to clean it all up and be "presentable" before she came in? Should the one with food poisoning only come in if their breath does not smell like vomit? So why do we tell people who come to the church to come in like they are already healed and fixed up? Why do we expect unrealistic things from the unregenerated? The church is a spiritual hospital, receive the wounded as they come and let Jesus heal them and set an atmosphere that will allow them to meet Christ. Only He can draw them closer to Him, and they can grow in Jesus, and ***HE*** will change in their lives what must change and that includes their attire!

We do not get to say how God will do that. Remember the Ethiopian Eunuch? Want to know why they were turned away from the Temple? Because he was castrated and dressed effeminately. He was truly hungry for God and even studied the Word. Philip met him where he was, preached to him and he was baptized on the roadside. Not once did Philip tell them that they needed to change their clothes. We need to be like Philip. We need to encourage people to love Jesus no matter how they first come. Get them in the Word of God. Worship God like crazy in spirit and truth around them. God is the Great Physician, and He will do what must be done. We should just do what He wants.

Before I leave this subject of attire, this is not just for the unsaved visitor, but too for the follower of Christ who dresses in their own way. Let me stop and say this. We are all working on our soul's salvation (Philippians 2:12), and we are in various places in our development or our life's journey. Some people need "church attire" to feel like they are "church people" and others do not. Let me be open and share my past experiences. I was criticized many times because I was a church official, and I did not wear a tie (some said suit jacket), or I did not seem "ministerial" in their gaze. Then after I open my mouth and let God use me, they "somewhat" treat me differently. I have ministered from the pulpit wearing sneakers, jeans and a printed t-shirt and never batted and eye (and it ***WASN'T A YOUTH SUNDAY***).

I am used to people sometimes prejudging me, but many others are not. It is hurtful for someone to "help" you by telling you that what you are wearing is offensive or inappropriate in the wrong way. The wrong way is when you are putting the decorum of the building ahead of the state of people's hearts and lives. If God truly leads someone to speak to someone, they should do that. If not? Keep your mouth shut and let God speak for Himself. I have seen whole families leave a good, Bible-believing and Spirit-filled church because of silly things like dreadlocks, casual clothes and even make up styles. That is a tragedy and lives could be at stake.

Good people with hearts burning for Jesus have been run out of churches over their outward appearance and that hurt takes a long time to go away. We quote the Scriptures that say that God looks at the heart, but many people do not follow that advice. The old saying "don't judge a book by its cover" only seems to apply to books or things outside of the church. Again, there is a major difference between judgement and discernment. If people need to be spiritually fed let them come even if they are wearing rags. We do not get to choose who God works in and through. Churches do not need a "dress code" to maintain holiness. Teach the Word, glorify Jesus and be like Jesus and Jesus will operate and do what needs to be done. Our ministries need to ***TRULY*** be earnestly in God's Will, and our opinions need to stay to ourselves.

Beyond what people wear is another long-standing tradition that is a little controversial and many might disagree with me here. Some people may be familiar with things such as the somewhat unofficial "twelve-year-old" rule where when a child reaches the age of twelve, they must go give the preacher their hand or be "confirmed" into their denomination. We all know where this twelve years of age concept comes from and that is from the pages of the Bible.

In Luke 2:41-52 we see the account of how when Jesus' family went to Jerusalem for a feast and when it was time to go home Jesus stayed behind and his parents didn't know it. When they went back looking for Him, they found the young Jesus in the Temple speaking with the doctors who were amazed at His wisdom and knowledge. This is where Jesus told His parents in verse 49, "How is it that ye sought Me? Wist ye not that I must be about My Father's business?" Many call this the Age of Accountability, and it is the model for this tradition of being twelve years old and ready to be about the Father's business.

Let's stop here for a moment. If a child is truly ready to receive Jesus Christ as their Lord and Savior let them be encouraged to go through the public declaration of ***THEIR*** personal faith when they are ready to express that affirmation of faith for themselves. Just shoving a child to walk down the aisle because that is what happened to you is not only ridiculous, but also dangerous if they are not ready. Here is why this is dangerous.

If someone is forced to "give the preacher their hand" and become a member of a church before they truly have accepted Jesus Christ as their Lord and Savior there is a serious risk that they will be so overcome by the "pageantry" of the occasion as well as the pressure of not wanting to disappoint their parents, the pastor or others these children may masquerade themselves as being saved or may even think that they are saved because they did what their parents or others have done before them.

This leads to spiritual confusion and could lead to limited spiritual growth in the future because of the delusion that repeating this traditional action always leads to salvation. Each person in this world needs a personal connection and a personal acceptance of Jesus Christ as their Lord and Savior as He leads them. Can children get saved this way? That is between them and God, but I know many that didn't get saved until later or a few that accepted Jesus earlier. To continue to practice this ritual nullifies the power of God to reach a soul when it is truly within His Will.

There is another outdated tradition that is linked by social constructs and the mindset of the patriarchy. I am sure that I will lose some readers at this point, but the truth is the truth. That outdated tradition is the function of women in churches. Many times, in our history women have been relegated to service roles as well as backup roles in churches. The origins of this are based in our history as human beings. When we look at the past men were the predominantly dominant people in society and women were just bearers of children servants and households and anything else that men desired. Even in scripture we see that women did not necessarily have leadership roles or roles where they felt that they had any kind of dominance over men.

Even the apostle Paul said that he did not permit women to teach or have room over men which was not necessarily what God had intended but if you look at what he said he was saying it was his opinion let's look at the passage together:

IN LIKE MANNER ALSO, THAT WOMEN ADORN THEMSELVES IN MODEST APPAREL, WITH SHAMEFACEDNESS AND SOBRIETY; NOT WITH BROIDED HAIR, OR GOLD, OR PEARLS, OR COSTLY ARRAY; BUT (WHICH BECOMETH WOMEN PROFESSING GODLINESS) WITH GOOD WORKS. LET THE WOMAN LEARN IN SILENCE WITH ALL SUBJECTION. BUT I SUFFER NOT A WOMAN TO TEACH, NOR TO USURP AUTHORITY OVER THE MAN, BUT TO BE IN SILENCE. FOR ADAM WAS FIRST FORMED, THEN EVE. AND ADAM WAS NOT DECEIVED, BUT THE WOMAN BEING DECEIVED WAS IN THE TRANSGRESSION. NOTWITHSTANDING SHE SHALL BE SAVED IN CHILDBEARING, IF THEY CONTINUE IN FAITH AND CHARITY AND HOLINESS WITH SOBRIETY. – 1 TIMOTHY 2:9-15 KJV

Before I continue, please understand that I know that the apostle Paul was a great teacher, and he was an apostle sent by God. However, I must also remind you that Paul was a human being. During that time in that region of the world that Paul was preaching to, women tended to have dominant roles, especially in a lot of the Greek and Roman culture. Women were exalted priestesses; they were leaders in different cults and other movements and men were relegated to minor roles.

With that said we need to also remember that in Hebrew or Jewish culture women were not allowed to be dominant in any way. Paul even alluded to this in the passage by saying that Adam was first formed then Eve and Adam was not deceived but the woman being deceived was in the transgression. In Hebrew society women were not allowed to be anything but the bearers of children and whatever the man wanted.

Notice in verse nine that Paul said, "but ***I*** suffer not…" He never said God said to not let a woman to teach, but he said that ***HE*** did not allow a woman to teach or usurp authority over the man but to be in silence. We need to recognize the difference between the opinion of a person versus the Will and Word of God. Now, let's put this into perspective. The writings of Paul in the New Testament of the Bible were letters, or epistles, to people and to churches all over the world. This means that we are reading Paul's mail to other people. These were his opinions and his feelings as he was being an apostle to the churches and to the people that he was raising up to do Kingdom of God business. He spoke to the needs of each addressee.

In the Bible women have been prominent and they have been dominant in the work of God regardless of the function. You had Deborah who was a judge of Israel. You had the first carrier of the gospel with the women who went to the tomb when Christ was resurrected. There are many other instances where women did things even in Jesus's ministry. Remember where it said that they supported the ministry of their own means? There has never been a time where God has restrained or minimized the contributions of women to not just society but to the willing work of God. We as our modern-day society still have a patriarchal opinion of how women should function.

We don't believe women can be real leaders because we think that they are too emotional or unstable or not smart enough or good enough to do the job that we know that they can do. Unfortunately, the same problem exists in today's church just like it did back in the days of the apostle Paul. Women are relegated to not be true functioning components of the ministries in many churches around the world. I have seen and known many powerful women of God who were restricted just because of their gender and that is unfortunate and is an injustice to them.

There are many churches and traditions that refuse to ordain women. To me, this is a major sticking point in issue because we cannot discount any vessel God has called into ministry. These same churches will ordain a woman to be an evangelist or simply a minister but never an elder or never installed as a pastor.

They will appoint women as deaconesses but never as a Deacon. In other offices, such as bishops or apostles or even overseers are usually reserved for men only regardless of how qualified a woman in that position could be.

In some churches they won't even allow a woman to stand in the pulpit but force them to use a lectern on the floor of the sanctuary. What sort of nonsense is that? Where does it say in the Scriptures say that only men can speak in the pulpit or on a platform? Why is it that short sighted male leaders will use the scripture to discriminate and exclude women just because they feel it is the traditional way to do things?

The concept of women serving in ministry hits close to home to me because one of my aunts was a powerful woman of God and an incredible pastor. I have known and served with other women who have been relegated to small bit parts in ministry just because they're female and not a male. I have known of other great women pastors who were not allowed to be ordained just because they were a woman and that, my friends, is a mistake. We don't have any business telling God who He can call and who He cannot use just because they are not a man. Yes, I know that there are passages in scripture where Paul gave the qualifications of a Deacon or an elder or Bishop or whatever you want to call them that they had to be the husband of one wife. I get that, but we also still must remember that the times that Paul was living in were traditionally male-dominated.

This does not mean that I am saying that the gospel that Paul wrote was flawed; I am not alluding to that in any way. What I am saying is that Paul was still a man he was still in the flesh, and he was still tied to his opinions and his own cultural influences from that time. How do I know that? Remember that Paul was a trained Pharisee. A pharisee an adamant and vigorous student of the law of Moses of course he would have adhered to the same social norms and customs that the law of Moses perpetuated in Jewish society at that time.

Not one time in any scripture will you find a woman being a priest or being a Pharisee or a Sadducee. Yes, I also know that during the time of Moses only the men were selected as priests in the temple to our knowledge. We know that traditionally it was the sons of Aaron who were chosen to serve as the first priest as well as the other members of the tribe of Levi. Yet we also need to remember that God Himself has never said that a woman could not serve in ministry; not one time.

Fast forward to modern times and we have situations where women who have been called by God directly and gave them a commission to serve in the Kingdom of God. These women went to the leaders of their churches or ministries and declared what God had said only to be turned down humiliated or embarrassed because those leaders said that they were not fit to do this because they were a woman. Some of those leaders were also women. There are many churches today that will not allow a woman to preach the word of God, serve in any type of leadership position, or be anything besides an usher, a nurse, a choir member, a Church Mother, or anything related to what is traditionally thought as a female role in their church. It doesn't matter what God does through them, and it doesn't matter what God manifests through them because some male pastors or leaders refuse to allow a woman to serve in positions in churches such as elders or ordained ministers or anything that has an ordination associated with it.

I have seen powerful women of God leave ministries in disgust, heartbreak, or disbelief because someone told them that what they heard from God was a lie because God would never use a woman like that. Conversely, there are many women who are discounted by men regardless of what God does through them just because they are a woman also. I have witnessed a powerful woman of God in a church begin to preach and certain men would refuse to hear anything that they had to say even if God himself was speaking through her mouth. I have seen men leave ministries that appoint a woman as a pastor or an elder or whatever it might be just because they're a woman. I have also seen many women who have been hurt or young girls who are growing up in God in these ministries who feel that they are not capable because of what men have said about the abilities of women, and that is very wrong.

These women are mistreated, discounted, and maligned to be either wicked or just completely wrong and it causes heart shame pain that should not have existed in the first place. It is a sad thing that men in some churches will turn their nose up at a woman being used by God and I personally feel that it's because of jealousy that God didn't choose them to do the job. There are a lot of churches in our world today that have more women than men and the lack of men causes a vacuum, and God will fill that vacuum by allowing a very capable, powerful, anointed woman of God to fulfill those roles. As men, we cannot be upset that God chooses a woman to do a role in the Kingdom of God just because she's female! It is utterly ridiculous that we just decide that a woman can't do the job just because she's not born with the male anatomy. It is foolish, it is abominable, and it will cause hurt in the church.

Any woman of God who is hurt by nonsense traditions like this can be seriously damaged by such backward thinking. These women know that God had called them, and they know that God is working through them, and yet they are denied by a leader who is short sighted and is not correctly hearing the Voice of God. We cannot let social traditions to cause us to break the spirits of people who God has called in these last and evil days to serve Him. Let us remember the words of the prophet Joel:

AND IT SHALL COME TO PASS AFTERWARD, THAT I WILL POUR OUT MY SPIRIT UPON ALL FLESH; AND YOUR SONS AND YOUR DAUGHTERS SHALL PROPHESY, YOUR OLD MEN SHALL DREAM DREAMS, YOUR YOUNG MEN SHALL SEE VISIONS: AND ALSO UPON THE SERVANTS AND UPON THE HANDMAIDS IN THOSE DAYS WILL I POUR OUT MY SPIRIT. – JOEL 2:28-29 KJV

These words were echoed by Peter on the Day of Pentecost in the Acts of the Apostles chapter two:

AND IT SHALL COME TO PASS IN THE LAST DAYS, SAITH GOD, I WILL POUR OUT OF MY SPIRIT UPON ALL FLESH: AND YOUR SONS AND YOUR DAUGHTERS SHALL PROPHESY, AND YOUR YOUNG MEN SHALL SEE VISIONS, AND YOUR OLD MEN SHALL DREAM DREAMS: AND ON MY SERVANTS AND ON MY HANDMAIDENS I WILL POUR OUT IN THOSE DAYS OF MY SPIRIT; AND THEY SHALL PROPHESY: – ACTS OF THE APOSTLES 2:17-18 KJV

In both passages Scripture clearly dictates that God's Spirit would be poured out on all flesh. That means male flesh and female flesh. There is not a single restriction placed on women here. Yes, I'm aware that he doesn't say anything about preaching or pastoring but it's compelling to see that God said He didn't care about your gender, but He only cared that you were willing to be used. It is not in dispute that we are truly living in the last days of Time. It cannot be disputed that God is not pouring out His Spirit and things that are happening now are some of those things that happen way back in the early church after Jesus ascended into heaven. Why then do some churches still limit women being allowed in certain positions or offices? Does it make any sense to deny anyone who God has called? Do these short-sighted leaders understand the hurt that they are initiating and perpetuating in those ministries?

Because of misinterpretations and misunderstandings of God's desires all because of a social, traditional construct is where we as humans go wrong. We need to stop thinking that God is limited to what we feel is right and instead we should be paying more attention to what God says is right! If we didn't call them or dismiss them let God handle who's been called! Now why the apostle Paul wrote what he wrote in first Timothy chapter 2 we won't understand, but the same apostle wrote these words in the book of Galatians:

THERE IS NEITHER JEW NOR GREEK, THERE IS NEITHER BOND NOR FREE, THERE IS NEITHER MALE NOR FEMALE: FOR YE ARE ALL ONE IN CHRIST JESUS" – GALATIANS 3:28 KJV

I can admit that seeing these passages of scripture like that seems like a contradiction but, again, we were reading Paul's mail to Timothy, and we don't necessarily understand all the reasonings around that letter. Yet I am convinced that whomever God has called in these times to serve in whatever capacity, whether it be as a pastor, preacher, deacon, or whatsoever it might be who are we to say who God has called?

Has it ever occurred to any one of these male leaders that the enemy is using them to cause hurt to any woman that God has called for a specific purpose in the Kingdom? Has it even registered that we are limiting the vision that God even gave to that man to further their own ministry that God has given to them as a caretaker? Where there is pain, there's division, and where there is division there is the breeding ground for Satan to do his best work and cause hurt, confusion, and destruction in the church.

What I ask of every male leader in churches to do is to simply ask God to show them who God has raised up. I asked them to look beyond outdated traditions to see where God is moving today. You must realize that God will hold us accountable for the pain that we cause regardless of whether it's a mode of dress or if its women serving in churches. We need to pause and realize that whatever God has done or whomever God has called or wherever God has sent any one we need to respect God's wishes and stay out of God's business. I realize that everyone won't be won over by this argument and that is your choice and your right. But if you refuse to allow a woman to serve as a preacher, pastor, or Deacon, do the best thing step aside and let them serve, if not in your ministry allow them to serve somewhere else. No one has the right to tell whom God has called that they cannot serve regardless of what they might be.

I almost didn't include what I am about to say next in this book, but I couldn't leave it out. I don't care about the backlash about this, and I will confront the outdated and dangerous practice of shaming people who were found to be in sin. Let me be clear about what I am going to say. I am not endorsing the overlooking of sin. I am not saying that the church should ignore sin, and I will go in-depth later in this chapter. What I am referring to here is the archaic and hurtful act of bringing someone before a congregation and having them to get on a microphone and confess their sin to everyone while they are just standing there in their shame.

I know that some will disagree with what I feel about this, but I also know what shaming has done to many people. If this works in the ministry that you attend? God bless you and I pray that all continues to be well. This has worked for some people and if they don't get hurt by it? So be it. I'd like to focus on the pain that shaming can cause people. When I look at the Scripture, what I find is that the Word of God is clear about how sin is to be dealt with in the church according to Jesus Himself:

MOREOVER IF THY BROTHER SHALL TRESPASS AGAINST THEE, GO AND TELL HIM HIS FAULT BETWEEN THEE AND HIM ALONE: IF HE SHALL HEAR THEE, THOU HAST GAINED THY BROTHER. BUT IF HE WILL NOT HEAR THEE, THEN TAKE WITH THEE ONE OR TWO MORE, THAT IN THE MOUTH OF TWO OR THREE WITNESSES EVERY WORD MAY BE ESTABLISHED. AND IF HE SHALL NEGLECT TO HEAR THEM, TELL IT UNTO THE CHURCH: BUT IF HE NEGLECT TO HEAR THE CHURCH, LET HIM BE UNTO THEE AS AN HEATHEN MAN AND A PUBLICAN. – MATTHEW 18:15-17 KJV

I realize that this passage was about dealing with individual sins between the offender and the offended. What I see here in this scripture is that Jesus advocated one-on-one discussions of sin ***FIRST***. When someone makes a mistake or a bad choice and commits a sin and gets caught in that sin, Jesus teaches that one person goes and talks to that person and that person alone. What I see here is grace at work, because it says that if the person heard you, that you would gain a brother (or sister). That is a restoration or establishment of a relationship. Sure, the person being confronted is not going to like what is said, but grace and love are being shown to allow them to have that space to hear, be convinced with the truth, and then be restored in private. Jesus taught this. Keep this in mind.

Notice next that Jesus said that if they don't listen to you that you are to take another or two people with you to speak with them. The other people are there as witnesses to what is being said on both sides of the discussion. Still notice that level of grace being given to the one in sin. I can see the amount of love and concern that could be shown by dealing with sin in this way and, most importantly, I can see that Jesus taught this method. The settings are intimate and only a potential two or three people know about the sin that was committed by the offender.

It is only at the last stage of the person not listening to counsel that the sin is told to the church. The Scripture didn't say how it was told to the church, but it does show that the church speaks with them as well. By this point, if the person doesn't want to listen after all this process, Jesus said to treat them like a heathen or a dreaded Roman tax collector. The person who sinned was given two chances before the church was told. Now, I can't speak for every church and situation, but my familiarity with shaming and those who have endured it has shown me that the person caught in sin was treated much like the woman caught in the act of adultery. They were brought before the court of public opinion almost immediately.

The old traditional way of shaming, or "being brought before the church" didn't involve one-on-one counseling or a chance to be heard by someone else to help drive the point home. No, these people were brought before everyone and had to confess their sins to each person in the church. When we are in sin, we automatically feel embarrassment and shame. Remember Adam and Eve? They felt shame because they had sinned (Genesis 3:7). They hid from God because they knew that they did wrong. For those who are truly repentant, they will accept that grace, listen and come to repentance. I can see why Jesus said that if they listen that you would gain a brother (or sister). There is a bridge being built because of the power of the Holy Spirit and the heart that has sinned can return to Jesus.

Every level after that initial one-on-one encounter shows a level of belligerence and even though there is grace, there is escalation as the sin is not overlooked and not forgotten until it comes to the point of telling the church. The major difference is a sense of fathering/mothering/parenting that occurs with the one who sinned. Even if we don't follow the model that Jesus described in the Scripture, there should be spiritual parenting going on when handling these sorts of situations. Every parent that loves their child and understands them will parent them according to what they can handle. God never punishes us beyond what we cannot handle or endure with His Power, and we shouldn't put more on our children than they can withstand because that sort of breaking is destructive.

I call this practice shaming when it is done without showing the love and care that Jesus would show when someone was in sin. Even when the church is told about the sin there is still care being shown. A lot of churches don't show that level of grace or love. They expose someone because it is what has always been done in the past. They put someone out there for the sake of exposition and that is where it is wrong. Shaming like this gives way to a culture of fear of sin or mistakes. Yes, we should never wish to sin, but Jesus never used fear or intimidation as a means of spiritual growth. I go back to the woman who was caught in adultery. The crowd wanted to shame her and have her killed, but Jesus wanted her to be reconciled to Him. Look at the differences.

The reason to not practice sin should be because of love for Jesus and not the fear of everyone knowing your business. This is when a ministry like that is more about legalistic practices versus relationship with God. When we know we messed up we are aware that we screwed up. When confronted with sin, a believer who has a relationship with Jesus ***WILL*** feel that weight of regret. That weight of regret, in my opinion, should be experienced just like it was depicted in the Book of Matthew, one-on-one with someone who is giving you grace. A crowd is not necessary unless the one who sinned refuses to listen. I can't imagine how many souls have been subjected to scars and traumatized because they sinned, and they know that they sinned and were embarrassed in front of their entire church.

Look, I know that many leaders do this practice and don't necessarily mean to cause harm. I get that. Lots of outdated traditions like this are done just because they are traditions. So, please, don't think that I am attacking everyone who does this to those in sin. Let's be honest, some people aren't deeply hurt by this and are helped by the experience. However, what about the one who witnesses this happening and fear creeps into their heart? What about the one who knows that they should be caught, and they leave their spiritual assignment because of that fear? This is not me making excuses for them but seeing how Jesus treated sinners makes me feel that there is a better way to deal with sin and not cause embarrassment. If Jesus doesn't expose us all in public, why should we?

It is when we allow our traditions to supersede God's Will is when we make the Word of God to be of no effect. We need to stop and realize that God is God. We need to understand that whomever God has sent or called in these terrible times is whom He has designated to serve in whatever role that God has designed for them. I have seen churches split and splinter because of this misogynistic practice towards women in ministry. I have seen women who God has anointed and called being veered off course because of the rejection of leaders who do not wish to hear God's wishes but instead wish to adhere to social constructs that should not apply in the Kingdom of God.

I just firmly believe that God can use anyone, and He is using anybody who is willing to uplift and build the Kingdom of God. Fragile men need to stop being afraid of women and realize that God can use any vessel that He wants to. Fragile males need to get over themselves and let God be the One who works through the vessel and stop discounting that vessel just because it doesn't appear the way that they feel that it should.

Regardless of what is being done in the past, we must see if it is truly fruitful for the Body of Christ. On the other side of this issue are those who don't mind and thrive on these traditions. To each their own. I think that it is best that if people in ministries don't wish to subscribe to these ideals or experience these traditions they should be allowed to move on with grace to where God will lead them next.

Keeping people bound where they don't wish to be causes pain as well. Just like other disagreements in Scripture, go your separate ways in peace. Grace, peace, and love will always be an aid to ministry. Bondage and fear will never fully equate to fervent and effective ministry.

Lack of Spiritual Connection

Not being connected to a power source when something should be connected creates a state of dysfunction. Without power something that was designed to operate with that power is ineffective and isn't very good for anything. The church is designed to operate and flow in the Power of God and for that power to be transferred, there needs to be leaders and pastors connected to God's Power to lead and shape the people. Some folks are what they are, and they are slow to adapt or change within the boundaries of those who lead them spiritually. Often those limitations are within the realm of a spiritual drive or connection to God. This goes beyond culture and race, which I will get to later. Here we will examine how people around the country are looking for more from God than what their house of worship is offering. This can lead to damaging hurt and pain in people who have their lights snuffed out due to deep spiritual hunger.

When God places in our hearts a hunger for Him when we accept Him as our Lord and Savior, we start this journey with an open road laid before us. God points the way and off we go doing the best we can to get where He leads us. For some, God has placed them in situations where friends, families, and even churches aren't equipped or ready for how God is raising them up. Depending on how and where they got saved or even their former lives have a lot of effects on how their walk with God progresses. Some connect deeply with God and worship like there is no one watching. Some want answers to things that they read in Scripture and have probing questions. Some are called by God into the ministry or to work in the areas of spiritual warfare or deliverance. The problem comes when people don't know what to do when God is pulling them in a direction that their family or church isn't capable of understanding.

Let's pause here for a moment. We, as people, cannot grow wild without leadership and teaching. What I am talking about isn't about people "going rogue" but is about people who legitimately are growing in Christ, and they are in situations where they are spiritually stuck and feel ostracized by their church or family. I add family in this section because most families are tied to a church or church organization. How often has it been heard that "this family is ***BLANK***" or we don't believe ***BLANK*** because that's not how we were raised. Still, there is such a thing as order and sometimes God wants people to stay bridled and confined while He grows them. Rebelliousness is a whole other animal.

For example, God can call someone from day one of being saved and let them know that they will be a pastor. God can do what he wants, but we always need to ask God for the context and timing of what He reveals to us. Some people go rogue and rebuke the structure God has placed them in instead of growing where He wants and going where He sends them. What I am talking about here is those who God is growing in a different direction than their church teaches of their family believes and it causes friction.

With spiritual growth there must be some fire. The problem lies when the enemy swoops in and redirects the lessons. People that God is calling are sometimes made to feel shame and endure guilt-tripping. They are isolated and demonized because they dare step out of the box people made to restrain them instead of into the realm God has designed for them. For example, picture someone in a church where people have a doctrine that doesn't embrace the five-fold ministry. A place where the church believes that the age of prophets and apostles is in the past and that God doesn't speak to ordinary Christians. Now imagine that a person who grew up there their entire life in that church had a God encounter that was genuine and true. For the first time in their lives, they heard the real voice of Jesus. They encountered the realms of the Spirit and were filled with the Holy Spirit.

Let's add a little extra to spice up the scenario. They were a respected leader in that church with many responsibilities and now they have been awakened to Jesus for the first time. Imagine that they are convicted by the Holy Spirit for the pastor's preaching. They see spiritual movements of darkness in the ministry because God has given them the ability to see them. Imagine them asking questions at Sunday School or Bible Study about these things and they are given "brush away answers" that try and tell them that this ministry doesn't believe those sorts of things. Think about how this person might be feeling. They feel alone, dejected and rejected. Their church and family have made them a pariah.

They pray to God, and He reassures them in the Spirit, but they must live in the natural world. They press on and begin to lift their hands in worship to the chagrin of others. They begin to share with others what God is revealing to them and are ridiculed. This person is getting talked about behind their back as being crazy, lost or misled. Their family confronts them and tells them that "this isn't how you grew up" and that "your grandmother is turning over in her grave right now" because of what they are doing. Then this person gets summoned before the Church Board and scolded for being an apostate and spreading a false gospel. They are told to abandon their ways or risk being "sat down" from their duties which comes with a heaping dose of shame. That humiliation being brought up before the entire congregation with "charges" being announced against them or being a topic in the pastor's sermons as being "against the Will of God" or "being unnatural" spiritually.

Here is this person, going where God tells them to go, and their church doesn't have the same spiritual connection that they do. They know that in their heart and spirit that they are where God wants them, but the coals of abandonment and shame are heaped upon their heads. Their church won't even hear about what God has been saying. The enemy goes in for the kill. He will either pour icy water on the fire on their spirit or let emotions drown their souls in pain, rejection, and shame or they will lash out in anger, leave that church, and separate themselves from their family leaving burned bridges and hurt feelings. That's just a general scenario as there are many others.

Often, it's not just about "dead" church situations. Sometimes it's a disagreement with doctrine or practices God has revealed to someone as incorrect. It could be plunging into worship and having a personal encounter with God. It could be a situation where people are connected spiritually, but don't accept the full Gospel. For example, picture a place where the Spirit of the Lord is high and yet prophets are condemned as being false. Or picture a place where prophets are accepted but casting out of demons is not. The permutations can go on and on without end, but it all boils down to a church not having a certain "level" of spiritual connection.

It can be very disheartening and frustrating when someone encounters a church or spiritual leader who does not connect to God in the same way as they do. Mind you, I am not talking about aberrant or spiritually deviant behavior that doesn't align itself with God's Word. What I am referring to here is when people have a closer relationship with God that causes jealous or spiteful feelings of rejection. Some churches are "stuck" at the spiritual "level" of their pastors. If the pastor doesn't get it? It doesn't exist.

Honestly, some pastors and leaders feel threatened by the growth of their parishioners. It's really a messed-up situation. Some pastors get ***JEALOUS*** of people who experience and work in a gift that they do not have. People who are God-sent and God-breathed are treated as rebels or trouble that must be "run out of the church" or silenced for good. Sometimes that jealousy isn't jealousy, but an awareness that if this person continues to grow, that the church might get exposed (we will talk more about that later too).

Religion is poisonous. It is a form of Godliness, and it is not what we need. Religion is what humans created to try and relate to God instead of directly going to God and seeking His way of relationship. So many people are stuck in the trap of religion and those who dare to try and break free are ostracized and ridiculed for doing such a thing. You see, when someone is in close relationship with God they also recognize and crave a deeper connection to the Holy Spirit. When we go to church we desire to encounter God corporately. This is why we are not to forsake ourselves to assemble (Hebrews 10:25). We have the inherent desire to worship God together and when we do it is often that the style of that worship or fellowship can also cause divisions.

A religious mindset is only focused on the precepts and tenets of religion and rarely does it see the movements of God in the Spirit Realm. The next section will talk about the lack of understanding, but in this case, this isn't about understanding the movement of God's Spirit but feeling and knowing that God's Presence is near. I have seen leaders who didn't seem to know that God was moving in their sanctuaries at all. When God is moving in the room it resonates with those who know how to sense and feel the Presence of God. It goes beyond a feeling or a process and those folks who have that relationship with God and His Spirit know these things all too well.

A religious mindset does not always allow the Spirit of God to operate freely since it is more focused on traditions and procedures. I have been in churches where a group of people will notice and react to the Presence of God while others are either oblivious or condemning of what is happening. Now, I am not saying that folks who are in a religious structure aren't saved or anything such as that. What I am saying is that those who choose to embrace God's Presence on a deeper level will want to go beyond the human constructs of what faith in God is all about. I will cover more about these things later, but it is because of the spiritual connection that people have to God helps them understand things about Heaven that religion cannot teach.

I can say that I have experienced this to a great degree in my walk on this road of relationship. I have felt isolated and misunderstood because my spirit would know that God is moving, and others would not be in the same place that I was. I have felt disappointment when leaders would pass over a God encounter or would not discern spirits that God was loudly spiritually warning about. I have had questions that I asked that were never answered and dismissed as nonsense. I have helplessly watched as some, especially the younger people, connect with God deeply only to be lectured by those who were older and told that what they were doing was foolishness.

I have seen people's heart break when they are treated like they are crazy because of what they said that they experienced in God. I have seen whole families leave ministries because they didn't feel welcome anymore because a ministry lacked a true and Biblical spiritual connection with God like either they had or desired. This is not about rebellion or a revolt, but people who want to stay somewhere and fellowship and build their relationships with God. Yet, when things like this occur it can spurn feelings of pain that can take a long time to recover from. When someone is hungry and spitefully turned away it burns into their hearts and minds the feelings of rejection.

The bottom line is that these folks don't want a watered-down message, a pseudo-connection to God, or pacifying traditions. They want a connection to Jesus, and they want more of Him right away! People today are hungry for God. They are thirsty for more and a "brush away" answer isn't going to do it anymore. People who are spiritually famished are searching for answers and prayerfully they are finding the right ones. Why do I say that? Because many who are searching for answers may fall into the traps of cults and "way-out there" ministries that lead to spiritual manipulation (more on that later). If you are this person all I can say is, please be careful and seek the Voice of God first before you do anything.

The pain of feeling strange or weird because they want a deeper connection with God and cannot find it in their church or ministry is just like every other church hurt that can be experienced. Satan can and will use this type of confusion to manipulate people into straying from the course that God has for their lives. Wherever there is hurt like this it can cause people to spiritually shut down and conform to a religious norm, flee from God because they no longer want to be persecuted, or they go off on a wild tangent that can harm them for life. My prayer is that they hear the Voice of God over their emotions and go where He sends them. If it is to stay where they are they get the strength that they need to continue the good fight. If it is to go elsewhere that they follow where God leads them. No matter what the scenario, it makes walking this broken road even harder.

Lack of Understanding

The Bible says that if someone wants wisdom, they should ask God (James 1:5). Sadly, we all don't ask God on a continuous basis for His Wisdom and when it comes to the church we need to constantly be kneeling at the altar and asking God for His wisdom. This subject is difficult because it can be so vast and broad so forgive me if I miss some things. Let me say first that this applies to all sorts of churches. I am not saying that these churches are "bad" and full of "ignorant" people because when we think about it, we are all doing our best to learn what is before us in this thing called life. Unfortunately, regardless of our good intentions terrible things like getting hurt from the church still happen because we don't understand things that people who are in our congregations need.

It is hard being a pastor or a church official. It is maddening what happens in the life of a church leader. The battles alone with a myriad of situations are some of the bloodiest and grueling that people can face. I know it isn't easy and what I am trying to say is for those in situations like these pray for your church. Pray for your pastors. Intercede for your leaders. Lay on your face for them all in ministries everywhere. There is a difference between a lack of understanding and apathy (I will get to that later), yet we still must learn what God has for us to do for the people He has entrusted ministries with. Pastors and leaders need to never be stagnant and grow spiritually just like everyone else on their road to relationship with God.

As it relates to a lack of understanding, I will start with a topic near and dear to my heart, which is worship. Worship is misunderstood and is defined incorrectly. Worship isn't a style of music, but a lifestyle in the Spirit. True worship is an intimate encounter with God, and many ministries do not fully understand what kind of experience that truly is. It is a way of life and worship can happen with or without music and cannot be pigeonholed into a genre. Worship is way beyond a space of fifteen to twenty minutes singing "slow" songs.

Worship is an act of closeness, it is divine motion, it is communion with God, and it is spiritual intimacy. Worship can happen at home, in the car, at work and in church. Worship is an offering of the heart and spirit prepared just for God. Sadly, it is misunderstood and causes friction in many churches. Worship is not "more important" than the Word or prayer. All of these are equal components to a relationship with Christ. Most people take praise and worship for granted and treat it like entertainment instead of cleaning the atmosphere so that the spirit of God can do exactly what He wants to do when He wants to do it.

Some churches are fire breathing, Bible centered ministries in action but treat worship like it's a waste of time. I've seen pastors who don't connect with the Spirit when worship is taking place. I've literally seen a group of pastors chatting about just like schoolchildren at recess while a powerful worship was taking place. People watch and take notice of what is happening and for many, who crave a closer connection with Christ via worship, are often demonized and the worship they need is stripped bare or cut short because the preacher is incessant on preaching. They aren't connected to the spiritual realm and worship is not that important to them. I have seen people leave churches because they hunger for corporate worship. I've seen worship teams feel hurt and rejected because their leaders don't get what worship is. Few things hurt as bad as loving a pastor or a church and seeing them brush their passion for worship to the side.

There have been a few ministries where I have served as a praise and worship leader and met resistance to allowing God to have His way. Now before we get too far, let me clarify exactly what I mean here. We all know the verse in the Bible where it said that we ought to worship the Lord our God in spirit and in truth (John 4:22-24). There are many interpretations people have had over the years concerning this verse, but I tend to believe that worshipping God should be a spiritual practice as well as a truthful experience as to why we are worshipping God. I believe that praise and worship should be our spirit reaching out to God's Spirit and seeking communion with Him, to fellowship with Him, and to experience Him on a greater level than our physical bodies would allow us to have.

When we allow God to have His way and to move as He desires to move, it truly reminds me of when Solomon's Temple was being dedicated, and the Presence of God fell on the temple so much that the priests could not minister (1 Kings 8:10-12). I could imagine that God's Presence was so heavy and so overwhelming that everything human had to halt to allow the spirits of those present at that dedication to truly experience God moving as He so desired. We too can experience things such as this where God's Presence can fill the room, and we can allow Him to have liberty to speak to us to minister to us to heal us to deliver us from the things that keep us bound. There is no greater reward of those who love God than to be able to commune and fellowship in His presence.

Sadly, a lot of ministries don't see it that way. They don't understand that a connection with God can happen with just praise and worship without there being preaching or teaching or whatever it is that ***THEY*** believe that should happen. I have been in services where the Spirit of God is incredibly high and moving across the room like waves over a tropical beach or seashore. I have seen where God is delivering people, healing people, setting people free of whatever it is that is holding them back and yet I have seen pastors and leaders indifferent and sometimes belligerent. It is as if they have absolutely no perception of God moving in the room unless those pastors or leaders are in the "spotlight". I have also seen the other side where a leader will say that true worship is too "edgy" when people traverse the realm of the natural into the Spirit and encounter God on a real and personal level. No matter which way it goes, a lack of understanding of God's Spirit is more than evident.

I have encountered leaders who shut down praise and worship because they wanted to retake the focus of a service for themselves. I have had leaders who questioned the entire process of praise and worship because they didn't seem to understand what it entailed. I have even seen some leaders who are intimidated by those who have that deep and intimate connections with God, and they don't seem to have that same connection themselves. There are plenty of ministries who also rebuff and are offended by the expressions of those who are connected to the Holy Spirit. This isn't just about leaders because many congregations corporately have these same types of feelings and ridicule those who do enjoy an intimate bond with God. People like this will refer to those who enjoy true worship as "holy rollers" or "wackos." Just imagine what the people that they are talking about feel like. How would you feel if you were ridiculed for your relationship to God?

Anyone who has true connection and understanding of worshipping God feels very personal about that connection. Worship is not just a thing to do or to fill time in the service as I have said before, but it is more than just a space of time. Give us an encounter like none other and when people are connected to that it can be very hurtful windows around them especially their leaders don't have that same connection or even understand what worship is about. I personally know many people who will attend certain churches just because of the connection to God and that includes praise and worship. This is truly about a relationship with God versus a relationship with religion.

Just like praise and worship when people are looking for a deeper communion with God and they are not finding it where they currently are they will go hunting for what their spirits are looking for. When there is a deep spiritual hunger, it cannot be satisfied by anything less than the spirit of God. There is no alternative, form, or function that will ever take the place of our true connection with God.

The human side of people will want things to improve or change where they are but eventually the tolerance for resistance will run out. Feelings get hurt and spirits get broken. Some people are left listless and adrift because they don't know what to do. They want the fellowship of where they worship but they also want to be able to worship where they go to worship in a way that truly connects them with God. The enemy knows exactly how to take advantage of these types of situations and cause nothing but hurt, heartache, and pain.

I know we talked about a lack of spiritual connection before, but often it is because folks don't understand why a connection even exists. Spiritual warfare is one of those things. Some folks are completely blind to the war in the realm of the Spirit. Some don't want to understand or see it. Some church pastors don't engage with it if they don't know how, or they have limited understanding. Being ill-prepared for spiritual warfare is dangerous. Not just for the churches, but for the people in them.

A spiritual war is being fought all around us and the church is ground zero. As a nation we don't send soldiers into battle without being trained, but in many churches that's exactly what we do. My personal belief is that a church that is compromised and blind to spiritual matters is a candidate to be the central hive of demonic activity for the community that church exists in. Without equipped saints to take challenges head on in the spirit realm those churches get whipped and beaten into demonic submission.

Where is the hurt from the church? Everywhere and across the spiritual and emotional spectrums. People who are in churches that don't engage on a spiritual level are full to the brim with people battling demons and possessions and don't even know it. They have experiences and challenges and don't even know why things are happening to them no matter what they do. Sickness and pain are shellacked over by a façade of being a regular attender or member of a church. These churches don't teach them how to pray, how to take authority over demonic forces and most of all they don't teach and demonstrate how powerful the name Jesus is. The damage for a lack of understanding of spiritual warfare can take a toll on a community. The person who is seeking answers instead gets empty rhetoric instead of deliverance.

This brings me to another touchy subject that a lot of churches don't handle well. People in situations of abuse are an incredibly challenging set of circumstances and need to be handled with the utmost care. I have seen people who were being abused and were in fear for their lives being told that they just need to pray about it, and everything will be fine. Folks being told to not leave their spouse or situation even though their lives were on the line.

Sometimes people are made to feel shame and scolded for what they must have done for this person to abuse them. They are told in some churches that God hates divorce and that they need more faith to see things through. People are publicly or privately shamed when they speak up about abuse of all kinds. Whether it is domestic violence, verbal, financial, spiritual or sexual abuse, a lot of churches don't understand the ramifications of these things and many genuinely don't know how to handle these situations.

Where there is abuse, there is pain. There is damage on a physical, mental, emotional and spiritual level. One of the worst feelings is coming to the church for help and there is no help to be found. I'm not saying that these churches don't care, but they aren't equipped to handle it and despite their best intentions people get critically hurt and suffer in silence with their knees bent in prayer and their mouths nailed shut by a lack of understanding. Churches need to remember that hurt people hurt people. Pain is like cancer that spreads from person to person like an infection carried by other people. If a particular church doesn't understand how to address abuse it is either full of abused people who bury what they are experiencing, or people leave that church in a trail of tears and go someplace else hoping for answers.

That leads me to another topic that many churches aren't equipped to handle. The topic is mental health. It's not just the church that is ill-equipped to handle mental health issues, but most of society as well. The first thing people think about when they hear the term mental health is the word "crazy" and it shouldn't be that way. Mental health concerns are connected to one's emotions and well-being as a person. There are people out there who have endured emotional and life traumas that a lot of folks don't survive. The pain is real and so are the aftereffects.

Let me say boldly that there is absolutely nothing wrong with being a Christian and having a counselor or therapist. Especially a counselor or therapist that is a Christian and certified to do the work. Some churches need to understand that just because they have a pastor that it doesn't automatically make them a counselor or therapist. Just because someone has lived a long time doesn't give them the skills to give advice and help treat mental health issues.

We should pray about things without question, but faith without work is dead. We must do something a lot of the time. Could God heal it in a split second? Of course, He can, but sometimes a part of our journey is to go through some things. These things could be traumatic and devastating, and we all could use some help along the way. Ministries that have a firm grip on how to deal with mental health issues with Christian principles is what so many people need today. There are some people passing through the doors of the church who shout, dance and praise themselves into a frenzy and still leave church with the burdens they came in with. Yes, you can praise your way out.

Yes, you can worship to get through. God gives us these avenues, and He also has given us the means to get help through people too. We need to lift the stigmas of depression, suicidal tendencies, anxiety and many more. Seek God first and tap in on a spiritual level and then (depending on what God reveals) work in the way the Spirit says to work. If that is deliverance? Work it through. If it's repentance? Work it through. If it's counseling? Work it through.

When people are earnestly searching for more in God the automatic byproduct is a deeper relationship with Him. When people want to know more about God, they will find Him in His Word. Remember, our repeated reference to John 1:1 which told us that in the beginning was the Word and the Word was with God and [is] God. So, to get to know God you must get deeper into His Word. There is no alternative to this. To me, reading the Word of God is like reading a diary. The pages contained therein are full of the thoughts, motives, feelings, and history of a person. The same goes with reading and studying the Bible.

The Bible is not just a book, but it is alive with the Power of God. The Bible is far beyond its pages because when we are connected to God through the Holy Spirit, who is the Great Teacher, He teaches us all things and reminds us of what has been forgotten. Anyone who deeply loves God will deeply love His Word and sadly, some churches or ministries don't have the same fervor as their congregants.

This can be a bit complicated, but many denominations and schools of religious thought don't see the Word of God in the same ways. For every group of humans there is an interpretation of what the Bible is saying to everyone. This is problematic in some cases because where there are disagreements, there is strife and conflict. We have divisions on which day is the Sabbath, how people are to be baptized, whether there are prophets or apostles in today's world and the list goes on and on. This can be denominational, or it could be at the same level of understanding or connection with God of the leaders of these ministries. Whatever the reasoning, there is always a remnant of people God raises up in every ministry that is always seeking to go into deeper depths and higher heights in God. Sometimes these people are met with love, understanding, and camaraderie and everyone comes together and grows together. Sometimes, it doesn't work that way.

One aspect of the church hurt that can come from a lack of understanding is the denial of the working of the five-fold ministry. Let's look at the passage in Ephesians that I am talking about:

And he gave some, apostles; and some, prophets; and some, evangelists; and some, pastors and teachers; For the perfecting of the saints, for the work of the ministry, for the edifying of the body of Christ: Till we all come in the unity of the faith, and of the knowledge of the Son of God, unto a perfect man, unto the measure of the stature of the fulness of Christ: That we henceforth be no more children, tossed to and fro, and carried about with every wind of doctrine, by the sleight of men, and cunning craftiness, whereby they lie in wait to deceive; But speaking the truth in love, may grow up into him in all things, which is the head, even Christ: From whom the whole body fitly joined together and compacted by that which every joint supplieth, according to the effectual working in the measure of every part, maketh increase of the body unto the edifying of itself in love. – Ephesians 4:11-16 KJV

This is one of the passages of Scripture that has caused a lot of controversy in today's churches. Most churches universally accept pastors, evangelists, and teachers in their ministries, but many reject apostles and prophets. There have been many arguments about this that said things like, "only apostles were directly raised up by Jesus", or "the prophets were only allowed before Jesus was born". When we look at what Paul said to the church at Ephesus, we see that Paul was saying that God would give some of each of the components of what we call the Five-Fold Ministry. Why would Paul say this if he was considered the "last" appointed apostle if apostles weren't needed in the church today?

The same can be said about the gift of prophecy. God has given that gift as He has seen fit to whomever He wanted to be used to build up the Kingdom of God. Prophets have been necessary not to just "see the future" but they also declare and proclaim what the Lord is saying in the Earth. There isn't a single place in Scripture that declares that there are no more apostles or prophets. God has not said these things, and I challenge anyone to find the chapter and verse where God declares this. God is still raising up apostles and prophets and sadly, many ministries will horribly reject those who God has called into those offices.

When God has called someone who knows how to hear from Him it is something that cannot be dissuaded easily by the words of others. The call of God cannot be ignored and when one heeds that call and acts on it, it begins a new phase of their walk on the road to relationship with God. It transforms their lives and to be told that they are in error, ridiculous, or blasphemous in the calling that they know they heard directly from God can cause a myriad of emotions and circumstances to occur. Again, we come back to the hurt and shame that Satan will try to use to either discourage, disenchant, or simply cause division within a house of worship. The arguments alone can cause churches to split and fall into turmoil. Hearts can be broken because a ministry who once loved someone can turn their backs on them because they now believe what is believed to be heretical.

Whole groups of people, including families, are divided by the issues of apostles and prophets being valid in today's churches. Instead of churches uniting behind scripture, they squabble and argue over who is right and who is wrong while countless souls are left in the crossfire. There is no reason for us to argue over whatever God said to someone that wasn't ourselves. If God called someone, who are we to argue? If it is for real, it will thrive under God's blessing and if not, it will fail. If someone doesn't understand what God is doing in today's world, they should ask God directly instead of referencing the traditions of human religion to make decisions or judgments on who God wants to use and how He wants to use them. If Scripture said something, then that settles it. We need to start letting God be God and let Him administer what is right and wrong when it comes to what He says to others. God can handle Himself.

In all these scenarios one thing stands out. We need to see things as God sees them. We need to ask God for more wisdom and more insight of the concerns of people. Too many people are walking in and out of the church just as broken and in pain as they did before and sometimes worse. What was good enough for mother and father may not be good enough today. Let me pause, I am not talking about the Word of God. The Word is alive and has all the answers we need and will ever need. Sadly, the attacks of Hell are evolving, and we need to evolve with them. People are hurting and we need to be a healing force in every situation. If we aren't equipped? Get equipped or find someone who is. Once we know that something is lacking, we have the onus to make the changes necessary to fix it.

Spiritual Manipulation

This is a touchy subject and requires a lot of care and I want to be careful. Sadly, many churches have been the perpetrators of the manipulation of their congregants for the acquisition of power and influence over people. They have taken the truths of scripture, the Spirit Realm, and their positions as leaders, pastors, prophets, or whomever they are to hoodwink, steal from, and keep people hungry for the truth of God under their brand of mesmerism to profit from them and satiate their egos. Many of these ministries are either willingly or unwillingly in league with Hell and its minions to bewitch and confuse the people of God or those searching for God. Before you label me as a "lost" apostate and throw this book away, let me explain. Satan is an expert deceiver and some of his best work is not in "the world" as many people think. He has done a skilled job misleading the "very elect" or those in the church.

We must understand the mindset of Heaven's primary adversary to truly see what is wrong here. Satan has already lost and has already been condemned to the Lake of Fire. He knows his fate and yet he is continuing his evil plans to deceive and tarnish the works of God. Why? If I could use the license of my imagination, I could see Satan being cast into Hell for the very last time never to rise again all while giving God the "double finger salute" as he falls in slow motion into the Lake of Fire while billions of human souls he has deceived (along with the angels he is corrupted) going with him. His goal is to try and "hurt" God by taking a sizable part of whom God created with him to destruction because he has nothing to lose. He does not want to go alone because he is petty and selfish.

Sadly, because of this childish behavior by Satan, billions of souls will perish because of his senseless war against God. No, this is not the rosy, sunshine-filled stuff you would expect, but it is real. It is not popular, and it is not full of rainbows, lollipops, and fields of wildflowers. The Bible says that many are heading to Hell on the wide road of destruction. That road will be filled with many who were hurt by the church and hurt by what I like to call Spiritual Manipulation. When I said that Satan has infiltrated the church I was not joking.

The sad part is that most people believe that his work is only in churches that do not teach about sin, have a watered-down, feel-good message that makes people feel rosy about their broken lives. Sadly, that is not his best work. Satan's best work is in Bible-believing, Holy Spirit-filled ministries tapped into the supernatural and the workings of the Spirit of God. Remember, the Scripture says that he will deceive the ***VERY ELECT*** or righteous. The ones who got it right. The ones who work in all that God has for them. The ones that know the truth. Think about that.

Let us unpack this and see it for what it is. Satan has infiltrated ideologies and concepts that should be used to build up today's churches. If a church is not teaching about spiritual warfare, spiritual authority, and the supernatural, it is doomed to be blind and ineffective. The problem comes when most people look at those churches that operate in those realms and they get scared off or hurt and they run away from those churches. Pentecostalism and the Apostolic movement are not wrong in their simplest forms and need to be advanced in today's church with a Biblical foundation. The problem comes with what happens to many leaders of these ministries and the mindsets that seem to evolve in folks in those circles.

Here is where Satan enters and distorts what is good and true. Let us look at demographics for a second. Where are many Pentecostal and Holiness churches found? Who are their primary congregants? Start digging and you will find that a substantial number of these churches are in the country, impoverished areas, and urban centers. I am not "picking on" anyone but notice the patterns. Most of the people who live here do not have much and are desperately searching for hope. I am not saying that everyone in those areas does not have money and on welfare, on drugs, gang-banging or ignorant. These are fertile areas that have folks that are searching for hope and answers. These are desperate for any change in their lives and that is where the issues start.

Where there is a sense of hopelessness, and people are spiritually hungry, our God loves to enter those places and transform lives. Look at Israel when Jesus walked the Earth. People were oppressed by Rome, mostly poor, and searching for answers for relief. Jesus taught a simple Gospel that awakened the power of God among the people. This is what normally occurs in fire-breathing, God-powered churches! People can get exposed to the Spirit in ways they never had before, and God changes lives. Do you think Satan will sit there idly and let that happen? Of course not. This is where the games of deception begin.

The verse that whenever I do good evil is present (Romans 7:20-22) is prophetic for the cause of ministry. Let us start at the first deception. When God uses us for His Glory, we need to stop thinking it is us that has the power. I have watched pastors, bishops, and apostles fall into the trap of the power trip. It happens so slowly over time that many of them do not realize it. Let us be honest, we are human, and we want to be loved and appreciated. We all do. We need to stop kidding ourselves and admit the truth. It is when these spiritual leaders start to allow people in churches to overly adore them like they were a god that things begin to change.

Remember when Jesus told his disciples to go out two by two to minister and He told them to accept whatever they were given? Remember how the Apostles were everyday people of all levels of society who lived humbly. Biblical figures like Peter were wealthy and married. Luke was a doctor. They were business owners and laborers, and they all did not flaunt themselves. Name a single place where people like James or John were elevated to the point of being exalted and showered with gifts. You will not find it. Jesus was said to not even have a place to "lay His head" (Luke 9:58) because it was about serving God and people and not being glorified on Earth.

I get so appalled when people start to elevate their leaders to a near God-like level. I have seen everything from people stopping to stand for when their pastor enters (late in many instances) no matter what is happening in the worship experience to people showering their leaders with hundred-dollar bills. The worst part? These leaders allow it to happen and there is a cadre of spiritual "celebrities" that groom and teach other leaders to allow it. This cult of personality is dangerous and allows Satan to waltz right in and cause hurt in the church. Pastors need to minister and be more like Jesus. Christ had help ministering and He had those who did things for Him, not once will you see Jesus allowing Himself being exalted (except on Palm Sunday which was fulfilling prophecy).

Jesus did not have an "armor bearer" (which is a medieval concept, and not a Biblical one and I am not against a pastor having help) nor did He get chauffeured or put up in the fanciest hotels. I am not saying that preachers don't deserve to be treated well, but many mandate it because of their position. I have watched some pastors get caught up in this mindset and this circle of influence and watch slowly as the enemy uses this to fragment away not just members in the church, but potential people away from their church. People notice this "worship" and "adoration" of pastors and leaders, and it begins to affect them. Where humility and servitude once were more than prevalent, they assert themselves in "high places" and spread that to their congregations. They transform from humble leaders to kings, queens, princes, and princesses overnight.

They demand to be driven around everywhere they are called to go. They believe that people need to "fear" their authority in whatever position they have been called to serve. They allow opulent displays of affection to be shown to them by spiritually hungry people who have genuine love for their pastors. I have seen ministry founders and leaders from their pulpits tell their people and their admirers that it is right for them to be showered upon lavishly because it is Biblical. I have been a witness at conferences where several hours of a worship service were dedicated to raising one-million-dollar offerings ***JUST*** for the pastors using the psychological tactics of "motivational giving" and coercion.

Leaders who think that they are so great that they deserve to be presented with gifts like the Israelites brought offerings to the Temple of Solomon to the Lord. "Sow a seed into ***GOOD GROUND*** (them) and God ***WILL BLESS YOU!***" is their mantra as those who are in need believe that giving their very last to a leader who thinks that they deserve it because they "paid their dues" and now it is their time to be blessed. It is appalling!

I can hear the naysayers talking about the account of Ananias and Sapphira in Acts Chapter 5 where things were laid at the Apostles' feet. Proponents of "taking care of their man or woman of God" will point out that the utmost care and showering of gifts on their leaders is paramount and Biblical. Many of these proponents are pastors themselves and use this to justify their lifestyles or their authority over the people they have stewardship over. I hate to tell you the unwelcome news, but there is some deception here and what they believe is not in Scripture. Go look at the end of Acts Chapter 4 which runs into Chapter 5. Money and goods were laid at the feet of the Apostles not for the Apostles themselves, but for giving to the ***POOR*** and ***NOT*** for the Apostles themselves.

Now, let us pause for a moment. If a pastor or leader has only one job (which is being that pastor) then by all means pay them and take care of them, but we must remember why the church has money to begin with. Ministry requires funding to work and function, but it should be for the spreading of the Gospel and helping those in need right around us or abroad as God leads. A church is not supposed to be a for-profit business. It is like a business, but it is to serve the greater good of the communities they inhabit.

Churches are never supposed to fatten the wallets of the pastor and the "first family", but minister to those who are in need physically, mentally, and spiritually. In my opinion, if a leader has plenty of resources, they shouldn't want the church to splurge on them so heavily and ignore the plight of the masses that are in need too. When Jesus fed the four and five thousand, they served the people ***FIRST*** and didn't even mention about He or the other apostles eating. That's just me.

Ministry leaders need to be Godly careful about this affluent lifestyle that comes from the pockets of the members of the church. I am not saying that pastors cannot be wealthy or live a nice and comfortable life. If a pastor does well financially on their own or blessed by any means other than just off the backs and contributions of parishioners, then they should live their best life. However, if you are a preacher and ***DEMAND*** to be treated in such a way because you are a pastor, bishop, prophet, or apostle and that it is Biblical for people to shower you with money and prestige I believe that you need to stop asking your ministry mentors and ask God directly about this. Whether or not you know it, there is a dark undercurrent to this ideology.

There are people using the gifts God gave them and acting on God's behalf that are looting and pillaging the church of its money. There are shady prophets and speakers going around ministering the Gospel with a twist. Yes, God can use them, and people are delivered, healed, and set free, but the people are covertly groomed to empty their bank accounts at an altar call after God has moved greatly not because of God, but because of greed.

The moment prophecy and the workings of the Spirit are mentioned in any connection to being hurt in the church, people tend to get defensive, and they begin hurling all sorts of things in your general direction. This is not a popular topic, but it is one that needs to be addressed. Let me state again that I believe in true prophecy, words of knowledge, and the entire five-fold ministry spectrum. None of these things can be denied and minimized in today's church and the world. They are vital to the advancement of the Kingdom of God.

The Spirit Realm is real. The Holy Spirit is real. Living the best and prosperous life God has for us is real. Speaking and declaring words of mustard seed faith over one's life and situation is real. Giving with heavenly reciprocity is genuine. Each of these things is not just real, but relevant. God can and will do whatever He sees fit to work miracles, give us prosperity, and give us good success. The problem is when people get caught up in pathways that the enemy has designed to lead us astray from these Godly principles.

There are some unscrupulous folks who "dedicate their lives" to the ministry and do nothing else, but travel from place-to-place ministering in the Name of Jesus using signs, wonders, and powerful manifestations of the Holy Spirit. This is not wrong. This part is how it should be done in ministry because people need to see God's Power in action. There is nothing wrong with being an evangelist spreading the Gospel of Jesus Christ and it is sorely needed in our world today.

The problem arises when this evangelist, prophet, or speaker is invited or deployed to draw crowds with big checkbooks to churches who need a financial boost or notoriety.

This guest preacher uses the Name of Jesus and their gifts to transform the atmosphere and change lives for Jesus and then has an altar call that tells folks that if they sow a seed of "X" dollars God will grant them "Y" while they know that they will get a "cut" or percentage of that altar call offering for themselves. The "bigger" the name or draw these speakers have allows them to command up to fifty percent or more of the offering as their "fee" and may even demand that the host church pays for the finest amenities.

Yet people hungry for God will travel for hundreds of miles, take off their jobs and believe that they must be there, or God won't bless them. This same level of adoration is allowed by those who are ministering, and some seem to feed off that energy. It's like the enemy has tapped into their egos and they feel that it is "their time" after so many personal struggles. Don't get me wrong, I think that it's okay to enjoy personal success, but I say don't do it at the expense of ministry.

The reason for this is that when people get a glimpse behind the curtain of what is really going on it causes disillusionment and chaos as people who pledged their lives to a leader, or a ministry get let down and it breaks them. It shatters their hearts, breaks their spirits and plants quick-growing seeds of confusion. Some people leave the church and never come back. Some leave a powerful, Bible-centered ministry and go to a watered-down, utopian ministry that is light on Bible and heavy on a pacifying "love" that doesn't translate into true evangelism or Holy Spirit power.

Next, I would like to speak about something that I know is very prevalent in a lot of churches and I am not afraid to delve into, but I would like to clarify like I did in the beginning of this chapter about giving. I believe in giving unto The Lord, but there are some who have twisted given into a form of perverted gospel that is founded in some truth. This perversion has caused pain and suffering to a lot of people and because of it they refuse to go to a bible-believing church with power to this day. I am talking about the perversion of the prosperity gospel. Notice that I said the ***PERVERSION*** of the prosperity gospel. There is truth in what the Word of God says about being prosperous and having good success

(Joshua 1:8) and there are controversial things that are being done in churches that are driving people away because they got harmed.

Here is what I mean about this. Just like I was just speaking about those who are not as well off as they wish that they could be, hearing the possibility of becoming rich and not wanting for things is appealing and when folks are desperate, they will do whatever it takes to make a change. Sadly, there are those who take advantage of that and use the right principles but twist them for their personal gain.

They twist the Word of God to get them to increase their monetary giving to fatten their church's or their wallets. The first issue that I have is that prosperity and good success is not only about money. We, as humans, have an idea what prosperity is, and it always involves being rich enough to buy any and everything that we want. The Bible doesn't explicitly state it that way. God does want us to live comfortably, and He promised that He wouldn't leave us or forsake us and that our children wouldn't be begging for food.

This is where the twisting comes, and it relates to what we discussed earlier about sowing into their leaders. I believe that dishonest leaders use the prosperity gospel as that vehicle to fleece congregants, and the manipulation goes to a greater level. Using the lure of the prosperity gospel as bait congregants are made to feel so obligated to empty their pockets that they are groomed to never question the "man or woman of God" and follow their directions without question. Some of these people heard absolutely nothing from God but are aiming to increase their take from a service offering.

There are usually two ways that situations like this end. The first being that God honors the faith of those being swindled by humans and blesses His people because of what they personally believe and declare in the Name of Jesus Christ. That is because God rewards faith wherever He finds it if it falls within His Will and that alone is a difficult topic to discuss. Let me summarize it like this. God is a Father of us all who are His legitimate children. Just like any good parent, He doesn't just give us whatever we ask for just because we asked for it. God is not a vending machine and if we aren't ready for riches or capable of managing a fortune, God will not give it to us. The parable of the talents illustrates this in a way. The master gave his servants the amount that he thought that they could handle. Think about that for a few minutes.

There is not a single verse of scripture that concretely illustrates how anyone gave money to Jesus or any other action of ministry and became rich. There isn't any place where God declares that if you don't give, that you won't be blessed and please don't get me started about the misconception of the passage of Scripture about tithing in Malachi chapter four.

Let me sum that up for you, the tithes originally were meant to support the Levites who worked in the Temple. They only had the job of serving the people of the Temple and "meat in God's House" was about food. When the people stopped giving their tithes of sacrifice because they strayed and went to other gods, the Levites had to go out and work outside jobs because where there were no burnt offerings, there wasn't food for the Levites. Google it and be amazed.

People have been hurt badly by the misinterpretation of the prosperity gospel. People have given their money, and many have gone broke. They have given up everything and had little to show for it. I am not questioning God's timing or His processes, but when a charlatan is orchestrating all of this it makes it painful if that crook is ever exposed. Satan loves to whisper in people's ears when pastors are coming to their churches in extremely expensive vehicles while most of the congregation takes the bus. A pastor can have wonderful things, but if it comes from the expense of deceiving their ministries, they are rich from filthy lucre. I have witnessed people who were hurt badly after hearing about what really happens to their tithes in a church.

I want to speak about another controversial topic for a little bit, and it may surprise the reader. Be careful of spiritual fakes who perform signs and wonders and are tapped into the powers of Hell itself. Think I am off base? Let's go to the Book of Acts, Chapter 8:

BUT THERE WAS A CERTAIN MAN, CALLED SIMON, WHICH BEFORETIME IN THE SAME CITY USED SORCERY, AND BEWITCHED THE PEOPLE OF SAMARIA, GIVING OUT THAT HIMSELF WAS SOME GREAT ONE: TO WHOM THEY ALL GAVE HEED, FROM THE LEAST TO THE GREATEST, SAYING, THIS MAN IS THE GREAT POWER OF GOD. AND TO HIM THEY HAD REGARD, BECAUSE THAT OF LONG TIME HE HAD BEWITCHED THEM WITH SORCERIES. BUT

WHEN THEY BELIEVED PHILIP PREACHING THE THINGS CONCERNING THE KINGDOM OF GOD, AND THE NAME OF JESUS CHRIST, THEY WERE BAPTIZED, BOTH MEN AND WOMEN. THEN SIMON HIMSELF BELIEVED ALSO: AND WHEN HE WAS BAPTIZED, HE CONTINUED WITH PHILIP, AND WONDERED, BEHOLDING THE MIRACLES AND SIGNS WHICH WERE DONE. – ACTS 8:9-13 KJV

What happened back then is happening right now. Let me make a statement that may shock you: Just because it looks supernatural doesn't mean that it's from God. The Enemy can imitate the works of God to those that are bystanders. Think that isn't true? Check out Exodus Chapter 7. Moses and Aaron went in the Name of the Lord and performed signs and wonders that Pharaoh's magicians could do as cheap impersonations. It makes sense that Satan wants to imitate God and how God manifests Himself in the Earth because Lucifer wanted to ***BE GOD***. The Enemy will do all he can to deceive as many people as he can with even miraculous signs, miracles and manifestations.

Bottom line, I don't care whether gold dust did come from the air and landed on you, or sparkly gems are stuck in your hair. I don't even care if someone who is dead got up again or if a secretly false prophet said something that came true. We need to try every spirit and manifestation and see that it comes from God (1 John 4:1) because the fakes are out there. While there are true experiences like this, we need to stay spiritually sharp. These charlatans who aren't from God are blinding folks into a demonic trance and calling it heavenly, which is causing them to be led astray. I know some folks who experienced these Christian shamans and once they discovered the truth, they didn't want anything to do with the Spirit Realm in any way and guess what? That's what the Devil wanted.

There are others who tell their parishioners that they cannot leave their ministry or their "covering" for fear that they will be cursed or not receive blessings from God. This is a lie from the pits of ***HELL!*** How can any person say that they won't be blessed or spiritually protected unless they go through ***THEM***? Who do they think they are? I challenge anyone to point it out in Scripture that if a pastor, bishop, or apostle who is a spiritual leader that leaving their "care" because what they are doing is abusive, non-scriptural or just plain wrong that God (in His infinite wisdom) will curse this person because of a human who is not obeying

Him and abusing His Name. I will eat my words and unpublish this book and any other book at once. This is abusive.

To brow beat people into submission to force them to pledge their fealty to a human leader who has twisted the Gospel of Jesus Christ and has perverted biblical principles to suit their needs, and their calling is abominable. It is detestable and evil. Pastors and churches ***CANNOT CONTROL*** people. Scripture proved this effectively. When the Apostles had serious disagreements, they parted ways amicably (Acts 15:37-39). There was no mention of God cursing them or each of them laying curses on each other. They just parted ways for the sake of peace. If you are reading this and your pastors or whoever, have you in a spiritual choke hold where you feel stuck and know that the Holy Spirit is telling you that things aren't right and that you need to leave? ***LEAVE!*** Don't wait!

Lastly, the other part of spiritual manipulation is the opposite of what we have been discussing. The other contrasting view on this topic is the lackadaisical spiritual manipulation of lulling people to sleep with fluffy, sweet, and unrealistic messages, ideologies and practices that don't prepare Christians to effectively walk on the road of salvation. Whole ministries are filled to the brim of people who never heard the whole Gospel of Christ or who are outcasts from churches like we were just talking about who abuse people into submission.

These "Bible Lite" ministries only give feel good sermons that make people laugh or feel good about their lives and believe me I am not against that at all. We don't need to be "beat up" every time we are in church. However, not telling the whole truth is like telling a lie. Clever anecdotes, funny stories and "soft blow" and powder-puff "hard hitting" stuff is all good for the flesh, but none of that will help a person who is under a spiritual attack. It won't help them break a generational curse. None of that will get to the root of a situation.

These folks are manipulated to spiritual sleep and shielded from the truth. These ministries and pastors watch their churches explode with population growth and not spiritual growth. They condition people to be afraid of spiritual manifestations and to be skeptical of things such as laying on of hands, rebuking spirits, and other aspects of spiritual warfare and life. They will refer to such things as "edgy" and look to change the subject or remove anyone that tries to influence others to the Gospel truth. They prefer lukewarm and powerless Christians who don't question their milquetoast doctrine because they want good-vibes people to come in and bask in a utopia of happiness where little goes wrong and there is nothing but smiles.

If there are issues or spiritual concerns, they want to hide them from view and quietly shuffle them to the background while they maintain the Happiness Hour of church services. These ministries strip people of their spiritual equipment, keep them blind to the truth and the Enemy rarely attacks their ministries. Why? Because a weak and powerless Christian is ***EXACTLY*** what he wants. That's less soldiers on the battlefield to fight his agenda to drag everyone he can to Hell.

It's the perfect scenario and these blinded ministries are leading the charge. Manipulation from the truth into a false sense of security is just as abusive as a ministry that chokes every penny out of its congregation. Using the ultra-abridged version of the Scripture to cut out the "disturbing" parts of the Gospel is in my mind ***WORSE*** than twisting Scripture to abuse and hurt people. No matter which way it goes, God is not pleased with any of it.

These ministries are run by leaders who are afraid to "offend" or "drive away" people because they either enjoy the control of having them there or it is because of things such as financial stability or popularity within other ministry circles. Often, these leaders know the truth and hide it to keep people satiated and coming back for more "positive energy" and goodness. For the sake of being popular they deny the truth and leave a wake of pain and destruction. While the numb and rose-colored glasses church attenders are happy, those who need a real revelation from the Lord are left to languish in a state of yearning. You may say that these people aren't being manipulated, but I must disagree. To be shielded from the truth of a very real God all while those leaders know the truth or are afraid of it is manipulative. Hiding the truth is just like telling a lie and when people find out about it, it will cause pain.

Whenever anyone discovers the lie behind any manipulation it will cause destruction. It will cause people to either be angry at church, God, or the people that lied to them. Possibly all three categories of this can be the target of their anger, rage, and brokenness. Those who manipulate others seek to have power over them and that my friends, is unacceptable. Every manipulative thing involves a lie and anyone who discovers that lie for what it is will react in a certain way. When the lie involves God and the faith of people, it can end disastrously.

To use the greatest truths of Scripture in a bid to manipulate or deceive people for the gains of others never ends well for those who lie. For those who are lied to it can end in brokenness and a possible exodus from a church into something better or worse. God can use situations of manipulation to provide an opening for His Truth. The path to that truth can be difficult if the person listens more to their pain than their God leading them to where He wants them.

From the exploitation of the Serpent in the Garden of Eden until now, being manipulated never ends well. It has broken many people over the years and that gut-wrenching feeling that you've been lied to can be hard for some to recover from. God has never bamboozled us or tricked us into anything. He has always been open, honest, and transparent with His Will and His Ways. All manipulation comes from the Father of Lies and everything that he does ends up in pain. That's why Satan has been hard at work in the Church to do all that he can do to drive people away from God. To be manipulated and then to find out that it was a lie is a deep betrayal, and we all know how that feels. That pain can be crippling, and it takes the Power of God to heal it.

Apathy

Earlier I talked about the problem of lack of understanding and now I want to focus on the other side of this coin which is apathy. Apathy is deadly when the souls of the vulnerable are at stake. I find it so hard to believe that any truly born-again believer would have apathy in their heart, but it is becoming more of an epidemic in some churches. To simply not care about people in my mind spits in the face of Christ. Scripture speaks plenty about not having love for your brother or sister and its consequences and yet we still have it manifesting. There are two forms of apathy: intentional and non-intentional. One is calculated and the other is the result of not knowing what to do or being afraid to do what must be done.

Let's start with intentional apathy or when we choose not to care. We say things like, "That's not ***MY*** problem!" or "Why are they seeking attention?" which comes to my mind. Let me pause here for a quick minute. Yes, I know that there are some pretenders and thieves out there that are doing their best to deceive and take advantage of people. I get it. Be wise. Let the Spirit of God guide you in all things. However, not having love in your heart for those who are truly hurting, suffering, and going through tribulation is just plain evil. Remember the Good Samaritan? Remember the apathy of those who were supposedly the servants of God? It was recorded that two leaders walked by and didn't seem to care. There was never a Biblically documented outcome to that story. All we know is that the traveler was recovering from being attacked and that the Samaritan was coming back to settle the bill.

People who "don't want to get their hands dirty" tend to look down their long noses of self-righteousness and judge people who aren't "like them" or aren't on "their level". I have seen and heard about many instances of this. Mind you, churches need to be wise and not go barreling into every situation just because people ask for help. There ***MUST*** be spiritual discernment and common sense before proceeding with anything. However, we must listen to the Holy Spirit for guidance and be ready to do whatever it takes to assist. This is where the errors set in, and people are damaged, and breeds hurt in the church.

Making a conscious choice not to help people in the church because they don't want to get involved is horrible. They think that people in need are like stray cats. They worry that if they "feed one and they bring others to their door". That sounds like real ministry to me because one brings many, but I digress. Yet I think that when we see someone who is covering a black eye with sunglasses or makeup, we should do ***SOMETHING***. If we see little kids who are obviously hungry, we should do ***SOMETHING***.

When we see someone going through depression and they don't care about living anymore we should do ***SOMETHING***. I say that it's better for a ministry to refer someone to somebody who could help them versus do nothing. Every ministry, big or small, should have an impact on the community they exist in. Whether they do it themselves or partner with another person or organization that can do it, it should be done.

I have known people in ministries who legitimately were living in their own personal Hell. They were folks who were in a crisis, and it seemed like there was not any hope. They went to their church, and the church either told them no or ignored their pleas and cries for help. Whether it was poverty, abuse, mental health or sexual concerns there are people who come to the church and find apathy. They come in drowning and get weighed down with shame or rejection. They come in broken and have people pretend like they didn't see them or their pain. They come in desperate, and people lie to them and tell them that they can't help them, and they need to find someone who can. It's disgusting!

A sad part of intentional apathy is when people choose to forget where they came from. Look, none of us have been saved and sanctified our whole life. We all have a past, and all of us were in a mess at one time. God had to pull all of us out of some things we had no business doing. The crazy thing is that some people get saved, get washed in the Blood and over time they forget where their journey began. It doesn't matter whether it's because they made a little cash or reached the upper levels of ministry or prestige. The grace that was shown to them when they were in sin, they seem to not remember how to give that same grace to someone else. Or someone forgot what it was like to be poor and on public assistance. They forgot what it felt like to be abused or did not remember when they struggled with their sexual issues.

Not all predicaments are committing sins as many troubles are situational. The issues could be socio-economic, spiritual, or they could be a specific health condition (mental or physical). The obvious one that comes up is financial. People who can't pay their bills for whatever reason will go to their local church and ask for financial assistance. As I said before, some people do try and scam churches out of their money, but there are many with legitimate needs and honestly need help. These people are sometimes turned away because of a range of factors. How they looked, where they came from, their ethnicity, or anything else you could imagine would be the reasoning.

This is a judging based solely on what appearance they have or what we have as past experiences with certain individuals we have encountered before. The problem here is that this perception may be more based on human discernment versus spiritual discernment. It is like when people marginalize people from certain parts of town and assume that all of them are crackheads or criminals. It is like thinking that all people from a certain part of the world are rapists and low-lifers. It is an extreme form of prejudice that can be ingrained unintentionally no matter what the person's ethnicity or background may be. Often, this is because of their own struggles with past, painful experiences where they were tricked.

In a similar fashion where we abhor prejudice in the world, we should be careful with it within the church. We should be connected to the Holy Spirit and let Him guide us to determining who is a crook and who is for real. When we don't listen to the Spirit of God, we are in a way a tool of pain and suffering. When someone is in a situation that they cannot see the way out of, they will reach out for help. It is when that person reaches out to the church because of those situations, and they truly are in trouble and are turned away or have noses turned up at them just because of who they are? A seed of hurt gets planted. Suffering can continue and what happens next is that a ministry that may be doing the magnificent work of Christ will get labeled as hypocritical or apathetic. This can be dangerous for the cause of Christ everywhere, because it spreads and affects other ministries. It affects and damages people which can go on sometimes for generations.

I feel that when we turn people away who ask for help and base that rejection on our own prejudices, we are rejecting the core meaning of what ministry is. Let's look at the Scriptures and see what the Word says:

For I was an hungred, and ye gave me no meat: I was thirsty, and ye gave me no drink: I was a stranger, and ye took me not in: naked, and ye clothed me not: sick, and in prison, and ye visited me not. Then shall they also answer him, saying, Lord, when saw we thee an hungred, or athirst, or a stranger, or naked, or sick, or in prison, and did not minister unto thee? Then shall he answer them, saying, Verily I say unto you, Inasmuch as ye did it not to one of the least of these, ye did it not to me. – Matthew 25:42-45 KJV

I know that many of us know this passage of Scripture, but imagine that we didn't do these things for someone who needed help because of our prejudices? Imagine that we would feed certain hungry people only. Imagine that we would give a drink only to certain people only. That we would take in certain people only. That we would clothe certain people only. What if we only visited certain people in the hospital or prison? What did we do to those "certain people" and what did we not do to Jesus? Now, picture that ***YOU*** were those certain people.

Exactly how would you feel if it was ***YOU*** that was hungry, thirsty, broke, in jail, in the hospital, naked, or whatever the situation may be. How would you feel and how do you think Jesus would feel about all of it. There would be pain and those who are turned away because of prejudices hurt even worse than rejection alone. That's what ministries need to think about. We should continually ask God for wisdom and discernment as to who we should help. Jesus even helped Samaritans and didn't care. I trust Jesus' judgement and He will never lead us wrong, but I digress (for now).

Some situations are spiritual in nature. I know that many churches are ill-equipped to handle spiritual warfare concerns. It may seem like the plot of a movie, but people do contact churches for help with what is suspected demonic possession or the experiences of witchcraft. Just like a lot of those movies or paranormal TV shows, they call a church or meet with a pastor and before they can finish the description of the situation, they are told that the church cannot help them and sometimes to please not call them back. Sadly, scenes like this happen all the time. There are quite a few ministries that don't seem to have a clue about spiritual warfare or even the Spirit Realm. If a church witnesses a service where someone begins to speak in other tongues as the Spirit gave them utterance and then must have their pastor on the next Sunday give an explanation about what happened that downplayed it? Yes, that's the sort of ministry that I am talking about here.

I talked about spiritual warfare in Chapter 1, but I want to reiterate that many people do keep their heads in the proverbial sand because they don't want to deal with the consequences of knowing what's really happening. Not to sound redundant, but I have seen many instances of ministries not knowing what to do when supernatural things happen. I have seen deacons run from their posts when a demonic voice came from someone being prayed for. I have witnessed ministry leaders duck and cover when someone mentions demonic possession or acts of deliverance. Let me be clear, anyone who is struggling with a spiritual concern is in serious pain and trouble. I am not talking about the stereotypical scene where someone's head is spinning around backwards, and they are throwing up pea soup either.

There are folks suffering from things like generational curses where demons are stalking bloodlines. There are folks embattled with addictions or hard to overcome situations with molestation or abuse. Unbelievably, there are some people who are dealing with strange things happening in their homes that cannot be explained. All these things are real, and people do experience them. When people who are terrified or oppressed and need help go to their church or a local church and get turned down because that ministry can't handle the problems that they have? Just think about how that can feel. I know that I have said that a lot in this chapter, but I feel that we need to put ourselves in the shoes of others to begin to see how deep the hurt and pain can get for people.

The church has always been a symbol of hope and safety. The church is supposed to know Who God is and how to reach Him. Where there are forces of Hell at work, people expect the church to be the place with the answers since they are supposed to be representatives of God. The unfortunate thing is that some churches will turn people away or tell them that what they are experiencing is in their minds or caused by something else. Imagine a victim who is not believed when they report something that has happened to them and put this situation in the same vein. They would feel rejected and alone. They would harbor feelings of outrage, abandonment, and fear that their torment will never end. Those are not positive feelings. There is pain in the hearts of anyone who is rejected, especially when they feel isolated because demonic things are happening to them and the church refuses to help.

It doesn't matter the "excuse" that people give because it goes against the principle of Grace. When people choose to ignore the plight of others and especially if their struggles are spiritual places the proverbial "blood on their hands" because they let an opportunity to minister pass them by. Ministry requires us to put in the work and "get our hands dirty" and help people from all levels of society. It sickens me to see churches ignore people who truly need help. The opposite of intentional apathy is unintentional apathy and that is because of the lack of teaching or instruction. We as humans don't learn something until it is shown to us either by a teacher or by being exposed to it in a real-world scenario. There are many ministry leaders and churches that don't know how to love with the Love of Christ. Love begets love. Love is a spiritual act on many levels.

Unintentional apathy is sometimes hard to point out because it mostly isn't seen as apathy but is more of a "this is just how we do/don't do" sort of thing. Sometimes it is because ministries are improperly equipped for something and don't realize their error. Other times it is because of ineptness and the inability to admit to themselves or others that they don't know how to handle certain situations. Here is an example scenario that can go in either direction. The chronological age of people in a church has long been an issue in ministries. It doesn't matter which way it goes because the results are remarkably the same. For example, let's say that there is a church that has a late-middle age to retirement majority population with leadership to match. They tend to preach and teach the Word of God in a way that favors the generation of the majority. Enter a major demographic shift in the neighborhood near that church that brings in a lot of families with young children.

Even though the complete Word of God is being taught let's say that a lot of the younger people don't feel connected to the church (rightfully so) because there isn't a Children's Church or platform. The youth feel like outsiders because there isn't a Youth Program or outreach that understands the challenges of their generation. Now, let's say that the church responds and tries to accommodate by enacting activities and programs like they had when they were that age and to no surprise those actions fail. The failure isn't in the Gospel, but in the methods and understanding of today's challenges. There weren't social media pressures twenty-five years ago. A virtual world that can be cruel didn't exist just a generation ago. Sexual issues were hidden in past generations but are fully explored today. Music is much different now than it was in the elders' generation and that's a big divide unfortunately.

When the younger folks try to let their voices be heard about what's missing they are treated like children who don't know any better because elders must know what's best for everyone. The result is that the younger generations begin to either organize activities on their own or simply leave that church hurt that no one listened to them even if they know that they knew that they heard from God. Now, let's pause. I'm not saying that the Elders were completely wrong here. Everything cannot be let into the church to appease people. However, the problem arises in not trying to understand ***AND*** hear from God. The Gospel has and never will change, but the method of how we reach people ***DOES*** change. In this scenario, the older generation did try but failed to reach everyone in their church and didn't know how to change or were afraid to do so. Their hearts were in the right place, but the results gave way to a negative result. We could flip this over and have older folks attending a younger church and feeling left out and cut out from the mainstream and the same sort of hurt is the result.

The difference of ages is not the only way that a ministry can unintentionally cast the specter of unintentional apathy. Some people seemingly aloof and blinded to the reality of things simply just don't know any better. I am not saying that people are mentally unstable or anything like that. What I am referring to here is that some people with the biggest hearts and love Jesus to their cores simply just don't understand how the world works and see the world with rose-colored glasses. There is an innocence here as some churches have been isolated from the rest of the world or have been hidden away from real spiritual issues and are deeply convinced that things cannot be as "bad" or "serious" as people say that they are. It reminds me of that movie where the poor man who didn't know that he was on a reality show grew up in a literal bubble. A falsely constructed world that until he escaped from it, he knew nothing else.

To folks on the outside, these ministries seem like they are totally averse to reality. The truth is too hard to grasp, and it seems like they play the children's game where they put their fingers in the ears and shout out, "***LA, LA, LA, LA, LA!***" They don't in real life, but their actions reflect that mentality. The world that they live in cannot accept certain things and situations exist and instead of confronting reality, they run from it. The confrontation of the truth is too much to bear and it's like something short circuits in them and they turn on their emergency safety protocol and run away.

I don't feel that people in this category can truly be held accountable for their actions. This is the world that they know and understand and only God can change their perceptions. A deeply ingrained, blissful ignorance of the needs of people around them can. However, it can result in disaster. I didn't put this in the lack of understanding section because here it is about a true and honest ignorance of things. A person cannot be held accountable until they are exposed to the truth, and they choose to ignore it. It is when a person actively decides to acknowledge what is true and then rejects it when it crosses the line of innocence into belligerence.

Ministries that do not understand something because of blissful ignorance can cause a lot of people to fester hatred towards churches. For example, those who seek help for domestic violence might encounter people who don't believe that people should ever just get divorced. Some believe that it was the victim's fault because they can't possibly see why anyone would react the way that they did. Others have no idea the plights of those in unfamiliar cultures or socioeconomic backgrounds. They make decisions about the needs of their congregation and despite their good intentions and their hearts, those choices cause pain in the hearts of people in need.

It seems insane, but when someone has been living in a microcosm for so long, it is nearly impossible by human means to cause them to change. Satan uses this to his advantage. He is the expert of illusion, and he will blind those whose hearts belong to Jesus but have yet to tap in to all the spiritual gifts and the power of the Holy Spirit. These folks have only experienced what they know and for many it has been that way for generations. Yet their good hearts and honesty are not enough to avoid causing hurt in their churches or communities. They act in their illusions, preach and teach their false truths, and unintentionally perpetuate hurt in their churches.

Unintentional apathy is very covert and sadly not always detectable unless we use spiritual eyes and ears. When people are on the receiving end of this form of apathy it feels like it's intentional when it really isn't. When the spiritual needs of people are ignored unintentionally it can feel like oppression. It can feel like cruelty beyond any imaginable degree. In many ways, unintentional apathy is a direct result of a lack of understanding. Pick any topic that isn't just about the lack of youth programs, and you can see what I mean. When there is a serious need among the people who attend ministries where the church doesn't know how to respond to those needs it puts folks in the middle of those needs into a state of suffering. Ultimately, this all boils down to the committing of poor on a human and/or spiritual level.

When we don't use our spiritual sight, we will miss what God has intended for us to see in the natural realm as well. To see beyond the natural into the spiritual requires a deeper relationship with Christ as well as understanding that is taught from the top levels of leadership all the way down to the pews. When we, as people, don't have the knowledge or understanding of what we should be looking for and are sensitive towards we will err and sometimes appear that we don't care when we just don't understand. It doesn't matter whether we choose to not understand or blindly do not understand, the results are the same. When people come with needs, we must be sure that we ask God what we should do and not act on what we think the answers are.

Politics

This is a complicated issue to address because of the current climate, not only in America, but abroad as well. Let me say first that we need Christians in government. True believers of Christ that don't have an agenda for power are ideal for our nation. We need good people with hearts wide open for Jesus to go outside the church and make a difference. This is different from the negative movement infiltrating our communities today. The ugly spirit of politics has not only entered the church, but in some places taken over the entire message of Jesus Christ and it shouldn't be that way. I can't tell you how many churches I have seen that are doing wonderful things for the Kingdom of God that are scarred by the political realm. Pastors are commanding people as to how they should vote, and what ideology they must have, or they are not Christians. It's abominable! Before we get too far in this section and for the record, I am a Bible-believing voter, and I take the stance that politics has no place in our churches. Period. No exceptions. Let me explain why I feel this way.

There is no greater model for ministry than Jesus Himself. Jesus had the most dynamic ministry by the fact that He never condemned a single soul even if they were in sin. Jesus hung out with everyone and met them where they were so that He could minister to them. Jesus never built a single building and fed the hungry, clothed the naked, and cared about the mental health of the brokenhearted and actively fought for the restoration of people's lives. Here is the ***ONE THING*** that Jesus didn't do that many churches are doing. Jesus didn't say or do one thing regarding politics. Go ahead, search Scripture and you won't find Him towing a single line politically even though the Pharisees tried to get Him to comment on the cruelty of Roman taxes. The government of Rome was evil. It was wicked and it was apathetic. It was the rich and powerful exploiting the poor and destitute. Why didn't Jesus say a word about it? Good question.

Just looking over Scripture it can be understood that the primary focus of the ministry of Christ was to not change a single government on Earth but set up one for the church. Jesus was about building up the people and dealing with the concerns of the people and never about the obvious corruption that was in the Roman and local Jewish governments. He dealt with the people and not their offices. He dealt with the issues of the everyday person and not the policies that compromised the Word of God or the people of God. In fact, Jesus met with tax collectors and government officials not to persuade them to change their policies or activities, but He was concerned about their souls. Imagine that.

What is happening today around the world is that we have a glaring problem concerning churches getting deeply involved in politics. Let's pause for a moment. Again, I do believe that we need Christians in the government on every level, but not for the reason you may think. I believe that we need Christians in government to live a godly life and spread the message of Christ to those around them. Their presence there is not to enforce laws on people who don't believe in Jesus, but to transform those in the positions of power to think with more compassion, more love and more Christ-like behavior.

Let's take America as an example. The United States is not a Christian nation. Sorry to burst your bubble, but the USA is a nation with Christians in it. Much of the population is not saved, not Christian and in many cases don't believe anything at all. That is the cold, hard reality. This is not to say that the United States wasn't founded on Christian morality or principles. The U.S. was not founded as a strictly secular nation. Many of the founders attended Christian churches and considered themselves as Christians. Others were deists who believed in a creator or some sort of deity that made everything. There are some who say that America was meant to be strictly atheistic and that is not the case. However, here is an interesting quote:

Indeed, each of the nation's three founding documents – the Declaration of Independence, the Articles of Confederation, and the United States Constitution – carefully avoided all mention of Christianity or Christ.

ARTICLE VI OF THE CONSTITUTION STATES AS DRAMATICALLY AS POSSIBLE, THAT "NO RELIGIOUS TEST SHALL EVER BE REQUIRED AS A QUALIFICATION TO ANY OFFICE OR PUBLIC TRUST UNDER THE UNITED STATES" –HARDLY THE HALLMARK OF A "CHRISTIAN" NATION. TO REAFFIRM AMERICA'S NOT BECOMING A CHRISTIAN NATION, CONGRESS AND ALL THE STATES ADDED THE FIRST AMENDMENT TO THE CONSTITUTION IN 1791, REITERATING THE NATION'S ARELIGIOUS CHARACTER BY BARRING GOVERNMENT ESTABLISHMENT OF ANY AND ALL RELIGION. ONLY THE DECLARATION OF INDEPENDENCE EVEN MENTIONS GOD--IN A SINGLE AMBIGUOUS REFERENCE IN THE OPENING PARAGRAPH TO WHAT DEISTS RATHER THAN PRACTICING CHRISTIANS CALLED "LAWS OF NATURE AND NATURE'S GOD."[1]

Clearly, the United States was not founded as a solely Christian nation and those who uphold and teach this are in serious error. There is religious liberty, but America was never intended to be a strictly Christian country. If this were the case, the Bible would be within the Constitution or within the laws of the country like a theocracy. A theocracy is a form of government in which the ultimate leader is a supreme deity, who rules either directly as a god in human form or indirectly through mortal servants—typically a religious clergy—who rule on the deity's behalf. With their laws based on religious codes and decrees, the governments of theocracies serve their divine leader or leaders rather than the citizens. As a result, theocracies are often oppressive in function, with strict rules and harsh punishments for rule-breakers[2]. Does this sound like the government of the United States? I think not.

Where is the hurt from the church you say? It's at Ground Zero. It is a funny (and yet not so funny) coincidence that the political overshadowing is happening in many churches that teach more of the true Gospel of Jesus. The tilt into right-wing insanity tarnishes the purity and wholeness of the Word by their twisted lies all the while God still moves and delivers because of the Name Jesus being called in faith and not because of their lunacy. These churches ostracize a substantial majority of the population around them and polarizes the rest into their perverted gospel. It's a catch-22 that hurts either people who need Jesus and are out of the church or good people who turn their backs on the church because of neo-conservatism. For the record, I will say that Christian Nationalism is dangerous all while using Jesus Christ and the Bible as a shield.

The majority of those involved in their collateral movements use a cloak of truth to cover powerful lies and effective brainwashing that is cult-like in its state. I have news for you; it is impossible to quote one Scripture to drive power down the throats of people and ignore the other verses that God spoke in the correct context. The unholy marriage of patriotism and Christian principles is a trick from Hell. Proclaiming that being decent to people regardless of their ethnicity or faith is "woke" and that diversity, equity, and inclusion should be wiped off the face of the Earth is appalling. Movements like this are hurting those in the church by forcefully polarizing issues that are the limited views of a small group of folks who use the bully pulpit to bludgeon people into submission to their ideals.

Christian Nationalism is a cult of absolutes. It's their way only or the highway and usually their principles are sprinkled with racist and exclusionist tactics (I will cover racism in the next section.) The thought that America has some sort of mandate to save the world is incorrect. Find it in Scripture and prove me wrong. Also, the Stars and Stripes is not an idol, the National Anthem is not a Christian hymn, and the Pledge of Allegiance is not a spiritual creed. Christian Nationalists edify the United States to the point that it is idolized and worshipped and that is wrong. Scripture told us to not make any other gods before Him, but they do it and use the church as their platform to propagate this nonsense.

When nationalistic music is played, such as the national anthem in the United States, people are expected to stand in reverence or awe of the national symbol, such as a flag, which is usually prominently displayed for all to see. Often a nationalistic song is sung to the accompaniment of [that] nationalistic music. People in the nation are often told how great the nation is, and how God is on their side and always has been. They are fed a very slanted, highly biased, account of the nation's history, which is sanitized of all unflattering facts. This brainwashing from childhood on causes a nationalistic fervor in many people and can become very emotional when nationalistic music is played. This indoctrination can make it very difficult to modify one's viewpoint, because the emotions run so deep. For example, in the United States, the national anthem is often played just prior to a public event, such as sporting event, serving as a pious hymn to turn the entire spectacle into a quasi-nationalistic religious ceremony[3].

Speaking of the flag, in so many Christian Nationalist churches it is proudly displayed in the highest place of honor. So, what about those who aren't American citizens that come to visit? I would think that it would make them feel like God is only with America instead of the rest of the world, especially if no other nations' flag is represented. That also could convey that the church identifies with Americans more than Christians in other countries around the globe and puts up a wall in worship. That flag also says that America has a very special place with God and while God loves us all, there is only one nation that is the apple of God's eye and that is the Israelite nation. Christian Nationalists idolize the flag to the point that they believe and preach that the cause of America is the cause of God. The flag is pledged to with reverence which broadcasts that allegiance to America is synonymous with allegiance to God.

The blatant imposition of Christian Nationalist beliefs hurts those who don't subscribe to their heresies. They believe that they have a mandate to take over every government by every means necessary. This puts a serious negative stain on the cause of Christ not just in America, but in the world. These groups ram which candidates and which issues that congregants should vote for right down everyone's throats who are in earshot. They will make people feel guilty because they are going against God if they go against their beliefs. I have heard some of these wild pastors even tell people to get out of their churches and never come back. They use anger and vitriol to embed their messages into the hearts and minds of people that are willing to receive it. Everyone else is left to wonder why it is all happening. Those who don't agree with the doctrine but love their church, their families, and the people in those churches are left with broken hearts.

Christian Nationalism is an extremist philosophy that uses the Bible as its weapon. I feel that it uses brainwashing techniques to brow beat people into feeling that not agreeing to their policies is not patriotic. To not be patriotic with a nation that they believe is mandated by God is disobeying God. That is a heavy tax to levy upon the hearts and minds of people. Whole families have been divided because of this nonsensical "doctrine" that has surged in recent years to the point that even those who aren't Christians are feeling the effects of it. When non-Christians point out the idolatry that Christian Nationalism has with political leaders and the acquisition of power, something is very wrong.

This case of hurt from the church is much different than just the actions of the church in spiritual life. This is the case where the Christian Nationalist movement is hurting those who aren't even interesting in going to church or knowing about God. Christian Nationalism is a quest for power and control and not about the mission of Jesus Christ. This isn't about winning souls but about winning elections. It is about enforcing their twisted views upon all people versus allowing them to accept Jesus on their own. Jesus said whosoever will, let them come. Jesus never forced His ways or His will on anyone. Whenever someone is forcing their will on someone, it is akin to rape. I hate to use that word, but it is the only one that fits.

There have been, there are, and there will be people hurt from this dangerous movement. This forceful acquisition of power by the means of deception and using Scripture and God to do it will end in disaster. It will drive many away from the one true God and it will destroy relationships at every turn. It does not demonstrate the true nature of Christ and is severely xenophobic, prejudiced, and evil. Many of these people claim to hear the Voice of God and they don't realize that no one in Creation knows how to mimic God's Voice like Lucifer.

There are so many who subscribe to the ways of hatred that hide behind Calvary's Cross to claim that they belong to Jesus, and it is blasphemous. Sadly, there are quite a few people who are in this cult and don't realize the truth. When Christian Nationalism gets exposed, it will be a major blow to Christianity everywhere and, in my opinion, helps fulfill end-time prophecies that those who confess and proclaim Jesus Christ as Lord will be executed. I weep for my country.

If you thought that I am assailing only the right-wing side of politics, I have a rude awakening for you. The left-wing side of political leanings is also damaging the church. I won't talk about specific sins here because Scripture does that already, but what I am talking about is the spiritual blindness of the political ultra-left. The Church must look at sin and still preach about it and not ignore it. Christ was compassionate to those who practiced sin, but He never ignored it. The woman at the well is the best example. He didn't condemn her but told her when she admitted to being with as husband that it wasn't hers. Jesus didn't hesitate and neither should we. If it is contrary to the Gospel of Jesus Christ a church shouldn't push it as the "new Gospel", and it shouldn't push the extreme political agendas that come along with it.

There is a serious spiritual blindness of the political ultra-left. The Church must look at sin and still preach about it and not ignore it. Yes, our God is a God of Love, but He is also a God of judgement, and He hates sin. There aren't too many things that God hates, and sin is the biggest one of those things. Christ was compassionate to those who practiced sin, but He never ignored it. The woman at the well is the best example. He didn't condemn her but told her when she admitted to being with a husband who wasn't hers. Jesus didn't hesitate and neither should we. If it is contrary to the Gospel of Jesus Christ a church shouldn't push it as the "new Gospel", and it shouldn't push the extreme political agendas that come along with it.

Churches should not be forced to adopt practices that go against their convictions as they currently are either. People are being hurt in churches that are so liberal that they fall outside of the Word of God. This may be a landmine, but I must step on it anyway because the truth is the truth. I believe that we should love everyone despite where they are in their lives. Jesus did that and so will I. However, churches should never promote any sort of lifestyle or principles that are not rooted in the Word of God. I am not just talking about one thing, but I am talking about them all. If it can't be found in Scripture, we shouldn't be doing it. To be sure that we are doing this right, we should be getting as close to God as possible and hear what He has to say about it before we preach it from our pulpits and live it in society. I stand firm on that, and I won't change because God's Word doesn't change.

Whole church organizations are splitting and fragmenting over things like gay marriage, gay clergy, and abortion rights. When a church splits because of political pressure people get hurt that way too. People who have been in a church for years or their families there for generations now leave it because they were oppressed over issues that are way too liberal for the Scriptures. Pastors who start a marijuana farm to entice people to come to church all because of the legalization of weed. That causes pain too people! I am not talking about positive liberal changes, but those folks who have differing motives and methods outside of the confines of the contents of the Holy Bible are what

I am talking about here. These things can be difficult for those who walk with God, and especially when His discernment tells them that something is not right.

A church should be a haven from persecution and pain, but it should not be a place to hide from the truth. We shouldn't warp the Gospel to fit our ideals. We should conform to the Gospel. Period. No exceptions. Those who have a deeper relationship with Jesus would be hurt by churches who are extreme left and possibly would end up running to the extreme right-wing because of emotional damage. The enemy has both bases covered including the milquetoast middle of the road churches that see nothing and only focus on love and not the core tenets of the Word.

When we alter the Gospel of Jesus Christ to not offend people or to appeal to those who aren't living holy lives is just as wrong as the overly conservative movements that squeeze grace out of the church. When churches are forced to adopt what is clearly against what the Bible says is a mistake that can cause pain as well. We shouldn't use the ballot box to force a house of worship to marry people that Scripture says shouldn't be married. The statehouse shouldn't force a ministry to not speak the truth with love because it offends people.

What makes it worse is that its people in the church that use politics to water down the message or actions of that church and other churches. When these churches compromise their doctrines or their message it causes hurt, and persecution and we know what happens after that. I could go on and on about the other side of politics, but the hurt of people is the hurt of people no matter which way the political philosophy goes. All these positions are dangerous, and all can hurt the people within and without. Remove the politics and maintain the Word of God. Straight with no chaser. If we focus on our communities and focus on the pain and suffering of sin and show God's Love that's all we need to do. Leave the politic arenas out of our pulpits.

So, let me summarize how politics can cause hurt in church. There is a buzzword that many people like to wield in America for the wrong reasons at times is the word freedom. We all want our freedoms of life, liberty and the pursuit of happiness. Yet some people want to impose laws on people who believe differently than we do. I won't get into individual topics here, but when church people start telling non-church people how they will live and how they will act it always creates a backlash.

If we told the flag-waving, snarling conservatives" that laws were being passed against their beliefs they would be in such an uproar that I am sure that would be loud and proud that they would happily go "1776" on the government. What nonsense and foolishness. These political movements have the church so blind and gullible that they believe anything that is said to them using other catchphrases such as abortion, ***BLACK LIVES MATTER*** (I refuse to abbreviate the term), ***CRITICAL RACE THEORY*** (I won't abbreviate that one either) or gender identification concerns along with many others.

There are many churches that are more focused on what's going on in Washington, D.C. than they are in their own neighborhoods. Sermons that are targeted at the various branches of government with loudmouths using Scripture to justify their hateful natures. Ideologies that are more focused on who is elected to a political office versus the number of unsaved souls that live up the street from them. Places that want to water down the Gospel until it is a soup of sugar, lollipops, and rainbows that never talks about sin, never talks about holiness, never wars in the spirit realm and never operates in the five-fold ministry.

Un-Christlike behaviors and principles are just what they are regardless of the "left" or "right" side of the political spectrum. These ministries and leaders are hell bent on changing politics but not changing the lives and hearts of people. Here is a parting shot. If your church's views are against how Jesus walked, Jesus talked and how Jesus worked your church is apostate. I don't care who the leader is, how many degrees they have, how loud they can get, how many followers they have if they aren't one hundred percent Bible? They are out of sorts. I said it. Period.

None of these political factions are Bible-based or Bible-focused. They are resolved to do one thing: achieve power. Jesus didn't get politicians on His side. Jesus didn't influence who was on the Sanhedrin Court. Jesus didn't instigate a single rebellion against Rome (and He had every right to do so). Jesus didn't meet with Pilate or King Herod to get political favors or influence policy. The Pharisees, Sadducees and the Sanhedrin did. They were doing back room deals and politicking and they killed Jesus like today's political movement is killing the True Church of Jesus Christ.

It causes pain when people who are politically different can't feel welcome in a church of a political ideology. Nothing illuminated this more than when the COVID-19 pandemic was raging at its height. I watched this basically insane pastor tell those in attendance that they were not welcome at his church if they wore masks or got a vaccine. He told them to leave. On camera. In front of the world. Imagine if that was you. How would you feel? Instead of focusing on the sick, bewildered, possessed, broken, and lost people, this pastor objected against wearing a ***MASK***. Think about that.

Racism

Racism is something that our society does not want to speak about. Most people don't want to acknowledge it because of all the pain, anger, and horror that it can bring to the surface. As an African-American man I don't just know about it, but I have experienced it on a very deep and personal level. The world, not just the United States, must come to grips with the fact that racism, hatred, and xenophobia is deeply intertwined and ingrained in everything. Every nation and every people on Earth are guilty of being racist. Yes, some nations have more blood on their hands than others and there is a lot of shame and embarrassment for many who don't wish to acknowledge it. All racism is evil, and it comes directly from Hell. The atrocities are real and the wake of destruction from racism is real. Humanity cannot and must not ignore the reality that racism is tearing all our lives apart.

Many nations, like the United States, are in a crisis with racism. People don't want accurate history being taught, other cultures being honored, or policies and ways of life to change. Racism is deeply entrenched and the only way for it to be defeated is for good people to stand up against this diabolical way of thinking. This vile poison has oppressed people and kept them bound over a fear that only Satan can concoct and use against us. The biggest problem, in my view, is how racism seems to be permeated and enacted using the Name of God, which is the greatest deception of them all.

There have been a lot of good books and series of books written about racism in religion and if you want to go in-depth, I suggest that you check those out for an eye-opening exposure of the depth of racism in the church today. What I would like to focus on specifically is the hurt and pain that racism causes in the church. The thing about racism is that most of it isn't blatant and "in your face", but it is covert, active and sometimes passive due to cultural misconceptions and a generalization of who people of different ethnicities and cultures are. This goes ***BOTH WAYS***, and it needs to be addressed. In countries like the United States, by a wide margin the day of the week that we are the most segregated and intolerant of each other is on Sundays with Saturdays being in second place. We all claim to love the same God and worship the same Christ, yet we are divided and separate in many ways.

So, let's get the unpleasant things out of the way first. Jesus Christ was a brown man. No ifs, ands or buts about it. If you were expecting some other answer, I am sorry (and not sorry) to disappoint you. This fact, by itself, is not racist at all. This is just a fact. Jesus, as a brown child hid out in Egypt for many years in a country that is in Alkebulan. You know, the place with lots and lots of brown people. Not to be offensive to anyone, but could a blond-haired, blue-eyed child and his parents hide in a country full of brown people? The answer is no. Jesus grew up into a brown man and not a fair skinned, wispy man who looks like you could beat Him up for His lunch money.

Jesus was a carpenter's son. He was a carpenter and basically, a construction worker and most likely had the build to match. Think about this. Could a frail and weak Jesus carry a huge wooden cross (even if He was a mere human) as far as He did (nearly a mile) after being mercilessly whipped until skin and muscle were torn off Him? Those beautiful icons and pictures that hang in a lot of homes and churches are incorrect. Honestly, many cultures have made Jesus look like them and unless they are Middle Eastern or original Hebrew, they are wrong too. Even the Scripture says that Jesus had skin on His feet like bronze and His hair was like wool (Revelation 1:14-16). The Word of God is truly clear as to Who Jesus is and how He looked.

If racists were to meet the real Jesus, they would not want to worship Him. If He tried to live in their country, they would most likely deport Him. Many people don't even realize that their approach to Christianity is tainted with racism. Many mainstream Eurocentric denominations have altered the narrative to suit themselves. Those who have been dominant have erased the truth and substituted it with what made them feel superior or better about all of it. This is where all the problems with racism and hurt and the church begin.

The dominant cultures in the world reshaped the original faith of The Way and made it into the Christianity of today. Jesus came and died for every nation and every language, but today the world sees Jesus the way that He has been portrayed incorrectly, which has caused hurt, pain, and hatred over these biases. This is systemic racism at its core, and it has caused more pain and suffering than most people are willing to acknowledge. When faith is the vehicle of hurt, when it should be the place of peace is the greatest evil of them all. Let's move on.

Next, let's talk about us being separated when we worship. That is partly how American society developed. White folks let slaves into churches, but they had to be separated from everyone else. They were usually in the balcony, and they were to be seen and not heard. They were preached a doctrine that said that Scripture advocated them being slaves and that they were cursed with the mark of Cain. Google all of that and be horrified. Slaves were finally given the chance to have their own churches after they protested for their own autonomy.

Even after they won that right they (in many cases) were still controlled and were generally mocked for their unique traditions. African-Americans were (and still are) seen as inferior, and their worship was considered backward, uncouth, and substandard. At least, from the loudest voices of "authority" because there were many who loved and appreciated what they experienced but had to remain silent as to how they felt. I'll get back to that point in a minute.

Fast forward to the present day after many, many changes and evolutions of doctrine and traditions and we are still separated culturally and racially. I'm going to leave the colors of skin out for a moment. One group feels that their counterparts' worship is dry and dull while the other side feels that it is a spectacle to be seen like a circus act. One group believes that the theology of the other is unrefined and incorrect, and the other group feels that their theology is rightly divined and needs no validation from other people. One group feels that their music reaches the Throne of God because of what it says and how it is performed while the other group feels that their music touches the hearts of people and the offering from those hearts reaches the Throne of God. You get the idea. Now that I have brought all of this out let's talk about visiting a church of a different group. How many signs have you seen with messages that say they people are welcome, but it turns out that it's more about "outsiders" being "assimilated" versus being truly welcome? How many churches say that they are inclusive when all they do is ostracize? Let's unpack this.

First, let's look at how many people feel when visiting a church that does this that is of a different race or culture. Immediately all eyes are on them because they are different. Whether they are truly prejudiced and just tolerate them or make them uncomfortable or both see if you can picture in your mind this scenario. The feelings of being watched or judged at every move. People reacting to how you dress or who may be in your family. The mostly awkward greetings that range from overly acted to terse and "thin smile" in nature. It doesn't matter the race or culture because usually the response is usually the same. How would you feel?

Next, let's look at cultural differences. Unless you are a devout Pentecostal, "shouting" in church or standing and lifting one's hands would seem very weird in many places of worship. The other side of that coin would be the silent and reverent worship with the shedding of occasional tears that could appear "dead" to another. Most African-American churches have a driving band of praise or worship music that would scare most European-Americans. Just one turn of the "Ma-Shon-da" would cause most folks to never return.

Flip it around and imagine most African-Americans sitting through Johann Sebastian Bach's chorale from the 1723 Advent cantata *Herz und Mund und Tat und Leben (Heart and Mouth and Deed and Life)*, BWV 147, *"Jesu, Joy of Man's Desiring"* and falling dead asleep or chuckling to themselves while creating a social media video. Let's not forget that how we dress is vastly different too. African-American churches are used to "church hats", dapper suits, Kwanzaa celebrations, and maybe a splash of Alkebulan attire. You get the idea. Lots of differences and both sides see more of what they don't like versus appreciating the differences.

Here is another scenario. In today's non-denominational church there is a blending of cultures and races that is a beautiful thing. People come together, worship and serve without boundaries. In some of those churches, however, there is a strange undercurrent. Churches like these love for people of different ethnicities to sing and play music if it doesn't make other certain folks uncomfortable. These churches don't mind worship or preaching in a style that most of the leadership feel "comfortable" with. Imagine being in a non-denominational church that is laid-back and has that coffee house feeling. Where love is abundant and hard-hitting teaching on sin and Hell is not present. Not Pentecostal.

Now imagine a slight change in the worship music program that features a more Pentecostal tilt and emphasis on the Spirit of God moving. Picture the reactions of "stunned" leadership who felt that it was "controversial" and congregants that are from a minority background who plunged in and tapped into the Holy Place began to worship and speak in unknown tongues. Imagine having that kind of communion with God in public and people treat you like you're weird or have people whisper about them. Think those folks would come back or feel comfortable again? Maybe not. The thing that I have noticed about many non-denominational churches is that the mostly have European-American pastors and love people of other ethnicities if they come to conform to their ways, and they rarely adapt to the cultures of others. They want people of color, but don't want who they are. It's shameful and wrong. That hurts people.

These are differences that instead of much of each group wanting to understand these variances, those who are racist don't want either side to come together and worship. Racism is fueled by a lack of understanding and lit with the torch of hatred. All hatred and confusion come from Satan. Before I get too far let me say this. Every cultural thing is not for everybody. People will still like what they like, but we should never let racism dictate our separation from one another.

If you like anthems and hymns? Go to that style of church. If you like rock-style worship and swirling lights? Go to that style of church. If you like reggae music? Go to that style church. If you love traditional gospel music? Go to that style church. Go where God is real and is manifesting in His fullness. Go where you are comfortable, but don't forsake yourself from fellowshipping with those who are different. We are all members of the Body of Christ no matter our ethnicity or culture.

Racism in the church isn't just limited to praise and worship, but it can be connected to the fabric of society itself. Another area of hurt from the church caused by racism is interracial relationships. This is the year 2025 and there are some churches where this is still an issue. It's sad that some people believe that the mixing of races goes against the Bible. How many people have seen the looks, the stares and the treatment that some mixed-raced couples endure? Some pastors even refuse to officiate wedding ceremonies for either outright objections or due to the pressures of social climates in their churches. I am not just talking about a church that is nearly one hundred percent of one ethnicity or another, but I am talking about multi-cultural churches too.

In some areas of the United States people are still just getting integrated together. There are some churches (no matter which kind) that being in an interracial relationship is too much to handle. I have heard people tell stories of how they couldn't get married at their church because they were refused for many abstract reasons, but it was understood as to why they couldn't get married there. Sometimes it's even the ministers that refuse to participate. That one is personal to me, and I will explain. I am married to a woman of a different ethnicity, and I remember that when we were getting things together for our wedding my wife asked her pastor about co-officiating the ceremony with my pastor. He refused. In fact, he stopped talking to my wife.

When I visited her home church for service I was stared down and made to feel very uncomfortable. I caught people staring at us or whispering the whole time and it was unnerving. Once we went to a special Christmas program and I brought my family, and we were not treated well by the pastor and some of the people. Some were nice, but the pastor sealed it for us. He hardly acknowledged us, and you could see in his mannerisms and speech that he did not like us being there let alone being together. It was obvious. We have never gone back to attend another service. Thank God my home church didn't treat my wife the way hers did me. My church embraced my wife although there are plenty of African-America churches and pastors that do the same things done to my wife and me.

To me the worst consequences come for any children that may be involved. Some churches will either outright make these children feel like mutants or they will try to isolate them from the majority culture of that church instead of embracing all of who they are and the cultures they represent. To me there is nothing worse than a child being hurt by a church. Couple all that together with a family unit that is hurt by the ignorance of people who refuse to accept that we are all humans regardless of the color of our skin and a disaster is made.

Ministries where the ugly fabric of racism is justified by Scripture and perpetuated by those who are spiritually blind is tragic. Being in a relationship with or married to a person of a different ethnicity or culture is not a sin and it is not a transgression to humanity. Love is love and God is love. Look through the Scripture and you will find cases where people married people of different ethnicities and God took zero objections. God looks at the hearts of people and so should we. The color of our skin is not determination of who we are as people. The church should never treat people this way.

Whenever racism uses the Church to perpetuate its evils it will propagate hurt and pain no matter whether the racism is blatant or not. The mentality and doctrines of racist origins have caused whole anti-Christian or opposing racist movements to come into being. Think about that, entire religions and movements have been started that preach an even worst gospel or fake gospel because of racism. Millions of people have adopted faiths that either perpetuate hate against those who are racist or the antithesis of the God of the Bible.

Many have adopted other gods or faiths that abhor racism but are not the true way that Christ gave us. People don't change from being a Christian who loves Jesus into a person who says that they love Jesus but reciprocates the same hate that was used on them back on others unless they were hurt. People who abandon Jesus for another god or no god at all don't do that unless they were hurt by the church in some way with racism at the core.

On the other hand, there have also been some positives as the result of racism causing hurt in the church. As I said earlier, I will not go into details about racism in the church, but I will highlight the fact that many ministries and movements were born because of racism experienced by those who attended churches who were prejudiced against them. The Azusa Steet Revival (1906-1916) gave rise to Pentecostal churches like the Church of God in Christ.

The National Baptist convention was birthed in 1895 after many independent conferences of African-American Baptists came together. The African Methodist Episcopal Church was formed in 1816. Those are just the major denominations, but there have been countless others not just in the United States, but around the world. Many churches didn't allow diverse leadership or ownership of the ministry of their faiths because of racism, and it caused pain that some people did something about.

Speaking of doing something about racism, it is largely accepted that the Civil Rights Movement in the United States was born out of Black churches who knew the pain of racism from their genesis and knew that it was outside of the church and did something about the issue. The greatest leader and martyr of the Civil Rights Movement was a pastor from the Dexter Avenue Baptist Church in Montgomery, Alabama. Even though he is known as a doctor, most forget that he was a minister of the Gospel of Jesus Christ. Of course, we all should know his name, and he is the late Reverend Dr. Martin Luther King, Jr.

We have the freedom of choice given by God, but Satan has perverted it into something sinister. Hatred and prejudice should not be the reason we "look down" on someone or refuse someone into our churches. If a church is Christ-centered, it doesn't matter whether they play Bluegrass or K-Pop-styled worship. It doesn't matter whether people shout, and prophecies come forth or it's silent and people just pray. If we are all chasing the same Jesus, following the same Word of God it shouldn't matter. Let us be where God has placed us and let us come together as one to gather in the harvest of souls that need salvation.

We are ***ONE BODY*** in Christ with many members. We are different, but we are still ***ONE***. We are of different ethnicities and cultures, but we all love ***ONE JESUS***. Here is my example that I use when telling folks that we are one. The word "hallelujah" is mostly the same in every language. It may be written differently, but it has the same exact meaning. There isn't a black or white "hallelujah". There isn't a Hispanic or Japanese "hallelujah". There isn't a Yoruba or Russian "hallelujah". There is only one. We are all one in Christ. We should see color and culture and appreciate it. We should never mock another person's offering to the Lord. We should never feel superior to one another. All our righteousness is like filthy rags (Isaiah 64:6).

When we discriminate, are prejudiced and hate or marginalize people for the color of their skin or culture we cause pain. I dare question the true salvation of those people who justify hatred using words meant for love. People who intentionally have hatred in their hearts and practice prejudice are the worst of the worst and make being a Christian difficult. There are so many people who don't realize that how they were raised or conditioned is racist. This systemic poison is hard to get rid of without the aid of the Holy Spirit as I feel that it is connected to evil spirits. I am not just speaking of people of European descent. It goes both ways from all ethnic groups, and we need to be wise and check our hearts and ask God to transform us.

Sin

Now we come to the biggest "elephant in the room" and while it may be the last on my list it is not the least of the churches battles with hurt from the church. Sin is a word that has many origins and yet has the same core meaning: to go against God's Law. Over the years my understanding and views of sin have been shaped by God directly speaking to me and my studies in Hamartiology, which is a branch of theology dedicated to the study of sin. Let me be clear as I can: sin is sin, and Jesus came to free us from the eternal consequences of sin. Period. Any and everything that isn't in the Will of God or against His Word is sin.

Sin can be defined as describes sin as an act of offence against God by despising his persons and Christian biblical law, and by injuring others[4]. or going in full violation of God's Law. Sin is even said to be an archery term and spoke of in "degrees of sin" from not hitting the target. I used to believe that to be an absolute truth, but it isn't. Sin is a subtle and yet blatant thing. Sin takes something beautiful that God created and corrupting it against what God designed it for. For every virtue God made there is a sin.

I will not "sugarcoat" or pacify the fact that sin is real, sin must be dealt with in our lives, and sin is sadly in the church. It doesn't matter which church, and it doesn't matter what denomination. It doesn't matter what the sin is and where it is being done. It doesn't matter who is doing it and who isn't doing it. God doesn't care about that because sin is sin. I will keep saying that over and over. The church can ignore it or confront it. The result of all sin is pain. This pain isn't the rightful conviction of our flesh concerning sin. That should ***NEVER*** be in the same conversation as being hurt in the church.

As I have said earlier, rightful spiritual conviction that causes us to feel shame or guilt is not hurt, but the spirit of the person detaching from the control of the flesh and listening to God. We cannot confuse this with hurt from the church. Anyone that tries to say that is under the influence of a lying spirit. The Word of God cuts like a two-edged sword and is designed to convict us and let us see the truth. This section is not about personal conviction in the hearts and minds of people. If anyone reading this and thinks that their hurt is coming to them because God rightfully pointed out their messes? They need to talk to God about it and let Him guide you. You aren't hurt by the Church that God planted; you are hurt from the delusion of sin being lifted from your eyes for the first time. Trust God to help you.

Sin is present because we humans exist. We are creatures born from sin that Christ offers redemption and salvation through the shedding of His Blood that we would have a right to the Tree of Life. We were commanded to live holy as Christ is holy. We are told that our righteousness is like soiled menstrual rags (yes, look it up because it's true). When sin permeates and corrupts the church all sorts of terrible things happen that will cause not just pain for people in the church, but pain for those outside of the church as well. As I have said many times before, wherever we do good, evil is always present. We are in our flesh and because of that we must remain vigilant to live as Christ has commanded us to live. This is a full-time job, and Christ knew that we would not always be successful. He sent The Comforter to teach us all things and bring them back to our memory (John 14:26).

Jesus knew that once He left the Earth that the real battle for our souls would begin. Internet memes joke about people straightening up when the commonly accepted, but universally wrong image of Jesus (I could spend all day on this) shows up and everyone starts acting right. Truthfully, many people feel that if no one is watching that we can get away with anything. We think that what we do behind closed doors or under sheets won't be known to anyone else, but God's eyes have never been dim and His ears aren't deaf. He sees us. He knows what we are doing. Instead of being angry He has compassion for us, which is why the Holy Spirit came to be with us. His Spirit is our gentle reminder that we should do this or that they way God desires for us.

The church is an extremely complicated place. Many of us that grew up in the church learned (or should have learned) what sin is and how we didn't want to disappoint God. God is a loving Father, and we are His children. Still, after a while we will cross the sin boundary and "not get caught" and we either choose to not go there again on purpose or feel that we can because no one said a word. How does this relate to the church, you may ask? These answers may shock you. Let's dig a little deeper and see.

Let me start off with a general rule: whatever a pastor or leadership allows in their church starts and ends with them. The pastor and the leadership aren't responsible for what people individually do but are responsible for what corporately happens. The same could be said (depending on the church's organizational structure) that the people are responsible for elected or appointed leadership as well. Whatever the case, intentional or unintentional, the climate for the tolerance of sin is a balanced relationship. If church attenders openly practice sin, and leadership and the pastor ignore it, they have allowed it to fester. If the congregation sees leadership openly in sin and do nothing, they have allowed it to be a cancerous head on the Body of Christ. If left unchecked this tidally locked dance of sin and allowance leads to corruption and consequences. God will speak to those who can hear Him and plead with them to take a stand and do His Will to move the people to return to the Heart of God. Meanwhile, those who aren't saved are watching it all.

This form of hurt from the church affects the saved as well as the unsaved. If sin is rampant or blatant those who hear the Voice of God and are in a good relationship with Him will either speak out or wage spiritual warfare against sin. They will face fierce opposition as the Adversary doesn't want to release territory that he has conquered. He will do all he can to smear those who speak out and impose consequences on those who are against his evil works. He will even use pastors, leaders and congregants to do the job. The illusion of sin is comfort. It feels good and pleases the flesh. Just like the body doesn't want to go run five miles for better health because it would rather sit on the couch, rest, and eat tasty morsels, the spirit in us doesn't want to please the Spirit of God, but it wants to please the flesh that it can feel directly.

Just like when someone is trying to get physically fit and fight their bodies, the flesh fights them to keep the status quo. Our flesh will never see Heaven. It craves to get all the pleasure it can right now while it is alive. Whether or not you know this, your flesh is intelligent and the Adversary whispers to it constantly and knows how to caress and manipulate it to his will. Revival in a church means that the flesh will lose out on what it wants because the spirit becomes saved. When sin is eradicated, sinful pleasures will be cut off for what is righteous.

People who practice sin will combat those who teach and preach against it. Those who are doing what's right in God's sight are candidates for hurt from the church that winks at sin. They see the people and they love them, and they love their church. They speak out because God lays it on their hearts to not allow things like this to continue. They know it's against the Word. They know it's against God. Yet they are fought against or dismissed as rogue elements or fools. It doesn't matter whether it's the congregants that speak up to leadership perpetuating or committing sin. It doesn't matter if its leadership that preaches and teaches against sin the results are the same. Pain.

When a culture of sin being permissible or overlooked in a ministry becomes pervasive it creates a Hell-designed system to create Christians who are blinded to the truth and lack spiritual power. These sorts of scenarios create what I see as two forms of hurt from the church. This first kind is that with a lack of spiritual foundation and a true measure of spiritual power, these people will be susceptible to spiritual warfare attacks, which in turn will lead to suffering in the spiritual and natural realms.

As I have said earlier, sin opens spiritual backdoors and allow the Adversary the means to pierce through our defenses and even cause Christians to be possessed or oppressed by demonic forces. These situations are painful for those who go through them. When the churches that these poor souls attend don't teach sound doctrine about sin or just ignore it allow those congregations to become a breeding ground for suffering. It may "feel" good to do what you want for a while, but consequences will come, and the payment can be their very lives.

This is like the second form of hurt from the church as it relates to sin. When it is rampant and leadership ignores it, participates in it, or leads it leads to similar painful results. Where there is a comfort culture of sin there will rise a veneer of godliness that looks good on the outside until the sin reveals itself. So many things can become deeply ingrained in people who are in ministries like this. When we, as humans, become so accustomed to something that could be bad for us it will cause us to see the truth as a lie and the lie as the truth (2 Thessalonians 2:9-13). You may ask what that means? Here's what I mean. When someone in a ministry lives in open rebellion to whatever the Bible says the ripple effects affect the one who lives contrary to God and those who observe them.

When a ministry leader is not living according to Scripture it sets a precedent that others growing in their walk with God will think that it is acceptable to be the same or to do their own thing. Others will possibly become victims of lives that live contrary to the Word of God because they can't control themselves. If their sin is predatory, they can become direct victims of their sinful actions. Others will imitate what they see as acceptable and practice it themselves. Scripture says that the wage of sin is death (Romans 6:23) and that doesn't necessarily define if the person getting paid is saved or unsaved. We will get paid what we earn in this life. Every choice has consequences and spiritually, we cannot afford to pay the high price for sinning. That price is always painful whether it is in this life or in eternity.

We can't ignore those who observe all this happening and try to speak out about it or feel that it shouldn't be as it is. Those who know in their hearts that what is happening is wrong have a heavy weight on their hearts. They can feel let down because leadership ignores what is obviously a sinful act or lifestyle. When I have experienced this sort of thing, I questioned how spiritual leaders could allow such sin and foolishness to happen in the church. I have witnessed people who were let down leave the faith or be heartbroken that their leaders don't do anything about what is obviously against the Word of God.

Here's another type of scenario. We've all seen the news and heard stories about how sin can tear a church apart. I am not going to focus on one sin or another because it's irrelevant. Does it really matter which sin it is? Some people pick on one sin over another, but God sees sin as sin. Just because someone's sin is a different "color" than theirs, they will look down on them and persecute them.

Just like every other situation that I have talked about in this chapter, the pain caused by the church and its errors have lasting effects. People's spiritual lives are at risk and when sin is involved it can be a much more complicated thing than others. Sin is completely opposed to God, and it is why Adam and Eve were evicted from the Garden of Eden. Sin blatantly committed and ignored is one of the worst.

From the pulpit to the door preachers will preach damnation on one specific sin while they are either covertly or openly committing another (or sometimes that same sin, but I digress). That, my friends, is called hypocrisy. The saved and the unsaved see this from different points of view and all roads point to disaster. "Do as I say and not say as I do" is tearing churches up from the inside out. How many have seen influential pastors who preach hard against a certain sin and then get caught red-handed committing that same sin?

What usually happens after that is that those people who followed them, modeled their lives after them, or went to their churches are left hurt, bewildered and either leave the church or abandon their faith. Conversely, those who don't know Jesus see their bad examples and then feel that they are just fine, and those church folks are all crooks and liars and ramp up their sin and may possibly die in it because they saw a person and put their faith in them versus Christ. They may even die in their sins and sentence themselves to Hell. The result is more pain.

It is sickening that people in churches feel that they can be what they want to be and not be concerned about the consequences of their actions. Sin is the culmination of being hurt in the church. People are coming seeking answers to life's questions and in some churches, they only find pain. I believe that when Jesus said that the Comforter would teach us all things and brings all things back to our memory. I believe that this is a big part of what He, an eternal God, saw coming. Hell is laughing as countless souls are steered away from the true Gospel and move away from the Love of Christ. Just remember, all pain is not just from hurt feelings. Hurt is also a damage that can leave horrible scars. When sin is involved, Satan is at work. Please never forget that.

In all these scenarios it is important to understand that walking this broken road is a marathon and not a sprint. We can either let things hurt us or let things grow us. We can choose to be the healers that God has desired for us to be, or we can perpetuate the unfortunate circumstances that cause pain and woe. Whatever your position may be in the realm of hurt from the church it is important that instead of being the victim in perpetuity, we need to turn the God as our refuge and strength and let Him show us what pain was and what conviction in the Spirit was. God will show us if we are hurting others because if we were hurt it is possible to hurt someone else.

The main cause and expert puppeteer of real hurt from the church is the Adversary. No one is better at manipulating the church into becoming a hurt locker than him. Because of that we must learn to always be on our guard and let God be our guide. We need to recognize that despite our feelings we won't be happy all the time as I have said before. Often it is our road to a strong relationship with Christ that will take us through a desert place and sometimes it is right in the church. The plans that God has for us are His and we need to understand that all that He has laid out for us is for our good. It all has a purpose and a plan for us to develop in the way God wants us to become. From a human standpoint, it seems crazy to go to a place that is supposed to be a refuge and discover that it is a place of conflict. Who goes to a hospital to get sicker or hurt worse? Who calls the fire department only for them to pour gasoline on your burning house? Yet, many Christians go to church broken and have brokenness open the front door for them.

As hard as it is to comprehend sometimes God will send us to a desert experience and we must stay there until He says move. Sometimes those places are within churches that have glaring problems, and we must endure what God lays before us on our journey. From a human viewpoint it seems unfair and even sadistic. It also feels ironic to witness a bigger mess in the church than outside of it. Our job is to trust God and His process. We may be getting grown into maturity or we may be sent to minister to a remnant that God is preparing in a tough place.

We don't know, but we should seek God before every step even while it hurts us. God never has and never will forget our pain, tears and struggling in our lives. God already knows and understands. If we believe in Him, He will reward us. If we walk the path we never would have walked unless God placed us there, we never will travel there. None of these excuses ministries that are hurting people and driving folks away from Christ, but it does let us know that wherever there is error and pain God is still there.

CHAPTER REFERENCES

[1] *The U.S. a Christian nation? Not according to the founders!* (2019, September 8). History News Network. https://www.historynewsnetwork.org/article/the-us-a-christian-nation-not-according-to-the-fou

[2] Longley, R. (2024, September 19). *What Is Theocracy? Definition And Examples*. ThoughtCo. https://www.thoughtco.com/definition-of-theocracy-721626

[3] Bible Authenticity. (2024, January 21). *Should Christians Honor Nationalistic Music And Anthems? - Bible authenticity*. Bible Authenticity. https://bibleauthenticity.com/nationalistic-music-national-anthems/

[4] Slife. (2022, September 27). *Christian Views On Sin*. The Spiritual Life. https://slife.org/christian-views-on-sin/

5

Purpose For The Pain

Those words don't make sense in any way. How can pain have a purpose? How can falling into an inconvenient situation be beneficial? No offense, but how can God use pain? I hear you and I am with you, but I also know that it is real, and pain does indeed have a divine purpose. As I have said before, we won't understand it at the time because while it is fresh, intense, and potent, the only thing we want is for the pain to ***STOP***. We could care less about what lesson it is teaching or any of the "who, what when, where or why" because the only thing we can focus on is staying sane or not dying. This broken road is much more than meets the eye and when it comes to understanding the purpose of the good as well as the bad will turn any mind upside down.

I have a theory about all of this, and I think that it goes all the way back to Adam and Eve in the Garden. Again, these are just my personal thoughts so take them as you like. Remember how Adam and Eve had everything in the Garden of Eden? Food was abundant, they didn't have to work, and I believe that they were created as eternal beings. They had it all, as far as we would think. Yet these people who God made with His own hands defied Him after He told them to not ever, never ever, ever (you get the idea) touch ***ONE TREE*** in the Garden.

Obey God's directive. That's all they had to do to keep living in paradise. A place where they didn't have to work, feel pain or anything bad happened. God would freely talk with them and they with Him and communicate on levels we can only get to by the power of the Holy Spirit. There was no money, no greed, no shame, and there wasn't any disease. Yet... They just had to ruin it for the rest of us because someone got hungry for some fruit they couldn't have while her husband sat there on his thumbs and did nothing. While bad advice was given to them by the Serpent the wheels were set in motion for the greatest lesson ever taught that we are still learning to this day.

Here is my theory: God tried telling us, but we didn't listen to His instruction so now He will show us what He wants us to learn. Sadly, the only way that humans seem to really learn is through pain. Let me explain. Adam and Eve learned the consequences of sin the hard way. God told them what each of them would now have to go through because they were hard-headed and then banished them from the only home they ever knew and posted a powerful guard to ensure that they would never return. Why? Because I believe that God made them walk out of the Garden of Eden to the rest of the world.

He let them cry and snot as they took the first Walk of Shame in human history from paradise. The irony is that because they walked away from Eden, they knew the way back but were denied by the angel with the flaming sword (I tend to imagine a blazing sword used by a giant lion-themed robot that flies in space, but I digress). God made Adam and Eve feel the regret, the remorse, the shame, and lastly, the separation from paradise and God so that they would never forget what they did. I can imagine that they often reminisced about Eden and all the great times they had there, but now? It was a distant memory. It changed them forever and not just because of sin.

This is an extreme example, but it makes some sense. Humans won't evolve unless they are forced to do it. Whether it be motivation or circumstance, we won't change some things until we meet some sort of obstacle. Think about little ones. They are born unable to walk and over time as their brains develop, they see us walking and they want to do it too. Why? Because they want to move like we do. Now, if we keep picking them up repeatedly and never let them try to walk, they will be slow to try. What would be the point? They are taken everywhere and don't have to do a thing. However, they want to move if we don't do it for them.

They will crawl first slowly and then quickly, but they know instinctively that's not enough. They will pull up on something to stand and get excited! They will giggle and laugh because they can stand on their chubby little feet. Then they let go and take a step and those wobbly little legs buckle, and they hit the floor. Bam! Then come the tears and the tantrum. Then after that? They get up again and try it repeatedly until they take that first step without falling and then another. One after another they stumble, but walk and we cheer them on, until they learn to run and we can't catch them, but that's another story.

Let's unpack this little scenario. If that little baby didn't fall, they wouldn't know that they wanted to stand again. They may have experienced pain, but it taught them to walk because they didn't want to stay there. In this scenario the pain of falling and disappointment of not walking causes the baby to learn until they get it right. Sometimes we must remember that when we fall it is not always about us being put down, but it is about being strong enough to get up. When we slip and stumble, we learn to watch our feet. We learn what not to do so that we don't end up on the floor again. Some pain that we experience is for us to learn not to be hurt anymore.

When we fail, we can also learn how to succeed. We can learn from everything and figure out a better way to go this time. They say that the difference between success and failure is one more try, right? Failing is the best teacher and sometimes God will allow us to fall and fail because He wants us to see the right way to stand and keep moving. How many of us have heard that a setback is just the prelude to a comeback? Failure isn't the end!

Look at what happened at Calvary. It seemed like Jesus had lost from the human perspective. From the outside it seems like a failure. Jesus was being executed, and it looked like Satan had won. The promised One from forty-two generations was dying on a wooden cross. He hangs His head and dies after saying that it was finished. Then Jesus, now lifeless, was placed in a tomb and buried. For seventy-two hours all seemed lost and defeat was imminent.

Oh, but after those three days! Jesus got up with all power in Heaven and Earth in His Hands! What looked like fail was the setup for victory! No, we aren't Jesus but look at what happened. Appearances are never what they seem when God is in the mix. If we could ask Lazarus about what happened to him, he would tell you the real story. Lazarus was sick and he knew he died. He had to because he was there. He felt breath leave his body and he transitioned into eternity. His family buried him and after starting to rot Jesus brought him back to life! God has destined Lazarus to rise again and when we fall or fail hard God intends for us to get up again! Not just get up the way that we fell to the ground, oh no, but be better when we rise.

When Jesus died, He got up with all power. When Lazarus rose again, he wasn't sick anymore. When that little baby falls, they get up a little stronger than they were before they fell. When we fall (whether we fail or fall into sin) God will empower us with the strength we need not only to stand again, but to stand stronger than before. That fall was repurposed from what it looked like into what it needed to make us better. We never forget where we fall. Even years later we can remember what we were doing, where we were, who we were with or what we were trying to do. When life trips us up God is still there even if we fail or stumble. He is there and sees our pain and no matter how long it takes God is there when He gives us the strength to get up again!

Getting up from a fall or failure is one thing but recovering from a circumstance that wounded us or nearly killed us is another. I will put myself out there again. I have endured some things that most people don't know about or see. I endured pain so severe that I could tell no one and many times when I was a child I was depressed and suicidal. My life seemed unlivable, and it didn't make sense. I had both of my parents who loved me, and I grew up in church and loved Jesus. I suffered for years and even though I was down I refused to go out. I held my head up the best I could and as I became an adult the scars of my pain were opened again, and I felt lonely and abandoned. I came home, cried until I couldn't anymore. I went home to see my family and I smiled and laughed and acted like I was full of life but was dead inside. Every time I felt one bit of happiness; I would get beaten down three times by suffering.

I got married, then divorced, and after that trauma, I spiraled downwards out of control. I wanted to die. I was angry at God. I was angry more at myself and I wished I was never born. I didn't see the point of being reality's whipping post. I was knocked down so much that being down felt normal. Being in the loser's column was becoming a regular thing for me and I foolishly started to accept it.

When it gets like that midnight starts to look like noon. Pain becomes an odd comfort because at least it is consistent. I was drowning and started to suck in water for air. It was nearly over. That's what I thought, and I was wrong.

God had a plan for me, and I swear that I couldn't see it back then. Even though I prayed and cried out for God and thought He didn't care, God was preparing me for my comeback. God was meticulously designing my future, and I didn't know that He was even moving in my life because He wasn't moving as I expected Him to move. Let me pause here for a second and unpack that a little bit. When we pray while we are suffering and saved, we ask God for deliverance, and we literally are only looking for God to do what we asked Him to do and not looking for His movement. We only want to see what we have requested by faith and often we don't see that God started moving when we prayed. We are still in a mess and may think that God didn't hear us or that our faith wasn't strong enough.

The Enemy starts whispering in our ears and tries to keep us distracted because I believe that the Devil can see God moving in our lives which is why he turns up the heat. He wants us to keep doubting or stay in despair. Yet God knows the exact spot and time that we will begin to come out of what is torturing us. He is right there just out of our vision and never leaves us alone. God knows the point where we will break and is ready to gather us up and start the healing process all while we don't know our limit and we still can't see God working. We just must trust Him.

For every "why" there is a reason, or purpose. It doesn't matter whether we understand it or not, for every question there is a definitive answer and thankfully, God is full of the answers that we seek in this life, and we all should be grateful about that. Many of us know Jeremiah 29:11 (some of us word for word), but do we understand exactly what that means? That God, the All Powerful, knows the plans that He has for us, and they are of good and not evil (Jeremiah 29:11)? I can honestly say that when I was young in Christ, I read those words and never truly grasped the meaning of them the way that I do now. In my naiveté, I thought that this was only about the prosperous and wonderful things that God has for my life, but after living for a little while and maturing in my relationship with Christ, I learned that it's not just the "good" times, but every waking moment we breathe has been meticulously planned out by God.

Let me pause for a second for the religious crowd who may read this and think that I am a bit off my rocker. I am not saying that our fates are sealed no matter what we do in this life. I do not subscribe to the concept of Predestination or anything like that. As I have said before, God is a being beyond the confines of time and space. He knows all before it happens, but that doesn't mean that He made it so. God's plans are His desires for us, but it is up to us to live them through or not. It is up to us to accept His promises or believe Hell's lies.

Either way, His plans are meant for our good even if we ruin them. Only we can ruin our destinies in Christ. Satan can't do anything to keep us from Heaven or our God-promised lives unless we choose to do the opposite of God's plans. Period. We are not hopeless hamsters on a treadmill. God gave us the choice to accept or reject Him and because of Who He is, God already knows the answer because of His relationship with Creation. To us, it is a paradox because our understanding is limited.

This broken road has a purpose, and that purpose is wrapped up entirely and totally in God. There are no ulterior motives or other primary stakeholders. When we are born, God has our lives ready for us to live, and His desire is that we choose Him over Hell to live in Heaven forever with Him. From our first breath until our last, Hell is waging a full-scale war against our every move and wants nothing more than blind or obfuscate the Will of God from our lives. Hell does its best work when what we go through, albeit in God's plan, isn't pleasant or its simply Hell on Earth for us. Satan wants us to avoid the hurt and the pain because he wants to trick us into thinking that we are unloved by God or being punished. He wants us to think that it's too hard and too much to walk the line God has drawn for us to walk in His word and through His guidance to us.

The answer to all the "whys" can vary, but it is God who knows the true answers and if we trust Him, He will show us the fruits of the labors to be harvested as we get through rough stretches of the broken road. Hell wants us to believe the lie that being saved is only good times, dancing, shouting unto God, and lots of windfalls and blessings. Mind you, those things do and must exist because God promised that He would bless us. He knows what we need and want and all we must do is ask (Matthew 6:8).

Let me give you a short answer as to why the pain has a purpose. Because the two results of all pain are healing and growth. In my walk with Christ these two things have always followed every dark and arduous period in my life. I am not just talking some of the time, but each time. I grew from what I went through, and I was healed not just from the painful situations, but from other spiritual traumas I had experienced that I either knew about or didn't know about.

Sure, my life may not seem bad to many people and those who know me personally would say that from outside appearances, I have had a pretty good life. While I have been blessed beyond what I can measure, I still have had trials that nearly destroyed me. Yet, when I count the cost of it all I see that I never lost, but I gained in every area of my life. Not just financially, but mentally and spiritually as well. What God set in motion for my life has shaped me, remade me, and put the right Spirit in me to serve Him and I am still not finished. There is yet more to do, and I await what He does next. I never would have seen what came into my life to shape me to what I am, and I have yet to see what is to come, but because I trust God with my life I no longer worry about the future because if He is in it? It doesn't matter. I may not like it, and I may cry many tears over it as I did in days past, but I know it is for my good. I want to encourage you, the reader, to embrace these truths and keep them in your heart.

The Jewelry Box

There is an example that God gave to me, while I was writing this section, that I want to share with you about being transformed from the beginning all the way up to the present and it blessed me so, I want to tell you the story about the Jewelry Box. We all know what a wooden jewelry box is, and we see them ornately decorated and full of personal treasures, we don't always think about what it took to get this wonderfully lacquered and decorated ornate box finished product that we can see with our eyes.

That box started many, many years ago as a seed, an acorn, for example, which was either planted on purpose or dropped to the ground from another oak tree.

That acorn had to die on the ground before it could take root into the earth. Its shiny outer shell and rugged cap would dissolve into the dirt and a tiny sprout inside of that dark seed would start to burst out of the acorn along with a root to absorb the water and nutrients from the soil. All of this is happening in relative darkness as the little acorn struggles to come forth from its tiny prison to become more than a seed.

As the tiny, budding roots began to grow deeper, the first green sprout appears above the ground and reaches towards the light, hungry for the photons that would activate the chlorophyll that is mixed with the water and nutrients from the soil that cause cells to divide and grow at a fast rate. It is here where the little oak tree is the most vulnerable. The little seedling can be crushed, eaten by animals, or starved by one good dry week of no rain because the roots aren't yet deep enough to tap into deeper moisture. Still, the seedling grows and grows, and it may lose a leaf or two along the way. It may even get partially or totally mashed into the ground by an animal or falling debris.

Still, it is within the DNA of that seedling to keep growing, keep trying, and follow the instructions in its genetic code. After a time, the green seedling begins to develop branches and even begins to produce bark as it grows from a frail seedling into a sapling with tiny little oak-shaped leaves on it. It is young and looks like an oak tree, but it is still very weak and if a brush fire came along, it would burn the sapling up and it may not recover or even die.

Time passes, and the sapling begins to grow higher and higher into the air. The roots go deeper than they ever had before, and good days come and go. Storms come and go with howling winds, rain, lighting, and the little young oak tree holds on for dear life. Years pass, and the little oak tree has branches and boughs, provides shade for those underneath its branches. It provides a home to birds and little creatures like squirrels who enjoy the acorns it produces.

It goes through seasons of spring, summer, autumn, and winter. Putting out buds, growing leaves, watching them fall and then enduring freezing cold winters with snow and ice. Some branches may even break off because of storms or snow. These little breaks can be easily recovered from, and new leaves sprout from what was previously broken. The oak tree has now become majestic and beautiful. Its wide and broad branches provide relief for those who need shade.

Its acorns produce food and new offspring. Its branches give homes to homeless creatures and even some parasites live in the tree, but overall, the oak tree stands tall and has grown tall, wide, and beautiful. Then suddenly, the logging truck pulls up.

You see, there have been others watching this tree grow taller and stronger in the woods. The logger has come because there is a need for wood products outside of the tranquil forest. This oak tree is straight, broad, and perfect to make many products from its wood, but those products cannot be made from the tree as it is right now. It has been slated to be cut down. I am sure that if the tree was like us, it would wonder why these people are looking at them differently than others that have come by before. The tree has seen humans walking by on their hikes or pitched a tent under its branches. It has heard campfire songs or seen scouts marching by. These people are different, and these humans have strange tools with them that are quite noisy.

Then, a shudder shakes the entire tree as one of those tools has sharp choppers and those teeth are slicing into the trunk of this tree, and it is not pleasant. The birds fly away in terror as this shaking is unlike any they had experienced before. The deep-woods squirrels saw them coming and they don't like people so they ran away as fast as their little legs could take them. The tree has been rocked in thunderstorms, survived a raging hurricane, and even a decimating tornado. This is different. This is hurting beyond any measure ever felt before and it is beginning to lose connection with its roots.

The loggers have chained the tree to fall in the direction they desire as the chainsaws cut deeper and deeper into the tree. Suddenly, a cracking is heard loudly as the now helpless tree feels itself breaking, splintering, and now falling to the ground below with a thunderous crash. Once, its boughs bathed in the glorious sunlight and now they are flat on the ground and it's not over. Every limb is lopped off one at a time painfully and the tree watches its many arms carved away and either shred into billions of pieces or tossed away to the side.

If the tree had emotions, it would be feeling utter defeat. It had survived many storms and rain. It endured being an acorn that fell to the ground. It had limbs torn off before, but it still stood where it was planted. This is a change that is hard to accept. Nothing this bad had happened to this tree before. I can imagine that the tree was bewildered and lost. Other trees had fallen before or have caught diseases and died, but the oak hadn't suffered calamity before. Why is this happening? This was still just the beginning.

More machines come and grasp the once mighty trunk and place it on a truck to be hauled away from the only place the tree has known as its home. This is terrifying as the truck shudders and pulls away while the tree sees the birds, deer, and squirrels watch in horror as their home, friend, and companion is now gone forever. The tree will never be the same and for a while, things seem to stabilize. The ride to the logging company isn't that bad now that the cutting down and cutting off limbs is over.

Now the oak tree trunk is unloaded from the truck, taken to a processing area, and observes as other trees are being placed one-by-one onto a very large belt that heads into a building. I can imagine that this tree feels lost by now. Taken from where it was comfortable and forcefully transformed from a mighty oak tree with innumerable leaves to a barren stalk going into the unknown. It was now covered with scars, maimed, and had no control over what was next, and that part was even worse than it had experienced before.

Up until this point, the tree still looked like a tree. It may have lost its limbs, leaves, and a few patches of scraped off bark but eyes could still see that this was a mighty oak tree at one time. Yet that was about to change as the conveyor belt was taking the tree trunk into the sawmill. The broad and mighty tree was split into many pieces. I can imagine the tree feeling ripped apart and flayed wide open exposing its inner flesh to the air for the first time. Every imperfection and every crevice were now laid bare.

The scent of the sap, the tree's blood, permeated the air as the saws sliced and chewed the tree's flesh apart piece by piece and shaped against its will into planks. These planks were then taken to other machines like planers that scraped off all the bark and shaped the oak wood into the desired shapes. Inspectors evaluated the quality of the wood as less desirable wood was used for products such as pressed wood pieces or things like toothpicks. Sturdier pieces were turned into specifically sized wood planks like 2x4's and 4x4's for building. Some pieces were turned into flooring and other related products, but the best and prettiest wood, the heart of this tree, was saved for a special purpose.

Imagine for a moment that this oak tree now feels decimated. All that it once was and was connected to is now gone. Most of it has been carved away and sent elsewhere or even discarded. The essence of the oak tree has now changed. It's not a tree anymore but now known as oak wood. It has a new designation. No longer is it what it was born as, but now it has been set aside for a special purpose that it doesn't yet know is coming. Now this precious oak wood is packed away and sent from the sawmill and destined for its purpose. The oak wood no longer bathes in the sunlight or enjoys the cool rain. It no longer can feel its roots in the soil that it had fed from for many years.

It is no longer a friend to birds or squirrels. It is alone for the first time and in the company of those it does not know. Torn apart from everything that it has ever known I can imagine that the tree is angry, sad, and in a mental state of flux. Why did this happen to me? Why didn't the pine tree get taken? Why didn't the maple tree get chopped down? I can imagine that the oak wood is going over memories of past storms and wishing they had perished earlier. That lightning that struck years earlier should have set that tree on fire, but it survived. I can imagine the oak wood wishing that it would have burned before suffering what it's going through now.

Little did the oak wood know, but all of this led to the carpenter's workshop. Even though the oak wood had suffered plenty already in its journey it still wasn't done from suffering pain. The carpenter saw the wood's quality and knew that they could use this wood for something special. They purchased the wood and took it home with them. Surely, the oak wood thought that this had to be the end of this long journey. The oak had suffered and at least it wasn't thrown away or left to rot, but the carpenter saw what the oak wood could not see: a masterpiece.

The carpenter began by measuring the wood and marking what still needed to be cut off and shaped. The oak was then cut by specialized tools more delicate than the ones from the lumberjack or the sawmill. Care was taken to cut only where it needed to be cut and not splinter the wood unnecessarily. Etchings were made and routers carved in rounded areas and special corners. The oak wood must have felt even worse than before because they thought that after being bought and saved from an unknown fate was enough. It wasn't.

The carpenter worked with love and care to follow their plans for the oak wood and assembled the wood in a way that the wood didn't understand. The wood had no influence as to how it was purchased, and they didn't have any say as to how it would be handled. They were in the hands of the carpenter. After a while, the oak wood began to see what was happening and began to get a sense of peace. They started to trust the carpenter because what was just wood was now taking shape.

The carpenter used sandpaper to smooth out rough spots and did so with their own hands. The wood was sanded, made beautiful, nailed with tiny nails, and glued together. Only the smoothest and prettiest wood was used to make this masterpiece. Then the oak was stained with a color that the carpenter desired. This was done over and over to ensure that the desired color was well represented in the oak wood. It was then left to dry as the carpenter continued their work. Before the last step, the wood was sealed with lacquer to preserve its color and beauty. The wood was no longer susceptible to water rotting it away or worms and parasites to eat its flesh anymore. It was now protected.

The carpenter didn't do all this instantly, but in stages. Measuring, cutting, sanding, assembling, staining, sealing, and then adding hinges, latches, and knobs the oak wood had never seen before. Screws penetrated the oak wood as if all the hardware is finally attached causing some more pain, but it was still being lovingly and skillfully done by the carpenter. This oak wood was now shaped by its master's hands and transformed from its original state. It has been quite the journey for this oak tree, and it seems that this odyssey was finally over, but it was still not complete. The carpenter still had more to do to this oak wood.

The carpenter had a purpose for this still rough wood that the wood didn't know. The carpenter needed a jewelry box and saw the wood best suited for the job. Even though it was no longer the tall tree that it once was it was still oak, and the carpenter saw and desired it even though it was still just pieces of wood. After creating their masterpiece in the image and likeness they desired, it was time to leave the workshop and be used for its purpose: a jewelry box.

The oak wood was no longer just wood, but now a jewelry box and placed in its special place set just for it to go. No longer outside to face the elements and no longer prey to parasites the jewelry box has had quite the journey from being rooted in the earth and even though the newly minted jewelry box could think that it has finally arrived, it still hasn't fulfilled its purpose. There was a purpose for being a survivor of being planted, growing up tall and strong, being cut down and disfigured, and being forcefully changed from what was comfortable into what was not.

This jewelry box was designed for jewelry! The carpenter now opens the box and places their special treasures inside. Rings of gold, chains of silver, diamonds and precious stones are placed in the jewelry boxes drawers, hooks, and cupboards. The insides of the jewelry box are lined with felt and other adornments the oak tree never had or seen before. The jewelry box finally sees what all of this has been for. At each step of the way the box could not see why all of this had been happening and was never meant to see it. Let me explain.

As an oak tree, it could not handle jewelry being placed inside of it. The oak tree was out in the open where thieves could take the treasure from it. The oak tree was unrefined, raw, and dirty compared to the jewelry box. Jewelry would have been surrounded by birds and other creatures and not fit for use where it was. The treasures were meant for safekeeping by the owners, and the oak had a mandate to be transformed. The carpenter had use of and demanded oak which sent the request to the supply which was the forest.

The supply was acquired but the carpenter didn't need all the oak tree. The jewelry box doesn't have any place for birds' nests or leaves. They had to go. The jewelry box had no need of bark, and it had to go. The carpenter only desired the best of oak wood, so what wasn't fit had to go. What the oak was used to doing didn't fit what the carpenter desired so all of it had to go. For the oak to be what the carpenter desired, the oak had to start a journey from the forest to the front room and that trip involved transformation as it went. The tree couldn't hold the treasure until it was transformed.

What was not needed or would impede the functions of a jewelry box were stripped away. The rough edges were made smooth. The jewelry box was not shaped like a tree but made from it. What wood that made the jewelry box was chosen by the carpenter. The tree could not see it because it was never meant to see it. The tree had no control once it left the forest and when its journey began.

It went through transformation after transformation until it was completed. Even then, it still would have to be repaired from time to time.

Hinges break, the interior soft felt gets damaged, and some pieces may need to be replaced or repaired. Improvements could be made and after time the jewelry box could be sanded down again and re-stained and lacquered again. Transformations and repairs are done until the jewelry boxes life is over. All the oak tree's journey had a purpose. Each step of the transformation had a purpose. That oak tree could not be used until it was changed. It didn't happen all at one time, and it had to occur in stages until it would perform the functions it was desired to do: hold treasures inside of it.

Examples in the Word of God

We are not jewelry boxes, but we do hold heavenly treasures inside that God has designed for us to carry. Just like that jewelry box, for us to be what God has intended for us to be we must be transformed, and we won't and can't always see those changes coming. When we look at the Scriptures, we can see many instances of where the people in the Bible from Abraham in the Book of Genesis all the way to the apostle John in the Book of Revelation. From the first Adam until now there have been many who have had to endure their own broken roads, and we could fill many books with their testimonies. Let's look at a brief list of them:

1. Abraham - Formerly known as Abram, God took him and his wife Sarai from their home in Ur into what would be the promised land (Genesis 12:1). Through it all God changed their names to Abraham and Sarah (Genesis 17:5, 15), and they were the founders of the nation of the Israelites via their descendants. Abraham was told to sacrifice his son Isaac on a mountain, and he almost did it until God stepped in (Genesis 22: 1-13). Abraham left everything he knew and had to trust a God he never knew before to be the Father of Many Nations.
2. Joseph - Grandson of Abraham and favored of his father Israel who made him his special, colorful coat (Genesis 37:3). God gave him visions and dreams that said that he would rule over his family (Genesis 37:5). Hated by his brothers for what God gave him, he was sold into Egyptian slavery and told by those same brothers that he was dead (Genesis 37:23-33). Was a slave at Potiphar's house where the woman of the house wanted to get fleshly closer to him. Joseph stood his ground, ran from

this woman, did the right thing and ended up in jail for it (Genesis 39:1-20). While in jail met a baker and cupbearer and used his gifts to interpret dreams and was forgotten by them until Pharaoh had a dream that he couldn't understand years later (Genesis 40). Got out of jail, interpreted the dream, and was rewarded by Pharaoh as the second in command in Egypt (Genesis 41:14). After a famine, Joseph met his long-lost brothers, and his dreams became a true reality (Genesis 42:6). Everywhere Joseph went he was blessed and went from the pit, to Potiphar, to the prison, and finally the palace. Had to be taken from where he was comfortable, endure pain, and elevated all while using his gifts from God.

3. David - The founder of the royal Davidic line from the Tribe of Judah started as a shepherd boy that was not called by his own father Jesse when the prophet Samuel came to anoint Israel's next king (1 Samuel 16:10-12). David said that he was born in sin and shaped in iniquity (Psalm 51:5) so it's possible that he was the product of an affair as his mother is never named. We don't know for sure, but David went from the killer of Goliath (1 Samuel 17:49-50), the favorite of Saul to the hunted of Saul and an exile. David had a man killed to get his wife, who he impregnated after watching her bathe from a rooftop (2 Samuel 11:1-5), lost the child he conceived in sin (2 Samuel 12:18) and endured his other son's attempted coup (2 Samuel 15 - 2 Samuel 16) and subsequent murder (2 Samuel 18:14-15). All of this while he wrote songs to God that we enjoy to this day. A man that was after God's Heart (Acts 13:22).
4. Sampson - The Israelite champion who was predestined before his birth to be a mighty man of God (Judges 13:1-5). Was incredibly strong and killed many Philistines (Judges 15:16). Sampson was a flawed hero that even though he knew his purpose, he had trouble with women, and horribly bad taste in them (Judges 16:1-4) and had a bad temper (Judges 14:19). He told Delilah his secret and was captured, blinded, and tortured by the Philistines (Judges 16:21). He finally wised up when he attended a banquet that celebrated the Philistine victory over them, prayed to God and killed over 3000 people via his suicide (Judges 16:26-30). Sampson learned his purpose once his gift was stripped from him after years of doing his own thing. Strife brought Sampson to the Heart of God at the time he needed to the most to fulfill his destiny.
5. Daniel - An exile stolen from Israel (Daniel 1:6), Daniel was a blessed young man and found favor with the king of Babylon (Daniel 1:18). Endured ridicule and persecution for being different. Proved that God favored him and that angered his peers (Daniel 6:1-5). Was targeted for living holy unto God and thrown in the lion's den to be eaten (Daniel 6:16). God delivered him and his persecutors were then made the lions' substitute supper since God kept their mouths closed overnight and they were hungry (Daniel 6:24). Engaged with angels that held up the answers to his prayers for weeks (Daniel 10:12-14). Daniel was one of the

greatest prophets and seers of Scripture all while being stolen from his homeland, given a foreign name, and persecuted for serving God.

6. Jonah – The prophet and preacher who was told to go to Nineveh and preach and deliver people that he despised (Jonah 1:1-2). Jonah knew how powerful God is and decided that he wasn't going to do what God wanted and jumped on a ship in another direction because he rejected his assignment (Jonah 1:3). God wasn't having any of that and sent a terrible storm while Jonah was running away and ended up getting tossed into the sea because Jonah realized that the storm that was threatening those around him was because of him (Jonah 1:9-10). We can assume that Jonah would rather drown than go to Nineveh, but God arranged a personal transport from the sea that swallowed Jonah whole and vomited him up near Nineveh after three days of being in the stomach of a great fish (Jonah 1:17). Fresh from being partially digested, the possibly bald, discolored, and ragged Jonah probably looked like a prophet of doom. Jonah operated like one because he knew that God was serious about his directive for Jonah to go and preach (Jonah 3:1-10). Then got upset when God moved, saved the peoples souls, and caused repentance to flow (Jonah 4:1-3). Jonah tried to ignore the assignment but was dragged into it because a whole city was on the line and Jonah's hubris was not going to stand in the way of God's plans.
7. Nehemiah – An exile slave who served in the king's court of the Persian empire who got permission to go back to Jerusalem (Nehemiah 2:6) and rebuilt the walls of the sacked and burned city of Jerusalem (Nehemiah 1:3). Nehemiah was not a prophet or a minister, but a prayer warrior and servant of God. Nehemiah had exceptional faith to petition the king, get written orders to go (Nehemiah 2:7-8), and organized a group to go back to Israel to rebuild the walls of Jerusalem (Nehemiah 2:11-12). Encountered hecklers and vagrants who wanted to keep the city destroyed and the temple unbuilt (Nehemiah 4:1-3). Defied the calls against his own life to fulfil the urging of God to embark on such a monumental task (Nehemiah 4:7-8). Even had people stand armed at night and work around the clock to rebuild the walls in fifty-two days (Nehemiah 6:15)! Nehemiah had faith to move, faith to work, and faith to stand in adversity even when his life was threatened. Nehemiah ended up as the governor of Jerusalem and a wise ruler of integrity because of all the lessons he learned from his oppressors.
8. Peter – Simon, son of Jonah (שמעון בן יונה or *Shimon ben Yonah*), was a fisherman who admitted that he was an unlearned man (Acts 4:13) was approached by Jesus while he was fishing with his brother Andrew (Matthew 4:18). He dropped everything and followed Christ from that point on (Matthew 4:19) and sat under Jesus' teaching for three years. Peter was a hot head and didn't hold things back when he was asked about them. Peter was quick to pull out a weapon and hurt someone to

defend Jesus (John 18:10) but was a coward and denied he even knew Jesus when he was asked after Jesus was arrested (John 18:15-18, 25-27). Later, Peter became one of the most prominent preachers of the Gospel as the Apostle to the Jews (Galatians 2:8). Was the primary messenger on the Day of Pentecost (Acts 2) and never looked back. He was still skeptical of God's direction when he was told to see Cornelius (Acts 10:19), but he had great faith and preached to the Jews and even his shadow could set people free from disease (Acts 5:15). Peter went from a simple fisherman to one of the Twelve Apostles and was crucified for his work building up the Kingdon of God. He worked through all his issues and God helped him through them.

9. Paul - Saul of Tarshish was a Pharisee and highly educated religious scholar who ended up being a serious persecutor of the followers of The Way (Acts 9:2), which we call it Christianity today. He watched Stephen get stoned to death and approved (Acts 8:1). Saul was responsible for seek-and-destroy missions as he orchestrated people being severely punished or murdered for being a disciple of Christ (Acts 9:2). While on the way to his next murderous assignment to Damascus he met Jesus on the road who spoke to him and blinded him while others with him watched (Acts 9:3-6). Saul went to a house in Damascus (Acts 9:8) and started to pray and heard from the Lord all while Annanias was being sent to the man who was famous for persecuting Christ followers (Acts 9:10-12). Annanias was told to pray for this man and baptize him and when he did Saul regained his sight (Acts 9:17-19), started going by his other name to Paul (Acts 13:9), and went out preaching the Gospel. At first, he was distrusted but proved himself and was relentless just like he was as an assassin as a travelling Apostle. He endured demonic attacks (2 Corinthians 12:7-10), was whipped (2 Corinthians 11:24), jailed (2 Corinthians 11:23), shipwrecked (2 Corinthians 11:25), beaten and left for dead (Acts 14:19). He got older and was nearly blind (Galatians 4:13-15) and wrote many letters to churches he planted and to those he served with in ministry. We still read those letters today. Paul went from persecutor to preacher, murderer to miracle worker, and apostate to apostle and suffered loss and tragedy along the way as he changed the Christian world forever. He was finally murdered by being beheaded.
10. John the Revelator - One of the greatest prophets in history, we don't know a lot about his life besides being one of the original Twelve Apostles. What we do know is that his ministry was so effective and so fervent that it ruffled enough feathers for him to be exiled to the remote Greek island of Patmos. John had visions that were not like most and while what he experienced had parallels to what Daniel saw, John was taken to places that hadn't been seen before. John spoke as an oracle of God to the Seven Churches of Asia Minor and foretold the End of Days, Eternal Judgement, and the New Jerusalem on the New Earth. John was

isolated after being persecuted and then punished for God to use him to write what was never known before. John was a prolific author writing the Gospel of John, First, Second, and Third John and of course, the Book of the Revelation of Jesus Christ. Many believe that John was the only one of the Twelve Apostles that was not martyred. Some agree, but disagree, but it took isolation and persecution for John to use the gifts God gave him to fulfill his destiny.

There is one person on this list that I left off on purpose even though we have already talked about him at length. That's because I want to dissect his story a little more than just a summary and I am sure that you know who I am talking about. That man is Job.

Job: Why Pain Has A Purpose

Job is a person that we never would have ever heard about in history at all if it weren't for his story recorded in the Bible. Why would we have heard about him otherwise? He was just another rich old guy with a great life and not many rich people are written about in such detail. While we have heard and read his account in Scripture, most don't understand his ordeal until they have their own Job-like experience. It was not even the riches-to-rags-to-riches story either that caused Job's story to be written. Job didn't do anything special but existed in his time and lived his life. Job was not a prophet, did not perform miracles, and did not lead an army or a nation. Job was just a man who lived a life devoted to God. Here, to me, is what made Job a person that Scripture was written about him. Job bent and buckled but never broke and that my friends is a miracle.

Let's back up for a few moments and examine Job carefully. Job was truly in a dark place and after he suffered loss, Job still exalted God. Job remarked that he came from his mother's womb naked and to the ground after death he would return naked. God gives and God takes away, and he blessed the Name of the Lord (Job 1:21). That makes me think about the old Gospel song with the line, "I've got Jesus and that's enough" and Job personified this completely.

Job was an upright man and that, by no means meant that he was perfect because he wasn't. He was still in flesh and very much human even though God bragged on him before the face of Satan. Job was continually offering sacrifices for himself and his family because he knew the consequences of stepping out of favor with

God and he didn't want that at all. Job's awareness of the troubles of others was more than present in his mind, and we don't know if he had suffered anything like he experienced in the Book of Job before. All we know is that this man was on God's lips as He told Satan that Job was a man like none other.

God then did something unique that we hadn't seen in scripture which was tell Satan that he had permission to test Job (Job 1:8). He allowed Hell to show up at Job's doorstep and begin to torture him and his family. Satan did this few times and God allowed Satan to go further and further in his level of torture until Job was left bankrupt, diseased and utterly broken. Covered with swollen, pus-filled and painful boils, Job's life was destroyed. Even his wife told him that he should just curse God and die (Job 2:9). Job wanted to die and wished that he was never born (Job 3:1).

Job wracked his brain trying to understand why he was suffering. If I could use my imagination, I could imagine that people who didn't believe in God made fun of that "holy roller" Job and his invisible God were "nuts". Job probably watched as the idolatrous and sinful were living large while he barely clung to his faith and was completely ruined. Job had every right to be angry (just don't commit sin of course) and I can't imagine what his level of sanity was at that point. I'm sure that he felt like he was losing his grip on reality.

I can't begin to ascertain how Job felt because the Book of Job was written most likely by someone else close to the situation. Whatever Job felt, he never completely gave up on God. He may have talked sideways to God a bit, but he never totally abandoned his faith in God. Job hung in there and even when his friends came at him wrong (even though they were still his friends) Job didn't let them sway him either. Weakened, struggling and holding onto his last strand of faith, Job persevered and was cracked, bent and overextended, but never broke. God knew that this was as far as Job could literally handle. Satan lost and God restored Job to better than he ever was giving way to the expression we now say in the Christian faith that Job "got double for his trouble" which he literally did.

Sure, this may be a remarkable story of triumph over tragedy, but for many in our world this is their current reality. There are several things about Job's account that I found to be interesting. The first thing is that we never knew how long Job's trial was. Scripture doesn't give us an exact approximation of when Job lived like many other accounts in the Bible. Abraham and Sarah were dated by their ages. The enslavement of the Hebrews in Egypt was annotated to the year. The wandering in the wilderness was denoted by how many years. Yet Job wasn't given a chronology.

I don't believe that this was by accident. I think God intended for us to see and realize that if we are allowed to go through tribulation that we will never know how long it is to last for us. Job could have had a month of Hell, or decades of suffering and we will never know, but what I do know is that no matter what God raised Job up from the ashes, restored everything that he lost and gave him even more than he had. Even Job's restoration isn't explicitly recorded. Regardless of any of this God won't give us a time we are to be in trouble like a prison sentence would.

We must live day to day not knowing if today the last day for the darkness is to pervade. Job didn't let loss get him down so far that he would stop praising God. That man lost his animals, his family and his property and he still loved God. He didn't change his attitude towards Heaven because of what was happening on Earth. It is hard to not do that, but seeing Job's account shows us that it is possible. No matter the material things or the failures God is still blessing us, and we need to keep blessing Him!

Job was also a man of incredible faith and fortitude. Job was practically in ruins at this point and said, "Though He slay me, yet I will trust Him!" (Job 13:15). Job was willing to trust God even if it meant that he would lose his life. He knew like Paul that to be absent from the body is to be present with The Lord (2 Corinthians 5:6-8). Job couldn't see the end of his suffering and didn't know the plan, but he knew that if God was in it there was no way he could truly lose. Job had a measure of faith that was uncommon among many on the Earth.

Job may have been down and may have been sad, but he wasn't out just yet. He wasn't perfect, but he refused to lose faith and lose heart in God. Disease may come, death may come, loss may come, but if we have Jesus we win. Plain and simple. Job couldn't see God moving, but he had faith that God would not let him completely go. Even if Job were to die, he would keep his trust in God. That's powerful. Those words, "God, I trust you" are so hard to say as well as believe because no one wants to die, but Job was willing to do just that.

Job was seemingly punished for no reason except that God bragged on him as being righteous. Job understood punishment too. Job 5:17-18 says this:

BLESSED IS THE ONE WHOM GOD CORRECTS; SO DO NOT DESPISE THE DISCIPLINE OF THE ALMIGHTY. FOR HE WOUNDS, BUT HE ALSO BINDS UP; HE INJURES, BUT HIS HANDS ALSO HEAL. – JOB 5:18-18 KJV

This often makes me think of a doctor performing surgery. When a surgeon cuts us with a scalpel, they cause us to bleed. They must open us up with knives, make deep cuts into our bodies that require anesthesia for us not to feel or remember the pain. The same hands that cut us open are the same hands that stitch us back together for our healing. That process of healing is progressive. We will still feel the results of the cutting, and we are never the same after leaving the operating room. When we meet the consequences of our actions God will allow us to undergo spiritual surgery through spiritual, physical, or emotional means to cut some things off or out.

He will cut us so that we can be reshaped and rerouted internally and then sew us back up again to be healed. He may even perform surgery, like those hospital shows on television, where they won't close the incision because the body must do some healing before closure. After being open but watched over closure of the incision is closed when the time is right. Job learned that his deliverance took some time, and his wounds were left open for a long time.

Here is something else that I find interesting… Job's story also showed us that God has Satan on a choke chain. He may act big and bad, but he still must obey God. Wait, the greatest rebel of them all who defied the God of Creation did exactly what God told him to do. This made me think about a lot of things. Hell cannot and will not run unchecked in our lives because God will draw a line, and they won't ever cross it. Think about that for a moment and let your mind wander back to situations you may have gone through or take inventory of what you are currently in the middle of right now. No matter how bad it may get God has limited Hell to what it can do to you. Our God is not the author of evil. Sometimes something good can come from something nefarious.

Let me say that again, something good can come from something evil that happens to us. When Lucifer and God had that conversation, he told the Devil that all that Job has is up to Satan as to what he does with it (Job 1:12). Take note that God gave the Devil the limits of what he could mess with. When stuff happens to us, and it is just plain awful to go through, we must remember something important. God set the boundary of what He knows that you can handle. Think about that for a moment. God drew a line in the sand and told the Enemy how far he could go to hurt you. That seems sadistic, but it's not. How God does things don't make sense to us, but God uses the Devil's toolbox to shape us into righteousness. We need to know that God has already prepared the treatment plan for healing. Job's healing came through what I thought were two remarkably interesting activities.

In Job 42:8 the Scripture says:

THEREFORE TAKE UNTO YOU NOW SEVEN BULLOCKS AND SEVEN RAMS, AND GO TO MY SERVANT JOB, AND OFFER UP FOR YOURSELVES A BURNT OFFERING; AND MY SERVANT JOB SHALL PRAY FOR YOU: FOR HIM WILL I ACCEPT: LEST I DEAL WITH YOU AFTER YOUR FOLLY, IN THAT YE HAVE NOT SPOKEN OF ME THE THING WHICH IS RIGHT, LIKE MY SERVANT JOB. – JOB 48:8 KJV

The first thing God asked Job to do before He brought him out of his tribulation was for him to give God an offering for Job's friends. God didn't ask Job to do this, but He obligated him to do it. Job was still in ruins and still in a mess and God directed him to pray for his friends. Wow! Job's pain and his suffering were immediately turned into ministry!

Look at what you've been through and rewind the video. See that every place that you were tested, beaten, broken, and battered is an opportunity for God to use you to help someone else. Ministry isn't just being a preacher or a pastor, but it is also being a prayer warrior, a worshipper, or a set of helping hands. It can simply just be a witness to someone who is going or endured what you did. There isn't a single class, degree or program that can be created through surviving hard knocks with Jesus in our lives. In verse 10 of the same chapter, it said that God ended Job's captivity when he prayed for his friends and God blessed him double.

This is the second thing, and it was recorded in Job 42:11. His family, friends and acquaintances came to eat dinner with him at this house, comforted him and gave him some money and one earring of gold. They all knew what had happened to Job because they came to comfort him over his ordeal. Notice that Job was ***STILL HEALING*** after it all went down. Job needed comfort and I am sure that he told those people exactly what he went through. We don't know who was there, but it is possible that the one that authored the Book of Job might have been there. Job shared what he went through, and I am sure that he told the people exactly how God brough him out of it.

Job himself made a difference. Sure, these people could have brought him money and helped him out, but it wasn't the right time. If Job was getting rescued by people instead of God, don't you think the story would have been different? Job ***HAD*** to go through it all because Jon ***HAD*** to see the salvation of God. These folks could have held him up and cheered him up, but God didn't allow it for a purpose. He was abandoned by people that knew exactly where he was and yet they only showed up after, but God! Job lived a long life, was richer than before and died in peace. What a powerful testimony!

I dare say that if it weren't for the Book of Job millions of people would not believe that God is a God of restoration. Job was one man God allowed things to tragically happen to him even though he was righteous. The story of ***ONE MAN'S PAIN*** has literally changed the lives of millions. Even though I had read about Job since I was a child, I didn't understand it until I lived through severe pain. Many have heard the church expression "double for your trouble" and yet many don't even really know what it means until they experience it for themselves.

Job's pain had a purpose which was to help those who are going through their own desert places to know that there is hope and salvation from the storms of life. What we may not understand is the "why" while we are going through, but we must trust God for the ***WHY*** we are going through it all. No matter how fierce a hurricane may be the Sun never stops shining even though the clouds above are torrentially wreaking havoc on the ground. While the rain is in one spot the light of day is in another.

Job's story is a testimony and a testament that if our faith doesn't waver that God will always come through. Job's heart may have been broken as well as his spirit, but he never gave up on God. Some will say that he argued with God, and he hated his life, but I have learned that we will argue with someone if we have love for them. Job loved God and was questioning why he was going through all of this.

God's reply was God being raw and uncut with Job. He let Job know where Job stood in the grand scheme of things and God reminded job that He was God, and He knew what He was doing. I got that reminder too that God was in control in my life too. Job's pain had a purpose to be a witness for millions of people that despite what they go through God will bring them out for His Glory. I am not saying that my story will change the world, but it might change the lives of a few people. Your story may change many or it may change the life of one, but the point is that your story has a purpose.

So, What's It All About?

Being a Christian guarantees one thing and one thing only: eternal life with Jesus Christ forever and everything else pales in comparison. I think that we often think of eternal life as the cherry on top, but it is the entire sweet reward. Walking this broken road requires sacrifice as we are foreigners in a strange land. The Earth at this moment is ruled over by Satan because Adam gave up his place when he sinned. The Kingdom of God is not an Earthly kingdom of brick and stone, but of hearts and souls connected to Jesus Christ. Jesus said Himself that His Kingdom is not of this world.

We must realize that what we live and fight for is not going to be here. Yes, The Kingdom manifests on Earth, but the Earth is captivated and overrun by sin. Why else would God have to renovate the Earth by fire? Where the Saints of God are, so is the Kingdom. Part of being a Kingdom Citizen is enduring suffering. That's not my opinion, but Scripture backs that up. We get to know Christ by the fellowship of His suffering (Philippians 3:10). This road was never meant to be easy every single day.

We don't know why God does what He does and why He will allow things to happen to us that seem like He hates us. On the contrary, God loves us deeply and we matter greatly to Him. He is the ***BEST FATHER***, and He knows what we need to be what He knows we can be. This will sound crazy, but we need to

THANK GOD for the test that seems unpassable. We need to bless God for the situation that seems impossible. We need to be grateful for the mountain that seems insurmountable. We need to tell our flesh to take a backseat and realize the truth. God chose us for this. Yes, it seems unfair, but God is beyond time. God sees the end and the beginning at the same time. He also sees what we cannot see and how our lives may seem insignificant to us but are not to God.

Sure, we may get lied on, betrayed, sick unto death or lose everything we have. We may lose everyone that we love around us, but we need to kick our own selves in the seat of our pants and remember that God is above it all. God is in charge and in control. If He brought someone else out? He can bring ***YOU OUT!*** Even if the fight ends in death we still win. Even if we never get it back, we still win. It doesn't matter because God gets all the glory. God will use our situations to let others know that things aren't as impossible as their senses and intellects say they are.

God will allow us to go through years of pain because He knows we can handle it. How we choose to respond is the key. How we stand for Him is critical. Of course, we will cry because it hurts. Yes, we won't always be the smiling Christian with a Bible under our arm and a praise on our lips. What we will be able to do is keep believing in God. We will keep faith in His promises. We will let others see that God is still good no matter what.

I have heard folks applying the lie that what happened back in the Bible days doesn't happen anymore and that simply is ridiculous. There are modern-day Jobs whose stories have yet to be told. There are many people who have had a very hard way to go and have kept their testimonies to themselves because of either pride, fear, or shame. It is interesting to me that most Christians are more willing to witness to someone who doesn't know Jesus versus witnessing to the goodness of God that brought them out of a very dark place in their lives.

While it is important to witness to others about Jesus, we should also tell others about how we survived what should have killed us. We should bear witness to how God can heal any disease and repair any relationship. We should speak boldly about our struggles with depression and suicide. We have too many people either going to Hell unsaved or living defeated lives because we don't share the goodness of God the way we should.

I never said that we should "over share" and tell all our business. We don't need to do that to get the point across that God can rescue anyone out of a mess or bring them through the darkest parts of their story. Believe me, there are parts of my story that will only come out if God commands me to do so. Condemn me if you want or call me a hypocrite, but it's true. It's that way for most of us and I believe that God understands where we are coming from.

Still, we can tell our story and let people know about the darkest days of our lives and we can do it in a way that will get the meat of the testimony across and not allow ourselves to relive the deepest parts of the shame or disaster again unless God leads us to do so. If we have developed a strong relationship with God, we will know when and how He is leading us. Some people may not understand what you've been through, but we need to be witnesses anyway, even though we felt like losers at the time.

I also want to encourage you all to stop crying, "Why me?" I want to let you know that when we are in the middle of a terrible situation, we can wonder why is it that we got to be the "winner", and I mean that sarcastically. It is here where Satan uses his best tactics against us. He knows how to make us feel like we are victims and that we are hated by God. He can make us feel like we are being picked on by Heaven and unwanted by Christ. When trouble comes it does get murky sometimes and it gets confusing to know which way is up. I've been there. I get it.

We just must turn down what our flesh is telling us, and we need to remember that God is a loving Father and that everything that we may experience in this life is for our good. I know that I have said that before, but it needs to be said over and over until we truly bury it in our spirits. We are not victims or a sick practical joke that God is playing on us. We were designed for this; built for this. We were made to be overcomers, and we were created to prove to everyone around us that God is God and that there is no one like Him. Period.

You had faith enough to endure the pain. You had the strength enough to carry the burden that no one else could carry like you can carry it. Only you had the fragrance of worship and ministry that God knew was in you that couldn't come out until you were placed in the press. You weren't chosen because you weren't any good. You were selected because God knew that He could trust you with the trial. He knew that you have it in you to win. God knew that if you just waited until your change comes that you can set things in motion that could bless someone's life by your testimony. We were meant to be on this road of life. God knew from the beginning where we would be and what we would do in our lives. We need to banish the feelings that we are victims and realize that we are victors.

So, why not you? God uses life situations to grow us in faith and practice. Faith is something that is built or grown and never given. Read Hebrews Chapter 11. All those people had to ***GROW*** faith and earn their stripes. I've yet to see anyone in the Scriptures that just magically had strength and faith to do it all. Sorry to disappoint, but that is not real life. Even Jesus had a moment in His flesh. "O my Father, if it be possible, let this cup pass from me: nevertheless, not as I will, but as thou wilt." is what He said (Matthew 26:39).

His flesh said no, but His Spirit said yes. Let the pain come and your mind and body may feel every drop, but let your spirit say, "it is well" and keep it moving. We are chosen. We are made for this. The walk is hard, but God is there to give us what we need to overcome it. If, by chance, it is for restoration? To God be the glory! If it is a loss? To God be the glory! Why? Count it ***ALL*** joy. Not just the flashy parts, not just the good parts, but ***ALL OF IT***.

When we give God the glory and amazing thing begins to happen. We start to see the unfiltered love of God, and it changes us. We see that God has been so much better than we could have imagined. We see that God has a love that cannot be calculated or explained in human ways. His Love is so deep that it never makes sense. His power is so vast that we cannot calculate it. The fact that God has wiped out entire nations of people for those He loves seems unorthodox and even weird but look at the evidence.

We have looked at Creation, Job, and so many more things and we have seen what God has done and will do for us. He has never abandoned us. He has never been an absentee Father to His children. It becomes liberating and it releases us into realms that we never could have reached before. Sure, we must get to this point and just survive what we are going through but trust me when I say that it will be worth it!

The Final Answer

I know that we have talked about Biblical figures and talked scenarios that seem like our own in modern times, but what does all of that have to do with us? What is the purpose of all this pain that we must endure on the road of life? Why does God oversee us going through all the struggles, tribulations, and more? Why must people endure the suffering of going through life in sin to meet Jesus only to find that it gets much worse even though it is better?

Why can't I just live my life and be happy? Why was I hurt in the house of God? Why do we need to go through all this stuff just to fulfill our destiny in God? Why can't God just speak a word, and it just happens in my life? Is this truly necessary? Why is Hell always involved? Why is spiritual warfare necessary when God is God and Heaven has already won after Jesus died on the cross? I can sum it all up with one word: ***TRANSFORMATION***.

Look at every person that I have talked about in this book and those that are in Scripture and take note of how they started and how they finished. Not a single person from Scripture remained the same. Not even one. Some started off wicked and ended up in God's service. Some started off as rebellious servants of God and ended up as faithful servants of God. Some started as timid sheep and ended as roaring lions. Some changed their names as they went. Many started in one land and ended in another.

The point to be made here is that their journeys transformed them from the raw materials that they were into the finished products that God wanted to develop. Sure, there are always variations and similarities to each story, but none of them saw it all coming as to how they were going to endure trials, and they certainly didn't all know how things were going to end up from where they started. Just like the jewelry box, we must go through a process that we don't want, we don't create, we don't have input for, and we don't control.

What may not always be documented, but I am sure happens in every scenario is that there is a point of surrender unto God to let Him do what He wants with us. God won't force the transformation on us, but we must want it. We must have enough faith to give God a "***YES***" to be perfected. We aren't like the oak tree that had zero say in this. God will let us press pause on our destiny if we don't want to go through with it. The thing is that if the calling is great enough and our faith is just enough to trust God, He will take us through whatever we need to go through to be perfected in the image that God has for us.

That's the purpose of the broken road. It is the teacher that has been designed to teach us the ways that God has desired for us to learn. We have the free will to walk away, but just like the examples the Bible has given us, if we press forward and not quit there is a great reward. We don't have to be a minister or have a position in God's Church. We can just be whoever God has made us to be for Him and serve where He desires for us to serve.

I would like to clarify that this transformation is not just for us alone. Just like we read in the Scriptures, the testimonies of those written in those words help us, like our testimonies to others will help them. Everything that we do is for the Glory of God. Everything on this broken road is a demonstration of God's power in our lives and can be both a blessing and a warning to others about their journeys. Our testimonies tell others about how we trusted God and He came through and delivered us.

They also talk about how we turned God down and paid a price for disobedience. Even though we may have recovered, we still suffered loss and learned valuable lessons that others can see. Testimonies show the power of deliverance and with all the tribulations and trials that we may encounter on the road of life others seeing how can changed us as we went and how He and He alone brought us out is empowering and proves that faith in God is the best spiritual investment that can ever be made.

Yes, we get our anointing on the broken road. Yes, we receive Holy Spirit power from the broken road. Yes, we acquire wisdom on the broken road. Yet it isn't all for us to hold on to and never let anyone else see it. Imagine if Job's story was never told? Or Paul's testimony? King David or Jonah's narratives were unspoken. Think about how different we would be. Without a testimony, the works of God are just whispers and unsolved mysteries. It's like a magician's trick. We see the result, but we don't see how any of it works.

We think that it's like a vending machine where we put money in it, push a button, and pop out a product. Sure, we can have faith that it works, but not

HOW it all works. God doesn't work in mysteries like that. Everything that we need to know about this life He has revealed to us in the Word. He reveals these things through the Holy Spirit. He shows these things through the testimonies of others.

If we don't understand how things work, we can take them for granted. We see the beginning and the end and never see the middle. We can start to want the result of a transformation and not know how that person got there. For example, as a worship leader I have had people say things like, "I wish that I had your anointing", or something along those lines and I always stop them and let them know that they have no idea about the cost of God's Oil in my life.

It is an opportunity to share my testimony as I am led to do with people to let them know about what I went through to get here. God uses our stories to illustrate our transformation. Without the broken road there would be no testimony to share. This is crucial to the building up of the Kingdon of God that is often hidden because that transformation on the road of life often involves embarrassment and shame.

We don't have to tell all our business to everyone, but as God leads us, we are compelled to share what God has done for us as we were (or are currently being) transformed by the road of life. Someone out there needs to hear our stories and hear and know that our God is real and unlike any other. Our transformation should give us the courage to bear witness to the wonderful works of God in our lives. We, as the Church of God, need to stop hiding our stories because part of that purpose is to share them and demonstrate to others about what God has done.

Today, our world needs to see that God is the powerful God that He is and that He is good and that His faithful love endures forever! The enemy wants us to hide our stories. He wants us to keep quiet from being delivered from things that should have killed us. He wants us to run away from the things that hurt us instead of waging spiritual warfare against them. He also wants us to keep quiet from us telling the mistakes that we made and how we corrected them through with God's help.

Each one of us are walking exhibits of how good God is. Every one of us. We may be tired, and we may be weary, but we have the peace of Christ in our hearts. We have seen faith work, and we have seen miracles happen in or around us. We have seen God change us from what we were into what we are becoming. We know what it is like to suffer various tragedies, survive, and then thrive. We know what it is like to pray and seem to hear nothing. We know what it is like to do everything right and still end up on the wrong side of things. We know what it is like to serve God with tears rolling down our faces. We know what the "midnight hour" means first-hand. Whether it is past, present, or future we understand these things and know them well. The one solid constant is that God has never left or forsaken us. Even when He didn't answer, He was there. Even when we felt all alone, He was there. Even when we lost everything and didn't know where to go, He was there.

We grew our relationships with God as we went down the broken road. We learned unwritten lessons on the broken road. We experienced things that we never imagined that changed us forever on the broken road. We were transformed by the broken road for the better even when we didn't see it. We may even have tried to "pray it away" or ran away from it for a while. The most necessary and hardest set of lessons that we have ever faced was always waiting for us with God reaching out His Hand asking us to trust Him. The road of life may seem unorthodox and cruel, but it is necessary. The transformation that I am receiving there is teaching me to love God even more than I did when I first got saved. I can hear God more clearly than I ever could before. I could see what God has had in front of my entire life that I didn't see. I can share the gifts that He has given for me to use with others. I can look back at my life and see that this broken road saved my life and gives me hope. That's transforming. That's what God does. He transforms us if we are willing to take one step after another.

Just like that jewelry box we must be changed to be what God has designed for us to be. We can't hold the treasures that God wants to place in us before we go through the processes that He has set up. What I want to convey to you, the reader, is that we need to trust God and let Him do his work in us. Know that God does want us to prosper and have good success. Know that God wants us to have great days and to be blessed. The life of the Christian is not all doom and gloom. The brokenness in life's road is the training ground, the perfector of faith, and the corrector of errors. It all is meant for our good!

Please don't think that all God wants to do is punish us and that is far from the truth. We are meant to enjoy life like the oak tree had sunny and warm days, but for that tree to receive nutrients the rains had to come too. Transformation comes with all the good and the bad in our lives and all of it is required. We cannot cut corners or take shortcuts. If we want to be what God desires for us to be we must walk where He leads us. We must endure what He takes us through. It is a mandatory assignment, but the rewards are massive.

It Isn't Over, Until God Says It's Over

Your story isn't over yet, and the chapter currently being written may still be in progress but change the narrative and let go and let God. Let God finish the story His way and trust His ending. Even if you don't like what He does with your life know that it is for your good., Know that it is all for God's glory. Rest assured that you aren't forgotten. Trust God and keep praying even if you don't hear anything back. God heard you. God sees you in the darkest of midnights and He hears you even if you don't say a word. If I can impart just one thing from all that was said in this chapter, just remember this: ***DON'T GIVE UP!*** You were made for this! God ordained you for this! Trust me, you don't want to give up too early and potentially miss out on the reward that God had waiting for you. God never made you to be a quitter and you should not start now.

Look, if you are still breathing, God isn't finished with you yet. It doesn't matter how dark it may get and how much it hurts. God has the final say. God is the beginning and the ending. People will tell you that you are wasting your time and that you must have sinned to get into this trouble and don't know what the real reasons may be that you are going through. None of that really matters because regardless of the cause, it is the effect that matters.

God has laid out your road for you to complete because of where He wants you to go and how He wants you to grow. When we quit on the process God has designed, we miss the fullness of His promise to us. His promises are solid and never changing, but we can miss them if we fail to meet the terms God has set.

God promised Israel that they would prosper and flourish if they stayed within His will. Mind you, staying in God's will is not an impossible task. God doesn't ask for our perfection, but that we seek perfection in Him.

We can be out of God's Will and not even realize it. We can feel that we are all good and we may not be where we think we are. This isn't a condemning thing, but it is true. God is perfect and flawless, and we are human and filled with imperfection. Even our righteousness is like filthy rags. God will push us until we flow where He knows we should be ***IF*** we let Him teach us. I know how hard the process can be. I know how demoralizing it can seem because it sometimes feels like we will never make God happy. That is a lie that Hell uses against us to try to make us forget that God loves us eternally. He knows what we are and what we will do, and He wants us to rely on Him to be our best. It makes me think about a drill sergeant in the military.

I never served in the military, but what I know about a recruit is that the one who trains them has been where they are at that moment. They are charged with making a soldier out of a citizen. The drill instructor knows that the strength they have now will not serve them in a battle. They know that the knowledge they have now won't allow them to defeat their enemies. They know that the stamina that they have now will not allow them to finish strong. So, they make them run, carry packs, get drilled on discipline, how to use their weapons, and change their mindsets.

They make the recruits run in the rain, crawl in the mud, work their muscles until they nearly explode, and let them hardly recover from the pain. They change their sleep schedules, expose them to the weapons and tactics of war, and more. Here is the part that is important. They aren't declared fit to be soldiers until they graduate from boot camp. Someone can start boot camp and quit, and they aren't fit for duty. Some will quit because it is too hard, and they aren't fit for duty. Some hit a wall and quit and end up doing something else.

Everyone who I have known that was in the military tells me that they were so glad to graduate from boot camp that they couldn't wait to leave. They hoped that they would never see their drill instructors ever again and wished to never look back. Those who served in war zones have told me that once they were out on the field of battle, they realized that their drill instructor wasn't so bad after all. They learned that all that painful training and harsh conditions made them stronger, faster, and more durable than they knew they were. They told me that when it came to a situation where their lives were in danger, their training saved them.

Many may not like their teachers personally, but many have said that they held a special place in their hearts for them. They owed their lives to them because the Hell they went through was for a reason. I have talked to some folks who went to see their instructors to show them the love and respect that they deserve. We need to look at this example and substitute our God for that drill instructor. We may not appreciate what is happening or has happened to us, but we need to understand that God loves us enough not to send us out on the road of life without being prepared. Boot camp for the military is a fixed amount of time, but the broken road of life is ours to travel until we transition from this world.

The major difference between a drill instructor and God is that God loves us unconditionally. An instructor can, if they want, let you slide by and pass when you aren't ready to get rid of you. An instructor can miss details and fail at their job. God won't let us slide and will never get rid of us. God makes zero mistakes, and He knows exactly what we must face and what we need to go through it all. God only wants the best out of us, and He knows that the broken road is the best training ground. It is all for His Glory and it is all for our preparation. I cannot say it enough. We will never be like we were when we first got saved and I thank God that I won't be like that when I take my last breath.

Lastly, the test won't end until God says it is done. We don't have the luxury or authority to question God as to why He does what He does and how long He does it. Frankly, we don't have enough understanding to question His wisdom. We are too limited and too unknowledgeable for any situation who can best God's knowledge. We can fool people that we have met the requirements for graduation, but we can't fool God. Some people graduate because they cheat or get lucky. We don't have that with God because He knows the horizontal and the vertical. Every step on the broken road of relationship is ordered and known by God, and we must come to terms with that.

Our opinions are worthless in the Presence of our God. God will listen to what we think, but the choice is still His. He will always have the final say and that can be hard for us. I don't know about you, but when I am going through things, I just want to know when it will end. When we get a shot at the doctor's office or a root canal, we want to know what we have to endure so that our minds can prepare ourselves as to how long we must suffer. When someone enters prison, they know how many years that they will spend behind bars before they get released. We like to know how long it will take, but God doesn't have to tell us anything.

If God tells us? Great! If not, we must hold on for dear life and keep our faith strong and our trust on maximum. Our faith is built strong when we must not know how long it will take and what we must face. When we can put all our worries and faith in God and His timing we will be transformed. We may feel pain, lose things, get mistreated, or whatever God has in store for us, but all we need to remember and keep close to our hearts is that God never fails. God never abandons and God never forgets. That level of faith is not something with which we are born. We don't necessarily get saved and immediately can start casting mountains into the seas. Whatever the situation for whomever it is designed for is what God desires and we must stay vigilant until God graduates us to the next level.

Let me encourage you about walking the broken road. Let me encourage myself too while I am at it. We all must finish the course. We can't give up before God gives us His reward. We can't afford to fall short of what he has promised because we are only hurting ourselves. Even though God will let us quit, we shouldn't give up. We should never surrender because God has given us the tools, and He gives us access to Him to be a winner. I have seen the end of some marathons, and it isn't all as glamorous as people think. People who cross that finish line may run across the line in triumph, but many collapse at the end and need medical attention. They collapsed because they are dehydrated, exhausted, sick, or mentally spent and knew that they had to keep running. Some have torn ligaments, tendons, and even broken bones but unless they pressed beyond the pain, they couldn't get to the finish line.

Not to be gross, but I have seen some people finish a marathon who have urinated all over themselves or defecated in their clothes because they couldn't afford to stop for even bodily functions. They knew that if they stopped, they wouldn't make the best time to their finish. They knew that they had to run no matter the cost. A runner can't say that they ran a marathon if they don't finish. Anything else is just another long run. No one can get a prize unless there is a finish line that is crossed. The race has a requirement that to win or place, you must finish. Now if something serious happens and you can't finish, it is what it is, but most of the time those folks try the race again.

Setbacks will happen, but to be a champion we must desire to meet the goal. It will hurt. It will cost us, but it is worth it. A boxer can't win a title bout if they are afraid of getting hit. A weightlifter can't get strong unless they keep lifting a weight that is heavier than what they have lifted before. A sharpshooter won't ever hit a target unless they learn how not to miss. A gymnast won't complete the routine for the perfect score unless they learn to get up from falling. The road of relationship with Christ will hurt, but to get what God desires for us, we must go through. We can choose to walk away and give up. We can choose not to endure going through the tough times. We can choose to "quit while we are ahead", but is it worth it?

There have been so many times that I wanted to quit. There were so many times that I wanted to give up. There are so many times that I want to take the easy route. Trust me, when I say that you are not alone in how you feel. Only a fool wants to live a life of misfortune, loneliness, and pain on the broken road of relationship with God. I am going to be honest, and I don't want you to misunderstand me. In the carnal world, it is easier to just do what the flesh wants, because the rewards are for right now. If I ate sweets and good-tasting, fatty foods now my tongue and my insides would enjoy them right now. But if I always ate like that, I would gain weight and suffer negative effects later after eating badly.

The darker days of life are never fun. The pain of walking alone and going through tings after becoming saved and in relationship with Jesus is hard! It isn't fair and it seems unjust some days. We all need to be honest about this! Serving god is not easy in a world that is ruled by Satan. We are a lot like salmon swimming upstream. We are fighting powerful currents to get to where we know we must go. It is difficult, but there will be good days and blessings. Serving God isn't all about suffering, pain, and woe. We just need to keep moving forward in

Christ. We need to not stay down too long when we stumble. We don't need to wallow in fear and doubt when it seems impossible. We need to realize that God knows when the time is right for us to exit the storm. He knows what we need and how we need it because He knows us better than anyone else.

We must wait for God to turn off the rain. We must wait for God to turn down the winds. We must wait and trust that God won't let us out of His Hand. We must believe and keep believing that He won't let us down. We must encourage each other that it will be okay, that God did it before and He will do it again. We must stay close to His Word and keep our ears to His Mouth for whatever He says. We must ignore what Satan says, and our emotions say about our situations. We must hold fast to God's track record. We must know that it isn't over until God says that it is over.

6

Healing As We Go

I am sure that the title of this chapter seems to be completely out of place in this book, and I can understand why anyone would think that may be the case. This chapter is going to be a bit different from the others because we are going to focus on restoration from the pain of life's injuries versus the causes of our difficulties on life's broken road. We have been talking about hurt, brokenness and pain and now we are talking about not just healing but healing as we go. I didn't understand this concept until I had to live through many dark experiences myself. I had to endure many hurts and pains to realize that on this broken road of life that will lead us to the prize of the high calling in Christ Jesus requires us to be resilient and prepared to suffer more than we could ever imagine. This includes knowing that we must heal while we still stay in the press and keep moving forward in our lives.

First Things First: Forgive Yourself

There is a major part of healing as we go that is often overlooked and taken for granted, which is when we must forgive ourselves for past mistakes that we have made in the past. We often carry the burdens of our shame and regrets of what was or should have been and it can cripple us and bring us to our knees in a way that God never intended for us to endure. This can be one of the hardest things to heal from in my honest opinion. When we carry guilt and regret it transforms us and, in my experience, it can damage worse than the original pain could ever have.

I know that I could have covered this in the section of this book earlier about when we did it to ourselves, but I wanted to unpack this in a different way here as we are talking about healing and restoration because I feel that of all of the pain that we will ever feel on our broken road of relationship, this is the scenario where it comes down to a conscious choice to recover or remain in a prison that we create for ourselves. So let me get this out of the way first and let you know that once we have repented of our mistakes and ask God for His forgiveness, we have permission to move on from that situation and walk and live in the freedom that only Christ can provide. This is where it gets tricky.

The best way to keep something hidden is to have it in plain sight but distract you from seeing it. It's like the adage of "not seeing the forest because of the trees" and Satan uses this in the best way possible and often he uses our faith in Jesus to do it. I know that this may seem to be a contradiction, but I can tell you from all that I have experienced that the misdirection used in hiding what God's forgiveness means is more prevalent than you could imagine. Hell's best weapon against us is shame. It is powerful and potent, and it is so effective that even the act of crucifixion used shame to render the victims and potential victims into fear. What do I mean?

Based on Roman literature as well as descriptions in the provinces, crucifixion was an established routine. There were special military teams led by a centurion, and in the provinces, the soldiers were selected from the local auxiliaries (natives who had joined the Roman army). The victim was stripped and then lashed (scourged). As part of the public humiliation, he/she was led through the streets and remained naked. Christian art portrays Jesus with a decent loincloth on the cross, but the nakedness was maintained as part of the humiliation[1]. Crucifixion was levied against those who committed a crime, and it could have been as simple as making a mistake but then having to suffer dearly for it.

Now, I want you to picture this. Imagine that you were tried and convicted when being crucified was a viable punishment. You were guilty of the crime you were accused of and were processed just like it said above. That means that you were stripped naked, beaten to a point near death and then paraded through the public streets while friends and foes saw you exposed to everyone on your way to death. Then imagine that someone runs through the crowd with a pardon by the governor before they hoist you up to die and lets you go because of an appeal that you made. The crime may have been wiped from your record and is no longer against you, but what about the shame and embarrassment of being brought to execution, but spared?

In this scenario you may be free and get to live another day, but the fact that people saw you wide open and exposed from what you hid under your clothes will never be taken back. Imagine people seeing you on the street and either showering you with pity or tormenting you over what you looked like without clothes. I know that this is an extreme example but stay with me. Imagine that while being whipped because you had soiled yourself and they refused to clean you up. Imagine that you a self-conscious about what you look like undressed. Then to be forgiven and covered in public and everyone is now supposed to be like nothing ever happened. Sadly, it did, and you have all those memories.

Many of us have made mistakes in our lives that have had public or even consequences. All of us no matter how long they have been saved or what office they hold in the church. When God forgives us after true repentance, we have our slates wiped clean and we can begin life again anew in Christ. Hell does not want that for us. Hell wants us to remember the faces of the crowd. Hell wants us to remember the mistakes that we made and stay focused on them instead of God's Grace and Love. It doesn't matter what the mistake was or if it was public or private. We were never meant to carry it after Christ has pardoned us from it. The sad part about this is that many other Christians don't understand it that way.

Even though there may be results from our mistakes we don't need to feel embarrassment or shame from them if we have truly repented to God about it. Some Christians feel like they must continually pay for it spiritually for the rest of their lives. They wallow in self-pity, shame, and plod along with their heads hung down because God is God and forgave them, but people are people, and they can't overlook their transgressions. They feel that it is "pious" or "righteous" to discount and look down on themselves as broken because of the mistakes that they made. These same believers then impose that feeling on others who make mistakes, and the cycle continues.

This was never in God's plans for us. John 8:36 says, "If the Son therefore shall make you free, ye shall be free indeed." Now, I know that I purposely said "mistake" instead of sin and I did so to make the point about how sin is a mistake against the Will of God. It is a choice that we make to go against God whether we realize it or not. We are made free by Christ we are ***FREE INDEED*** (John 8:36). God won't hold us to what has been forgiven even if we can't forgive ourselves. Part of the healing process is knowing that because Christ forgave us, we must forgive us. We must accept the blessing of forgiveness and let it go and move on.

Look at Abraham. He was promised by God that he would have a son even though he was of advanced age (Genesis 22:17). Both he and Sarah thought this was insane and Sarah brough Hagar in to get pregnant instead. Ishmael is born and God and Abraham have frank discussion about it all. God was disappointed, but Abraham repented, and Isaac came years later. Ishmael didn't just go away empty handed as he was also blessed, but the consequences of that mistake still live with us today as Jewish and Muslim peoples are at war to this day for the same promise made to Abraham.

Peter denied three times that he even knew Jesus, but Jesus still forgave him and blessed him. This same disgraced Peter went on to boldly preach to the masses in the Book of Acts and beyond. Peter came out of the shadows of that crucial mistake and never seemed to look back from it. Neither did Abraham let his mistakes keep him down for long. The consequences of sin are not permanent disqualifiers for those of us in Christ. God has a long track record of reconciliation and new growth from the times we have messed things up.

Sure, the child we fathered outside of our marriage didn't vaporize when we repented, but God will bless us anyway. No, the eye that was lost because we drove drunk didn't come back because we fell before Jesus and repented, but God will bless us anyway. That private sin that no one knows about except Christ and Hell may never have been exposed to the public. Yet the regrets that eat us up slow us down when we think about what we did is because it is we that are holding on to it even though Jesus said that we were free. That doesn't mean that it may take more than a personal declaration to get over traumas like this.

Sometimes seeking mental health help is what we need to wipe away the stains of our very good memories of what we did in the past. No matter what we do, we must continue to pray to God for restoration and know that it is Hell that wants us to relive our mistakes over and over and not Christ.

Not once has God ever used guilt to make us holy. Look in Scripture and you won't find a single place where God has levied shame against us after we have been forgiven. Yes, His prophets have warned people of the future punishments of shame and regret if they didn't repent, but even after being in spiritual court, forgiveness was available, and God wiped the slate clean again. To those who feel that they need a little shame to stay humble or holy, I have a word for you. To feel that way is a mistake. Holiness is never deployed with shame is the same way salvation cannot be achieved through fear.

God has designed it so that we can recover from any sin and mistake we make in our life's journey. We used to sing an old song by the late Rev. Milton Brunson when I was growing up that said:

I'M FREE. PRAISE THE LORD, I'M FREE.
NO LONGER BOUND. NO MORE CHAINS HOLDING ME.
MY SOUL IS RESTING. IT'S JUST A BLESSING.
PRAISE THE LORD, HALLELUJAH, I'M FREE[2].

I have had people who did me wrong and have apologized for their actions and I forgave them only to find out that even years later they were hesitant around me because they thought that I would regurgitate what they did wrong to me and hold it against them. Although I am human, I did let it go and never held it to them again, but in their hearts, they still felt bad and carried it for years that they thought that my forgiveness was true, but that I would still somehow use it against them. Satan does this to us, and I know that he did it to me in several areas of my life.

Sometimes I feel so embarrassed about things that I did that were clearly stupid and when the thoughts come into my mind, I feel dejected, and I tend to degrade myself because of what I did wrong. I must remind myself and get out of that funk that even though I cannot change the past, I can change my future. That I can learn and grow from what went wrong and foster what can go right. The enemy uses my super critical nature of critiquing myself to his advantage and make me replay every misstep and every error while my brain calls me stupid over and over. It used to rule over me and make me feel bad about myself and in many ways, I still get that way sometimes, but I do my best not to stay there.

There have been things that I did wrong at home and when I think that my wife would be upset with me, she grabs hold of me, kisses me, and tells me that she doesn't hold it against me and never did. We need to get that from God sometimes and we can only get that from God if we stay close to Him and stay in fellowship with Him. Why? Because He always shows us that we are forgiven. We have new mercies every single day we wake up (Lamentations 3:22-23). He smiles on us and loves us as we are because we belong to Him. When He forgave us, He expunged our records and then gives us another chance. We don't have to stay bound anymore, but we stay in the personal prison that we created out of guilt and shame.

The sad part about it is that many are still bound by chains that they forged within their hearts and minds. We can't heal if we can't move away from the place where the pain started. To me, it's like walking around with a rain cloud we made over our heads and be sad as to why we get wet all the time. Sure, the mistakes were mistakes and the sins were sins, but we need to live in the forgiveness and freedom that Jesus gives us when we repent. It is still human to remember what happened and feel shame for a moment. We aren't machines and it is more than okay to be human, but we cannot stay in that place for long.

We must change our mindsets and our spiritual status about what happened yesterday. Hell will use our shame as a tactic and be innocent of any wrongdoing because we are the ones who made the choice to wallow in the pain of not forgiving ourselves. We cannot live up to our full potential in Christ while we are saddled with a guilt and shame prison that we built brick by brick on our own. Just like the Israelites that came back to Jerusalem in the time of Nehemiah, we must not weep too long at the brokenness that we see of what happened back then. We must focus on building our lives in the ***RIGHT NOW***.

We often reopen wounds that God is actively trying to close. We may even do so with the intention of being pious or virtuous when it is counterproductive to our spiritual journey. There is enough trouble on our road of relationship with Jesus that we must carry self-inflicted burdens too. To whomever is reading this, please know and understand that if you truly repented your mistakes to God, ***YOU ARE FREE***. It is time to let guilt and shame go. You have lived through what killed many. You are still standing when others had fallen away. You are still here and breathing and that is nothing to be ashamed of.

Recognizing the Need for Healing

When the storm is over and the dust settles for yet another tragic or horrifying moment in your life and some sort of calm arrives with the worst of the trial being over the question that comes to mind is, "What do I do now?" When the pain or the grief that held you by the throat seems to be resolving at the behest of the Hand of God it can feel surreal or even unreal that the answer to many prayers has finally arrived and the figurative dawn begins to wash away the darkness.

In our walk with Christ these moments will come and go as time goes on and we "keep on living" as the old folks used to say. With the ebb and flow of life happening in real-time we must not just be grateful to God that our test has now finished, but we need to begin to clean up the debris and bind up the wounds that happened to us in the dark night of suffering we just survived by the Grace of God.

We must understand that healing is a necessity for us all no matter what the injury. Caring for our injuries and beginning the healing process of not just what was hurt, but all the things connected to it are essential for walking this broken road. The journey to recovery can many times be a trial as there may be many aftereffects. From my own worst times in my life there were many areas that needed to be gathered up and presented to God for spiritual and emotional healing. That healing involved time, dedication, spiritual grounding and unpacking the experiences that traumatized me deeply.

From my own experience, healing was just as difficult as the times of tribulation, but instead of getting worse things would get better, but it would take work, and it would take a level of dedication that I did not know existed. Sometimes God just breathed into the situation, and everything was instantly healed, and all the wrongs were made right. I do not minimize that in any way, but as people we need to be prepared for either end of the spectrum because all of it is still in God's Plan and we must endure it until the process ends.

Recognizing the need for healing is to understand that healing is a cooperative effort. It doesn't matter whether we are conscious or unconscious we must agree to be healed and to fight for our recovery. Those who get gravely wounded and survive are said to possess an elevated level of tenacity or gumption and a "never say die" attitude towards life.

Then there are others who run to the nurse's office crying and wailing at a simple paper cut and fall into a proverbial pile and simply quit. Lastly, on this broken road journey, we need to choose which of those attitudes we will employ as we fight for our very spiritual lives in this world. As with anything we must grow into either of these philosophies and what we pour the most effort into will be what our realities will become.

We all must keep in mind that we must consent and submit ourselves to be treated and receive the treatment and let it do its perfect work. This, of course, is depending on the environment that we are injured by and how close we are to the aid that we need for our injuries. For example, the best place we can be if we get injured or discover an injury is wherever medical doctors and life-saving equipment are nearby, such as a world-class hospital complex. One of the worst places we can be if we get hurt is a remote, desolate place where we are alone, and the resources are few. This would include places like a wilderness and even a battlefield where imminent dangers are all around you. Let's unpack these scenarios and look at how we can equate them to spiritual concerns.

When we think of a world-class hospital, most of us think of a place with the best doctors, the best nurses, innovative medical technology, seemingly endless depths of medical knowledge and the most accommodating facilities to address virtually every disease or injury. It doesn't matter whether a person gets sick or hurt in the hospital complex or is rushed there because of a situation that happened away from the hospital, we as people tend to feel more at ease when we know that we or our loved one is at the right place to get the care that they need. We breathe easier knowing that the best of the best will address the condition no matter how bad it may look.

How many of us have seen all those hospital shows on TV where people either walk in or get carried in by emergency vehicles with the most bizarre or life-threatening illnesses? Those patients get swarmed by doctors, specialists, technicians, and nurses and after getting worked on they recover. What I have found interesting is that some patients who refuse to die seem to endure or recover more than the ones who have given up hope. Even if they don't make it, you see a patient who is defiant to the end and tells everyone they meet that they won't die today. Some patients they say are "fighters" and even if they aren't conscious, they seem to defy the odds and survive surgeries or procedures that they weren't supposed to make it through.

Then there are patients who get hurt or sick and they commit themselves to the grave before any doctor can see them or even attempt to help them. They hear the word "cancer" and think that it's over no matter what the cure rate may be. They see all their blood on the floor and immediately start picking out caskets to be buried in. They have no hope and no faith in anything positive, and these patients usually don't make it. They either get treated and die on the table, so to speak, or they refuse treatment and go home to die even though help was right there waiting to aid them. It is apparent that to be healed it is required to have faith that recovery is possible and to also allow oneself to be treated. Doesn't this sound familiar? It should…

A true House of God and true followers of Jesus Christ are like a world-class hospital. When someone comes across their paths that is trapped in sin, hurt by circumstance, or fighting a spiritual war that is trying to destroy them is the best place for God to commence healing and restoration for whatever that person is facing. A person seeking relief not only has to volunteer themselves to be present, but they must also allow themselves to be helped by God through the hands and faith of those around them. At some point in all our lives we will need to go to a physical and a spiritual hospital. This is not saying that God can't heal us on the spot wherever we are either. Yet God chooses to do things differently according to the circumstances of what His plans are for us. All the healing and restoration power come from God and only God can authorize that power as He desires.

Still, there is power in coming to where the Saints of God are to get what God has for us. This involves us giving up our personal shame and allowing God to work on us. When we go to a hospital or a doctor there are a lot of times where we must be in a compromised position to get treated. If we get a nasty cut or a broken bone treated it will depend on where the injury is located and what must be done to treat it so that we must endure a little embarrassment. What do I mean? Let's say that the injury is on our arm. We will have to expose that arm to allow treatment to occur. If the injury is on our leg, we will have to expose our leg to be treated. If it is in our torso our torso will have to be exposed for it to be treated. Whatever clothing may be covering the area that presents any risk of infection must be removed and replaced with a clean and prepared garment.

Let's look at a car accident, for instance where someone gets hurt badly, but they are still conscious and can communicate with a first responder. That first responder will assess your condition and see what caused the injuries. They will check your vital signs and see what your alertness levels are and ask questions to determine if you may have a brain injury. They will most likely ask you if you are okay with them helping you and depending on what is injured like a broken leg, for instance, that's bleeding badly they will grab scissors out of their toolkit and cut your clothes to expose the area that's hurt to see what must be done next to stabilize you for transport. This can be embarrassing to have a person who you have never met before have to cut off clothing so that they can treat your wounds. Its humbling and makes you remember your mother's advice to always wear clean underwear.

Sometimes when a person is triaged, they will need to put leads on your skin to monitor your heart and breathing and they may not have time to ask you to remove clothes, and they will cut them off because time is critical to save your life. I have personally been driving by a horrific accident where bodies are mangled and have seen people's pants cut as far as you could imagine while they are setting bones and bandaging wounds. Even though EMTs do their best to keep everyone from seeing them in a state of compromise it has to be a humiliating experience for the person being treated. The secrets of what is hidden under their clothes are no longer secret. The state of their personal hygiene has been revealed. Even what garments they hide underneath their visible clothes are known to at least one person.

It doesn't end there as a hurt person is put in an emergency vehicle and transported to the nearest and waiting hospital. Once there, a team begins to treat that person and one of the first things that is done is to take off every piece of clothing they arrived in and replace it with a hospital gown (that famously opens in the back) and sometimes they have to wash the person down to remove any extra blood, dirt or contaminants from their skin to reduce the chance of infection. It doesn't matter what position they hold in society; it doesn't matter whether they are rich or poor. It doesn't matter what their ethnicity or gender may be. If their injuries are severe, they will go through this sort of scenario.

It is revealing and embarrassing. If they consent because they are conscious or if they are unresponsive and are brought in without their consent, it doesn't matter. To be treated, exposure is imminent where the injury has occurred. Whatever is covering or shielding the injury from plain view of the doctor must be removed. We don't get a choice about anything because our life is in danger.

I am going to pause here for a quick second and insert something that I have heard other nurses and doctors say about patients being treated that sometimes annoys them. I have heard that medical professionals are often the worst patients. Coming in a close second are the ones who think they know what the problem is and know nothing at all but swear that they are right. I have heard stories of people who say that medical personnel will argue with the doctors treating them about every step that is taken in their care especially if they are in denial. This doesn't mean that they are always wrong, but it makes it difficult to treat a patient that wants to waste time arguing about what they think when seconds are ticking by, and their life is at stake.

The person who thinks that they know what their problems are better than anyone else are the ones who have either looked up on the internet on someone's blog or web doctor site and determined in their minds what the troubles are or think they know what their body is saying, and they convince themselves of what their diagnosis is. Here is the problem with both types of folks, the treating doctor has the test results, images, and eyes to see what the problem is and their medically trained patient or the one who thinks they know will argue with them and refuse what they truly need because they have a right to not be treated at all. Sometimes, when people encounter folks like this, they do what they ask and send them out of their doors hoping that they get the help they need somewhere else because they have lost patience in their dealings with them.

Now, let's bring this to the church. There is a humbling that must happen when we come into the House of God or encounter His people because we must admit that we need healing or restoration. It takes courage to come to the altar during church service or ask someone for prayer or counseling. Even if that person doesn't share all the details of their circumstances, it is embarrassing and revealing to others that there is trouble and sadly, the Adversary capitalizes on that.

When God has ordained that we seek outside help for what has hurt us on this broken road the enemy will do everything that he can do to discourage us from getting that help. He will whisper in their ears that, "People are going to talk about you like a dog," or "You can handle this on your own. Just keep praying." While these things may be true that yes, people will talk about you and that if they keep praying that God can and will fix it, the solution to your needs are whatever God has determined. If He intended for you to expose your infirmity to others? That is what must be done.

What makes it worse is when we get to church or around believers who God has set in place to help us recover and be restored that we make up in our minds that we know what is best for us and not what God has spoken to them. We will ask God for healing for our sadness but not ask God to restore what was taken from us when we were violated. We will ask God to pay our bills instead of showing us how to manage our money better. We will come crying to the altar about the person we lost and how we want them back when God has someone new that He has for us that we have yet seen. We will ask God for the temptation to leave and not ask Him to close the spiritual door that we opened when we messed with that thing that we shouldn't have touched in the first place.

Just like a medical hospital or doctor's care, we must allow exposure to get healing. Exposure comes first with admitting that we are in pain. We must surrender our pride and our shame to get what we need to continue this journey. It doesn't matter whether it is to God or others that God has placed in our paths because whatever God wants us to do to get healed? We must do it. I don't think that a person who was in a massive car wreck liked being exposed like that for medical treatment, but they do appreciate the ones who saved their life. The embarrassment they endured is eclipsed by the fact that they are on the road to recovery.

I think about a colonoscopy. It is ***EMBRASSING*** in every sense. To be examined we must empty out our digestive system and then take off our clothes and exchange them for an open back gown all for them to have a room full of people see a doctor shove a camera up our backside with the full glory of our rear end in full view. All of this while we are often unconscious and at the whims of those treating us. Yet, after the colonoscopy is over. We are grateful for whatever they find because if we are in the clear we can celebrate. If they detected something they can send it off to be tested or if it is obvious that treatment must happen that experience of being exposed could have saved our life. Do we really dwell on the fact that we had to be exposed to others or are we grateful for the results? Was it worth it to get exposed to either confirm good health or to detect a problem before it became too severe?

Let's stay with the colonoscopy example. If a polyp is detected before it bleeds and metastasizes the chances are very high that after treatment your life could be spared. If we only get checked after we see blood in our toilet when we use the restroom the chances of us surviving are normally not as good, unless God intervenes. Waiting too late for help can be costly and cause us to abort our purpose too early because of pride. So, when we are on our road of life, and we can get the help that we need we should go to God early and go often as we need to get to the root of what ails us. Humbling? Yes! Necessary? Also, yes! When life's tests come our way, and we begin to succumb to them we need to not be ashamed and go to God as He has prescribed for us. Even when it may embarrass us to ask for help it is necessary that we go.

Remember when I talked about how it could be needed to cut off the clothes of a person in triage? I didn't forget about that, and I want to explain the reasons how this applies to us spiritually. Just like in the natural realm where whatever areas need treatment need to be exposed, the same goes with the other reason we are stripped down and often bathed before we get treated: infection.

An open wound is a dangerous entry point into the body for infection to set in and possibly kill us. It is important and proved that whenever a person is treated for injury or disease that the area, instruments, and person should be sterile and clean. If the person who is already wounded or sick is exposed to outside germs it can make things much worse. Ever read in history books about field hospitals in wars over one hundred years ago? More people supposedly died from infections from being treated in filthy environments than the injuries themselves. Here is an example that comes to mind about something called Cat-Scratch Fever.

Cat-scratch fever is an infection caused by a kind of bacteria called *Bartonella henselae* (it's also sometimes called *Bartonella henselae* infection). You can get it if a cat that has this type of bacteria licks an open wound on your skin or bites or scratches you. About 40% of cats and kittens carry *Bartonella henselae* in their mouths or under their claws. They get this by scratching or biting at infected fleas. They can also pick it up by fighting with other cats that have it. Most cats that are infected don't show any symptoms. Human symptoms manifest like this. The first sign is often a red bump, sore, or blister at the site of the scratch or bite. This may not hurt, but it often has a crust and could contain pus. Within the next 2 weeks -- and even after the bump has healed -- you could have a fever, headache, fatigue, poor appetite, and swollen glands (lymph nodes). In very rare cases, CSD causes serious problems that affect your bones, joints, eyes, brain, heart, or other organs.[3]

All from a small cat's scratch or if they lick an open wound. One little cut could lead to greater sickness all because of a tiny open wound. I am sure that you have heard about people catching a flesh-eating bacteria and other ailments from being treated in a setting where something was left unclean and caused severe sickness, injury, and even death. Spiritually, we must let God wash us clean and guide us to where there is a "clean" spiritual environment for His work to be done.

When we get wounded or sick on this road of life there is always a residue that comes with it. The Adversary always looks to pounce on our human weaknesses to make things worse for us. Hell will take a wound we had in our early life and make it a festering disease in our later years. We could have been teased as children for being too short and growing up with hatred in our hearts for people like the ones who teased us.

We could have found a porno magazine as a preteen and grow up with a silent sex addiction that would wreck our marriage later. We could have been coerced into playing with a spirit board at a sleepover in middle school and be tormented by demons throughout our lives and not understand why. Worse than all of that, we could come to be delivered from a demonic spirit and not deal with the root of the problem and that demon would take advantage of that open spiritual door and come back with seven more demons wickeder than they are and make things worse. Whatever the situation and whatever the cause we must recognize that we need to be healed before things get out of hand. We need to see that God is our Healer and that He will use many methods to get us healthy in every aspect. Now let's look at some various methods that God will use to heal and restore us.

Wartime Medicine

So, why even call this "healing as you go" to begin with? My inspiration from this is imagining a besieged soldier on an active mission and does not have the luxury of a doctor, hospital, clinic, or even a medical kit. I picture in my mind a soldier performing field medicine on themselves like removing bullets, tending to lacerations, or treating fevers until they can get to the proper place where they can rest, feel safe, and get the treatment that they need to fully recover.

When a soldier is on a mission, and they are far from home or from their unit they must learn to survive and deal with whatever comes what may as they endeavor to complete their mission and reach their destination. They must find food, shelter, and tend to injuries as I said earlier. When a soldier is behind enemy lines they must survive and rely on their training to make it.

We must remember that as Christians we are in a war that won't end until we die. We are soldiers in a war older than time, and we are strangers in a foreign land. We are constantly under fire and when we are attacked, we will get hurt. I know that I covered that earlier in this book, but now we will focus on how do we stay sane, stay spiritually well, and stay effective for Christ? That is not always an easy answer as many of us learn this as we gain experience as God's children who truly belong to Him. It doesn't matter how long we are on our Christian journeys; we will have to heal from what hurt us and we still must keep moving because life continues whether we desire it to or not. If we stop and fall in a pile it could lead to serious spiritual consequences that we don't necessarily have to face.

What do I mean by that? When I read Philippians 3:14, it speaks of "pressing towards the mark" and the word pressing alludes to a continuous process. This doesn't mean that we can't rest, but if we look through Scripture, rest was only taken when there were periods of safety or a lull in what was happening around them. From my experience of being around military personnel, there is an enormous difference between being on duty in peacetime and being on duty in a war. When there is peacetime, there are regular duties with regular times of rest. There usually isn't a perceptible enemy and there is a general sense of safety. War time is different as "all hands" are on deck because the enemy is attacking, must be repelled, and defeated.

I remember seeing the old black-and-white movies about World War II where sailors were on their way to their operating area, or they were stationed at a port or with a battle group where some sailors would be asleep in their bunks while others were performing tasks. Some were enjoying time off with shipmates playing games while others were eating a meal. Then, suddenly, the alert would go out that the enemy was spotted or unexpectedly an enemy shot hit the ship and immediately every person ran to their stations and began to engage the threat.

No more time for rest, regular meals, or fun. It was time to fight. While in the fight if a minor injury (to that person) happened, they would have to either patch themselves up or fight through the pain. They knew that they had to keep going to win against their foes. I remember seeing the heroic characters fighting through burns, fires, cuts, and other various injuries. They would stop for a moment, take care of what they could and keep going.

This is what I mean when I say that we must heal as we go. When we know that we can't stop moving forward and that we cannot give up because our lives or spiritual callings are depending on us staying on the course, we may not have the luxury to stop and take care of what hurts us. Often, we must keep moving, trust God's plan and not lose hope. This life cannot work without God on our side. The only true healing that we can receive comes from Him. Period. There is no other source of healing that can repair the damage that the broken road can cause us, but how God disperses that healing can vary depending on the person and the situation. The biggest takeaway from this is that God urges us to keep going knowing that He will come to our rescue.

This is where it can get a little complicated. God can and will heal us instantaneously or He will do it in small bits at a time. Why the different approaches? Why does God sometimes heal us all at once and other times in small increments? The straight answer is that it's God's prerogative to do as he desires for us. He is God and that's it. He controls the horizontal and the vertical, but I have learned that He has His reasons, and they don't make sense to us at first as I have stated earlier. However, while we don't understand His reasoning, God has made ways for us to use His resources to patch us up and help keep us moving on this road of relationship. The biggest thing that we must do is adopt a culture of unshakeable faith to make it through the storms of life. We must know that God's has His Hands on us and won't let us die in defeat if we trust in Him.

Since we know that pain has a purpose how do we heal while we are still getting battered and bruised daily? In the natural realm, it all comes down to one word: training. Let's shift back to our soldier/sailor example and look closely. When a person becomes a recruit into the military they go through basic training. These are the fundamentals of how to be a soldier or sailor. Instructors teach people how to train, learn the basics of combat, field medicine, hazards, and terminology. Notice that the word ***BASIC***. Ground level training for everyone to get started. Once they graduate from basic training, specialized or advanced training can be taken to expand learning, gain advancement, or make someone eligible for special service. It is here that people can learn advanced techniques related to their concentration and learn how to deal with escalating levels of conflict or types of war.

The old church saying, "New level; new devil," can be connected to a saying of my own: "New dealings, new healings." As we progress from a "baby" Christian to deeper levels in Christ we must learn how to recover from the deeper wounds that we will receive on our war journeys. That comes from the relationship with God that I spoke of earlier. As we grow in relationship with God, we learn the ways in which we can get healing for our souls. Sometimes that healing is nothing more than reinforcing our faith to endure the pain.

I know that sounds harsh, but it is true. I can remember the times when I took shots from Hell and all I could do was cry on the inside and not let it show. I had to stiffen my upper lip and "walk it off" even though I was hurt down to the core of my core. There are times where the act of falling in a pile isn't an option because it could be life or death. Stopping to tend to an unbearable pain can't always be done and it is a test of faith to keep walking despite your eyes being nearly blinded by tears.

This isn't about pride, and this isn't about ego. It's about strength. Strength to endure evil when Hell itself is trying to whip you to death. The Apostle Paul dealt with a situation where he dealt with his thorn in the flesh and couldn't stop moving even if he wanted to (2 Corinthians 12:7-9). Most of us know this story, but I want to focus on this part in Verse 9: "My grace is sufficient for thee: for my strength is made perfect in weakness." Paul prayed for relief and God said no. That's a hard pill to swallow when God says no, but His Grace is all that you need.

Paul had to deal with the messenger of Satan for the rest of his life. Paul had to hear the insane whispers of a demonic spirit in his ears for the rest of his days. The only thing that he had was God's grace to sustain him. It was God's grace that got him through it all. Paul had to patch himself up with God's grace to keep preaching and teaching everywhere he went. All of this while the messenger of Satan kept bothering him.

It almost reminds me of a kidney transplant. I learned a very interesting fact from people that went through the procedure. When they receive a donor kidney that the diseased ones aren't removed. The new kidney is placed in a different spot of the old ones, and it replaces the function of the dead ones. Just like every transplant recipient, that person take anti-rejection drugs for the rest of their lives. The things that were killing them stay in them while they get a kidney from someone else and must take medication to keep the new one alive. This now becomes their daily routine, and they must carry with them dead kidneys even though they don't want to, or they had prayed for God to restore their original ones to full strength.

When have deep emotional and spiritual wounds that are killing us, God will transplant in His Spirit to take up residence in us to give us what we need to survive. What hurts us is still there, but His gift of His Spirit and Grace sustains us and restores what we lost. Like Paul, God may have us still deal with what hurts us, but God provides what we need to endure going through it. In Paul's case, his torment was sent, and it was meant to keep him humble. Paul trusting God through it all was the key to his purpose and the fuel for his ministry.

Even though it wasn't fair from a human standpoint it was all in God's plan that he endured it. There have been many things in my life that God hasn't removed from me that hurt me, but I know that God has a purpose for them somewhere. I don't understand it all and sometimes I have moments where I want to quit and fall in a pile, but I remembered that I can't stop. I must trust his process and that trust is a healing salve to my spirit. The more that I have faith in that trust, the more it comforts me.

Also, it seems almost cruel that we must return to a healed place while we are still moving along this road or even possibly dealing with another storm already in progress. It is not uncommon to be dealing with more than one set of issues at the same time and trying not to succumb to any of them. Often, life doesn't give us the luxury of being able to triage and rest and we must patch ourselves up and go through God's process of restoration one step at a time. For anyone who may be going through tough times right now I want you to know that in Christ there is always a period of restoration. God will never allow us to stay in a personal Hell longer than we need to be there.

We may never understand why things have happened, but when the darkness abates, we need to be ready to accept what God had sent our way and that is not easy. Acceptance that the challenge that was faced is over, in my mind, is the first step to recovery. To acknowledge to God first and then everyone else around us that the worst is now over, and that God deserves all the glory for our survival is paramount. When we bless God with gratitude it causes things to shift. Gratitude is not just for the now, but it is also for the future of what has yet to come. Being thankful that God didn't forget us even when we didn't see Him moving is powerful. To bless our God when He spared you what could have been worse or even fatal is the purest offering that we can give. Being thankful and praising God for restoration and recovery should be the first thing that passes our lips into the atmosphere.

Restoration Via Gratitude

How you thank God is up to you, but when we look back at where we had just come from and see the lingering darkness, we see the tears that were shed in the midnight hour and the prints our knees made in the floor as we prayed for help and strength should move you to tears. To see where your blood was spilled in battle and to witness those who didn't make it through what you did should cause your spirit to leap for joy that God didn't let you go.

When you see the staggering steps that you made in the desert of loneliness or the wilderness of pain and the places where you fell but got up again with all the strength that you could muster should turn your heart to the heavens to Jesus. When you can look back and see that it wasn't just you in this fight, but you can see Christ holding you up, steering you away from death, or wrapping His arms around you when you cried it should change you. It should burn away the doubt that God had forgotten you. It should drown out the whispers of the Enemy who told you countless lies that God doesn't care about you.

I believe that giving thanks to God for bringing us out of our troubles is like cleaning out a wound with antiseptic medicine. It cleans out the doubt and feelings of abandonment and turns our face to God who is the author and refiner of our faith. Honestly, it may even seem silly to be giving God thanks after we have lost things or was severely hurt by trauma, but I can tell you from my experience that it works. Others may see you and think that you're crazy but let them think what they want to think. This is between you and God and truth be told only He can truly begin the healing process in our lives. He is the Balm in Gilead, and He can (and will) heal anything, but there is a slight catch and it's on us and not God. We must let the pain go. We must release to God everything we genuinely want Him to heal, and I know that may sound a bit crazy, but let me explain.

God has given us the choice of what we give to Him and what we don't. He gave us free will and because of that when we turn things over to God, He will work on what we give Him. I know that this is a head scratcher, but it is true. God is unlimited, but we are limited. When we give our situations, pain and issues to God He respects our decision to hold on to what we hold on to. I can hear someone balking at that idea but think about this for a minute.

If we go to a doctor and get examined, we will be asked a series of questions about how we are feeling and what we answer is what we receive in treatment. If we don't tell the doctor about a certain pain in an area they may never know until it is inevitable and something harmful shows up in a test result. Even then, if we refuse to get treated for it, a doctor will not tie us down and make us get treatment for it even if they already know what ails you.

If we don't release our wounds and our pain to God, He will wait until we let it go, or He will stand by to aid us as we carry a burden we may not have been meant to carry. What we don't turn over to God may in fact be a self-imposed struggle that we allowed because we wouldn't surrender it all to Christ. I know it is easy to say, "let the pain go", but I know that it is much harder than the words, but it still must be done to be truly healed. I can speak for myself that I didn't let certain things go that nearly destroyed me. I held on to literal hatred for some people that did things to me. The situation was over, but I let my own pride and emotions make decisions for me that I should have made. I held on to grudges I should have put down. I latched onto pain that I should have let go. God was waiting with outstretched arms to receive it and heal me, but I refused and held it close to me. The wound was fresh, but I polluted it with what I should have turned over to God.

Let me be clear and be completely honest with you. Being human means that any of us and I mean ***ANY OF US*** can fall into the trap of holding onto things that we should have let go. Don't be fooled by anyone who claims otherwise because it doesn't matter about the position or how long they may be saved because anyone is susceptible to this situation. Pain and trials can occur in a way that exposes and reveals the deepest parts of someone. The things that they thought that were never be, will become more than clear when "the chips are down" come to the surface and they must either fight them off or fall prey to them.

When we are deeply in pain and seriously tested, we are not ourselves and depending on the situation we will turn our rage and hatred to what caused us pain. It is the human condition and if we don't listen to the Holy Spirit and let Him guide us, we will embrace what we never would before. I hated those who hurt me, and I know of many who despised people, companies, people in positions of power, the church and sometimes even God. We tend to want to assign blame in whatever we cannot understand and each of us is prone to feel that which is unthinkable.

God will always provide for us a means to escape these feelings or even actions, but it is up to us to follow His call and heed His Word to us. When we don't do what He has directed us to do we can be corrupted by the things Hell has sent our way. When a wound is cleaned and continually exposed to the elements something dreaded can happen to it called infection. Sometimes the result of infection is worse than the wound itself. We all have heard about things like MRSA and gangrene which will send shudders of fear through anyone.

I know of a friend who had major reconstructive surgery that was lauded as a success until they noticed that the area was swollen and filling with fluid. It turned out that they had a serious infection that is hard to eradicate. To make things right they must go in surgically and remove all the new reconstructive parts, scrape out anything that shouldn't be there and then treat the remaining bacteria with antibiotics. Then they must wait a while and then go back in and replace all the hardware they had put in with new hardware. The process they must endure is longer than the original treatment phases.

Now I know that my friend didn't cause the infection themselves, but if I could use their story as an allegory to what spiritually happens maybe it can help illustrate my point here. This person suffered pain and loss of function of their limb, and it was painful to the point that it was unbearable. They went to get evaluated and treatment was devised, and they got the surgery that was needed to fix the problem. They dealt with the pain of recovery and had to learn how to do things again in physical therapy, but all the time something wasn't right.

An infection was building silently and when it was discovered it was advanced and it was threatening their life, so they sought the doctor again. They were told what they had to do, and it would take twice as long to heal. Because of the infection and the result of taking out this hardware and leaving nothing could cause them to lose that limb. Scars that were healed would have to be opened again and now new ones would eventually take their place.

Let's look at this from a spiritual standpoint. When we come through a trial in victory, that victory can be tainted by holding on to something God meant for us to release to Him to be healed. It could be emotions, habits or even sin that we still hold on to even after God has brought us out of the darkness and into the light. Whatever it is that we hold onto can cause our now healing wounds to get infected with a specific spiritual concern. When I held on to hating someone for hurting me it damaged my heart.

I had every right to hate them after what they did to me. I failed to release it, and it stunted me and caused me to drift away from God because we can't love God and hate someone else. I claimed that I was healed from the situation, but my hatred of them festered and affected me in ways that I couldn't see. I clung to the pain like a security blanket, and I let it define me. It warped my spirit and when I took notice of what was happening, I had to stop and repent to God because it was wrong. It was sin and it was affecting me, my relationships and my personal ministry.

I repented to God and turned it all over to Him and the weight was lifted from my soul, and I was totally free. I let God take control of not just the original wounds, but the new ones that I created myself. I had to let go of the pain, the rage, the anger and the hate and let God fill all my empty places. Here is the funny thing, God literally put these people in my path, and I genuinely greeted them with kindness. One of my other friends thought that a rumble might have broken out when one of them approached me, but him and I saw God's restoration in action.

When the other person showed up, I embraced them cordially and that was that. No words of rebuke, no thoughts of malice, but genuine kindness. Not that I will ever associate with them again (because you can forgive and release and refrain from seeing them), but I don't have the hatred for them anymore. I allowed God to clean out the infection of my emotions from the wound they caused, and I give God all the glory for His restorative power!

Again, I know that it is easy to say that we need to let things go. I get that. I do. Yes, God can close the deepest wound with one stitch of His Love, but sometimes God allows us to go through a process to heal. Regardless of the path that God has for us the healing is for our testimony. The thing that will help someone else that is going through now what we went through back then and survived by God's Grace. Still, to be truly healed we must let it go to God and trust Him to restore us. It doesn't matter about what was lost, who was lost, who hurt you or what hurt you we cannot cling to the things God has meant for us to let go.

These things can do great harm and damage to us not just spiritually, but also in the natural realm. It's not wise to hold on to sheer terror of a person who harmed us seriously. Yes, being cautious and vigilant is one thing, but living in a prison made by our own stress is another. Despising someone's gender or organization because of what they did willfully or unwilfully only hurts us and not them. Shaking our fist at God for who died or losing everything only harms us.

Seeking Professional Help

As we go along this broken road, we need to be reminded that God may not lift your situation from you but give you the means to overcome it. God doesn't erase the event that hurt us from the sands of time, but He will give us a way to overcome what happened to us. Hell's forces only want us to dwell on the bad that has happened, but God is pointing us to the restoration of what we lost behind us. Whether it is instantaneous or through the long way around, we need to put our hands firmly in God's Hands and let Him do the work. God can do the work supernaturally in the Spirit or in the natural realm through the hands of others. What I mean by this is that when we go through traumas, we need to be cured in both the spiritual and natural worlds. God has placed people in this world that are poised and ready to be used by Him for our human concerns.

To everyone that I meet and minister to concerning going through struggles and trauma, I always stress the need for counseling and mental health help. When demonic forces that ravage our lives use our emotions and mental states against us why are we afraid as Christians to seek mental health aid? I am not just talking about any sort of help but help that is Christian-focused or done by true Christians and there are more out there than you think. When Hell tears up our lives, we need mental health help to help restore the human damage left behind. Just like any other kind of healing this can be done through the Divine Power of God, or God can use people. There are many healings where Jesus spoke over people, touched people, or told them who to see or what to do and they were healed. This is no different. Whatever way God sends healing we need to receive and accept it.

What I have discovered is that there is such a continual stigma in the Christian world to seek help for recovery. Calling on God is the first and right choice but sometimes letting God guide you to a mental health professional is also in His plan for us. Church folks don't seem to want to recognize the word "therapy", and it is such a shame. Our mental health is a big component of our spiritual health. When we carry the baggage of pain from our past it will most certainly affect us spiritually. It is more than okay to seek help from a therapist that God has led you to see.

Some pain was never meant to bear alone and a licensed professional as well as a God-lead Pastor or other Christian may be just what a person needs to get well after getting delivered. This is not denying God's power in any way. God certainly can do it instantly, but many times He doesn't. Naaman had to dip in the Jordan seven times (2 Kings 5:10). The ten people with leprosy had to go show themselves to the High Priest (Luke 17:14). The Shunamite woman had to go chasing after the prophet (2 Kings 4:22-27). God is not averse to using a process that involves other people or unorthodox methods to heal, restore and set free.

The stigma of mental health among Christians needs to stop ***NOW!*** I personally believe that there are many people who have sadly committed suicide or abandoned their relationship with God all because the religious stigma of seeking professional help with their mental health. Christians need to realize that while spiritual warfare casts out the demons it is mental health services that can help clean up the damage.

Just because someone throws out a squatter from where they don't belong doesn't immediately restore any damage that may have happened to that property. If a building or house is damaged by a storm or an accident, it could possibly collapse if the core of the structure of the place is damaged. If walls are wide open because of holes anything can sneak back in and cause even more destruction. If the damage goes unrepaired in a person, it can cause them to be susceptible to the same sorts of demonic oppression that they dealt with before they were delivered.

As the Bible has shown us God will use anything or anyone to restore a person so a therapist or psychologist can be one of those methods. I hate to break it to people, but an unqualified pastor is not the only hope for counseling for Christians. Yes, I said it. There are too many pastors putting themselves up as counselors and they have no business trying to help people who have gone through trauma. Now before someone gets mad with me, let me clarify something. There are some "untrained" pastors that God has given spiritual gifts to offer great counsel, so I am not talking about people like this. If God has ***TRULY CALLED*** a pastor to be a counselor, they will be effective and lead by God to restore people. If a pastor doesn't have that calling or those gifts? Relegate the mental health of their parishioners to someone who is gifted or trained. God is the source of all knowledge so we cannot overlook or dismiss where that knowledge comes from.

As I told you all before, after I went through separation and divorce, I was emotionally devastated and spiritually broken. I was depressed, angry, and unsettled within myself. I was prone to periods of deep depression that caused me not to leave my home for the days that I didn't have to go to work. I would sit in the dark for days as the heavy clouds would swirl around me. While my soon-to-be-ex-wife seemed to be living large, I was not. I contemplated suicide many times and even planned on how I would do it. I was wrecked and I didn't have the mindset to "pray my way" through it. My friends and family didn't know all that I was going through this pain as one-by-one people turned their backs on me and I was left alone. Reality stopped making sense as I flew into a fantasy realm, and I was numb to everything around me.

I was a high-functioning dead man that was still leading worship and still ministering in church. My emotions had been ripped out of my heart and soul, and I didn't know where to turn. I didn't have a pastor I felt comfortable speaking with because of the things I was feeling and how I felt about the stigma of mental health. I had convinced myself that I was saved and that I didn't need to get a therapist or seek a counselor. I just sat there day after day stewing and brewing a toxic potion of feelings that was affecting me deeply. Yet the few that knew what was happening prayed for me and never let up their support of me. My friend Pastor Russell would come to my door and pray for me even when I wouldn't open the door. He encouraged me and he wouldn't quit. I had hit rock bottom and had started to dig deeper with my bare and bloodied hands. The Enemy was laughing at me the whole way.

When my breakthrough through God finally came and He lifted my dark shroud of doom, I was led to an ad on social media for an acquaintance that was starting a business as a life coach. I sent a message to them and set up an appointment. While I was working on my spiritual issues with God, this person helped me put my life back together. I learned how to love myself again in the natural while God reinforced that He loved me even more. I learned healthy routines and how to not be so negative about myself and other things around me. I believe that it was God who led me to seek her out, because I needed to talk to someone and rebuild my life. In parallel I began to see a therapist for my mental anguish. For the record neither of these people were affiliated with a church. I never expected that God would use those two people in amazing ways.

I worked through my feelings, talked out my frustrations and dealt with the results of the situation and they gave me ways to accept what God had allowed to happen to me. I was allowed to safely release my rage and deal with my deep sadness and depression. God used them to rebuild my self-esteem and self-worth as my time with them helped me set new goals and open new possibilities that I never saw before. I still prayed, I still worshipped God, and He gave me deeper insights to what was happening in my sessions. I never told anyone (especially in the church) what I was doing because I didn't want to face any backlash.

It was His plan that I seek those professionals, and it was His leading that revealed them to me. All while I was doing these things, I was also seeking God about them as well. Slowly, but surely, I was turning corner after corner and God was leading the way. I know that He used that life coach and therapist to help me where I couldn't help myself. It was when I finally learned to love myself again and be healthy that I met the love of my life, and we got married. Where I was hollowed out and empty God had filled my spiritual empty places and used other people to help heal my emotions and my mind. I still have things to work through, but God is showing me what is possible if I just trust Him. If I rely on Him and whatever He sends me to be restored, I haven't looked back.

Each day I have gained strength from God's healing process and so will you. It isn't always easy, but it is necessary for healing and strength to come for us to walk this road not in shame and defeat, but in power and faith. Everything is for the glory of God and provides a testimony for those we know and don't know. Those we see and don't see. It seems extreme sometimes when we look over all that we must endure as humanity and that God seems to do nothing and that's not the case. We can't understand God's mind and motives, but the one thing we must keep in mind is that it all is for our good. We aren't failures or destined to never succeed in life because God has never broken a promise to us. Even at its darkest God will see us through anything. We may not agree with His timing, but He knows what's best.

When God lays out the plan for our restoration it is up to us to take it seriously and trust Him and follow it. Spiritual processes are not always instant as I have said before. Instantly or not, we must walk the program that God has tailor-made just for us because I believe that it is our purpose to do so. Look throughout Scripture and you will find many instances where people came out of a mess and went straight to work. I remember when the prophet Elijah was troubled God immediately sent him to anoint people and so forth (1 Kings 19:15-16). Elisha watched his mentor taken up into Heaven and simply picked up the mantle and immediately started ministering to people (2 Kings 2:11-12). I could go on and on, but I cannot imagine that any of these people didn't receive some sort of healing for the traumas that happened to them.

The healing process doesn't always feel fair. In fact, it can hurt much worse than the original injury. It sort of reminds me of what happens to amputees after they lose a body part which is called phantom pain. Phantom limb pain is pain that a person feels in a part of a limb that was removed after an amputation[4]. When phantom pain strikes, the part that is missing is not there, but the person experiencing it feels the pain of what is not there anymore. When we are recovering from what hurt us in this Christian walk the phantom pains of the losses, deaths and injuries will still feel real. The flashbacks and the moments of despair feel real. When we look at the photos or visit places where our loved ones once were will trigger painful memories and feelings of loss. When we look in the mirror the feelings of uselessness, unworthiness and regret will flood our hearts. Even years after something happens the phantom pain of it all can still feel very real and very present.

All of this can happen while we are being charged to minister to others. We can feel the pain of abuse and neglect while leading worship. We can feel gripping pain while we encourage another brother or sister that is going through what we went through. We could be praying for the loss of someone else's family member and feel the grief of others from afar. Whatever it may be for you just know that God has a purpose for it all. Whether God frees us from the echoes of the past or keeps it relevant to the present it is up to God and that alone can be painful to hear and experience. Yet we must stay in the press and stay moving forward and live out God's plan and purpose for our lives. Here is the most important thing I must share with you concerning your healing: Don't fall in a pile and stop moving.

If there is one thing that I have learned from nature it is that if one doesn't stay moving, they will get stagnant and possibly die. The body of water that stops moving will get stagnant and can eventually die. If a wounded animal cannot or will not keep moving the buzzards will begin to circle and wait until they stop, die and become a meal. In nature everything keeps moving. From the atom all the way to the galaxies of the Universe everything is in constant motion. Where there is motion there is life. Where there is action there is potential. Even the smallest amount of movement is an improvement. As it relates to spiritual and emotional healing, I have discovered that appearances are deceiving as on the outside things can be moving one way and emotionally and spiritually, they are going another. For example, we could be successful at business or our professions but be depressed and stagnant spiritually. Our connection to God can be the best it has been, but emotionally we are an open wound.

We Have To Keep Moving

There can be an unlimited number of scenarios and combinations of things that could equate to your life, but one thing is certain. We cannot lay down and die. We cannot allow the situations in life to get the best of us, and we may or may not have time to stop and patch up our hurts. We often must "faith it until we make it" because God is working in the background. Just like the ten people with leprosy, we must allow healing to happen as we go. Is it what we want? No, it is not. Yet God gets the glory from it all. The salve that our emotions need may not be the best, but it is what we need. The wound so deep that it cut us to the bone might leave a scar that can be seen. Our flesh may still have echoes of phantom pain from a violation that destroyed our world. Whatever God has designed for us to carry on our journey we will carry. We must be unmovable in our faith in Christ because He alone is the solution to it all. He will give us the strength to carry the heaviest burden. He will hold us together where it seems that we are coming apart at the seams.

Once, I had a dream about a person that I didn't know and they were walking in the darkness, whistling as they went down a lonely road. Even though it was dark, I could see the person's face, and I could see the grooves under their eyes down to their cheeks where tears once fell. I could see the scars they had all over their body. I observed the limp that they had with each happy step. It seemed like such a paradox to see such a person who was disfigured by what they experienced, and you could see the remnants of the tears once shed in agony. What came next blew my mind.

Another traveler was crying out in the darkness, and this person heard them calling. They opened the doors that were on their chest and inside was something I never expected. It was a jagged, cracked, broken and brilliant heart filled with light. There were broken shards of glass and twisted metal that were in assorted colors and existed in a state of brand new to rusty. This heart-shaped lantern made no sense to me. It looked like a pile of scrap that if it was set on a table, it would fall apart.

While I observed this person with this impossible lantern, I watched how the light was so bright that it pierced the darkness. The lost soul in the dark cried out louder and the impossible lantern sought them out and found them. Once they were found the person picked up the lost soul and embraced them and tears of joy flowed as this person held this wayward traveler up in their hour of need. As they embraced, they pulled out a bag of scraps and trash and put it in their own chest and the impossible lantern got close to it and the fire leaped from their heart in they too had an impossible lantern formed with a small, but brilliant flame that started to grow.

I remember that I turned to God to help me to understand what I was seeing. A Voice calmly said, "That impossible lantern is the heart that was broken into pieces and reassembled and healed by My Love. It is My Fire that is their flame that holds their hearts, minds and spirits together, and their job is to seek out others that are broken so that I may set their hearts on fire for Me again!" I was speechless as I heard God speak and the dream immediately ended, but I carried so many things away from this dream. The impossible lantern is not supposed to make sense to us. When God heals us, we are walking miracles.

We are the results of His handiwork and there is none like it anywhere. The Fire of His Spirit is what burns on the inside for Him which sends us to others. The happy traveler I saw was still hurting and still healing and still crying every now and then. They didn't have a perfect look, but they were in the perfect position. They didn't ignore the call of the broken and they went to them limping, full of scars, and imperfect. They embraced another who was down with a shattered heart and God lit them on fire again.

Both hearts look like they shouldn't even work. Shattered, rusted, twisted and marred. When we recover from pain it doesn't make sense to have joy again. When we recover from abuse it doesn't make sense that we can stand again. When we lose everything, it doesn't make sense that we can be restored again. When we were victims before it doesn't make sense that we can be champions now. What God restores doesn't make good human sense, but it is only held together by His Spirit and that is ***ALL*** that is needed. But just like that traveler, we must keep moving and we must keep healing. We must not be ashamed of God's restoration because someone may need to see your scars. Seeing that it is possible to be restored can heal them and heal you. When God turns your pain into purpose and your shame into power miracles begin to happen for them and for you.

Whether it be alone or with others go where God sends you. Do what God tells you and listen and not just hear. What was your greatest defeat is potentially your greatest ministry. Where you may fall is where God wants you to stand. Whatever God prescribes? Take it; use it; become your destiny. Walk the broken road as fast as you can or are allowed to go. No one way works for everyone so be patient. If we are trying to help someone else let God lead you and don't step out of the boundaries that He has set. Scripture says that one plants, one waters, and God gives the increase. It works the same if you are the one healing. One prayer might not "do it" and one visit to a counselor might not "fix it", but whatever the plan God has for you? ***GO THROUGH***.

But let's look at another aspect of healing as you go which is restoration as we step. The best example of that is in Luke 17:11-14:

AND IT CAME TO PASS, AS HE WENT TO JERUSALEM, THAT HE PASSED THROUGH THE MIDST OF SAMARIA AND GALILEE. AND AS HE ENTERED INTO A CERTAIN VILLAGE, THERE MET HIM TEN MEN THAT WERE LEPERS, WHICH STOOD AFAR OFF: AND THEY LIFTED UP THEIR VOICES, AND SAID, JESUS, MASTER, HAVE MERCY ON US. AND WHEN HE SAW THEM, HE SAID UNTO THEM, GO SHEW YOURSELVES UNTO THE PRIESTS. AND IT CAME TO PASS, THAT, AS THEY WENT, THEY WERE CLEANSED. – LUKE 17:11-14 KJV

The account of the Ten Lepers is well-known in Scripture, and it talks about ten people with leprosy that Jesus met one day and asked for healing. These men were cut off from their communities with a disease that at the time was most certainly fatal and could spread quickly to others. They cried out to Jesus who gave them instructions to show themselves to the priests, which was according to Jewish Law. They weren't healed when Jesus spoke to them, but as they pressed closer to their destination their leprosy progressively vanished until they were healed. Notice that this healing went as they went where Jesus told them to go that they got better.

The Scriptures don't necessarily say that they went immediately or when they exactly went. It just said that as they went to show themselves to the priests that they were healed. I can imagine that these people with leprosy knew that Jesus could heal immediately. I know that they heard the stories and knew of those that He had healed. Jesus was famous at the time and people knew that God was with Him.

Yet I can imagine that if I could put my human hat on for a minute some of these people with leprosy had their doubts. The Bible doesn't say that all ten people with leprosy went at the same time. Sure, the one who came back knew the other nine, but nothing specified anything except that one came back. Their healing all came from the journey of their God-given promise. Jesus said go show themselves. He didn't speak healing over them. He didn't say that they would be healed. He told them to go as if they were already healed. They had to just go the way Jesus said, and the rest was up to their faith.

When we encounter pains that wish to cripple us and separate us from everyone else because what we have can bleed over into someone else's life it can make it difficult to exist and we often travel with those like us because there is little comfort or welcome anywhere else. Yet, when God gives us a direction to go; a destiny to attain our healing comes from the journey. When we see that we are getting better, albeit slowly, we learn to move with more faith and more zeal. I am sure that those people with leprosy started to rejoice and even started telling others in their leper community about this Jesus who spoke to them. When we are recovering from pain, and we are on task to reach our destiny or ministry God gives us what we need to keep going and do it with strength and power.

Healing Ourselves by Healing Others

For some of us, if we got healed immediately, we wouldn't work the ministry into which we were called. We wouldn't operate as God's ambassador to the ones that He sent us to minister to. We wouldn't operate with the faith that we are because we had nothing to build it on. It took faith to go like they were healed when they clearly were not when Jesus first spoke to them. To the carnal, this was stupidity. This was the definition of insanity. When we are cut down to the spiritual bone and God says, "get up and go", it makes no logical sense whatsoever. It almost feels ridiculous that this is what God wants us to do. That's almost like going to urgent care for being sick and the doctor tells you to take a long walk instead. When we are hurt, we want medicine, painkillers, something to take the edge off right then and not to take a journey. God doesn't always give us what we want, but He will give us what we need which will get us what we want.

When I was gravely emotionally hurt from an early age, I remember praying and asking God why I was suffering like this and instead of healing, God called me into ministry. I was a teenager, and God answers my prayer with a call to His service. I didn't understand why, but as I have lived a little while I can see the healing that is taking place, but I know that I am not all the way there just yet. I have had to pour all my tears and anguish into leading worship and writing.

I have had to bind up my wounds by service to God and helping His people. Remember the prophet Elijah in 1 Kings 19? He had called down fire to burn up altars and killed the prophets of Baal. Yet, when Jezebel sent a messenger that she was going to kill him Elijah ran and hid in a cave. God showed up, displayed His power, and then sent him to anoint a king over Syria, anoint Jehu to be the king of Israel, and Elisha to be his apprentice. God didn't speak healing over Elijah; He gave him things to do that would bring him healing over time.

Later, Elijah recovered from his pain and lit the flame for his successor, Elisha, to blaze a trail of ministry that left an indelible mark on the world. Elijah's healing as he went and fulfilled his purpose, and destiny was designed to heal him and ignite another for their journey. God doesn't always provide the healing that we need in the ways that we want it to come to us. He has a prescribed method just for us in a way that has been designed for us, and we don't get much say in the matter. It is a human thing to want things the way we see them because we feel that we know what is best for us. What we must understand is that God is bigger and greater than we are. His eyes see much farther than ours and His wisdom is deeper than ours could ever be.

When we cry out to God or are under His watchful care, we don't get to have an opinion on how He works. He is God. That's it. We can ask God for what we want, but it's up to Him and Him alone. Will he hear our requests? Absolutely! We can apply the maximum amount of faith and tell God what our desires are for help when we are hurting and need help. What we need to accept is that what God sends isn't always what we pictured or asked for.

Yes, I know that the Scriptures tell us that whatever we ask in His Name, He will do it. The Word doesn't lie and won't ever lie. God is still God, and he can do what He wishes, especially if He knows what's best for us. That is something that maturity in our relationship with God brings. The longer we walk with God, the more we see that God will do things for our good even when it isn't what we asked for.

I am sure that Elijah wanted God to vaporize Jezebel or let the prophecy come true about her demise to come at that moment, but God had other plans. When Elijah left that cave Jezebel's threat was still there, but God gave Elijah peace of mind and spirit. It is that peace that can also bring healing and restoration to our souls in ways that removing the threats can never do for us. God's peace, as in Philippians 3:14, is the peace that goes beyond understanding. The human mind cannot understand it from an insider or outsider's point of view. God's Peace is special and unique. It is beyond assurance, and it is beyond a "fix" for a broken situation. God's Peace is directly connected to the activation of faith. When we turn our face to God and lay our troubles at His Feet and trust Him, something amazing begins to happen.

Don't Forget About Jesus

Finally, the greatest and best way to heal as we go along this broken road is one that should be obvious, but it often isn't as apparent at first. That way is ***THE WAY*** Himself, who is Jesus Christ. He is the great healer and the author and finisher of our faith (Hebrews 12:2). It is only through Christ that we can truly be restored and healed as we work out our soul's salvation. It seems paradoxical that the road of relationship in our lives that has the pitfalls and dark days on it is also the source of our most effective healing. Will the pain be there? Yes, they will, but as we get to know Christ through our lives in Him, we realize increasingly that Jesus wasn't kidding when He said that He would be with us ***ALWAYS*** even until the end of the age.

The farther we go along in this life we will realize that we are far from being alone. This isn't a cliche as many would like to believe. As for myself, the more I grow with God, the more I can see Him in every area of my life. Even in the darkest days where my vision was cloudy and my heart was failing, and I felt abandoned and hopeless; God was right there. My sorrows and my situations were like cataracts and blocked a part of my spiritual eyesight, but God was still there, and I am learning to feel His Presence more than I can see Him. Even then, if I can't feel Him there, I know that without doubt, He is still there for me. That He is working on my behalf and that it can all come crashing down and I could be in agony, but I won't be forgotten.

That hope is a powerful medicine to a sick spirit. It is the salve that soothes every wound and binds up every injury. It reminds me of how a little one will run to Mommy and Daddy when they have a boo-boo that hurt or scared them, and they begin to cry and wail uncontrollably. Often it is when that little child gets scooped up into their parents' arms that they stop crying after a little while because they know that comfort and help is now here. Most likely their little bodies are still registering the pain, but because they are in Mommy or Daddy's arms, they know that everything is going to be all right. The tears can stop even if they still sting or bleed. They can lay their heads on their chest, put in a pacifier or whatever they do and calm down and recover.

Jesus wasn't kidding when he said that the Kingdom was like little children. It makes so much sense to me now because we are like the little ones and God is our Father. When we are hurt or scared instead of sitting there and thinking that we have this on our own we need to do two things. We need to cry out and signal that we are hurting, and we need to run to Him. We cry out to God when we pray. We cry out to God when we praise and worship Him despite our situation. We cry out when we search for the right Scripture to ease our pain. We cry out when we seek His face and not look for a bottle of liquor, a dose of drugs, or illicit sex.

While we are doing these things we are spiritually running to God for help. When we run to Him, we stay focused on where He is. We don't care what we look like, and we don't care how loud we are doing it. I have never seen a toddler wipe the blood off a scraped knee before they ran to their mothers. I have never seen a scared child "fix their face" before they ran to Daddy for safety. A baby who soils themselves don't change their own diaper before crying when they make a mess (normally). Those little ones will run or cry because they realize that they can't fix what's happening, but the ***DO KNOW*** who can. Mommy and Daddy can make it better. They may not even truly understand how or why, but they have such trust in the ones who gave them life, shelter, and nourishment that they don't care how they are, because they need help, and they need it right now.

We need to be like this more when it comes to God. I will use a dirty diaper to demonstrate, and I apologize if this is a bit awkward to you, but it is a good illustration. Adam was ashamed when he messed up and hid from God and we need to not follow that example. When our spiritual diapers get soiled from what we did we need to need to call out to God loaded with our mess and dripping with our accident. We need to surrender and realize that we can't clean this up. Like the little ones, we need to be unashamed that we made a mess. Even if we figured out how to take the diaper off, we still have the remnants on us. We aren't clean. We are still stained with what we did and now we are going to get exposed.

If you talk to my Mom, she will tell you of a time when I was a toddler that she caught me trying to change my own diaper. I was ashamed to make a mess, and I didn't want to get caught, so I saw where the clean diapers were and thought I could do this on my own. When my Mom caught me trying to put the tape on, I couldn't get it right. One side wouldn't adhere correctly, and I was struggling.

I never knew what I did with the dirty diaper, but it was at that moment that my Dad knew that it was time to potty train. Mom said that I even tried to clean myself with a baby wipe, but I botched it up badly because I couldn't reach everywhere to wipe away all the mess. I am sure that the image of me standing there embarrassed to be caught and guilty that I knew it was bad had to be a funny moment that I am glad came before the Internet was born.

Let's look at this from a spiritual standpoint. A diaper change is a humiliating experience that prayerfully we, as adults, won't have to endure, but as children we did. Someone must pick you up, lay you down and take off your clothes and diaper with all its messy glory. The child must have their most hidden areas exposed to the one changing them. They must stay laying there while someone must lift them up by their legs, wash them clean, and remove all the stuff that defiled them.

They must lift you up in ways you couldn't do yourself and make sure that every piece of fecal matter or urine is cleaned off the baby's skin to prevent a future infection. It also makes sure that the smell of being soiled is removed from those areas. Then they must examine you to see if you have a diaper rash or have any other issues and then put on a fresh diaper and often new clean clothes and once that is done, they take you off the changing area and life returns to a clean normal.

This whole experience is one the child cannot do on their own (even though I woefully tried) and puts them in a powerless position. When we mess ourselves spiritually, we either cry because we recognize it (repentance), or God smells our mess and comes to get us (correction). God must pick us up and exposes our shame but does so with compassion. A baby is most likely changed in privacy where no one else can see what's underneath their diapers. It's not always that way.

I have been in strange places where a parent changed a diaper, and I immediately cringe or look away because I always feel that they shouldn't have a little child's business out there like that for people to see. I have been on buses, in airports, and even in the food court of shopping malls where a parent would use a table, chair or even the floor and strip a child down, changing them and getting them processed. I would never change my little one that way, but when I think about God in this way, I know that sometimes He will change our spiritual diapers in the public for them to see. Even though it is embarrassing and exposing it is still for our good. It is humbling for God to correct us, or we repent openly to what we did, but we must remember that like those babies who are changed in public, that their exposure is for a moment and then they are cleaned up and dressed again.

God will never leave us exposed like that because He means everything that we endure to be for our good. No one takes dirty diaper off a child and leaves them without clothing. They change them to get them clean and to smell like little ones should. Fresh and clean. This is why just taking the soiled diaper is not enough. There must be a bath as well to remove the scent of defilement. Repentance and correction require admittance of error, submission to Godly change, spiritual cleansing, and God's resetting of our lives. If we just took off the dirty spiritual diaper, we would still have disgusting remnants on us that could break us out in a rash or get us infected with something far worse than a soiled nappy.

We also want to have the right fragrance on us. The Holy Spirit is a fragrance that comes from God. God is all about fragrance and if you read the Scriptures there are many instances where burnt offerings were made, and it was a "pleasing aroma" unto the Lord. When we receive the Holy Spirit when we are saved, we carry His aroma on our lives. When we defile ourselves, we take on the odor of sin. Even if we wipe it away ourselves, we can still carry the aroma that's detestable to God on our lives. The smell of excrement is on our skin and if it stays too long it will stay there until it is cleaned off with the right product. We can hide our mistakes, but the scent is still on us until God cleans it away. When God has us clean, we smell like Him. We have His Spirit, and it bears witness with Him. We have a lot of people walking around with the wrong scent on them.

Let me put this in the context of a relationship. When I am with my wife, and we go out together and because we are close anyone who meets me can faintly smell her perfume on me because of how close I am to her. We have all experienced this where we will kiss our husband or wife goodbye for the day or whatever and because were close to them, we have an imprint of their fragrance on us. It is when we meet someone else with a different cologne or fragrance that we get close to that causes that fragrance to be imprinted on us. In church I have had people hug me and when I get home or in my car, I can faintly smell their perfume on me and even though it was accidental, the proximity stuck with me.

Just like a soiled baby bottom that isn't properly cleaned, a dabble in sin or the wrong fellowship leaves its scent on us. It may not be there any longer, but without God's cleaning to remove it that smell will linger. So, like the perfume example I spoke of, there have been times when I came back home to my wife and has told me that she can notice when another scent is on me. Now mind you, she isn't the jealous type, but I do my best to ***NOT*** let those imprints get on me because I care about what she thinks of me even though she knows that I have never, nor will I ever stray from her. Spiritually, there are a lot of people who claim that they belong to Christ and have His scent of the Holy Spirit in them, but the evidence reveals that they have gotten the Devil's cologne on their spirits.

This is not condemnation, but we all have smelled a little one who didn't smell so fresh but didn't wear a soiled diaper. We all have had one of those "not so fresh days" where we didn't shower as well as we should have or forgot to put deodorant on. The same thing goes spiritually as we can look good, be in a good place, but we have a whiff of the wrong scent on us. When all these things happen, we must submit like the priest in Zechariah that had to be stripped down and made clean. On our broken road, this is where healing comes. Getting cleaned by God restores us and makes us feel fresh and neat again.

Everyone feels superb after a bath or shower. We smell good, we feel empowered when we are confident that we are clean. That's how God wants us to be all the time. Whether we get cleaned publicly or privately, we need to know that it is for our good and for our spiritual health. A clean little baby is one of the most wonderful things ever. They are happy, smell good and in fresh clothes. So, in the natural, it is in the spirit.

We need to stop being embarrassed about the dark times of life. We don't have to tell everyone about it, but we should tell God. He already knows, but He is waiting on us to reach out to Him. I imagine a little one who has a snotty nose, or a dirty face and their parents see them and immediately clean them up. That child, just like the diaper change, gives up control to them and allows them to fix the issue and get them cleaned up again. There is healing that comes from surrendering to God. When we lift our hands in worship or our voices in prayer to God, we get freed from what is holding us down and we allow God to pick us up again. The experience of voluntary surrender binds us to the heart of the one we surrender to. To surrender voluntarily there must be trust and faith in them to not hurt us.

Even if we are hesitant, we have tipped the scales of uncertainty enough to allow ourselves to be subject to someone else's will. Over time we lose the tendency to hesitate because we know that they have not let us down and they haven't hurt us when we needed them. As we go along the road of relationship we learn to value and trust God and see that He is a God of His Word. He is a loving and caring God that will take us as we are and make us whole again. There is a powerful medicine in knowing that God will love us and get our wounds bandaged and our messes cleaned up. There is healing in knowing without any doubts we can come not just with our mistakes, but with every situation. When we are innocent, we can come and get comfort like the child who fears the monsters under their beds. We can come to Christ when the foreclosure notice comes, or the diagnosis is terminal.

We can come to God when our spouse walks out of our lives for an affair. We can find solace in our God when we've lost our job or our home. We can find rest if we've run away from our destiny or abandoned our faith. We can find peace even if there is exposure to our nonsense. We can allow the shame to fade away from whatever it is that broke us down on the broken road. As we grow in our relationship with God, we can rest assured that He is our help and our place of safety. The God that spoke everything into existence is here and works on our behalf as He fathers us like no one else could. This is why I love Psalms 16:

PRESERVE ME, O GOD: FOR IN THEE DO I PUT MY TRUST. O MY SOUL, THOU HAST SAID UNTO THE LORD, THOU ART MY LORD: MY GOODNESS EXTENDETH NOT TO THEE; BUT TO THE SAINTS THAT ARE IN THE EARTH, AND TO THE EXCELLENT, IN WHOM IS ALL MY DELIGHT. THEIR SORROWS SHALL BE MULTIPLIED THAT HASTEN AFTER ANOTHER GOD: THEIR DRINK OFFERINGS OF BLOOD WILL I NOT OFFER, NOR TAKE UP THEIR NAMES INTO MY LIPS. THE LORD IS THE PORTION OF MINE INHERITANCE AND OF MY CUP: THOU MAINTAINEST MY LOT. THE LINES ARE FALLEN UNTO ME IN PLEASANT PLACES; YEA, I HAVE A GOODLY HERITAGE. I WILL BLESS THE LORD, WHO HATH GIVEN ME COUNSEL: MY REINS ALSO INSTRUCT ME IN THE NIGHT SEASONS. I HAVE SET THE LORD ALWAYS BEFORE ME: BECAUSE HE IS AT MY RIGHT HAND, I SHALL NOT BE MOVED. THEREFORE, MY HEART IS GLAD, AND MY GLORY REJOICETH: MY FLESH ALSO SHALL REST IN HOPE. FOR THOU WILT NOT LEAVE MY SOUL IN HELL; NEITHER WILT THOU SUFFER THINE HOLY ONE TO SEE CORRUPTION. THOU WILT SHEW ME THE PATH OF LIFE: IN THY PRESENCE IS FULNESS OF JOY; AT THY RIGHT HAND THERE ARE PLEASURES FOR EVERMORE. – PSALMS 16 KJV

We can't say things like this unless we are truly close to God. This takes time and doesn't happen overnight. This is why the road of relationship exists, in my opinion. We need the road to find our way to God in a manner that we build up trust in His Word, and we fall hopelessly in love with Him. As I have said before, everything is not bad in the walk of the Christian. Most of it is joy, but even in the storms and darkness God will give us healing from every wound and relief for every scar. We get to know Him and the power of His resurrection, and the fellowship of His sufferings being made conformable unto His Death (Philippians 3:11) and that, my friends, is healing for our spirits. The Three Keys that I spoke of earlier unlock a joy that is unspeakable and is our relief and restoration on the road of life. The road may be broken, but God's promises are intact.

What I would like to do is encourage you to stay the course that God has you walking. It may seem contradictory as to why god has you enduring such pain and darkness, but I promise you that it is for something that He has intended for your good. God makes zero mistakes. Whatever you struggle with or struggles with you is under the gaze of Almighty God. His Hand is on you regardless of whether you can see it or not. Don't allow your faith to be "deconstructed" to nothing because of our human logic can't understand the Mind of God.

It will never make sense to us until it is over and done. It reminds me of when I see people get cosmetic surgery on those reality programs. The surgeons carve a person up in specific ways and when the patients are recovering, they are left with stitched up wounds, swelling, and often fluid drains filled with all sorts of stuff. It is not pretty, but as they heal the features they desired come through and they have been thoroughly transformed.

Let the broken road be your genesis to your next. Let the broken road be your process to where God desires for you to be. Let the broken road be your altar upon which your living sacrifice is laid. Don't hide from a God that already knows all about you and despite that, He loves you dearly. He does things His way (Isaiah 55:8–9) and we must keep that in mind as we go through things that don't seem to make sense to our human minds. We need to not look at the whole journey, but at one step at a time. I remember my father telling me that if you look at the whole ditch that must be dug you will get tired before you start. As people, we want to know when a rough patch will be over, and it won't work that way. Part of our relationship with Christ is trusting Him for every moment, every hour, and every day we walk this road. We must know deep in our hearts that it will be okay. God will not let our end be worse than our beginning.

That faith and trust in God is all we need to continue. That hope is what sustains us. It helps us to shout with praise in the sunshine and through the rain. It is when we, like the old song says, "walk where He leads me" that we know that it will all be all right. We can't say that until we know Jesus on a deeper level. We can't bear witness to it when we haven't encountered Christ like that. Believe me, I tried as I am sure many others have before, but I always ended back in the arms of Christ because He has been the only stable and true Person in my life. No matter what will happen in this life it will always be Jesus and me. Everyone and everything else can fail me in this world but give me Jesus! When we peel back all the layers that have been discussed in this book, the only constant that will never fail is Christ Jesus. Let the road be broken and let it cut your feet. Let the enemy camp at your house. Let Hell forward its packages to your address. If Jesus is with you? Who could ever defeat you?

CHAPTER REFERENCES

[1] Denova, R., & Art, W. G. O. (2024). Crucifixion. *World History Encyclopedia*. https://www.worldhistory.org/crucifixion/

[2] Bady, Percy, & Townshend, Pete. (1988). I'm Free [Recorded by Rev. Milton Brunson & the Thompson Community Singers]. On *Available To You* [CD]. Nashville: Word/Epic (1988).

[3] *Cat-Scratch Fever*. (2022, April 26). WebMD. https://www.webmd.com/skin-problems-and-treatments/cat-scratch-fever

[4] Cleveland Clinic. (2023, September 8). Phantom limb pain: What it is, causes, treatment & prevention. https://my.clevelandclinic.org/health/diseases/12092-phantom-limb-pain

7

Final Thoughts

For a few moments I would like to leave you with some things that God has laid on my heart to share with you, the reader concerning the broken road of relationship and a bit about me. I know that we have talked about many facets of the broken road, but I want to leave these few words with you from my personal perspective. I can say that my life hasn't been as hard as many others that I have encountered in my fifty years on this planet. In all accounts, my life has been a blessed one and I can agree with that wholeheartedly. I graduated high school, went to a prominent Historically Black College and University in Hampton, Virginia. I have had a wonderful career in information technology, and I haven't been seriously ill over a lengthy period. I am not hilariously rich, but I am not woefully broke either. All I know is that you need to never give up and stay in the race.

The broken road we travel isn't easy, but thanks be unto God that His burden is light. It may not seem like it is easy while we are going through the desert and dark places, but God has never left us and never forgotten about us. I have told you a few things about me in earlier passages of this book, but I would like to retell my story a little and fill in a few blanks as my testimony.

I, like many other people, believed that being saved would put me on easy street and I was so wrong. I suffered trials and tribulations from the start of my life, and I still endure them to this day. What do I mean by that? Let me take you to the beginning of my story. My childhood was full of mental and emotional torture and as an African American who was raised in a heavily racist and conservative area, I suffered persecution from Day One. It was to be expected that came from growing up as an African-American male in a county that still has Confederate battle flags flying and a Confederate traitor soldier's monument guarded twenty-four hours a day by right-wing extremist wingnuts.

I was reared in a home with both of my parents who were devout Christians who lived the life they professed to others. I had an untroubled home and a wonderful family. Yet I was at war with life. I have endured physical and emotional challenges from the time I could remember anything and yet, here I am as an overcomer. I was a smart Black kid that felt unwanted and unloved by everyone except his family. I was never a social butterfly and when I got saved as a young boy, things (to me) seemed to get worse.

I was ridiculed because I was different, I was ostracized because of how I spoke and the fact that I took advanced classes, and I didn't do what everyone else was doing made me the butt of many jokes and persecution. My life has had a calling to serve in ministry from a very young age. I remember when I was around four years old that I would practice preaching by using the back of the large armchair in the living room of our home. I have been an avid reader since the age of four as well and I can recall myself reading the Children's Bible and encyclopedias just to ingest knowledge.

I remember being in kindergarten and exposed to other ethnicities besides my own and being tortured and persecuted as being different. My parents did isolate us from a lot of things to keep us Christ-centered and no matter what, there will be good and not so good consequences from that. I was a bit sheltered, but I know now that it was for my good. So, I didn't wear all the latest fashion trends or have expensive video games, and I was "well spoken" which made me an outcast. I was a social reject who was put down by my peers and treated unfairly by those who held racist beliefs in the core of their beings. I hated my life outside of my house growing up.

I hated life in my hometown, and I was depressed often, and I kept it all hidden from everyone including my family. I was a sad child most of the time. Even though I grew up in church and seemed to love living the "Jesus Life" the entire time I was fighting for my life from inside my mind. I was angry at God. I remember once that I was alone riding my bike on a country road through the woods, and I shook my literal fist at God and cursed the day I was born. I hated my life and wondered why God would do these things to me. I was bewildered and confused, and I didn't know it at the time that God was setting me up for something greater and that my pain had a purpose.

There was one exception. My home church, Zion Baptist Church in Cardinal, Virginia, was one of the only other bright spots in my life. My church family was and still means everything to me. I served in everything from Sunday School, choirs, Usher Board, and was appointed as a Junior Deacon. You would think that life was okay for me, right? Wrong. I had accepted Christ as my savior at the age of nine years old and I feel in love with Jesus and life took a turn. I was emotionally bombarded with the spirit of rejection, and I retreated to eating as a coping mechanism. I ate and I never stopped as I felt empty inside. I remember kids would give me their lunches just to watch me gorge like a feral pig. This was the genesis of my severe weight problem that persisted throughout most of my life.

I just wanted the attention because no one seemed to like me for me. It took over my life as I was awkward, obese, isolated, and Black. I still loved Jesus and the only relief I got was at home and church. The Call of God was still there and through many prophetic words and dreams I knew what God had in store for my life. It was all around me as my family was ***FULL*** of deacons, prophets, ministers and pastors. I grew up with a family that was filled with the Holy Spirit and worked in the Fivefold Ministry as their lifestyle. I remember that whenever they came together as family, they would have what they called a "prayer meeting" which I didn't understand back then, but I do now. It was more than just prayer; it was a God encounter that I didn't get normally where I grew up.

My family would get together and bombard Heaven to receive from the Lord. I didn't know what speaking in tongues was back then, but I remember when as a kid that I could hear all that chatter, and I was mesmerized by it. I didn't know what it meant, but it called me. I remember that I would sit as a little one while they spread around a living room and began to pray in English first and transition to the Heavenly language. I remember that sometimes there would be tape recorders in the room to catch the prophetic downloads that were being given. My little heart was captured by this and then I didn't know why. My family would bring us kids in and pray for us within their prayer circle, and I remember the many times things were spoken over our lives that seemed wild then but make sense now.

I remember when my late aunt, the wonderful Pastor Sarah McShaw, was praying for me one time and for the first time I felt something that I never had before. She was speaking life over me because at that time I was around twelve years old, and I started getting rebellious and defiant. She never touched me but looked at me with her kind eyes through her round spectacles and declared that God has big plans for me. That I was going to be a force for Hell to reckon with. While she was praying a wave of fire passed through me and I lost track of where I was. Time stood still and the voices around me were drowned out until I heard a voice that I never heard spoke clearly, "You are mine and I will never let you go."

The voice was unlike anything I had ever heard before, but it was calming, peaceful and it shook me to my bones. I was afraid and felt safe at the same time. It was the Voice of God and He let me know that He had me and was holding me close. It was after that day that everything got worse in my life. I was a social pariah at school, and I felt so alone. I never dated in high school because no one would even consider me. I was mercilessly teased by Black and White students alike. I would come home and close the door to my room and cry ugly tears. I felt so hated and so rejected. I was doing wonderful things in Marching Band and in my classes and yet I felt alone, and I was dejected. As I said earlier, I contemplated suicide ***MANY TIMES*** during this part of my life.

I had to take my niece to my high school prom because I couldn't get a date. Even then, some of the mean girls cornered her in the bathroom and asked her how much I paid for her to go with me. You get the idea. So many times, I pondered ways to end my life. At the same time, I was growing in God, serving increasingly in church and yet, I felt incomplete. In my mind and heart, I was a torrent of chaos while on the outside I was a seemingly calm person. I hid my feelings from everyone. I tried to do it on my own. I knew that I was set apart by God but didn't understand what it meant. I didn't realize that isolation is where God prepares us for promotion. Still, Hell was working overtime to kill my spirit and prevent me from doing what God had for me to do.

Even when I graduated high school the pain continued. Some people took advantage of my kindness and a few mentally tortured me there because I was different, and I didn't do all the things they did. Most people don't know about what I am about to say here, but for the building of others I want to share a part of my testimony most of my church people have never heard. While I struggled with depression through most of my life I went to college and got introduced to alcohol. While I still dealt with obesity, I was now drinking to satiate my pain. I was still coming home one weekend a month to play for one of the choirs at my home church, but every other weekend I would drink alone or with a circle of folks who weren't necessarily God-centered. I just wanted to fit in. I just wanted to belong. I didn't know yet that God never meant for us to fit in with the crowd. I hadn't learned enough yet.

I hated my life. I despised my existence, and I was still mad at God on one hand but loved Him on the other. I could never shake or break my connection to God, but I still hadn't surrendered my humanity fully to Him. Yes, I had surrendered to my calling as I got into adulthood and started my career, but I didn't surrender my pain. After college I was still awkward and an outcast and I connected with a woman whom I never should have married. I wasn't right for her, and she wasn't right for me. Our marriage was a disaster and looking back I see that all that experience did was prepare me for my life now. I suffered many heartaches and brokenness, but here I am thankful for all those experiences. Not just my first marriage failures, but for my entire life.

I would go to work and come home to sit in the dark and cry. The only "friend" I would have would be the food delivery driver who mocked me. I would eat and cry myself to sleep in my dark living room. My best friend Russell would come to my house to see me because I had hit rock bottom. Sometimes I wouldn't let him in, and I slammed the door in his face because I didn't want to hear what he had to say. He would stand at my door praying for me and wouldn't give up. I am glad he was there for me. I demeaned and deprecated myself because many others did in my past. I counted myself out for what God has called me to do because I believed the lies of a now distant yesterday meant to derail my future which is today.

My family saw what was going on when I finally told them and my Dad (God rest his soul), my Mother, and my sister and brother were there for me while I stumbled along my life's journey. I had uncles and aunts who were praying for me and with God's help I crawled out of the valley on that broken road and clawed my way back to sanity and joy. God led me to the right people at the right time including life coaches and therapists.

I reconnected with an old friend who turned out to be the love of my life and we got married. God remembered every tear I cried and kept record of everything that I lost and today I can say that while everything isn't always perfect, God has restored what I lost and given me more. I can see that there was a purpose for my pain and a reason I went through what I did and will go through in the future.

Yet thanks be unto God for His staying power! I bless God that He did as he promised me the first time that I heard His Voice as He has never let me go. He has never abandoned me. I am His and He is mine. Even when I didn't see Him or hear His Voice, He has been right there for me. He picked me up when I stumbled and watched over me as the recipe of my life was cooking and I was maturing. I can admit that I should have come to this conclusion earlier, but out of fear, I was afraid to step out for God. I let my early years poison the well of my today. I allowed what my eyes and other people's mouths try to dictate to me what God saw in me, and I was in error. I believed the bluster of Hell's whispers over the comforting Voice of God. Why? Because of what my humanity told me.

I remember the spiritual leaders that muzzled me for being too "edgy" or didn't understand what God had placed in me. I took their rebukes as condemnation at the time and began to question who I was in God. Thankfully, God has built me back up as I trusted Him to restore what the cankerworm and the palmerworm have stolen. I can look back on every time I was so weighed down with depression and wanted to die and count it all joy. I can look back at when I would drink alcohol so much that I would be sitting or lying on my bed and feel the room spinning like a top and I can see where God brought me from. I can look at every rejection, insult, put down, muzzling, and mean word as a brick in the fortress that God has built around my spirit to prepare me for the work that he has for me to do.

When I look back at the road that I traveled on I can see all the smooth places and the cracked places. I can see where my feet were cut and bled and where I stumbled and fell in the rain and in the storms. I can see where I wandered off the road in the darkness and where I was left for dead in the desert places. I also could see where Jesus picked me up repeatedly and never left my side. Even when I didn't see Him, He was always there. When I didn't feel Him, Jesus never took His Hands off me. When I battled my giants, Jesus had my back and was fighting them for me. As a Psalmist and Minstrel, I now understand that pain, suffering, and tribulation are a part of building my spiritual resume. They are a part of building all our spiritual resumes as God does His thing in our lives and shapes us into the image that He has destined for us.

I look back on my broken road, and I see where I stumbled, wobbled, stepped off the path momentarily and even took many wrong turns that I never should have taken. Yet, I can see that in my reflexive part of my spirit, my commitment to Christ wouldn't let me falter for too long. Sure, there were many times that I fell on my face in defeat. Yes, my faith wavered, and I strayed. I hid my ministerial calling from many people. Hell made me feel that I wasn't good enough based on the seeds planted in my early childhood. The enemy tried to kill me off by coercing me to gain ludicrous amounts of weight as I have been obese for most of my life on Earth. Careening to divorce and utterly alone the Adversary planted thoughts of suicide and loneliness on levels I had never experienced before.

My journey cannot be your journey, and I would not dare try to tell someone else how to complete their walk in Christ. However, even though we are all different we will all face the same types of obstacles and the same principal enemy. I also want you to know that I am by no means finished with my journey. I have not arrived, and I know that God still has a whole lot of stuff that He must get out of me and refine me into what He has desired for me to be. We are ***ALL*** works in progress, but we can testify about how God has brought us so far. I believe in transparency and those who know me closely know that it is a major part of my ministry. The days of keeping our scars covered and our shame secret are over. There are millions and millions of people out here searching for answers and may miss their breakthroughs if they can't see that they are not alone; and that what God does for one, He will do for them too.

Being Birthed From the Broken Road

I can bear witness that God uses isolation as the birth canal to destiny. To be set apart, you must be isolated. A baby in the womb is safe and taken care of and must go through pain, compression, torsion and pressure as they transition to the real world. Eviction from the womb means going through a place that is not meant to be the destination to life. God planted me into a family that nurtured me and fed me spiritually before and after I got saved. I went through struggles and trials that I never could have imagined. Just like a baby, only one can pass through the canal at a time. Just like that infant I was squeezed to wring out the oil that God placed in my spirit. I was contorted by temptations and illusions like the baby must twist out the shoulders and arms to pass through as their little bones must nearly dislocate and spiral around their little bodies to pass through the birth canal.

I often look at the prophet Elijah who repeatedly felt alone and wished he was dead. The same man who killed the four hundred-fifty prophets of Ba'al ran from Jezebel who threated to kill him. I've felt like that too. I've felt like Jeremiah who was told that he was too young to serve God. I've felt like Samuel who heard God's Voice young and didn't know what to do. I've felt like Daniel who was persecuted for staying true to his faith and punished for it. I have felt like the humanity of Jesus who asked His Father to let the cup of His destiny pass from Him, but had to quickly say not His Will, but God's Will be done. Look at the isolation. Look at the trials. Look at the times of the lives of all these people and more were isolated and alone. I learned that I really wasn't alone after all. Like a midwife or doctor in delivery, that baby being born was never alone.

When a baby is born, they are not just pushed out and allowed to fall and hit the floor or the ground. Care is taken to receive them with love and attention. Hell made me think I was like excrement which will just fall to the ground with gravity taking it over and the excreter leaving it where it fell. The Devil lied to me that I was nothing and that I wasn't fit for what God had called me to be. I learned that Hell was wrong and that if I trusted God, that I would be not just all right, but received by Him to do the work for my destiny. Instead of being dejected and rejected I was delivered and received. Here I am still not done with my journey but starting to truly do the work. I admit, I waited longer than I should, but I won't stop now.

Just like that little one born into the world, we are spiritually born into destiny via isolation and then received with love and care. A baby is first stimulated to breathe air for the first time with a little spank which makes them cry. As a psalmist and minstrel, I can see the parallels with this in the Spirit. When God is transitioning us to a new season the first thing we should do is praise and worship Him. Sure, we need to be cleaned up like that newborn infant, but they don't clean us up first before the birthing cry. Every birth ***MUST*** have that cry first before anything else happens. If not, resuscitation methods need to be employed. Still, every season and new level requires a birthing and in that birthing process, isolation is required to get there. That is the broken road my friends!

I had to learn that nothing in my life was an accident. Nothing was outside of God's knowledge and will for my life. My journey isn't done yet and neither is yours. There are still new seasons to encounter, more life to live, more struggles, and yes, more joy and blessings to come. I look back at my broken road, and I thank God every day for what it has taught me and still teaching me. I have said all this my friends to give this advice: Hang in there and trust God. This is not cliche and it is not boilerplate stuff here. When God urges us to go forward? Do it no matter what you may think the cost is. Do it even if it seems that God is missing, because He is not and is still right there. Weather the storms and know that you won't faint or fail. Know that like that midwife or doctor that you will be received into loving hands that won't drop you. That won't let you fall abandoned and forlorn.

Don't let the static and the noise overwhelm you. Draw closer to Jesus. If you don't know what to do? Just call His Name and tell Him that you need Him. It doesn't have to be fancy, and it doesn't have to be "churchy" for God to hear you. Keep persisting like Jacob and keep pressing until He is ready to answer you. I know that you may be dealing with the worst things of your life. I know that you may be ready to give up and let death swallow you whole and I am here to tell you to rethink that decision. It may be insurmountable, but our God is greater than ***ANY*** situation. It may seem hopeless but out God has ***MORE POWER*** than any force in Creation. God loves ***YOU***. Yes, ***YOU***! It doesn't matter what the mirror says, your mama or daddy says, or your spouse says about you. I don't care what your pastor may have said or anyone else. You are valuable to God and He desires ***YOU!***

Why would God give His own Son to save messy people like us? Why would He even bother if He didn't love us so deeply? We matter so much to God that He orchestrated thousands of years of history just to save us from eternal life in Hell. While we want to play and win the short game with instant results, God does the long scenario for reasons that only He truly understands. I won't dare to try to explain the mind or logic of God. The only thing I can say with assurance is that He has proven His Love for us. Time after time and season after season God has verified His credentials as loving humanity. The Bible is full of many things, but God's Love shines through most of all. Even when people screwed up and went against God, He still loved them even if they had to suffer the consequences of their sins. He never turned His back on others, and He won't on you! What we need to do is to share with others that He loves them too.

Listen, Hell only attacks threats to its kingdom. The greater the attack on you means that you are a greater threat than you think. It will start from your first breath and will continue until your last breath, but our God is ***FAITHFUL*** and will be there for us all. In my life I have learned to ***WAIT*** on God. That is hard to do, and I get that. Everything can and will fall around you, but don't let things fall in you. Keep calling on Jesus even if you feel that He is silent. Keep worshipping and keep praying even when it seems to keep getting worse. Stay in the press because your life depends on it! Don't let Hell's nonsense cheat you out of your destiny on this Earth! Let your faith stretch and grow as Christ prepares you for your next. ***IT WILL BE WORTH IT!***

Also, don't be seduced by false doctrines that contradict the very Heart of God. There are many lies wrapped inside of viable truths and this is Hell's war against God's Church in our world today. Satan will use your situations and sorrows to lead into spiritual whoredom that sounds like virtuous truth. God doesn't use fear, intimidation or control to do what He desires to do in the Earth. Cling to

God like the life raft that He is in the stormy seas of life. Stay focused and determined to hear straight from His lips because He does and will speak to you no matter what it is about. Stay in His Word and never let any organization, loud lying prophet distract you. God speaks truth through truthful and God-sent prophets and revelations through the Holy Spirit.

I write this today a changed man and I thank God every moment of every day for my life. I can admit that I almost gave up and gave in. I nearly let my pain destroy me, but God is faithful and just. He never let me out of His Hand and He loved me just as I needed to be loved and restored. My spiritual scars are prominent, and they are deep, and they hurt at times. I am not free from being in error or making mistakes, yet God chose me and uses me for His Glory. I am a blessed man because of all that God has blessed me with. I have learned who I am in Him and what He desires for me. I now know my purpose that Satan tried to hide for many years with all the tricks in his toolbox. I am not there yet, but I am running towards Christ as He leads me to my purpose. You can and must do this too. Get ready for the battles for the doubts will do everything to distract and obscure God's truth for you.

I am what God says that I am, and I fight my human nature to not believe the lies of Hell that have been trying to hinder me for decades. It is an uphill battle, but I have a relationship with a battle-tested God who made the hill. I am learning to stay still and let Him fight my battles. I am learning to trust even when my physical eyes or discernment can't see. I am acting on and working in my callings not just as a psalmist and minstrel, but as a spiritual warrior and soon to be a pastor. The breath in my lungs is not mine and I owe it to God to live for what He desires. I offer that same advice to you, the reader. While you are alive, you have time to do what God has for you to do. Step out and trust Him completely.

Develop a faith that can speak to a mountain and have it thrown into the sea. Step and place your feet where God will guide you to walk even if there doesn't appear to be any ground to walk on. Push your humanity to the side and let your spirit take over. Wipe your tears and know that God sees you. That He hears you and is there for you. Take the leap even when everyone discounts you or calls you crazy. You may be beaten, downtrodden or even defeated. Get back up again! The strength will come to your spirit and empower your bones. Fear is a liar, and you should ignore everything it says. Depression is the result of the root of rejection. Know that God has chosen you before you were born, and He knows who and what you are and what you will become. Don't let Satan tell you that your imperfections disqualify you because those are just more lies.

God made ***YOU*** just as He intended, and He makes ***NO MISTAKES***. The first thing Hell does is mess with your identity and make you doubt what God created or called you to be. It is a struggle in all areas of our lives, and we need to ask ***HIM*** what we are and not tell ourselves what we think based on our experiences or feelings. For too long I discounted myself as not good enough and I am learning to stop that and just walk where God says to walk and do what He says to do. Grow closer to God and He will show you what He sees in you and what you are. I let the Devil lie to me that I was too fat, incapable, unlovable, too dumb, and unwanted for far too long. I pray that you don't make the same mistakes I made. God doesn't make a mess when He makes us. We are designed to be used for His Glory, and we need to stop second-guessing our Creator!

If God is calling you? Answer Him. Let's not be like Gideon and make excuses as to why we aren't good enough. I don't care what color your skin is, where you grew up, or how much money you may have, God has something for you! Everyone isn't called to be, and everyone isn't called to be a preacher or in public ministry, but we are called to what God has designed and destined for us. Whatever He has for your hands and feet to do? Go forth and trust His judgement for your life. Get so close to Him like Moses and speak with Him mouth-to-mouth. Embrace God as your Father and Friend and stop being ashamed of who you may have been or who you may be right now. God doesn't care about any of those things and loves you despite your own flawed self-criticisms and self-assessments.

Again, please ***DON'T GIVE UP!*** Don't quit. Fight your way through the pain. Stay close to God and He will never leave you. I promise you that God did it for me and He will do it for you. Stay on the broken road. It may hurt and it may leave you feeling alone. It may have troubles come your way looking to take you out of here but know that God is still right there. Even if you take a hit or two, stay on the road. If you make a mistake and get burdened by shame, stay on the road.

Someone may take advantage to you or hurt you even in the church, but I implore you to stay on the road. Life may chew you up and spit you out and leave you to die, but you must stay on the road. Chase after God's Heart like it is the only thing that you want. Embrace what God has told you and throw away the whispers of Hell. God ***WILL*** restore you no matter what state life leaves you in.

You were born for this.

God's Promises

Assurances begin to appear where we saw none before. Where the constant bombardment of Hell's missiles used to cause you to wince in pain at every turn now cause your praise of God to grow stronger. When setbacks used to throw you to the ground in agony wondering what happened now cause you to smile and realize that God is working like never before. When the mention of the person or place that hurt you once sent you into an anxiety spiral now causes your spine to steel up and your boldness to overcome to rise. Where once when your mind wanders to the things you did in shame that the enemy used to remind you of how awful you were, God's Peace tells you that He turned it around for you and now you have a testimony that Jesus is the answer to recover from anything.

God's Peace doesn't change the storm, but it changes us. Where before the rain was a sign that the sun is gone, His Peace reminds us that the sun will shine again. When God gives us Peace, nothing will stop us. Nothing will phase us. Let the failures keep coming because God's promises are "***YES***" and "***AMEN!***" Let others try to discourage you as you seem to travel alone, but God reminds you that, "I am with you always, even unto the end of the world." (Matthew 28:20) Let the winds that we once feared would tear our lives apart now come and sweep away the things that hindered us in the past. God uses the storms and the rain to bring us new life. God used the execution of Jesus on the cross to give us eternal life. What seemed like the end was just a glorious beginning. The Enemy wants us to see trouble as the first stage of failure, but God's Peace teaches us that trouble is the beginning of what is greater that is coming.

I have learned a strange lesson in my life that seems weird to those who don't understand the heart of God. Where trouble arises in my life is where God wants to use me or the situation to help someone else. When trouble arises, it wasn't because I was unlucky, but because God sees that I can handle it and still be thankful and bless His Name. I love what the Scripture says about this:

TO APPOINT UNTO THEM THAT MOURN IN ZION, TO GIVE UNTO THEM BEAUTY FOR ASHES, THE OIL OF JOY FOR MOURNING, THE GARMENT OF PRAISE FOR THE SPIRIT OF HEAVINESS; THAT THEY MIGHT BE CALLED TREES OF RIGHTEOUSNESS, THE PLANTING OF THE LORD, THAT HE MIGHT BE GLORIFIED. – ISAIAH 61:3 KJV

God will always reward us for our troubles. He has never failed to do that for ***ANYONE*** and even those who think that God has abandoned them I can assure them that He hasn't. God has always come through, and His promises are better than money. Let me explain…

Whenever we feel like giving up remember:

WHEREFORE COMFORT YOURSELVES TOGETHER, AND EDIFY ONE ANOTHER, EVEN AS ALSO YE DO. – 1 THESSALONIANS 5:11 KJV

When we feel abandoned remember:

AND THE LORD, HE IT IS THAT DOTH GO BEFORE THEE; HE WILL BE WITH THEE, HE WILL NOT FAIL THEE, NEITHER FORSAKE THEE: FEAR NOT, NEITHER BE DISMAYED. – DEUTERONOMY 31:8 KJV

When we feel weak remember:

HAVE NOT I COMMANDED THEE? BE STRONG AND OF A GOOD COURAGE; BE NOT AFRAID, NEITHER BE THOU DISMAYED: FOR THE LORD THY GOD IS WITH THEE WHITHERSOEVER THOU GOEST. – JOSHUA 1:9 KJV

When we need comfort remember:

BLESSED BE GOD, EVEN THE FATHER OF OUR LORD JESUS CHRIST, THE FATHER OF MERCIES, AND THE GOD OF ALL COMFORT; WHO COMFORTETH US IN ALL OUR TRIBULATION, THAT WE MAY BE ABLE TO COMFORT THEM WHICH ARE IN ANY TROUBLE,

BY THE COMFORT WHEREWITH WE OURSELVES ARE COMFORTED OF GOD. – 2 CORINTHIANS 1:3-4 KJV

When we feel tired remember:

COME UNTO ME, ALL YE THAT LABOR AND ARE HEAVY LADEN, AND I WILL GIVE YOU REST. – MATTHEW 11:28 KJV

When we need help remember:

I WILL LIFT UP MINE EYES UNTO THE HILLS, FROM WHENCE COMETH MY HELP. MY HELP COMETH FROM THE LORD, WHICH MADE HEAVEN AND EARTH. – PSALM 121:1-2 KJV

When we feel that what we do is hopeless remember:

THEREFORE, MY BELOVED BRETHREN, BE YE STEADFAST, UNMOVABLE, ALWAYS ABOUNDING IN THE WORK OF THE LORD, FORASMUCH AS YE KNOW THAT YOUR LABOR IS NOT IN VAIN IN THE LORD. – 1 CORINTHIANS 15:58 KJV

When we need directions remember:

I WILL INSTRUCT THEE AND TEACH THEE IN THE WAY WHICH THOU SHALT GO: I WILL GUIDE THEE WITH MINE EYE. – PSALM 32:8 KJV

When we see another brother or sister struggling remember:

AND LET US CONSIDER ONE ANOTHER TO PROVOKE UNTO LOVE AND TO GOOD WORKS: NOT FORSAKING THE ASSEMBLING OF OURSELVES TOGETHER, AS THE MANNER OF SOME IS; BUT EXHORTING ONE ANOTHER: AND SO MUCH THE MORE, AS YE SEE THE DAY APPROACHING. – HEBREWS 10:24-25 KJV

When we have lost hope remember:

BE OF GOOD COURAGE, AND HE SHALL STRENGTHEN YOUR HEART, ALL YE THAT HOPE IN THE LORD. – PSALM 31:24 KJV

When we feel fear remember:

WATCH YE, STAND FAST IN THE FAITH, QUIT YOU LIKE MEN, BE STRONG. – 1 CORINTHIANS 16:13 KJV

When we feel like we will never win remember:

These things I have spoken unto you, that in me ye might have peace. In the world ye shall have tribulation: but be of good cheer; I have overcome the world. – John 16:33 KJV

When we are scared and feel alone remember:

Yea, though I walk through the valley of the shadow of death, I will fear no evil: for thou art with me; thy rod and thy staff they comfort me. – Psalm 23:4 KJV

When we are searching for His Peace remember:

Peace I leave with you, my peace I give unto you: not as the world giveth, give I unto you. Let not your heart be troubled, neither let it be afraid. – John 14:27 KJV

When it feels like it will never end being bad remember:

For our light affliction, which is but for a moment, worketh for us a far more exceeding and eternal weight of glory; – 2 Corinthians 4:17 KJV

When we feel unloved by God remember:

Since thou wast precious in my sight, thou hast been honorable, and I have loved thee: therefore will I give men for thee, and people for thy life. – Isaiah 43:4 KJV

When we need God's favor remember:

And let the beauty of the Lord our God be upon us: and establish thou the work of our hands upon us; yea, the work of our hands establish thou it. – Psalm 90:17 KJV

When we feel forgotten by God remember:

Are not five sparrows sold for two farthings, and not one of them is forgotten before God? But even the very hairs of your head are all

NUMBERED. FEAR NOT THEREFORE: YE ARE OF MORE VALUE THAN MANY SPARROWS. – LUKE 12:6-7 KJV

When we feel that we are losing heart remember:

FOR WHICH CAUSE WE FAINT NOT; BUT THOUGH OUR OUTWARD MAN PERISH, YET THE INWARD MAN IS RENEWED DAY BY DAY. – 2 CORINTHIANS 4:16 KJV

When our backs are against the wall remember:

WHAT SHALL WE THEN SAY TO THESE THINGS? IF GOD BE FOR US, WHO CAN BE AGAINST US? – ROMANS 8:31 KJV

When we feel that our lives on the broken road are for nothing just remember:

THEY SHALL HUNGER NO MORE, NEITHER THIRST ANY MORE; NEITHER SHALL THE SUN LIGHT ON THEM, NOR ANY HEAT. FOR THE LAMB WHICH IS IN THE MIDST OF THE THRONE SHALL FEED THEM, AND SHALL LEAD THEM UNTO LIVING FOUNTAINS OF WATERS: AND GOD SHALL WIPE AWAY ALL TEARS FROM THEIR EYES. – REVELATION 7:16-17 KJV

If you are reading this and life has just been unkind, horrific, awful, and punishing I want to let you know that God has not forgotten you. He knows your name and God knows exactly where you are. God doesn't care about what condition you may be in, and He doesn't care about what you may have done because He loves you and He wants what's best for you. It may not seem like it but hang in there and don't lose hope and don't lose the fight that He put deep inside of you. You are made to win, and God will not forget His promises that He made to you. You can't die until what He promised comes true. Even in the middle of the darkness and the Hell that you have endured I can assure you that hope is just around the corner.

When your strength seems to be giving out and life is fading away from your eyes call on Jesus. He will help you and He will answer you in your deepest despair. Even if you don't hear the angelic choir or see a ray of light, Jesus is right there with you. Know that He heard you and that He is working on your behalf. When you accepted Jesus Christ, He made a covenant with you that is unbreakable. It goes both ways, and He won't ever let you down. Even though all that you have suffered and endured there is more than hope, there are His

Promises. The trial is hard, and the fire is hot, but God will bring you out like pure gold. You will endure the worst of it, but His rewards make us forget all about what we endured.

Our scars are our testimonies and believe me, I have many of them. I've been hurt so much it is a miracle that I have any feelings for anyone at all. My scars are deep and painful, but God is my Healer and He is my Comfort. In Him I have found joy in the storm, peace in the terror, and water in the desert. The broken road is hard, and I still have a long way to go because I am still alive, but I am content in knowing that my God will be my everything and He will be your everything too. Just remember that Satan wants to kill you and your testimony. The more people tell their story about how God brought them through struggles discredits the Devil. His argument looks weaker and weaker because when we tell others about the trials, failures, and pain on the road of life and how God carried us over despite our messed-up selves? It ignites the fires of faith in others.

Don't fear your story. Don't fear the help that comes your way. Don't reject God's hand in your life even if it isn't what you expected it. God loves you and you matter deeply to Him. You are on His mind and in His Heart. The road may be broken, but not His Love for you. The way may be hard, but it is easy to love our God. Know that the journey is the story that you tell when you share your testimony. The great psalmist Clara Ward wrote a song[1] that sums up life on the broken road:

How I got over
How I got over
My soul looks back and wonders.
How I got over
Soon as I can see Jesus (oh yes)
The man that made me free (oh yes)
The man that bled and suffered (oh yes)
And died for you and me (oh yes)
I thank Him because He taught me (oh yes)
I thank Him because He brought me (oh yes)
I thank Him because He kept me (oh yes)
Thank Him 'cause He never left me (oh yes)
Thank Him for the holy bible (oh yes)

THANK HIM FOR GOOD OLE REVIVAL (OH YES)
THANK HIM FOR HEAVENLY VISION (OH YES)
THANK HIM FOR OLD TIME RELIGION (OH YES)
I'M GONNA TO SING (HALLELUJAH)
YOU KNOW I'M GONNA SHOUT (TROUBLES OVER);
WELL I THANK HIM FOR ALL HE'S DONE FOR ME

CHAPTER REFERENCES

---

[1] "How I Got Over" by Ward, Clara; b. Apr. 21, 1924, Philadelphia, PA, d. Jan. 16, 1973, Los Angeles, CA; gospel singer and pianist; ©1951 by Andrea Music Co.

Acknowledgements

I want to always thank my Lord, Master, and Savior Yeshu'a Hamashiach (Jesus the Messiah) for being my everything and head of my life.

To my darling wife, the Queen, and my First Lady, Mrs. T. L. Foster for loving me for who I am and putting up with the person that I am. God used my wife in my healing process and God has used me in hers. I love you, Baby Girl, and I am blessed that we can live this life together.

To my daughter, H. A. Foster, I thank you for allowing me to be your Dad. You are so amazing, and I love you and you will always be a part of my heart.

To my father, the late Deacon James A. Foster (1927-2020) and my lovely mother, Deaconess Clemmie B. Foster, I thank you for bringing me into this world. Thank you for living a Godly and upright life before all of us kids. Thank you for raising us the way that you did with a house full of love, Bible, music, and laughter. I love you, Mom! I miss you, Dad!

To my siblings (***YOU KNOW WHO YOU ARE***), I love you all so much for the love that we share for each other and for the times that we have had. I bless and thank God every day for what He has put in you and how you enrich my life, and I know that we still have more to do for the Kingdom. Stay strong!

To Apostles Dwayne and Brenda Ward of the Believer's Heritage Kingdom Training Center in Cobbs Creek, Virginia I want to say thank you for being my spiritual leaders and family. God has used your leadership, mentorship, kinship, and fellowship to my life that has grown me beyond any place that I thought were possible. I love you both to life and the entire BHKTC Family! There is no ministry like BHKTC, and I love being in covenant of such a wonderful group of people. I love you all!

To Rev. Dr. Johnny A. Wallace, thank you for your brotherhood and friendship. God used you to begin the shifting process in my life and ministry. You have taught me so much.

To the Zion Baptist Church of Cardinal, Virginia which is the first church that I ever knew. Zion is the genesis of my personal ministry and the place where I started, my "old landmark" and incubator for my walk with Jesus Christ. I love you all. You mean so much to me in more ways that I can count.

To Pastor Russell Slade, Sr. and Minister Latasha Slade, and family, I love you and the whole Foster Family loves you. Thank you for being such good friends and family to us. Thank you for always having our backs and you know that we will always have yours. I am so excited for our futures in life and ministry.

To every apostle, bishop, pastor, reverend, and ministry leader that I have ever served with or served under. Thank you for all that you have poured into me. I have learned from each of you and my life and ministry are better because of you. Each one of you has taught me lessons that I will never forget. Thank you for what each one of you has done in my life. Every encounter, lesson, or whatever made me better.

To every person who has been in my life for a reason, season, or a lifetime, I thank you. God did what He did best and crafted our lives. No matter who you are, you were sent to me, and I am grateful for every moment. Good or bad, healing or hurtful, for my profit or for my loss I thank you! God bless each of you tremendously!

About The Author

Sean R. Foster is an ordained Elder, worship leader, musician, poet, songwriter, and teacher who has dedicated his life to the advancement of the Kingdom of God. He has served in music ministry since the age of fifteen – as a choir member, worshipper, choir director, and instrumentalist – going wherever God has called him across churches in the Mid-Atlantic region.

He has a deep passion for educating and blessing others with the gifts God has given him and has mentored and taught many worship leaders and musicians, both in the classroom and from the podium, at the invitation of organizations seeking to grow their music ministries.

He is also the author of *Consecration in the Refiner's Fire: A Thirty Day Journey*, a thirty-day devotional written to prepare worship leaders and ministry workers for a season of consecration.

A Virginia native, Sean is happily married to his wife, the love of his life. He enjoys spending time with his family, studying the Word, reading widely on many subjects, playing video games, and watching Doctor Who.

Connect with Sean at linktr.ee/srfosterwrites

www.ingramcontent.com/pod-product-compliance
Lightning Source LLC
LaVergne TN
LVHW020503100826
845148LV00003B/694

* 9 7 9 8 2 1 8 9 1 9 2 6 9 *